THE PEOPLE'S PRINCES

THE PEOPLE'S PRINCES

Machiavelli, Leadership, and Liberty

JOHN P. MCCORMICK

The University of Chicago Press
Chicago and London

The University of Chicago Press, Chicago 60637
The University of Chicago Press, Ltd., London
© 2025 by The University of Chicago
Published 2025

34 33 32 31 30 29 28 27 26 25   1 2 3 4 5

ISBN-13: 978-0-226-84235-6 (cloth)
ISBN-13: 978-0-226-84237-0 (paper)
ISBN-13: 978-0-226-84236-3 (e-book)
DOI: https://doi.org/10.7208/chicago/9780226842363.001.0001

Library of Congress Cataloging-in-Publication Data

Names: McCormick, John P., 1966– author.
Title: The people's princes : Machiavelli, leadership, and liberty / John P.
  McCormick.
Description: Chicago : The University of Chicago Press, 2025. | Includes
  bibliographical references and index.
Identifiers: LCCN 2024059232 | ISBN 9780226842356 (cloth) | ISBN
  9780226842370 (paper) | ISBN 9780226842363 (e-book)
Subjects: LCSH: Machiavelli, Niccolò, 1469-1527—Political and social
  views. | Political leadership—Early works to 1800. | Democracy—Early
  works to 1800.
Classification: LCC PQ4627.M2 Z743 2025 | DDC 320.1—dc23/eng/20250118
LC record available at https://lccn.loc.gov/2024059232

For Susannah

CONTENTS

Part 3. Imprudent Leadership in the Florentine Histories

PROLOGUE

The Italian republic of Capua was in crisis. Machiavelli recounts how, during the Second Punic War, Capua was beset by the dual threat of civil war and foreign conquest: the common people were about to take up arms against the republic's senate, and Hannibal's Carthaginian army was poised to besiege the city. Pacuvius Calanus, the city's chief magistrate, would have liked to persuade the people to set aside their anger toward the overbearing senate and rely on the senators' diplomatic and military expertise to address the menace of Hannibal. Yet he was sufficiently prudent to recognize that the people were simply too furious with the city's domineering elites to entertain such a direct appeal. Therefore Pacuvius publicly affirms the people's indignation over the nobles' arrogance and, having locked all the senators in their chamber, invites the assembled people to indict and execute as many senators as they deem especially oppressive.

Machiavelli intimates that when Pacuvius asks the people to pause and procedurally judge the fate of the city's senators, he effectively asks them to also consider a different question: What do they desire most in the present moment—vengeance against obnoxious elites or freedom from foreign conquest? Once Pacuvius "opens the people's eyes" in this unspoken manner, Capua's citizens become fully aware of these two critical if somewhat conflicting alternatives. In response, the people decide to absolve the senators (for the time being) and avail themselves of the senators' expertise in facing the impending military threat.

Machiavelli highlights how Pacuvius's subtle—in fact, silent—presentation of political alternatives and his deference to popular judgment produced two salutary political consequences: outcomes much more civically beneficial than had he attempted to harangue the people to achieve his objectives, or especially had he employed force. On the one hand, the senators have been compelled to accept the precedent that they should tolerate popular judgment over their offices (and lives). And on the other hand, the people have enlightened themselves regarding their own immediate political priorities.

Had Pacuvius wished, he could have exploited the current civil strife and foreign threat to usurp civic authority and become Capua's sole ruler. But despite his reputation for advising leaders to maximize their personal power at all costs, Machiavelli praises Pacuvius for resisting the opportunity to become a tyrant and for granting the people themselves the authority to decide a critical matter of public policy. Pacuvius serves as one of Machiavelli's principal exemplars for defending a republic's liberty against both tyranny and anarchy in times of crisis. This vivid if too little studied episode, along with numerous others I discuss in *The People's Princes*, illustrates the core of Machiavelli's theory of democratic leadership.

PREFACE: MACHIAVELLI'S RECONCILING OF LEADERSHIP AND DEMOCRACY

There was a time when Niccolò Machiavelli (1469-1527) was considered a cynical adviser of ruthless tyrants: an immoral or at best amoral strategist who counseled leaders to aggrandize themselves by any means necessary, at the expense of their subjects and citizens. This book continues to challenge this traditional understanding by demonstrating that Machiavelli's conception of political leadership is fully compatible with, and indeed uniquely enabling of, both democratic politics and what the Florentine called the "free way of life." Picking up where my previous studies of Machiavelli left off,[1] this book further illuminates radically novel aspects of Machiavelli's corpus that are broadly studied, if still too often misunderstood. Perhaps reluctant to give credence to traditional tyrannical, or even excessively autocratic, interpretations of the man, scholars contributing to the recent "democratic turn" in Machiavelli studies have largely eschewed the place of leadership in his political thought.[2] *The People's Princes* fills this conspicuous void by engaging Machiavelli's understanding of the mutually reinforcing relationship of civic leadership and popular government.

Whereas my previous studies of Machiavelli identified the kinds of civic engagement and political institutions that the Florentine thought necessary for democratic republics to flourish, this book delineates the interactions between leaders and citizens that Machiavelli considered indispensable for realizing liberty within popular governments, and it accentuates their relevance for contemporary democratic politics. Through Machiavelli's discussion of exemplary leaders—both "virtuous" and "imprudent"—I demonstrate how the influence political leaders exert at key historical junctures does not necessarily usurp democratic politics. Rather, such interventions, in conjunction with reinvigorated or newly established popularly empowering institutions, should serve as necessary complements to popular government.

From Machiavelli's major political works—*The Prince,* the *Discourses,* and the *Florentine Histories*[3]—I cull a normative standard for leadership that is urgently needed today as democracy faces intense plutocratic and oligarchic threats. Machiavelli insists that democratic leaders, after firmly establishing their political usefulness (P 9, P 15, P 18),[4] should enhance and solidify their reputations by making themselves obsolete. Specifically, civic leaders should effect their own obsolescence by establishing institutional means through which common citizens rule themselves more directly and substantively. This Machiavellian criterion for judging proper versus nefarious forms of leadership is especially relevant in our present moment, when democracy is challenged by plutocratic encroachment, creeping authoritarianism, and a crisis of political representation and accountability.

"Populism" is often touted as an appropriate answer to both the socioeconomic problem of plutocracy and the political problem of oligarchy. Populism is frequently championed as an antidote to the rampant corruption plaguing contemporary democracies, where socioeconomic elites wield increasing power over common citizens and political elites flout their obligations to behave responsively and accountably toward those citizens. In these circumstances, corporate interests and affluent individuals commandeer politics (and politicians) for their own selfish, particularist concerns at the expense of democratic majorities. To be sure, Machiavelli himself often assailed "the ambition and insolence" of individuals or groups who persistently "transgress the laws" of republics, and he frequently denounced the "corruption" generated by socioeconomic elites in such circumstances (e.g., D III.1).[5]

Yet the Florentine's doctrine of exemplary democratic leadership exposes the deficiency of simplistic "populist" solutions to plutocratic and oligarchic corruption in contemporary democracy. Populism merely embraces the dubiously accountable authority of a charismatic leader (or an outsider political party), attempting to impose such extraordinary authority over the corrupt political system that, throughout successive generations, has illegitimately stifled democratic expression. In particular circumstances, such populist leaders and parties may or may not speak or act more effectively on behalf of the common citizens who have been systematically disempowered over the course of decades. However, whether populist leaders ultimately prove to be genuinely public-interested statesmen or simply self-aggrandizing quasi-tyrants, contemporary populist leaders almost invariably do not—as Machiavelli insists all genuine "people's princes" must do—provide novel legislative, judicial, and electoral institutions through which the people directly participate in ruling themselves.[6] Such direct participation and rule must not simply entail arbitrary exercises of popular judgment but, as in the case of Pacuvius and the

Capuan people, must facilitate substantive modes of popular judgment through which citizens enjoy the opportunity to prioritize their own preferences regarding public policy before they formally enact it.

I intend this work to serve as a contribution to the fields of intellectual history, democratic theory, and contemporary political science. First I delineate Machiavelli's method of "political exemplarity" through detailed analyses of his case studies of leaders and their interactions with populaces throughout history. I demonstrate how Machiavelli conveys the full meaning of political success (and failure) through explicit and often implicit comparisons and contrasts among myriad examples of ancient and modern political leaders (e.g., Romulus, Brutus, Camillus, Agathocles, Cesare Borgia, Cosimo de' Medici, and Piero Soderini). In this manner I present for the first time a Plutarchian Machiavelli, a political theorist who primarily conveys his most essential lessons through exhaustive cross-comparative political biographies of history's most prominent (and often lesser-known) civic leaders.[7] By elucidating Machiavelli's method of political exemplarity, I show how he, perhaps even more than his Greek predecessor Plutarch, often leaves his most important lessons concerning salutary political leadership to be deciphered by his readers themselves rather than pedantically foisting such lessons upon them. Much like Pacuvius Calanus, Machiavelli consistently "opens the eyes" of his readers in an oblique, unspoken manner regarding the "effectual truth" of virtuous political leadership.

Second, the book elaborates Machiavelli's prescriptions for appropriate leadership within popular governments, ancient and modern. Machiavelli's model of leadership, I argue, enhances both the status of civic leaders and the welfare of common citizens. Machiavelli specifies the mutual deference that leaders and peoples ought to afford each other (e.g., Camillus and the Roman people); and he prescribes the appropriate means through which leaders and peoples must, in collaboration, sharply diminish the political influence of the wealthiest and most powerful citizens within democracies (e.g., Marcus Menenius and the Roman plebs against the nobles). Machiavelli considers both this mutual deference between leaders and peoples and the political ferocity with which both must confront oppressive elites to be vital for maintaining civic liberty within popular governments.

I draw from Machiavelli a theory of democratic leadership built upon the collaboration of two sets of political actors: "princes of republics" (D II.2) and "guardians of liberty" (D I.4–5). Machiavelli's exemplary civic princes—such as Lucius Brutus and Furius Camillus—seek to win personal acclaim through unwavering service to their republics. And his guardians of liberty—virtuous citizenries such as the Roman, Athenian, Syracusan, and (sometimes) Florentine peoples—directly decide matters of office-holding, lawmaking, and political trials. Machiavelli's basic guidelines for civically beneficial leadership and optimal popular participation require *both* civic princes and empowered peoples to scrupulously assess the motivations of a third set of political actors—the *grandi* (wealthy and politically prominent elites who invariably conspire against the common good)—and to spiritedly pursue policies that thwart their incessant efforts to oppress the *popolo* (ordinary citizens who generally wish to live free from elite domination) (P 9, D I.4–5). Unlike most authors in the history of Western political thought, Machiavelli, I show, does not confer an active political role exclusively upon the leaders of republics while confining the common people to a narrowly passive one.

For instance, Machiavelli attributes the freedom and greatness of the Roman Republic and Athenian democracy to each polity's affording common citizens the power to appoint officials, initiate and decide over lawmaking, judge individuals accused of political crimes, and, furthermore, to speak out publicly on all such matters in assemblies. Moreover, contrary to widespread misperceptions that Machiavelli unvaryingly reduces leadership to the unilateral exercise of force and fraud, he regularly accentuates crucial historical moments when political leaders, rather than manipulating the people or simply persuading them, are themselves wisely convinced or directed by public opinion to change their course of action in ways conducive to the common good (e.g., D I.53, F III).

Machiavelli suggests that intimate, affective bonds often form between leaders and citizens after the citizens have angrily dismissed the leaders from office, only to subsequently reappoint them. Furius Camillus, one of Machiavelli's chief examples, whom I discuss in chapters 3 and 4, gained unprecedented trust and authority from the Roman people by allowing them to exile him, then faithfully returning when they summoned him back in a time of crisis. As I show, Camillus certainly enjoyed much more trust and authority than Machiavelli's patron Piero Soderini gained from the Florentine people by entreating them—with flattery and obsequiousness—to allow him to hold office indefinitely, regardless of circumstances (D III.30).

Machiavelli demonstrates that Camillus's deferential leadership subsequently reinvigorates Rome geopolitically and domestically: he leads the republic to numerous military victories and institutes civic reforms that further empower the Roman people. By contrast, Soderini's obstinately selfish leadership permitted both a Spanish invasion of Tuscany and a successful Medici coup against the Florentine popular government. The Camillus/Soderini contrast exemplifies Machiavelli's notion that leadership in a democratic republic requires a certain embrace of indeterminacy; an acceptance that a leader's authority is always uncertain and reversible—but also potentially retrievable. This insight speaks to the fundamental tensions and risks of democratic politics for both civic leaders and common citizens.

* * *

In part 1 I weave together the disparate strands of Machiavelli's exemplary model for autocratic leadership within principalities. In a manner that may alarm certain "republican" readers, I ultimately show how Machiavelli's prescriptions for salutary *tyranny* prove strikingly relevant for civic leadership in *republics*. Chapters 1 and 2 outline Machiavelli's model of a successful Greek tyrant, whom he contrasts with the prototypically unsuccessful Roman reformer. This contrast imparts Machiavelli's lesson that republics often suffer such irredeemable corruption, initiated by socioeconomic elites, that they can be reformed only by princely or even tyrannical means. His writings exhibit a distinct affinity for Greek tyrants like Agathocles of Sicily, whom I discuss extensively in chapter 1. He presents the tyrants of Greek cities like Syracuse, Sparta, and Heraclea as sufficiently prudent to recognize that they can eliminate rivals to their own authority and gain the favor of the common people by eliminating their republics' senators and richest citizens and distributing their wealth to the people. When one analyzes Machiavelli's interpretations of the historical sources on his preferred exemplars of Greek tyranny—especially Agathocles, but also Nabis, Hiero, Clearchus, and Cleomenes—a general repertoire comes to light.

Overall, Machiavelli's Greek tyrants suppress their cities' nobles and distribute their wealth to the people; they decrease or terminate their cities' dependence on mercenary arms; they expand the ranks of their citizen-subject armies (often freeing slaves to do so); and they fight off much more powerful foreign enemies, whether Rome, Carthage, or the Achaean League. Through such means, in Machiavelli's assessment, these Greek tyrants properly found their reigns on the common people, ensuring that the people enjoy security from the prince and the prince gains security with the people (P 8-9).

By contrast, as I discuss in chapter 2, when the Roman Republic succumbed to rampant corruption engendered by growing socioeconomic inequality after the Punic Wars, Machiavelli indicates how the republic's aspiring reformers—the Gracchi, Scipio Africanus, and Julius Caesar—showed excessive deference toward the Roman Senate. As a result of this imprudent reverence for senatorial authority, these prospective reformers either were murdered or were ruined by the Roman nobility—such that oligarchic corruption proliferated unimpeded until the Roman Republic eventually collapsed. Many commentators note that Machiavelli ostensibly criticizes the uncivil motivations and actions of Agathocles and Julius Caesar (P 8, D 9–10). On the contrary, I will argue that he champions the career of this wildly efficacious Syracusan tyrant, and that he considers the political offenses committed by this egregiously failed Roman reformer to be reticent sins of omission rather than overbearing sins of commission.

When Machiavelli introduces the crucial concept of "cruelty well used" in *The Prince*, he describes how Agathocles orders the elimination of his republic's assembled senate, which enables him both to free Sicily from Carthaginian domination and to establish a relationship of mutual "security" between himself and the Syracusan people (P 8). When Machiavelli more explicitly makes the case in the *Discourses* that princely action is sometimes required to reform a corrupt republic, he discusses Clearchus of Heraclea. Confronted with "the insolence of the aristocrats," whom as chief magistrate he could "neither satisfy nor correct" in any civic manner, Clearchus decided to assuage the "rage of the people" by publicly eliminating the nobility in its entirety (D 1.16). Machiavelli thus asserts that republics sometimes reach a point where elites "cannot be corrected by laws." In these cases, he argues, republics require "a quasi-monarchical power" to effect the "correction" of wealthy elites, as Cleomenes undertook in Sparta and as Agathocles and Clearchus did in Syracuse and Heraclea (D 1.18). Attempting to reverse efforts by magistrates and senators to accelerate inequality in Sparta, Machiavelli describes how Cleomenes, in a "just and praiseworthy" manner, killed many of these nobles and distributed their wealth to the common people (D I.9, D I.18).

Perhaps counterintuitively, Machiavelli's prescriptions for salutary tyranny illuminate his recommendations for civic leadership in republics. In this light, I suggest, contemporary debates over "the democratic Machiavelli" and age-old disputes over "the tyrannical Machiavelli" effectively converge. As I demonstrate in part 2, the tyrannical Greek exemplar raises the bar on the level of severity that Machiavelli thinks appropriate and necessary for keeping republics uncorrupt, or for reforming them once they have become egregiously corrupted. If popular governments need not necessarily kill their entire nobilities through arbitrary violence, Machiavelli argues in no uncertain terms that they ought to legally indict and execute a single noble, or even some significant number of nobles, for treason to stem the process of oligarchic corruption.[8]

Specifically, magistrates and common citizens should indict elites on capital charges for seeking absolute power, for exacerbating socioeconomic inequality, and for thwarting efforts to redistribute wealth among citizens. When formally accusing members of the *grandi* and adjudicating their lives in political trials, Machiavelli insists, civic princes and assembled peoples must act more aggressively than prevailing norms permitted in the republics of his age—in fact, they must act even more assertively than countenanced by the rather aggressive norms of ancient republics.

Popular governments, in Machiavelli's estimation, should imitate Greek tyrants to a certain extent by threatening their nobility with formally conducted, popularly decided capital trials—and by often following through on such threats. As I show in chapters 3 and 4, Machiavelli praises Lucius Brutus for indicting and overseeing the execution of his treasonous sons and other young nobles who conspired to overthrow the Roman Republic. Moreover, he suggests that prudent statesmen like Camillus or Menenius ought to permit themselves to be put on trial, or suffer exile, to demonstrate their fidelity to the common good. Machiavelli is adamant in asserting that civic magistrates ought not fail to put enemies of liberty on trial, something he sharply reproaches the Florentine civic prince, Soderini, for failing to do (D III.3). Neither should such leaders abjure popular judgment over political trials, as did the Florentine civic prophet Girolamo Savonarola. Machiavelli criticizes the friar for preventing the people from deciding an important political trial out of fear that their judicial verdict would prove unfavorable to his personal or partisan interests (D 1.47). Machiavelli does not insist that political trials in republics must always result in executions of prominent citizens. As shown by the example of Pacuvius—mentioned above and closely analyzed in chapter 6—his republic's crisis concludes with the Capuan people's hatred for the nobles being assuaged, and the senators' arrogance toward the people being tamed, without a single noble suffering physical harm.

On Machiavelli's controversial views regarding property and wealth distribution in republics: If popular governments do not confiscate and redistribute all of their nobilities' wealth to common citizens, as did Greek tyrants, Machiavelli nevertheless insists that such polities must allocate and redistribute enough of their property to sustain relative socioeconomic equality among all citizens, thus maintaining a level requisite for civic liberty. He suggests that Roman reformers ought to have imitated Greek tyrants in more aggressively instituting and making effective agrarian reforms that prevent economic inequality from too readily translating into political inequality, a pernicious form of inequality that ultimately resulted in the Roman Republic's collapse (D I.37)

In sum, parts 1 and 2 demonstrate the following Machiavellian precepts for leadership: Civic magistrates should vigorously prosecute the nobles in popularly judged political trials; they should allow the people to judge the veracity of the smears that oligarchs inevitably spread against popular, reform-minded magistrates; and they should prepare to use force through mobilizing popular militaries should elites conspire to overthrow the republic via extralegal, violent means. Machiavelli prefers that socio-economic affairs not come to such dire straits that republics can no longer observe a fully civil way of life. However, a popular government where nobles exacerbate corruption and resort to violence to maintain inequality may be better off becoming a populist principality, which—so long as the people remain militarily armed—Machiavelli considers more desirable than an oligarchic republic that endeavors to disarm the citizenry in order to protect the status and wealth of its nobles. Machiavelli often reminds readers that a popularly armed principality may easily be reconverted into a republic (e.g., D II.2).

Machiavelli's examples of Greek tyrants display the unilaterally violent means necessary to reform an incurably corrupt republic. However, Machiavelli also suggests that such means may be routinized in formally legal and collectively decided ways as part of a republic's customary functioning; that is, as severe anti-oligarchic procedures that may in fact stave off poisonous civic corruption indefinitely. Readers of Machiavelli must not shy away from his endorsement of Greek tyranny, I argue, because such reluctance undermines our ability to understand the corollaries between popularly salutary tyranny and civically beneficial leadership. Machiavelli's ultimate lesson seems to be that the political actor most likely to successfully overcome oligarchic corruption in a republic must be part tyrannical prince and part civic reformer, and both, he insists, must be backed by an armed common people.

Part 3 of the book is devoted to Machiavelli's examples of imprudent leaders—negative examples that are just as illustrative as his examples of successfully virtuous leadership, if not more so. In the *Florentine Histories*, he presents Giano della Bella and Michele di Lando as well-intentioned leaders who fail to imitate the ancient examples of Moses, Romulus, and Brutus; consequently they fail to become successful founders or reformers of the early Florentine Republic. Machiavelli suggests that naive or undifferentiated notions of goodness or patriotism prompt Giano and Michele to spurn the common people's support, to exhibit excessive deference to rapacious elites, and eventually to exit—leaving the city much worse off than before (FH III.13, 22).

More wildly ambitious Florentine figures such as Corso Donati and Walter Brienne evince defective notions of self-interest that prevent them from acting in ways that could have benefited Florence's civic and geo-political welfare as well as their own political reputations and authority. Machiavelli indicates that Corso and Walter both arouse harmful popular hatred against themselves rather than inspiring salutary popular respect; they neglect to organize broadly public, civic-military forces rather than merely sectarian ones; and they both rely too extensively on foreign support for their defectively established authority (FH II.21, FH II.33–34). Machiavelli declares that a "wise legislator" could have imposed a proper constitutional order on the Florentine Republic (FH III.1). Nevertheless, both Florence's imprudently well-meaning and unwisely selfish leaders, Machiavelli laments, consistently foster a significant deterioration of liberty in his native city.

Throughout the book I employ excurses that sometimes qualify my interpretations of Machiavelli or extend such elucidations in alternative directions. These digressions, I hope, will dispel the notion that my account of Machiavelli's "political exemplarity" is in any way overdetermined and will help me skirt the perception that I'm reducing Machiavelli's prescriptions for leadership to something like an algorithm. I intend for these excurses—concerning Camillus's status as Rome's "most prudent captain," the consistency of Machiavelli's character study of Soderini, or Machiavelli's self-affiliation with Agathocles, and such—to allow me to fully communicate the flexibility and fluidity of Machiavelli's conception of political leadership.

PART 1

SALUTARY TYRANNY IN *THE PRINCE* AND *DISCOURSES*

1. AGATHOCLES AS PRINCELY EXEMPLUM

(AGATHOCLES, HIERO, CESARE BORGIA,
LIVEROTTO DA FERMO, NABIS THE SPARTAN)

Machiavelli frequently uses historical examples to impart lessons on leadership only partially conveyed by the general rules he so (in)famously sets forth throughout his major works, especially in *The Prince*.[1] Machiavelli deploys a controversial figure, Agathocles the Sicilian, to establish, throughout his writings, an elaborate cross-comparative web of leaders in similar political circumstances that are unavoidable and dangerous but also potentially advantageous (P 8). The vast network of comparisons and contrasts, at the center of which Machiavelli places Agathocles, conveys (at different textual moments, in multiple registers, and with varying levels of emphasis) the core of his advice regarding leadership, especially in principalities. Agathocles is the first of many princes and magistrates in Machiavelli's corpus to find himself, as the author describes the situation in the *Discourses*, positioned between "the insolence of the aristocrats . . . and the rage of the people" (D I.16). The domestic intensity and geopolitical context of aristocratic-popular conflict prevailing at any moment determines, Machiavelli suggests, whether, when, and how leaders—bearing in mind the example of Agathocles—should resort to cruelty, criminality, and oath breaking in managing their polity's class relations and civic-military operations.

In this chapter I demonstrate how Machiavelli presents specific political actions and particular historical circumstances in ways that often affirm and extend, but sometimes qualify and even contravene, his own political precepts and his own explicit evaluations of many individual actors discussed throughout his writings. These cross-comparisons, in which Agathocles figures prominently, enable Machiavelli to challenge conventional assessments of such individuals offered by previous writers and, concomitantly, to redefine traditional notions of virtue, glory, liberty, and even good and evil. Machiavelli often relies on historical details provided by previous writers when discussing the political actors he places in conceptual proximity to Agathocles (just as he subtly entreats his audience to again consult such sources—especially when indicates that he has omitted pertinent details). But Machiavelli almost always winds up contradicting, either directly or by implication, the moral-political assessments offered by these rival authors—and very often questioning his own initially ventured moral-political assessments of such leaders.[2]

At the simplest level, in chapter 8 of *The Prince*, Machiavelli presents Agathocles as a criminal; a morally reprehensible example to be condemned, not emulated. Machiavelli places the Sicilian in a chapter explicitly devoted to individuals who gain power through "crimes" and "violence" (P 8, P 9). Agathocles, generally considered a "tyrant" by ancient authors, seems to be a prince who achieved significant political success at the severe cost of forfeiting the opportunity to be considered truly excellent, virtuous, or glorious by posterity.[3] Yet besides explicitly accentuating Agathocles's "virtue" at crucial junctures, Machiavelli concludes the chapter by dramatically altering his evaluation of the Syracusan prince. After qualifying his remarks with the curious proviso "if it may be permitted to speak well of evil," Machiavelli proceeds to uphold Agathocles, without any equivocation, as a master of the practice he calls "cruelty well used" (*crudeltà bene usate*) (P 8)—a tenet of central, perhaps even preeminent, importance within *The Prince*.

Why does Machiavelli initially present Agathocles as a criminal example deserving of blame, only to subsequently praise him as a princely example worthy of notice and even imitation? Moreover, what precise role does "evil" play in Machiavelli's political lessons that enlist Agathocles, and to what extent does his mode of writing make it permissible for his audience to learn to think well of such evil (that is, evil reconstructed in Machiavellian terms)? To address these questions, I examine the rhetorical and literary techniques through which Machiavelli bids readers to evaluate various leaders in light of his account of Agathocles (and, conversely, through which he consistently invites readers to reevaluate his initial disapproving depiction of the Sicilian). Prominent among such figures are leaders I discuss in this chapter—Cesare Borgia, Liverotto of Fermo, Nabis the Spartan—and figures I will examine in chapter 2—Scipio Africanus, Clearchus, and Julius Caesar as well as, perhaps surprisingly, Machiavelli himself. Such rhetorical techniques include linguistic cues, intellectual tropes, and literary (often biblical) allegories; constant recurrences of similar circumstances confronting princes and magistrates throughout history; and consistent re-presentations of comparable actions undertaken (or shunned) by this diverse set of figures.

Sometimes Machiavelli directly entreats readers to consider, through the prism of his Agathocles, the behavior of other political actors such as the modern Italian *condottiere* Liverotto, whom Machiavelli places in the same chapter of *The Prince* as the ancient Sicilian prince (P 8). In other instances, Machiavelli induces his audience to make comparative considerations through less immediate textual associations: for example, Machiavelli implicitly asks readers to consider why he deems a criminal Agathocles, who appears in a chapter between those devoted to Borgia and Nabis, when he fails to overtly condemn the latter two—even though they behave quite like Agathocles. On other occasions Machiavelli elicits comparative reflections even more indirectly, as in the case (set forth in both *The Prince* and the *Discourses*) of Publius Cornelius Scipio. This Roman consul, like Agathocles, invaded Africa to free his patria from a grievous Carthaginian threat; but unlike Agathocles, Scipio succumbed to domestic "controversies" and "conspiracies" initiated by envious senatorial elites that cut short his illustrious political career (P 17, D I.29).

Machiavelli applies similar words or phrases to individual leaders at disparate places throughout his works, prompting readers to ponder their conceptual-political relationship. For instance, Machiavelli refers to the "hardships and dangers" (*disagi e periculi*) that both Agathocles and Machiavelli himself incurred in public service performed on behalf of their respective cities (P dl, P 8). While Agathocles's arduous efforts on behalf of his patria enabled him to successfully outmaneuver aristocratic opposition to his policies and fend off foreign domination, Machiavelli had to stand by helplessly while an aristocratic coup and foreign invasion put an end to the Florentine Republic that he served so diligently; a coup and an invasion that, as we know, also resulted in Machiavelli's being sacked, imprisoned, and tortured.[4]

A thorough examination of these other political actors whom Machiavelli links with Agathocles suggests that, in Machiavelli's estimation, Agathocles is much more than a mere criminal deserving of moral disapprobation; rather, he serves as Machiavelli's chief exemplum of the appropriate political action to establish a long-lasting principality and, perhaps more remarkably, to reform a corrupt republic. According to Machiavelli, conflicts inevitably arise in every polity between the insolent great, the *grandi*, and the enraged people, the *popolo*; that is, clashes between social classes who wish to dominate and those who desire not to be dominated (P 9, D I.2–4). Therefore both would-be tyrants aspiring to usurp republics and sitting civic magistrates committed to maintaining them will, Machiavelli insists, invariably find themselves situated in volatile circumstances where aristocratic *insolenzia* provokes popular *rabbia*. Machiavelli advises individual leaders to favor the people in such situations and to check the nobility whenever possible (P 9). But precisely how should would-be princes and civic leaders carry out such a perilous but necessary task? Machiavelli's answer seems to be that the political actor most likely to successfully manage such circumstances must be part tyrannical prince and part civic reformer.

Agathocles is the first prince to whom Machiavelli attributes a particular course of action that intellectual authorities, both traditional and recent, would unequivocally consider tyrannical: Agathocles usurps a republic by slaughtering his city's senators and wealthiest citizens (P 8). In full accord with established writers, Machiavelli at first condemns Agathocles's actions, but then, as I noted above, he seems to condone them as essential and appropriate exhibitions of cruelty well used. How can readers determine with any confidence which assessment of Agathocles is most fully Machiavelli's own? Machiavelli's ultimately positive endorsement of Agathocles's behavior, I demonstrate, is borne out through, among other things, his overt praise of other individuals that he previously and subsequently discusses who act quite similarly when confronted with the competing, often irreconcilable claims of oppression-driven nobles and freedom-seeking peoples. Machiavelli's praise for Agathocles is also manifested by his sometimes explicit, sometimes barely concealed condemnation of individuals who failed to adopt Agathoclean measures in such circumstances.

Slaughtering rich and prominent citizens is clearly useful to aspiring tyrants: Machiavelli coldly remarks that every new prince must eliminate potential rivals among the elite and that he ought to gain favor with the common people (P 6, P 9). More curiously, however, Machiavelli also intimates that similar action may be necessary to preserve and reform republics (D I.9, D I.16). In fact, he often affiliates such behavior with the recurrent need for republics to punish or eliminate "the sons of Brutus": nobles who are driven by an insatiable appetite to oppress (P 9; D I.2–4); who exacerbate socioeconomic inequality in their cities (D I.17–18, I.55, III.24); and who bitterly resent the liberty enjoyed by the common people within democratic republics (D I.16, III.3).

Machiavelli's discussion of Agathocles, and the cross-comparative network within which he situates him, suggest that the appropriate and necessary action a prince or magistrate must take vis-à-vis the nobles and the people is in fact "evil" political action as conceived by traditional writers. In other words, the Agathoclean exemplum permits Machiavelli, in a certain respect, to transform evil into good. By elaborating and amplifying his account of Agathocles through similar examples (such as other successful Greek tyrants) and through counterexamples (such as failed Roman and Florentine reformers), Machiavelli redefines the model of a good prince in ways that contravene the political preferences and moral injunctions of previous writers. As we will observe, not only does the "good" princely founder or tyrannical reformer crush or exterminate a city's leading citizens (which, unsurprisingly, always alarms nobles, as well as writers, their principal clients), he also extensively arms or rearms his common citizen subjects; and he uses fraud and force to fight back against or vanquish often numerically superior foreign powers.

MACHIAVELLI'S POLITICS OF EXEMPLARITY

Machiavelli communicates the political lessons described above—lessons guaranteed to provoke aristocratic outrage and scholastic disapproval—through the literary practice of exemplarity.[5] The best way to understand a particular example like Agathocles, Machiavelli seems to suggest, is not only or even primarily through what he initially and explicitly writes about that figure (say, either in a chapter heading or in a seemingly definitive normative evaluation). Rather, Machiavelli also invites, but does not necessarily demand, readers to evaluate Agathocles through careful consideration of similarly situated political actors and the means they employed or refrained from employing in such circumstances. Machiavelli never instructs us to directly compare, for instance, Scipio Africanus and Agathocles. But prominent similarities and differences in their behaviors subtly entice us to do so: both invade Africa to relieve their cities of an existential Carthaginian military threat; but the former permits the preferences of senators and writers to dictate how he conducts himself publicly whereas the latter, as we will observe, most certainly does not.

To be sure, the individual leaders with whom Machiavelli compares and contrasts Agathocles in constructing his exemplum do not exclusively serve one particular purpose. These other cases inevitably exhibit complexities of their own that problematize the very exemplary model I am delineating here; and they also play important roles in other theoretical strands that make up Machiavelli's political oeuvre.[6] This ambiguity corresponds with the very essence of "exemplarity": although it may initially appear that one example suffices to convey an author's political and moral lessons, multiple examples and counterexamples prove to be imbricated in a network of associations that impart conclusions that are more profound, but also potentially more tenuous and elusive.[7]

Nevertheless Machiavelli, as I will show, differs profoundly from previous (and later) theoreticians who enlist exemplarity while imparting their political lessons; this is so, most profoundly, because he unequivocally declares that he intends his advice to conform with "utility" (D II, Preface); he intends his advice to prove "useful" for those who "understand it"

(P 15). After all, Machiavelli separates himself from previous writers most emphatically when he professes an unprecedented concern with "effectual truth" (P 15). But what do "unequivocal" and "emphatic" mean within a literary-rhetorical framework that often deploys exemplarity in the indirect and implicit manner I just outlined? Will it ultimately be possible to reconcile Machiavelli's obvious recourse to exemplarity, a practice that always complicates as much as clarifies the relation between theory and practice, with his explicit motivation to put theory into practice more directly than ever before?[8]

One initial point of contrast between Machiavelli and previous writers illustrates this. In the *Discourses* Machiavelli explicitly states his intention to present models of "imitation" and not merely "admiration": specifically, imitation of "the most virtuous deeds illustrated by histories that were performed within monarchies and republics by kings, captains, citizens, lawgivers and others on behalf of their cities" (D I, Preface). Livy, in the preface to his history of Rome (Machiavelli's ostensible model),[9] declared his intention to highlight "good examples" from Rome's past that should be imitated, as well as "abominable ones" to be avoided.[10] By contrast, Machiavelli's emphasis on "virtuous" examples—unfolding from the exemplar of Agathocles—combines in a novel fashion what is conventionally considered morally good or reprehensible. Exempla that combine good and evil, it seems, are more "useful" than those that accentuate the traditionally understood differences between those qualities.[11]

OVERVIEW OF PART 1: CRIMINALITY CONDEMNED AND VIRTUE REVERED

Allow me to preview the major Machiavellian cross-comparisons, in which Agathocles figures prominently, that I will discuss in part 1, as well as to indicate some of the central themes these comparisons/contrasts raise. Machiavelli places his account of Agathocles's career in a chapter of *The Prince* (chapter 8) bookended by those in which he explicitly endorses the crimes of Cesare Borgia (chapter 7) and implicitly condones those of Nabis the Spartan (chapter 9). Yet in the intervening chapter Machiavelli condemns Agathocles's crimes even though these crimes earned the Sicilian greater and longer-lasting political success than either Borgia or Nabis ever achieved (*far greater*, in fact, than Borgia).

Moreover, Machiavelli emphasizes that Agathocles successfully invaded Africa to compel the Carthaginians to abandon their siege of Syracuse, his native city—a feat that immediately calls to mind the later actions of Scipio, actions that attained for the Roman commander both the glorious title "Africanus" and the eternally exalted status of consummate citizen/statesman/captain.[12] As I will argue in chapter 2, Machiavelli's criticisms of Scipio's affability suggest that, for Machiavelli, the much crueler Agathocles was more genuinely virtuous than Scipio, although the Roman won "glory" in the estimation of traditional writers and the Sicilian did not.[13]

Besides the relationship of Agathocles, Borgia, and Nabis, I discuss below Machiavelli's pairing in *The Prince* of Agathocles and Liverotto and their respective usurpations of republics. At first blush Machiavelli simply seems to be offering ancient and modern examples of criminal usurpers of republics. But the subtle details of his contrasting accounts of Agathocles's impressive long-term success and Liverotto's rapid demise insinuate, without openly displaying it, something very different: Machiavelli demonstrates, without explicit commentary at this juncture of *The Prince*, just how pernicious he considers the influence of the Roman Catholic Church to be in contemporary Italy. The prevalence of mercenary arms and the relations of dependence and duplicity that mercenary politics engender—both of which are fostered by the church—prevent a petty criminal like Liverotto from ever rising to the rank of a founder, conqueror, or liberator comparable to that of (the otherwise also criminal) Agathocles.

Furthermore, Machiavelli's implicit grouping of Agathocles throughout *The Prince* and the *Discourses* with other Greek "tyrants" like Hiero, Nabis, Clearchus, and Cleomenes—most of whom eliminate their cities' nobilities, end their dependence on foreign mercenaries, and expand the ranks of their armed citizenry—subtly indicts Roman figures such as Scipio, the Gracchi, Gaius Marius, and Julius Caesar. As I will argue in chapter 2, Machiavelli criticizes the Romans—unlike their Greek counterparts—for failing to decisively overcome (through force, criminality, and cruelty well used) senatorial opposition to their attempted pro-popular socioeconomic and military reorderings of their republics. Machiavelli intimates that the deference to the "senatorial order" of their republic displayed by the aspiring Roman princes-cum-reformers—deference vigorously eschewed by their more successful Greek counterparts—ensured the decline and fall of the Roman Republic.

Machiavelli demonstrates that the expansion of Rome's imperial conquests eventually, and to his mind unfortunately, extinguished the considerable political and military achievements of these Greek tyrants and the civic-military orders they reinvigorated. However, Machiavelli also suggests that the failure of Rome's reformers, after the Punic Wars, to imitate the actions of precisely these Greek tyrants ensured that a different, more pernicious model of tyranny—that of the Roman emperors—would smother civic liberty at home and more or less throughout the world for centuries to come—indeed, perhaps forever unless trends established across millennia were corrected by radical civic-military measures in Machiavelli's day or the near future.

Indeed, Machiavelli makes it a point to call the supreme civic rank Agathocles ascended to in Syracuse praetor, a name believed to be the original title of the Roman consuls and of the supreme magistrates in the other ancient Italian republics that Rome eventually conquered. Later praetor was the title bestowed on Romans who served as military governors of Rome's conquered provinces—and Machiavelli himself uses the term this way.[14] By attributing this title to Agathocles, Machiavelli faintly foreshadows the fact that Agathocles's dominion, like all of the Mediterranean, would eventually be swallowed up by Rome's empire—and therefore presided over by Roman "praetors"—thereby signaling the chief reason why Greek princes like Agathocles would never be remembered in the manner of a Moses or a Romulus.

Machiavelli likewise may be intimating that the success and longevity of the cities, peoples, and empires established by the great founder-prophets—Moses, Romulus, Theseus, and Cyrus—served to whitewash their criminality. The writers who chronicled these long-lived orders were beholden to their success and hence downplayed the crimes of successful founders and attributed to them great (often supernatural) acts that they may never have performed. Conversely, eventual political decline, not entirely or directly the fault of Greek petty tyrants such as Agathocles, permitted historians to accentuate their crimes. Or, in Machiavelli's estimation, it permitted such writers to overlook the necessary political actions that the Greek princes, like all protofounders, must undertake—whether they come to be viewed by posterity as immortal prophets or lowly usurpers.

AGATHOCLES AND "CRUELTY WELL USED"

Machiavelli's evaluation of Agathocles is a perennially perplexing problem confronting readers of *The Prince*.[15] On the one hand, Machiavelli declares that Agathocles's criminal behavior cannot be deemed virtuous; on the other hand he does just that, twice invoking the Sicilian's "virtue" (P 8). Agathocles's crimes notwithstanding, Machiavelli certainly seems impressed by the Sicilian's career: he recounts how, through cruelty, military prowess, and yes, crime, Agathocles, the poor and abject son of a "simple potter," rose through his city's civic military to become praetor, or chief magistrate, of the Syracusan republic (cf. D II.13). After noteworthy civic and military accomplishments—including fighting off the mighty Carthaginian Empire—Agathocles ruled securely over the island of Sicily into advanced old age (P 8). If Machiavelli's evaluation of Agathocles's "virtue" appears ambiguous, other aspects of his assessment are quite straightforward: he declares unequivocally that Agathocles is not counted among history's "most excellent men" and that, while the Sicilian's actions may have gained him power, they did not earn him "glory" (P 8).

One might expect that someone like Agathocles, who started from such lowly origins, would be fully gratified by his astonishing rise to the height of civic and military power in so important a Mediterranean city. Isn't it satisfying enough for a base craftsman's son to have become the Syracusan equivalent of an Athenian strategos or a Roman consul? After all, this potter's son ascended to command military forces that, not long before, had defeated the Athenians at the height of their empire. Nevertheless, according to Machiavelli, legitimate civic and military authority proved insufficient for Agathocles's ambition. He decided "to become prince and to maintain with violence and without obligation to anyone else that which had been given to him by consent" (P 8). Indeed, even supreme magistrates like *strategoi*, praetors, and consuls are bound by collegial obligations and confined by finite terms of office. Agathocles aspires to a kind of rule that is nearly unlimited—an aspiration, note, that is fully consonant with Machiavelli's definition of *virtù*, understood as unfettered political autonomy (P 6).[16]

While Agathocles was praetor, Machiavelli reports, a Carthaginian army occupied much of Sicily and threatened Syracuse's security and independence. Agathocles informs the Carthaginian commander, Hamilcar, of "his plans," but Machiavelli keeps readers in suspense by neglecting to tell us the precise content of those plans. Agathocles then calls a formal assembly of the Syracusan Senate and the people to decide important public matters—among them, presumably, hostilities with the Carthaginians. At this public gathering Agathocles orders his soldiers to kill "all the senators and the richest of the people" (P 8). In other words, in full sight of the *popolo*, Agathocles murders the wealthiest and most powerful citizens of his republic—collectively the social class that in the very next chapter of *The Prince* Machiavelli will identify as "the great," the *grandi* (P 9). In so doing, Agathocles firmly establishes his principality in Syracuse.

While Agathocles supposedly aspires to act in a manner not beholden to anyone else, he clearly depends, at least initially, on the consent of a foreign power. We may now surmise that Agathocles had asked Hamilcar to indulge his coup, and in return he would offer Syracuse to Carthage as a client city.[17] Furthermore, Agathocles seems to assume the continued consent and even cooperation of common citizens, the people, who directly witnessed his crime: Machiavelli reports that after eliminating the Syracusan elite, Agathocles holds the principality "without any civil controversy"— that is, with no popular protest. Indeed, once Agathocles betrays Hamilcar and refuses to surrender Syracuse's independence to Carthage, he withstands serious initial defeats and sieges without incurring any popular revolts (P 8). Then, turning the besiegers into the besieged, Agathocles invades Africa and harasses the Carthaginians into accepting his terms for peace; specifically, he imposes a truce that wins him hegemony over the island of Sicily (D II.12).

Agathocles's military acumen is unimpeachable. Indeed, when Machiavelli first invokes his virtue, it seems to pertain only to his military skill, to his indisputable status as a "most excellent captain" (P 8). Machiavelli mentions Agathocles's "virtue in spirit and body" (*virtù di animo e di corpo*) in reference to his martial prowess; he accentuates the "virtue of Agathocles [*la virtù di Agatocle*] in confronting and escaping danger . . . [and] his great spirit in sustaining and overcoming adversities." Machiavelli attributes Agathocles's success primarily to his favor with the Syracusan citizen soldiers, which he gained for himself through many "hardships and dangers" (P 8). Both the ancient sources and Machiavelli himself underscore Agathocles's remarkable improvisational skill in conducting the arts of war.

Yet Machiavelli also provides the Sicilian with a not inconsiderable domestic résumé. Machiavelli notes that despite (or maybe because of) Agathocles's "infinite betrayals and cruelties," he remained securely in power throughout his nearly three-decade reign—most astoundingly, even while he frequently left Syracuse to wage war on another continent (P 8). If Agathocles were not both an excellent captain *and* prince, why would the Syracusans endure his rule even while he was far from the city? Why wouldn't they have rebelled against his imperium and impeded his return? These armed citizens, who not long before had repelled the Athenian navy, could certainly have prevented Agathocles's reentry if they considered him a tyrant.[18]

Machiavelli provides an answer to this conundrum. Agathocles was never "conspired against by his citizens" (*da' sua cittadini non li fu mai conspirato contro*) because he employed cruelties well used: specifically, cruelties that are initially performed "all at once"; moreover, cruelties that, when reverted to subsequently, result only in "as much utility for subjects as possible" (P 8). Agathocles's rapidly and surgically applied cruelties, Machiavelli avers, benefit rather than harm the majority of his people. Agathocles may kill some citizens, but he also earns the tacit consent and perhaps even the overt support of very many others. Machiavelli's use of Agathocles in *The Prince* as his first leader who exemplifies cruelty well used toward his subjects suggests that the Sicilian possesses not only military virtue but also domestic or even civil talents more generally indicative of princely virtue. What else should we expect from a thinker like Machiavelli, who elsewhere declares unequivocally: "Where there are good arms there are always good laws" (P 12).

Furthermore, Machiavelli upholds Agathocles in *The Prince* as the chief example who proves the following somewhat paradoxical rule concerning domestic policy within a principality: A truly independent prince cannot live securely with his people unless they live in tangible security from *him*. Machiavelli insists, with the Sicilian expressly in mind, that "one can never found oneself upon his subjects [*sudditi*] if, as a result of new and continual injuries, they are not safe against him" (P 8). To be truly autonomous, Machiavelli declares, a prince may not simply treat his subjects however he pleases; to avoid conspiracies and insurrections, he must permit his subjects or citizens some tangible autonomy from himself. It is noteworthy that in these passages Machiavelli uses "subjects" and "citizens" interchangeably, just as he often calls individuals who enjoy armed peoples as their "friends" alternately "princes" and "tyrants" (e.g., P 9; D I.40).

Depending on which classical sources were available to him, Machiavelli may have been aware of this remark attributed to Agathocles: The Sicilian declared that he employed no bodyguards because the people themselves served as his bodyguard.[19] Employing bodyguards was traditionally considered the earmark of tyranny, yet the writers who established this criterion still identified as tyrants certain princes, like Agathocles, who did *not* maintain them.[20] In any case, perhaps this factor ranks prominently among the reasons Agathocles, according to Machiavelli, "lived securely for a long time in his patria" (P 8). Despite his cruelty and criminality, Agathocles remained until the end a benefactor of his "fatherland." If he was a tyrant, as the writers so often called him, then Machiavelli seems to suggest that he is a peculiar kind of tyrant. Rather than the title of tyrant bestowed on Agathocles by history, Machiavelli writes as if the Sicilian behaved more like a constitutional monarch.[21] And yet, as I mentioned above and explore further below, Machiavelli never, in his own voice, explicitly recommends Agathocles as a model prince whose behavior others should emulate.

AGATHOCLES, BORGIA, AND WHAT MAY "BE CALLED VIRTUE"

Machiavelli does not, of course, present his account of Agathocles's career in a vacuum. Readers of *The Prince* first encounter Agathocles after almost certainly being shocked, outraged, and perhaps a little exhilarated by Machiavelli's breathtaking description of the ruthless, deceitful, and murderous Cesare Borgia in the book's preceding chapter. In chapter 7 Machiavelli declares that he can give "no better example" than Borgia, who deceives, bribes, poisons, strangles, and outfights virtually anyone who obstructs his "high intentions" to become the undisputed ruler of Italy (P 7). Machiavelli attributes the utmost "ferocity and virtue" to Borgia, whom he prefers to call by the exalted title "Duke Valentino," or simply "the duke." He refers to him as a "prudent and virtuous" prince, one whose actions should be imitated despite his initial reliance on fortune, and even despite an ultimate political demise perhaps attributable to his own poor judgment (P 7). Machiavelli certainly knows that any reader who possesses a relatively healthy moral compass would be, to say the least, distressed by his endorsement of the duke—especially, Florentine readers, who, within recent memory, had been terrified by the duke's aspiration to add Tuscany to his princely holdings, an annexation that would have entailed the wholesale subjection of Machiavelli's own Arno republic to the duke.

In chapter 7, Machiavelli distinguishes Valentino from the great founder-princes of chapter 6: Moses, Romulus, Theseus, and Cyrus. Unlike those semilegendary figures, who relied solely on their own *virtù*—that is, their own arms—to establish long-lasting religious or political orders, Valentino ultimately fails because he relies too extensively on *fortuna*. More specifically, the duke relies on the mercenary arms provided by his father, Pope Alexander VI, and the auxiliary arms lent to him by the French king. Notwithstanding the disadvantages imposed by Borgia's military dependence on others, Machiavelli goes out of his way to emphasize that Valentino possessed so much virtue that he nearly overcame his dependence on fortune to establish an independent, free-standing principality in Central Italy.[22]

Considering Machiavelli's favorable account of Borgia's indisputably criminal career and the controversy this likely would have stirred among his readers, the next chapter on criminal princes—chapter 8, in which Agathocles figures centrally—seems intended to alleviate any concern his audience might harbor regarding Machiavelli's apparent endorsement of criminal immorality in chapter 7. In chapter 8 Machiavelli expands his typology of new princes to include not only those who attained their principalities through either virtue or fortune, but now also a third, apparently morally inferior, category: those who attained their new principalities through crimes. Machiavelli initially presents the ancient and modern princes discussed in chapter 8—Agathocles and Liverotto of Fermo—as mere criminals who attained varying degrees of princely success but who, because of their crimes, especially against republics, are not worthy of praise or emulation.

As we know, crime is hardly absent from the repertoires of successful princes whom, in previous chapters and elsewhere, Machiavelli deems either virtuous or fortunate. As Machiavelli notes in the *Discourses*, Romulus murdered his brother, Remus, and his coregent, Titus Tatius (D I.9, I.18); and, as he explains in *The Prince*, Borgia strangled competing condottieri and dismembered his problematically capable henchman, Remirro d'Orco (P 7). More intriguingly, Machiavelli insists that without these crimes Romulus would not have successfully laid the foundations for Rome's free republic and glorious empire, and Borgia would not have effectively established "good government" in the Romagna and provided "well-being" for its inhabitants (P 7).

Machiavelli was certainly also aware that writers in his own day vilified Borgia and would continue to do so.[23] At first glance, he seems willing to contravene contemporary moral disapprobation for Borgia by emphasizing the good outcomes that resulted from the duke's crimes. But he doesn't work as hard to counter the negative opinion of Agathocles voiced by "the writers" of the past (historians, essayists and philosophers), who tended to denounce or ignore him—or at least tried to minimize his achievements and significance.[24] Yet Machiavelli, who seldom misses an opportunity to distinguish himself from other writers, here seems to follow the example of ancient writers when he compliments Agathocles less robustly than he does Valentino—even as he defies contemporary convention by bestowing fairly lofty praise on the duke.

Although Borgia serves as Machiavelli's prime example of a prince who came to power through fortune, he presents the duke as sufficiently adept at force and fraud to compensate for such initial dependence—so much so that he deems Borgia virtuous with little or no hesitation. If Machiavelli were still operating in chapter 8 with the opposition of virtue versus fortune that he employed in chapters 6 and 7, he would have been logically compelled to judge Agathocles as virtuous without any qualification. After all, he demonstrates that the Sicilian owed much less of his political success to fortune than did Borgia. Agathocles did not, like the duke, inherit arms procured by his father and borrowed from a foreign king to establish his principality; the Sicilian rose from the very bottom of Syracuse's military to seize such arms for himself and use them to establish his own principality, successfully discarding any inhibiting relations of dependence that he incurred along the way. Agathocles retained his principality much more successfully and for much longer than did the duke, whose kingdom evaporated with his father's death.[25] Moreover, Agathocles seems to have provided the Syracusans as much "good government" and "well-being" as the duke bestowed on the Romagnoli, whom he ruled for a much shorter time.

Again, despite Agathocles's remarkable effectiveness as a captain and a prince, Machiavelli points to the objective fact that he is not "celebrated among the most excellent men" (P 8). Moreover, despite all of Agathocles's impressive self-earned success, Machiavelli himself appears to hedge about his status as a virtuous prince. In one of the most quoted sentences from *The Prince*, Machiavelli declares with respect to Agathocles: "One cannot call it virtue to kill one's fellow citizens, to betray one's friends, to be without faith, without compassion, without religion" (P 8).

However, Valentino, whom Machiavelli deems virtuous with no apparent qualification, and Agathocles, whom Machiavelli does not readily acknowledge as a fully virtuous prince, both—more or less equally—violate these standards of religion, compassion, faith, and friendship. So how truly decisive are such principles in Machiavelli's evaluation of a prince's prospective virtue? In the effort to better understand his evaluation of the respective "virtues" of Agathocles and Borgia, and therefore the quality of Machiavellian virtue itself, we should now apply the standards he invokes in this famous sentence more specifically and more directly to each of these figures.

Working backward through the qualities Machiavelli insists a virtuous prince should possess, who is more directly associated with religion, Agathocles or Valentino? The duke was the natural son of a pope, and he commanded the papal armies. This certainly gives Borgia some direct affiliation with religious institutions. However, Borgia had served as a cardinal before renouncing churchly office to pursue a military career.[26] This implies some diminution of Borgia's religious association over the course of his life. Somewhat surprisingly, Agathocles maintained greater ties to religious authority than did Borgia: according to historical sources, the Sicilian held a high priesthood when he seized control of Syracuse, and the only crown he wore during his tenure as prince was the ribbon signifying this civic-religious office.[27] Perhaps Machiavelli has this in mind when he claims, otherwise inexplicably, that Agathocles's actions ultimately acquitted him well "with both God and men" (P 8).

Who was more compassionate? Almost as much as Agathocles, Borgia serves as a prominent exemplar of the Machiavellian principle of "cruelty well used." Both commit sudden acts of violence against prominent elites that consequently result in a form of kindness for the common people. Borgia eliminates the corrupt petty lords who despoiled and misgoverned the residents of the Romagna, and he vivisects his lieutenant, fellow Spaniard Remirro, who offended the people while instituting Borgia's rule in that province. As we know, Agathocles exterminates Syracuse's ruling class and rescues the people from the threat of Carthaginian domination. Both Valentino and Agathocles, Machiavelli notes, resort to violence at a stroke while gaining control of Cesena and Syracuse; as a result, both princes avoided the kind of persistent, widespread, and intensifying violence that necessarily harms "the universality" of people (P 8). Both commit instantaneous acts of cruelty toward the few in ways that exhibit long-term compassion for the many.

What of faith? Machiavelli demonstrates that both princes are accomplished liars. Borgia, whom Machiavelli claims "knew so well how to dissimulate," lures disloyal condottieri to Sinigaglia on the pretense of making peace with them, only to murder them en masse; Agathocles calls the Syracusan *grandi* to a formal assembly on the pretext of discussing public affairs, only to perpetrate a similar crime on them. Which of the two is more guilty of betraying friends? Borgia rewards Remirro's effective service on the duke's behalf by eliminating him in a spectacularly bloody fashion. He also evades fulfilling his obligations to the French king, who had provided him with arms: Machiavelli favorably describes how, rather than enthusiastically aiding the king in his territorial designs on Naples, the duke pursues his own conquests in Central Italy with French troops—conquests that the king, in fact, expressly proscribed (P 7). Besides betraying the trust of Syracuse's nobles by eliminating the city's elites, Agathocles breaks whatever word he gave Hamilcar by renewing hostilities with Carthage after the Carthaginian commander had permitted him to seize the Syracusan principality.

In summation, Borgia, whom Machiavelli deems virtuous without any apparent qualification, and Agathocles, whom Machiavelli does not acknowledge as a fully virtuous prince, both exemplify (or violate) the qualities of religion, compassion, faith, and friendship that are supposedly dispositive in his evaluation of a prince's virtue. Further complicating matters, he arguably holds in higher regard than any of these qualities the following two modes that he insists Agathocles most certainly observed with great care: the exercise of cruelty well used and the guarantee of personal security to most of his subjects or citizens. These modes of action are more conducive to virtue as expounded by Machiavelli throughout *The Prince* than are actions conforming to religion, compassion, faith, and friendship, about which Machiavelli notoriously expresses considerable ambivalence (see, e.g., P 18).

As many astute readers of *The Prince* have noted, several princely exempla from previous chapters, not only Borgia but Moses and Romulus as well, are all criminals—at least if one considers murder a crime. Why do Agathocles's crimes, which Machiavelli insists he committed "at every stage" of his career, render him a prince unworthy of evaluation along the virtue-fortune continuum and instead relegate him to the separate category of criminality? The only crime Machiavelli specifically attributes to Agathocles is murdering all of Syracuse's senators and wealthiest citizens (P 8). Quite possibly Agathocles's murders differ in kind from those committed by Moses, Romulus, and Valentino: the latter three murdered (among many others), respectively, a slave overseer (D III.30), a rival sibling (D I.9), and a troublesome henchman (P 7) in the process of creating

new peoples and—in the long run—possibly new republics. Agathocles, for
his part, murders "fellow citizens" in the process of usurping an already
established republic. Perhaps this is a crime that not even Machiavelli can
overlook.

IS "KILLING CITIZENS" COMPATIBLE WITH
PRINCELY VIRTUE AND CIVILITY?

Obviously Agathocles's rule most certainly did not guarantee the security
of *all* his would-be citizen subjects: he massacres at a stroke the richest and
most powerful Syracusan citizens. Therefore a serious impropriety that
Agathocles commits, which Borgia does not—an act that may indeed un-
dercut the Sicilian's credentials as a fully virtuous prince—is the following
crime: "to kill one's fellow citizens" (*ammazzare e' sua cittadini*), and in so
doing overthrow a republic (P 8). From the pen of Machiavelli, who in certain ways favors republics over principalities (D I.58; D II.2), this is potentially a devastating charge indeed.[28]

In the *Discourses* Machiavelli, following well-worn republican tropes,
declares that leaders should wish to be praised, as Scipio Africanus is, for
defending and maintaining republics rather than to be denounced, as Julius Caesar is—whether overtly or subtly—for usurping them (D I.10).[29]
History may forgive a founder like Romulus who commits crimes while
laying the foundations of a future republic; but crimes committed while
usurping an existing republic bring blame upon princes like Caesar. From
this perspective, Valentino looks more like Romulus and Agathocles more
like Caesar. The former's crimes enable him to establish the foundations of
a principality in Urbino and the Romagna that—but for his ultimate ill fortune (or poor choices)—might have eventually become a republic. Whereas
Agathocles overthrows a republic and kills "fellow citizens," Valentino, by
bringing peace and civic institutions to his conquests, initiates the process
of making citizens out of the formally subjugated peoples of the greater
Romagna (P 7). Borgia cleaned up the corrupt, petty lords of those provinces (cf. also D I.29), whereas Agathocles killed elite citizens and usurped
an existing Mediterranean republic.[30]

This sharp contrast between the two figures may be mitigated somewhat because both Borgia and Agathocles enhanced the civic-military
institutions of their dominions: the duke begins arming his new subjects
in the Romagna (P 13),[31] and the Sicilian expands the civilian ranks of his
military—in fact, he even frees slaves to serve alongside citizen soldiers.[32]
Moreover, Agathocles may have inflicted less harm on the common people
of Sicily while consolidating his rule there than the duke imposed on "the
vulgo" of the Romagna: Why else were the people so angry at the duke's

henchman, Remirro d'Orco (and possibly at the duke himself), that Borgia needed to purge them of their "ill spirit" by eliminating Remirro in an infamously spectacular fashion (P 7)?[33]

When founding a people, as opposed to simply establishing a principality-cum-republic, a prince may be compelled to behave cruelly toward the people as well as toward elites. Note, for instance, the "infinite" numbers of his own people whom Machiavelli insists Moses needed to kill to establish his laws (D III.30)—many more, it seems, than did Romulus. Of course, Machiavelli sets strict limits on how deeply into the populace such cruelties should penetrate and for how long they ought to persist (P 8)—especially when such "rigors" pertain to subjects' property and women (P 16, P 19). In short, the rule of no prince can long endure pervasive and persistent abuse of the common people.[34]

Be that as it may, even if Valentino's cruelties may have affected a larger number of subjects than did Agathocles's, the latter's cruelties harmed already established citizens, usurped civic institutions, and overturned a republic. Criticisms of Agathocles along these lines abound in the works of scholars associated with "Cambridge school" interpretations of Machiavelli.[35] I suggest that such criticisms are premised on a widely held, but potentially faulty, assumption that Machiavelli maintained a rather undifferentiated notion of both "republics" and "citizens."

On the issue of republics: Machiavelli does not simply prefer republics to principalities; he favors certain republics over others, namely democratic republics like Athens, Rome, and the German-Swiss cities over oligarchic republics like Sparta and Venice.[36] Furthermore, he may favor certain kinds of principalities over these latter, oligarchic forms of republics—especially principalities that convert unarmed polities into armed ones; and he may prefer principalities that transform republics governed by the few into those where the many enjoy more extensive and robust political power. All the ancient sources, whatever their conflicting accounts of Agathocles's career, concur on at least this point: the Sicilian overthrew a republic where the senate and richest citizens had recently amassed more power for themselves at the expense of the Syracusan demos. In short, Agathocles overthrew an oligarchy that had formerly been a democracy.[37]

These distinctions between types of republics, among different kinds of principalities, and between different classes of citizens are especially relevant in our evaluation of Agathocles. After all, Agathocles's reign in Syracuse, which Machiavelli describes with feigned ambivalence in chapter 8 of *The Prince*, shares many characteristics with the "civil principality" that he favors more explicitly in the very next chapter; that is, a principality in which an individual comes to supreme power with the support of some citizens over others—most preferably, with the armed support of the common people against the nobles.[38]

A single fact nevertheless remains: Machiavelli declares that one "cannot call" Agathocles's actions "virtuous," nor can any individual who perpetrates them ever win "glory" (P 8). However, this judgment is not exactly straightforward: again, if one cannot attribute virtue to someone like Agathocles, this does not prevent Machiavelli from explicitly doing so himself. Moreover, glory is not an unqualified good in *The Prince*, as Machiavelli strongly intimates within its pages that several individuals who won glory, like Ferdinand of Aragon and Scipio Africanus, did not actually deserve it (P 21, P 17). In contemporary social science parlance, for Machiavelli excellence and glory are descriptive categories while virtue is a normative category.

In this light it may be significant that Machiavelli uses indirect speech to deny Agathocles virtue but direct speech to bestow it on him. Moreover, cross-comparisons with other figures invoked in *The Prince*, like Scipio (discussed in chapter 2), suggest that for Machiavelli winning glory is not an infallible guide in confirming the actual merit of an individual political leader. Glory, after all, entails a kind of dependence on others, namely writers of the present and future—a form of dependence not compatible with true political *virtù*. One must always keep in mind that Machiavelli considers himself the first author to full-throatedly impugn the judgment of such writers (P 15; D I.58).

Returning to the comparison of Valentino and Agathocles more specifically: I am fully persuaded by the renowned interpretation by Victoria Kahn.[39] Machiavelli, in her view, engages in a kind of rhetorical sleight of hand when he feigns criticisms of Agathocles's crimes; he undertakes a diversionary tactic in criticizing Agathocles's crimes immediately after forthrightly endorsing those of Borgia. By praising Valentino and blaming Agathocles, Machiavelli absolves himself, rhetorically, of overtly recommending the evil means employed by *both* political actors—hence affording himself plausible deniability against accusations that he "speaks well" of evil as such.[40]

Kahn provocatively argues that Machiavelli's denunciation of Agathocles in chapter 8 mimics Borgia's theatrical act of moral disavowal that Machiavelli depicts in chapter 7. By spectacularly murdering Remirro, Borgia exonerates himself, in the eyes of his subjects, of responsibility for the crimes Remirro committed at his behest. Machiavelli famously reports how Valentino left the people of the Romagna "satisfied and stupefied": satisfied that Borgia brought "good government" to the Romagna, but stupefied over whether Valentino or Remirro was ultimately responsible for the cruelty necessary to establish it. Likewise, Machiavelli performatively disavows his endorsement of Agathocles's crimes by imitating Borgia's disowning of his actual complicity in the cruelty Remirro commits in the Romagna.

Machiavelli, according to Kahn, similarly satisfies and stupefies his readers: the outrageous spectacle of Agathocles's antiaristocratic massacre seemingly substantiates Machiavelli's ostensibly severe criticisms of the Sicilian—criticisms that, on inspection, prove barely credible given the precepts that Machiavelli propagates, the actions he recounts, and the outcomes he describes. Machiavelli obscures for readers the fact that both Borgia's and Agathocles's crimes were necessary to establish good government in the Romagna and in Sicily. As Kahn rightly suggests, Machiavelli forswears his endorsement of this fact by pretending that the crimes of Valentino are somehow less deplorable (even if obviously less efficacious) than those of Agathocles.[41] Thus morally fastidious readers may be satisfied by the appearance that Machiavelli's endorsement of virtuous criminality is more restricted, more limited, than it really is.

Through further scrutiny, just as Machiavelli seems to qualify Agathocles's virtue, he also subtly indicates a certain lack of virtue on Borgia's part—a lack of virtue not fully attributable to the fact that the duke began his career with borrowed arms. On the one hand, Machiavelli explicitly calls Valentino virtuous throughout his account of the duke's career, and he seems to insist that Valentino's ultimate political failure was "not his fault" (P 7). On the other hand, however, Machiavelli ultimately attributes the duke's political demise *not* to any specific "malignity of fortune," but to a fairly clear deficiency of virtue: Borgia, he claims, errs in his choice of who would succeed his father as pope. Valentino, Machiavelli claims, could have prevented the election of a pontiff who would have posed a grave threat to his nascent principality: he could have permitted the accession of a French or Spanish cardinal who would have more readily tolerated Borgia's territorial gains than did an Italian like Giuliano della Rovere, who became Julius II. Instead, Borgia permits the election of della Rovere, a man his father had previously exiled and who would, in retribution, strip the duke of his state. Indeed, there are sound reasons to believe Machiavelli judges Agathocles to be a far greater success than Valentino: Agathocles conquered and governed the entire large island of Sicily for his whole long life, never suffered conspiracies by his subjects, and ultimately proved victorious against invading foreigners (P 8). Borgia could not consolidate the much smaller territory of Romagna-Urbino, which he in short order allowed Pope Julius II to expropriate (P 7).

So, to offer a provisional summary of Machiavelli's assessments of these figures: on the one hand Machiavelli denies Agathocles the full praise to which his actions, by Machiavellian standards, ought to entitle him. But

Machiavelli exaggerates his praise of Borgia, whose actions, by those very same standards, ought to condemn him as a rather foolhardy failure. In the end, however, Machiavelli bestows on Agathocles the virtue that he seemed to be withholding throughout his evaluation, then withdraws from Borgia the virtue he initially granted him.

Indeed, if one looks more closely at Machiavelli's evaluation of Agathocles, it is hard to say whether he ever actually criticized the Sicilian at all: Machiavelli employs indirect speech when he claims that "one cannot" call Agathocles virtuous; but then, *in his own voice*, Machiavelli emphatically calls him virtuous. Machiavelli's rhetoric suggests that it may, in fact, be a third party or parties, not Machiavelli himself, who denies Agathocles's virtue. He expresses his own view when he directly attributes virtue to the Sicilian. Considering these *giveths* and *taketh* on Machiavelli's part, it proves exceedingly difficult to provide a definitive answer to the simple question, "Who is more virtuous, Agathocles or Valentino?" Clearly one is more virtuous than Machiavelli first makes it seem and the other is less so. But we do not know conclusively which one Machiavelli deems more virtuous.

We cannot, I argue, venture a final word on this issue—if such a word is indeed possible—until we examine Machiavelli's other example of a leader whom, like Agathocles, he initially claims to be neither strictly virtuous nor fortunate; another individual whom Machiavelli deems a mere criminal. Liverotto da Fermo shares notable attributes associated with both Borgia and Agathocles, and Machiavelli's account of his career sheds light on two issues raised above: first, the extent to which Machiavelli thinks that all "*cittadini*" are always worthy of the reverence bestowed on them by civic humanists; and, second, the ramifications of papal power for contemporary Italian politics. More specifically, the case of Liverotto highlights how far Christianity and the Catholic Church have constrained the possibility of princely virtue's emerging in the Italy of Machiavelli's day. The issue of the papacy's political role in modern Italy leads us to closely examine the second major figure with whom Machiavelli compares Agathocles: Liverotto of Fermo.

AGATHOCLES, LIVEROTTO, AND PAPAL "PARRICIDE"

The contemporary counterpart to Agathocles, who also, as Machiavelli explains in chapter 8, acquired a principality by criminal means and by usurping a republic, is Oliverotto, or "Liverotto," da Fermo. At the most superficial level, the only two factors distinguishing their respective coups are that Liverotto usurped Fermo's republic with mercenary arms rather than, like Agathocles, by rising through the ranks of a domestic civil military; and that Liverotto's criminally acquired principality was remarkably short-lived. These differences, however, turn out to be not so superficial: in fact, they draw attention to other salient similarities and differences between the two figures that accentuate the added difficulties that the papacy, and the political-military conditions it creates and perpetuates, poses to new princes in Italy.

Although not a lowly craftsman's son, Liverotto, like Valentino, overcame somewhat disadvantaged origins in becoming a prince. While both were scions of aristocratic families, Liverotto was an orphaned child, and everyone knew that Valentino was the "natural" son of Pope Alexander VI (P 7–8). Liverotto was raised by his maternal uncle, the nobleman Giovanni Fogliani, who thought his ward could make good learning military arts under the tutelage of the mercenary captains Paolo and Vitellozzo Vitelli (P 8). "Ingenious and hardy in body and spirit," Liverotto proves himself an exceptional soldier fighting for others. But because he, Machiavelli declares, "considered parity with others tantamount to servility," Liverotto decides to seize his hometown entirely for himself, gaining the backing of the Vitelli and conspiring with some of Fermo's first citizens to do so.

Liverotto deceives Fogliani into believing he wishes to enter the city in a manner, Machiavelli reports, that would bring honor to himself, his uncle, and his patria. Thus, exploiting norms of patriotic duty and filial obligation, Liverotto arrives in Fermo at the head of a military parade, accompanied by a large band of troops (P 8). After an elaborate homecoming dinner, Liverotto lures his unsuspecting uncle, as well as the leading citizens who were not his confederates, into a private room where his men, lying in wait, murder them all. Backed by the troops with whom he entered the city, Liverotto then compels Fermo's civic magistrates to surrender authority to him. While Liverotto betrays his adopted father, Fogliani, the leading citizens, with whom Liverotto conspired, simultaneously betray their fatherland by contriving to hand it over to a mercenary usurper. Machiavelli denounces Liverotto's accomplices as "certain citizens [*alcuni cittadini*] who esteemed servitude more highly than the liberty of their patria" (P 8). To underscore the theme of crimes committed against both a father and a fatherland in these circumstances, Machiavelli deems the murderous plot carried out by Liverotto and his fellow conspirators a parricide.

This emphasis on a group of duplicitous, corrupt citizens potentially undermines the exalted status to which the civic humanists of Machiavelli's day (and contemporary "neorepublicans") might morally elevate, without qualification, the notion of *cittadini*. Furthermore, it may raise the question of how much Agathocles should be rebuked for killing "citizens" per se. Machiavelli introduces here, and explores further in the next chapter, the idea that there are in fact *two* kinds of citizens in republics: those who crave oppression and those who strive to resist it (P 9; cf. D I.5). The evidence and arguments from these two chapters (P 8 and 9) suggest that the former should be dealt with more sternly.

Liverotto certainly proves to be an intriguing parallel to Agathocles: like Agathocles, Machiavelli declares that Liverotto equates obedience, and even collegiality, with servility. An orphan, the usurper of Fermo compensates for a disadvantaged upbringing by excelling in military arts, albeit as a mercenary rather than under civic auspices (P 8). Moreover, like the Sicilian, Liverotto eliminates his city's ruling class—or at least that part of it that was not complicit in his coup. As Machiavelli shows elsewhere in *The Prince*, as well as in the *Discourses* and the *Florentine Histories*, while the nobilities of ancient Italian republics remained united by their shared antagonism toward their cities' armed populaces, who constantly challenged their privilege and authority, papal meddling in domestic politics splits the nobles of modern Italian cities into antagonistic factions, most notably the Guelf and Ghibelline parties (P 11, P 20). Whereas class conflict between the *grandi* and *popolo* produced outcomes conducive to liberty in ancient republics, Machiavelli maintains that continual sectarian strife among the *grandi* or *ottimati* undermines the civic health of modern republics.

However, despite these general criticisms of modern republics, and of individuals like Liverotto who exploit their civic deficiencies, Liverotto is not, in Machiavelli's estimation, entirely reprehensible. After forcibly compelling Fermo's magistrates to grant him full authority, Liverotto, like Agathocles, reorders the republic with civic and military reforms (P 8). Also like Agathocles, Liverotto governs without insurrection and with notable military success. He was poised to expand his principality beyond Fermo, Machiavelli informs us, only to be undone by the deceit of none other than Duke Valentino, who entraps and murders him at another purportedly celebratory gathering a year later, in Senigallia (P 8). This outcome, Machiavelli intimates, would have been highly unlikely without the intrigues associated with mercenary, warlord politics continually instigated by the papacy (cf. P 13, 24). Of course Liverotto would never have had the opportunity to overthrow Fermo's republic in the first place without such intrigues and without the aid of the Vitelli's foreign mercenary arms. By contrast, although Agathocles may have used Carthaginian mercenaries to help perpetrate his coup in Syracuse, he then attacks Carthage with a largely civic military force.[42]

Machiavelli elaborates the full ramifications of this point with considerable delicacy. Unlike Agathocles, who gains imperium over all of Sicily, in Machiavelli's account Liverotto's own ability to secure even a modest foothold within the Marche region of Italy is constantly shadowed by papal authority: Machiavelli dates Liverotto's political rise by citing the reign of

Pope Alexander VI; the Vitelli brothers, mercenaries in the service of Alexander, sponsor Liverotto's coup in Fermo; and, finally, Liverotto toasts the "greatness" of Pope Alexander and his son, Duke Valentino, at the "solemn banquet" where he deceives and murders his uncle and half of Fermo's *ottimati* (P 8).

Liverotto's tribute or blessing honoring the Holy Father and his son of questionable birth prompts a debate among the dinner participants over contemporary papal politics, a controversial topic that then gives Liverotto the pretext to move such sensitive discussions to a "more secret place" (*in loco piu secreto*). In this antechamber or private room, Liverotto's hidden soldiers strangle his uncle and the other leading citizens in attendance.[43]

Rather chillingly, Liverotto's toast is a blessing that proves to be a curse. It rings out as a death sentence for many of Fermo's first citizens, who are murdered almost immediately; and it foreshadows Liverotto's own deception and strangulation by Cesare Borgia, whose greatness the toast invokes. Moreover, Liverotto's blessing also proves a curse for Duke Valentino. In fairly short order, all of these people will have been deprived of either their lives or their authority. After Liverotto assassinates the *ottimati* of Fermo, Pope Alexander and his son quickly snuff out Liverotto's nascent principality, just as Pope Julius will, soon thereafter, do the same to Cesare Borgia's reign in the greater Romagna.

Machiavelli emphasizes the corrupt clientalism and servile dependence rife within papal-mercenary politics by revealing that, in the end, Liverotto is little more than an extension of Vitellozzo Vitelli's mercenary power and influence (P 8): at Senigallia, as Machiavelli reports elsewhere, while both of them were being strangled by Borgia's men, Liverotto pleaded for mercy; from his knees and through his tears, Liverotto protested that he was only doing Vitellozzo's bidding in challenging the authority of the duke and the church.[44] Through his own confession, Liverotto confirms that, all along, Vitellozzo had been, in Machiavelli's words, "the master of both [Liverotto's] virtues and his crimes." Plainly, his insolent and insubordinate nature notwithstanding, Liverotto never managed to fully extricate himself from servile dependence on his mercenary patrons, the Vitelli, who likewise never successfully freed themselves from subservience to the nefarious patronage of the church—which, through Valentino's actions, hastened their collective demise. Furthermore, in the *Discourses* Machiavelli similarly declares Cesare Borgia ultimately to have been little more than the instrument of his not so Holy Father, Alexander (D III.29; cf. also P 11). Within Machiavelli's worldview, it seems, until one is truly a prince, until one attains full autonomy—as Agathocles enjoyed in Sicily—one is always merely the tool of some more powerfully situated political actor.

Despite his own revulsion toward servitude, Liverotto's prostrate, tear-ful confession bears witness to the naked fact of his own lack of autonomy, his own servility, at the very moment that others relieve him of his life. By contrast, Agathocles "lived securely for a long time in his patria" (P 8). Not only did Agathocles die an old man in his bed, but he also pronounced the restoration of the Syracusan republic, which he left in better civic and military condition than when he usurped it.[45] Machiavelli never remotely accuses Agathocles, as he does Liverotto, of committing "parricide," perhaps precisely because the Sicilian leaves his patria better off than he found it. To put matters simply, Machiavelli's contrasting the accounts of Liverotto and Borgia with that of Agathocles demonstrates that princely independence and longevity—as well as the civic benefits these may confer on *citizens* and *republics*—are much more difficult to attain in Christian Italy than in the pagan Mediterranean.

As both Liverotto and Valentino discover to their considerable dismay, a curious combination of power and weakness enables the papacy to prevent an Agathocles from emerging in modern Italy. Speaking generally, Machiavelli observes that the church was too strong to permit another political actor to unify Italy, but too weak to do so itself (D I.12).[46] For our purposes this means it is difficult for a modern usurper of Fermo, like Liverotto, or a redeemer of the Romagna, like Borgia, to become lord of the entire region—more difficult certainly than it was for Agathocles, the ancient usurper of Syracuse, to become master of all Sicily.

Machiavelli's contrast of Agathocles's and Liverotto's careers highlights the thoroughgoing corruption and denigration of Italian politics wrought by the papacy (P 11–12). Throughout his writings, Machiavelli not only observes how the church sows seeds of disunity among the nobles of Italian republics by splitting them into parties like the Guelfs and Ghibellines, he also shows how the papacy abetted the military disarming of modern peoples: even when urban guildsmen managed to vanquish their cities' nobles in medieval cities, they relied increasingly on the arms of private, hired mercenaries to protect their republics (P 12–13).[47] The church may have religiously legitimated the cause of "the people" in such conflicts, but in the service of their cause, Machiavelli insists, it would not—indeed, could not—provide them with arms or knowledge of how to use them.

Precisely because the church divides modern nobles and disarms modern peoples, new princes like Liverotto seldom enjoy the opportunity to usurp republics in ways that substantively improve them long term, both civically and militarily. Modern usurpers-cum-reformers rarely face the circumstances seized by Agathocles; that is, the opportunity to publicly—and hence with all the dignity that *publicitas* confers—eliminate, overthrow, or correct their city's entire nobility. In the Christian republics of

Italy, supreme magistrates never wield robust civic-military authority over armed citizens, and they never confront their city's entire nobility formally collected in senates under the bright, cleansing light of the sun.[48] Instead, new princes must, as Liverotto is compelled to do, dishonorably lure their adversaries to banquets held in private chambers or secret rooms, where they strangle them in the dark (P 8). In other words, modern princes encounter few opportunities to become genuine civil princes, as defined by Machiavelli in the very next chapter of *The Prince*: chapter 9.

Machiavelli's Liverotto also intriguingly serves as a compelling allegory for Christian Italy as a whole: orphaned by the collapse of pagan Rome, Italy, like Liverotto, is put in the inconstant, treacherous, and civically corrupting hands of mercenary commanders by an *effeminate* father figure, the pope. (Recall that Machiavelli carefully but otherwise inexplicably identifies Liverotto's adopted father, Fogliani, as his "*maternal* uncle," his *zio materno*) (P 8). Destined to remain the hopelessly hobbled instrument of the church, Liverotto is literally and figuratively both a strangler and the strangled: as a mercenary he helps the church undermine functioning republics like Fermo by asphyxiating their leading citizens; conversely, as a potential princely threat to the church's authority he himself must be suffocated by the church's latest mercenary tool, Cesare Borgia.

In short, whatever flowers of political virtue might be planted or cultivated in Central Italy by some ambitious individual pope must, to preserve the authority of the church, be cut down subsequently by that very same pontiff or a succeeding one. These "Alexanders," "Juliuses," and "Caesars" prove in the end to be shallow, impotent imitations of their ancient pagan namesakes. International influence over papal elections and the short term of a single pope's reign, Machiavelli indicates, undermine any political actor, however virtuous, who might threaten to supplant the church's self-anointed role as imperfect but seemingly permanent ruler of Italy. To emphasize this, Machiavelli demonstrates how previous princely, would-be "rulers of Italy," such as Braccio da Montone or Francesco Sforza, in their day fared no better at wresting the peninsula's fate from the hands of the church than Liverotto and Valentino did in theirs (P 12).[49]

Let us then reevaluate our previous comparison between Agathocles and Borgia with the example of Liverotto in mind. Agathocles is more virtuous than Valentino in the strictest sense of Machiavelli's use of the term: he winds up beholden to no political actor but his own armed people; he gains mastery over an impressively wide territorial expanse; he is crueler to the entire nobility than to the majority of his people; no one conspires against or overthrows his "state" during his long life; and he leaves his polity better off than he found it—immune to threats from both oppressive domestic elites and rapacious foreign powers.

However, Agathocles never encountered the peculiar kind of "senatorial order" that confronted both Liverotto and Valentino. The Court of Rome is a seat of collegial power that can neither be outmaneuvered nor eliminated as easily as were the senate of Syracuse, the Signoria of Fermo, or the petty lords of the Romagna. The papacy's influence, Machiavelli indicates, will constantly work to severely constrict any civic or territorial gains a new prince might secure within Italy. Moreover, it will continue to empower mercenaries or foreigners to ensure that the church retains its dominant if ultimately limited geopolitical position on the peninsula. Invariably, the papacy will either figuratively or literally strangle such a new principality in its cradle. Liverotto's career emphasizes just how much Christianity diminishes the quality of political virtue in contemporary Italy and how much the Catholic Church severely restricts the possibility of grand geopolitical success in the Mediterranean world.

The Liverotto episode from chapter 8 seriously diminishes but does not fully disqualify the Borgia example of the previous chapter of *The Prince*. Machiavelli's presentation of Cesare Borgia's virtue is genuine: he accomplished so much despite obstacles that never stood in the way of ancient princes, reformers, and founders. In this light Valentino is somewhat absolved for his flawed judgment in permitting an Italian rather than a Frenchman or Spaniard to become pope. Perhaps, as Machiavelli suggests, the latter would not have seized the duke's provinces in the Romagna; Borgia did in fact enjoy diplomatic ties with the French throne and filial ties with the Spanish one. However, even if we bracket the doubts Machiavelli raises about the durability of diplomatic and filial ties throughout the episodes discussed above, neither the French nor the Spanish monarch was likely to allow his own pope to sit idly by while Valentino expanded his holdings in ways that threatened French or Spanish interests on the peninsula. Again, the church is too strong relative to Italian political actors and too weak relative to foreign ones to serve as a reliable participant in the unification of Italy.

Notwithstanding the political constraints imposed by the church—or precisely because of them—Cesare Borgia, Duke Valentino, rather than Agathocles the Sicilian, must be Machiavelli's exemplar for political success in the Italy of his day. This may account for Machiavelli's rhetorical accentuation and perhaps even exaggeration of Valentino's virtue, even though, in otherwise objective terms, it falls far short of the virtue exhibited by Agathocles. Machiavelli's Duke Valentino shows how far one can ride papal authority toward becoming ruler of Italy; but he simultaneously serves as a cautionary tale for how much further one must go to fully realize such a goal.

Ultimately, Machiavelli's narratives in chapters 7 and 8 of *The Prince* intimate that the church is a more intractable opponent than one of the fiercest, most successful military powers of all time, the Carthaginian Empire. Recall that Agathocles managed to impose his will on Carthage, which along with Rome and Macedonia was one of the three most formidable military powers in ancient history. Yet individuals like Borgia and Liverotto, princes who possess "virtue and spirit of mind and body" perhaps comparable to those of Agathocles, stand nary a puncher's chance in combat with the Holy See.

AGATHOCLES, NABIS, AND THE "CIVIL PRINCIPALITY"

Let us return to the one crime discussed above that, it seems, potentially separates Agathocles from Romulus and Cesare Borgia as praiseworthy and emulable princes: the crime of "killing fellow citizens" (P 8). Does Machiavelli believe that killing fellow citizens entirely disqualifies a leader from being considered truly virtuous and a princely example worthy of imitation? It is certainly this crime that places Agathocles most firmly in the company of other Greek princes Machiavelli discusses, princes whom previous authors generally considered "tyrants."[50] Machiavelli himself often calls such individuals tyrants, but not necessarily to criticize their actions; in fact, he often praises their conduct and upholds them as figures to be emulated.

Machiavelli's most overt praise for a Greek tyrant in *The Prince* occurs in chapter 9, the well-known chapter devoted to the topic of civil principalities. Here Machiavelli extols the political achievements of Nabis the Spartan, but he demurs from specifying the precise means Nabis used to attain his ends. According to Machiavelli, Nabis satisfied the Spartan people and avoided being "hated and despised" by them; as a result, he withstood military assaults and sieges by "all of Greece," even by the Roman Republic's "most victorious army." Nabis successfully defended "his patria and his state" against such formidable enemies for a decade and a half (P 9, P 19; D I.10). Yet, somewhat curiously, Machiavelli declares that he cannot provide the details of how Nabis drew the people to himself, and how he fought off superior numbers of previously victorious foreign enemies. Machiavelli fumfers that there are simply too many means available in comparable cases; and, even more unhelpfully, he declares that there are no "fixed rules" that apply to circumstances like those confronting Nabis. This is the best effort Machiavelli can muster in the world's most famous "how-to" book on politics? Or perhaps Machiavelli need not explicate such means in chapter 9 because he has already provided such details through the example of Agathocles in the previous chapter.

Machiavelli's hesitation to stipulate the precise details of Nabis's political success in *The Prince* echoes his unwillingness to elaborate in the *Discourses* on the "many dangers and much blood" that reformers of corrupt republics must endure and spill (D I.17–18). The only way a corrupt city can be reformed, Machiavelli writes, is if one very long-lived virtuous individual, or two successively virtuous individuals of normal life spans, provide a republic with "new life" through such hardships and bloodletting. Reminiscent of how he treats Nabis in *The Prince*, Machiavelli here declares: "it is almost impossible to provide rules" in such cases: since corruption is a matter of degree, he states, the appropriate remedies will necessarily vary given a republic's level of civic health at any particular moment (D I.18). How can we compensate for Machiavelli's reticence in these two instances? What does he consider the secret of Nabis's domestic and military success? And what, more specifically, are the dangerous and bloody means he deems necessary for reforming a corrupt republic?

If we consult Polybius and Livy,[51] we find that Nabis, Machiavelli's exemplar of a civil prince in chapter 9, behaves in very much the same way as two Syracusan princes whose morally questionable actions Machiavelli recounts in preceding chapters: Hiero and Agathocles. In chapter 6, Machiavelli describes how Hiero rose from private to princely status through Syracuse's civic military; and later he relates how Hiero ended his city's dependence on mercenary troops—"cutting [them] to pieces" and thus further winning over Syracuse's citizen soldiers (P 13).[52] After having these mercenary forces massacred, Hiero, now in command of an exclusively civil military, prevents the ever voracious Roman Republic from conquering all of Sicily. His martial virtue compels the Romans to accept him as a military ally rather than as a vanquished foe.[53]

As we have already observed, Machiavelli describes two chapters later how Agathocles, earlier in Syracuse's history, rose from even humbler beginnings than Hiero to become prince of the very same republic: Agathocles, no better than a carpenter's son, won the city's citizen soldiers to himself through dangerous military exploits and by publicly murdering all of Syracuse's senators and wealthiest citizens (P 8). If we reconsider Nabis, the primary example from chapter 9, in light of the historical sources, and mindful of Machiavelli's accounts of Hiero and Agathocles in preceding chapters, we observe that all three Greek princes liberate their peoples from both domestic and external oppression in ways that are similar if not identical.

All three enhance the civic quality of their cities' militaries: Hiero slaughters unreliable foreign mercenaries (P 7), and both Agathocles and Nabis make former slaves into fighting subjects to expand their military forces.[54] All three resort to fraud in foreign affairs: Agathocles revokes an

unfavorable alliance with Carthage (P 8); Hiero switches allegiance between the Romans and the Carthaginians at his convenience (P 6); and
Nabis betrays the Macedonian monarchy to the diplomatic and military
advantage of his patria (D I.40).⁵⁵ In short, all three princes—often treated
as petty tyrants by ancient writers—impose advantageous truces upon,
arguably, the greatest military powers in ancient history: Macedonia, Carthage and Rome.

But what about domestic affairs? As we observed, Machiavelli expresses
considerable reservations in chapter 8 over the violently criminal means
Agathocles employed in winning over the Syracusan people. Then, in the
very next chapter, he deems Nabis a "civil prince" for eschewing "criminality or other intolerable violence" while successfully expanding and
gaining to himself Sparta's armed populace—even if he does not specify
exactly how Nabis does so (P 9). Recall, moreover, that Agathocles ultimately earns Machiavelli's praise as a practitioner of "cruelty well used"
precisely because he perpetrates his crimes and exercises violence in one
fell swoop—that is, he murders his city's nobles "all at once" (P 8). Agathocles directs his cruel and violent behavior only to one specific subset of Syracuse's citizens, and he confines such cruelty and violence exclusively to
the start of his reign; when he resorts to such behavior subsequently, Machiavelli notes that he does so exclusively for "the utility of his subjects."⁵⁶

By contrast, according to Polybius, Nabis takes a much less efficient and
expeditious route toward similar ends: Nabis, in notable contrast to Agathocles, intermittently, and over a much longer period, kills, tortures, and exiles the richest and most powerful Spartans and redistributes their wealth
to the people.⁵⁷ This seems to seriously undermine Machiavelli's claim
that Nabis, unlike Agathocles and Liverotto, the criminal figures discussed
in the previous chapter (P 8), comes to power and gains popular support
without recourse to "criminality or other intolerable violence" (P 9). From
the standpoint of conventional morality there seems to be little difference
between the criminal princes Machiavelli ostensibly criticizes in chapter 8
and the civil prince he praises in chapter 9: both types of princes gain popular favor by killing prominent fellow citizens.

From the standpoint of *Machiavellian* morality, however, there is a pertinent difference between the types of princes described in chapters 8 and
9: Agathocles, the so-called criminal prince, uses violence and cruelty
much more economically—at a stroke—than does Nabis, the so-called civil
prince, whose violent cruelty persists over time (even if neither Agathocles nor Nabis ever commits violence, intolerable or otherwise, against
the common people). By the Machiavellian standard of cruelty well used,
Agathocles's "violence" is much less "intolerable" than was Nabis's because he deployed it much more quickly and efficiently. Put another way,

the criminal prince, Agathocles, practices "cruelty well used" much more *civilly* than does Nabis, the civil prince. This fact invites readers to question Machiavelli's sharply drawn moral-conceptual distinction between the two figures and consequently his apparent praise for Nabis and ostensible condemnation of Agathocles. We would be justified in concluding that Machiavelli's superficial contrast between Agathocles and Nabis gives way to a more substantive pairing of the two figures.

Keeping this in mind, readers might consider the following: However uneconomically or unexpeditiously a prince may or may not deploy violence against rich and powerful citizens, Machiavelli's close pairing of Agathocles and Nabis suggests that what makes them *both* examples worthy of imitation is the care each exhibited in refraining from using cruelty and violence against their own common citizens and subjects. The rigors of extensive civic-military service opened by both princes to the poorest and most abject members of their polities suffice in this regard. It is worth noting further that, in evaluating and somewhat closely affiliating the reigns of Agathocles and Nabis, Machiavelli intriguingly employs fairly "republican" language. In foreign affairs, Machiavelli emphasizes how Nabis and Agathocles each benefited not only himself, but also his "patria"; and when discussing their domestic policies, Machiavelli interchangeably calls those who live under the reigns of these so-called tyrants, subjects and citizens (P 8, P 9).

Thus, setting aside whatever ethical misgivings Machiavelli may profess regarding the behavior of these figures individually, we may conclude the following about all three Greek princes discussed early in *The Prince*: Hiero, Agathocles, and Nabis all resort to cruel and criminal means to achieve political ends that Machiavelli emphatically condones. Each of these Greek tyrants incurs massive hardship and sheds copious amounts of blood to improve his city, both domestically and internationally: they all either massacre mercenaries or murder rich, prominent citizens; none of them hesitates to betray powerful foreign allies; and they all successfully enlist their enlarged civil militaries to defend their fatherlands from external domination.[58]

Furthermore, Machiavelli's apparently lesser examples, Hiero and Agathocles, prove more successful than Nabis, his explicit exemplar for a *principato civile*, in at least one important respect: both Hiero and Agathocles lay the groundwork for the future reestablishment of republics in their cities. Diodorus and Justin report that Agathocles restores Syracuse's democracy from his deathbed rather than permitting any of his unruly progeny to succeed him;[59] and, in the *Discourses*, Machiavelli implies that Hiero kept Syracuse sufficiently well ordered that its citizens and soldiers reinstituted "a free way of life" after overthrowing his corrupt grandson,

Hieronymus (D II.2). Thus Machiavelli suggests that the armed subjects of a salutary tyrant may very well restore a republic once the tyrant's successor proves excessively oppressive, effecting a transition from tyranny back to a reformed republic. Ultimately the princely interregnums of Agathocles and Hiero initiate and guide the transformation of formerly weak, externally vulnerable, oligarchic polities into better armed, better defended, more democratic republics. Nabis, for his part, was prevented from doing so, had he been so inclined, when his life was cut short by foreign assassins.[60] In the long run, at least two of these three so-called tyrants left their republics, by important Machiavellian standards, in better civic and military condition than when they first "seized" them.

In chapter 9 of *The Prince*, Machiavelli explicitly and implicitly contrasts the politically successful examples of Nabis and Agathocles with the failed examples of the Gracchi in Rome and Giorgio Scali in Florence, a contrast that illustrates just how daunting and dangerous a task it is for civil princes to reform a corrupt republic or establish a fresh principality. Put simply, all civil princes who would reform republics that have become increasingly and maleficently oligarchic will encounter "kill or be killed" circumstances regarding the senates and richest citizens of their cities. Agathocles's actions, I submit, must be evaluated keeping in mind this "do or die" dilemma. Agathocles must also be judged in light of other important Machiavellian distinctions: (1) the difference between democratic and oligarchic republics; (2) the distinction between princes who favor the people and those who favor the nobles; and (3) the difference between the opposing motivations of noble and common citizens.

From this perspective there may be certain circumstances in which Machiavelli condones, nay encourages, actions through which a prince may *ammazza e' sua cittadini*, or kill one's fellow citizens. As we will observe in future chapters, a would-be prince of a republic may in fact do so through legal rather than illegal means, through collectively decided rather than unilateral modes, and hence avoid the designation "tyrant." But first I will address how Machiavelli, in the *Discourses*, conceives of Greek tyranny as a potential solution to the problems of civic corruption and economic inequality, problems he subtly criticizes potential reformers of the Roman Republic for failing to solve.

2. GREEK TYRANTS AND ROMAN REFORMERS

(CLEOMENES, CLEARCHUS, THE GRACCHI,
SCIPIO AFRICANUS, JULIUS CAESAR)

Machiavelli's magnum opus, his *Discourses* on Livy's history of Rome, has prompted readers to deem him the greatest modern champion of the ancient Roman Republic. Less acknowledged, and potentially more controversial, is the possibility that the *Discourses* reaffirms Machiavelli's admiration, already expressed in *The Prince*, for certain ancient Greek tyrants.[1] I suggest that these two distinct preferences—for Roman republicanism and Greek tyranny—are not as contradictory as they might first seem. In Machiavelli's estimation, once republics, including those ordered along Roman lines, succumb to oligarchic corruption, they must be reformed by princely figures reminiscent of the tyrants who ruled ancient Greek cities such as Syracuse, Sparta, and Heraclea.

This hypothesis challenges interpretations that present Machiavelli as more or less a faithful late medieval or early Renaissance civic humanist.[2] Scholars associated with the Cambridge school—most notably Quentin Skinner—are the most famous but by no means the only proponents of the civic humanist, or traditional republican, understanding of Machiavelli.[3] Yet Machiavelli departs decisively from the thinking of civic humanists on the question of republican renovation.[4] The civic republicans of Machiavelli's milieu, following Cicero fairly closely, hoped that rather conservative princely figures would assume the task of setting aright republics beset by corruption and insoluble social strife: for example, "fathers of their country" like Furius Camillus, Caesar Augustus, and Cosimo de' Medici, or the republican reformer—the *rector rei publicae*—of Cicero's literary imagination, Scipio Africanus the Younger.[5] Most civic humanists hoped that a patrician "first citizen" would step forward to settle the social crises of their cities, anticipating that such an individual would act with equanimity toward all classes—or, barring that, at least in ways that advantaged their republic's most noble, that is, wealthiest and most prominent, citizens.

Machiavelli, on the contrary, is perhaps the only "republican" who offers the ancient Greek tyrant as a model reformer of corrupt civic orders: specifically tyrants like Hiero, Nabis, Cleomenes, Clearchus, and the figure he discusses at greatest length, Agathocles. Drawing an ideal type from Machiavelli's descriptions of these individuals and from historical accounts available to him, in the previous chapter I suggested that the perfect Greek tyrant-cum-republican reformer performs all the following feats: he crushes the nobility and distributes their wealth to the common people; he eliminates reliance on mercenary arms; he greatly expands the ranks of citizen soldiers—especially by freeing slaves; and he manipulates diplomatic alliances with militarily more powerful foreign empires. Machiavelli intimates that the conservative, Ciceronian-humanist type of republican reformer—exemplified in his day by the Medici—usually takes the opposite course: he disarms common citizens, reinforces their status as mere clients of their city's nobles or senators, and leaves their polity vulnerable to domination by foreign powers.

Machiavelli is often considered to be a fairly faithful civic humanist, or traditional republican, because he supposedly devotes his most important work, the *Discourses*, primarily to the cause of promoting republics over principalities. Moreover, on this view Machiavelli confines his endorsement of unilateral, often violent and criminal, behavior to *The Prince*; the *Discourses*, on the contrary, is presented as a book in which deadly political action occurs almost exclusively within legally circumscribed bounds. But there is a seemingly insurmountable problem for proponents of this view: the *Discourses* offers advice not only to republicans but also to princes— and, even more problematic, it explicitly offers advice to *tyrants*[6]—advice concerning the effective use of extraordinary violence.[7]

In this chapter I will pursue Machiavelli's intimation that the lessons offered by the examples of Greek tyrants were apparently lost on *all* potential Roman reformers—reformers who set out to ameliorate the economic inequality that would eventually destroy the Roman Republic for good. Machiavelli frequently rehearses and pays homage to traditional civic-humanist criticisms of the likes of the Gracchi, Gaius Marius, and Julius Caesar for seeking to exert undue, even tyrannical, influence over the Roman Republic.[8] As exhibited by his explicit contrast between Scipio and Caesar, Machiavelli often closely follows classical republican and especially Florentine humanist tropes by criticizing Caesar as the Roman Republic's consummate usurper. However, bearing in mind the Agathoclean exemplum emerging from the amalgamation of his discussions of various Greek tyrants, Machiavelli indicates that what most interests him about

the examples of Scipio and Caesar is how remarkably similar they turn out
to be. Both are thwarted in their efforts to institute socioeconomic reforms
necessary for the civic revitalization of the Roman Republic.

Here I suggest that Machiavelli harbors more than a little sympathy for
a very specific kind of tyrant, one who kills a very specific subset of fellow
citizens—that is, the kind of tyrant exemplified by the Greek princes he discusses who suppress nobles and militarily empower the common people.
As I have already suggested, Machiavelli begins to show in chapter 8 of *The
Prince*, then confirms decisively in chapter 9, that he believes there are in
fact *two* kinds of citizens, not one. In his discussion of Liverotto, recall that
Machiavelli distinguishes "certain citizens" of Fermo who crave oppression and other citizens who strive to resist it. Moreover, in his account of
Agathocles he seems to differentiate between the "senators and richest"
citizens of Syracuse and the city's common citizens or subjects. Most famously, in chapter 9 he distinguishes more specifically between two types
of citizens who constitute "all cities" or, as he adds in the *Discourses*, "all
republics": the *grandi*, who are consumed by the appetite to oppress, and
the *popolo*, who are motivated to not be dominated (P 9).

To make the case that Machiavelli condones the behavior of tyrants
who violently crush the nobles and militarily empower the people, I argue
that the figures of Cleomenes and Clearchus in the *Discourses* complete
lessons Machiavelli offers through the examples of Hiero, Nabis, and of
course Agathocles from *The Prince*. These individuals—tyrants, as Machiavelli frankly calls them in the *Discourses*, or civil princes as he somewhat
ambiguously refers to them in *The Prince*—do not invariably establish monarchical dynasties that suppress civic liberty. Intriguingly, several lay
the foundations for republics that are healthier and more vigorous—that
is, more egalitarian and more martial—than the oligarchic and weak republics they initially usurped. In words that Machiavelli uses in a related
context, such princes "keep the public rich and the citizens poor" at home
(D I.37), and they successfully "withstand sieges" by the largest and most
successful enemy forces of their times (P 9).

CLEOMENES, THE GRACCHI, AND CORRUPTION AS
ECONOMIC INEQUALITY

In *The Prince*, Machiavelli discusses Greek tyrants such as Agathocles,
Hiero, and Nabis to illustrate how princes should befriend peoples, check
or eliminate elites, and withstand the military threats posed by imperial
hegemons. Throughout the *Discourses*, however, Machiavelli embeds his
discussion of Greek tyrants within a broader account of the unavoidable
corruption that all republics succumb to. Republics, Machiavelli repeatedly

insists, inevitably experience rising inequality over time (D I.17–20, I.55). At first he describes this pernicious inequality in purely civil terms—all republics, even Rome, are destined to suffer a serious decline in equality before the law (D I.18). But, much more subtly, he also intimates that this rise in civil inequality can be traced to an underlying expansion of economic inequality (D I.17–18, I.55, and III.24).[9]

As Machiavelli ultimately demonstrates in his chapter on Rome's agrarian laws (D I.37), economic inequality is a republican disease not readily amenable to a strictly republican cure. Tiberius and Gaius Gracchus harbored good "intentions," Machiavelli claims, when they sought to address the economic inequality that was corrupting Rome's civic-military virtue in the wake of the Punic Wars. But he concludes that they exhibited a mortally woeful lack of "prudence" by expecting the Roman Senate to sit idly by while they passed legislation aimed at stemming this economic inequality. The Gracchi basically asked the Senate's permission to legally redistribute to the increasingly impoverished Roman plebs the vast wealth controlled by Rome's senators.[10] The Roman Senate, of course, responded by murdering one Gracchus brother and, a decade later, compelling the suicide of the other—in these episodes killing hundreds, even thousands, of their followers as well.[11]

Elsewhere in the *Discourses*, Machiavelli recounts how the Greek prince Agis suffered a fate not unlike the Gracchi's: at the behest of the Spartan nobility, the republic's chief magistrates, the ephors, killed Agis before he could reinstitute Lycurgus's laws and so restore Sparta's foundational economic equality (D I.9). Cognizant of this, a subsequent, more prudent Spartan prince, Cleomenes—"using his authority well," Machiavelli writes—took the initiative in murdering the ephors, as well as members of the senatorial opposition, rather than, like his imprudent predecessor, waiting for them to eliminate him (D I.19). Through such actions, which Machiavelli deems "worthy of praise and conforming to justice," Cleomenes, unimpeded by aristocratic obstruction, then set about reestablishing socioeconomic equality in Sparta.[12]

Of course Plutarch provided the classic juxtaposition of the Gracchus brothers and Agis/Cleomenes—Roman versus Spartan statesmen who attempted to address socioeconomic inequality in their republics.[13] But Machiavelli expands this contrast by making central to his own account of ideal-typical Greek versus Roman reformers the examples of Agathocles and Julius Caesar. By the time we fully assimilate the Greek examples of Clearchus and Cleomenes in the *Discourses* to those of Agathocles, Hiero, and Nabis in *The Prince*, it becomes fairly clear that Machiavelli favors Greek tyrannical action over Gracchan imprudent inaction. But as we will observe, Machiavelli is much more circumspect when incorporating

Julius Caesar into his negative exempla of the ideal-typical, *failed* Roman reformer, which also include Scipio Africanus, the Gracchi, and Gaius Marius.

Machiavelli's example of Cleomenes, in the *Discourses*, better specifies the role redistribution must play in the quasi-tyrannical reformation of a corrupt republic—a republic where corrosive inequality has taken hold—an idea Machiavelli only intimates in *The Prince*. The historical sources Machiavelli points to in the *Discourses* illustrate how both Agathocles and Nabis redistributed to their extensively rearmed common citizenries the wealth each prince had expropriated from their cities' recently eliminated or debilitated nobilities.[14] Similarly, the example of Clearchus of Heraclea (D I.16) completes a lesson concerning class allegiance that Machiavelli leaves only partially taught in *The Prince*. To fully understand how Clearchus's example functions in the *Discourses*, we must return to Machiavelli's discussion of the "*principato civile*" in *The Prince*.

THE MEDICI, CLEARCHUS OF HERACLEA, AND THE CIVIL PRINCIPALITY

In chapter 9 of *The Prince*, Machiavelli defines the civil principality as a regime where an individual is elevated to princely authority by "fellow citizens"— more specifically, by either one or the other of the competing social classes of every city: either by the nobles, who are driven by the intolerable humor to oppress the people, or by the people, who are motivated by the decent humor to avoid aristocratic oppression. Machiavelli provides reasons, both strategic and moral, why a prince should establish his civil principality on a popular rather than an aristocratic basis (P 9). But he also opens the possibility that a civil prince, who was elevated by the nobility to oppress the people, might improve this politically disadvantaged and ethically inferior position simply by switching sides once in power. In fact, Machiavelli insists, the people will show even greater affection and devotion to a prince who defies their expectations of intensified oppression and instead completely alleviates them of aristocratic domination: "Because men who receive good from one that they thought would bring them evil are more obligated to their benefactor, the people immediately wish him well more than if he had been made prince through their own support" (P 9).

Leo Strauss perceptively notes that in chapter 9 Machiavelli uncharacteristically provides no historical example of a *modern* political example—in this case of a modern civil prince. Machiavelli usually presents both ancient and modern examples that, at least in a preliminary fashion, bear out his political lessons in a particular disquisition. Strauss suggests, if I surmise rightly, that Machiavelli need not do so in chapter 9 because the most proximate example of a prince who comes to power through the support of "fellow citizens" is the very addressee of the book, Lorenzo de' Medici.[15] But Strauss misses, I think, the more specific point Machiavelli is making through this notable omission, this pregnant absence. The Medici not only are modern princes who came to power through the support of fellow citizens, they are princes who recently came to power, more specifically, through the support of the nobility. That is, according to the stipulations of chapter 9, Lorenzo is an example of a defective civil prince, one who confronts the people as enemies rather than as friends.

The Medici, after all, were brought back from exile in 1512 by an aristocratic coup that overthrew the democratic republic, the *governo largo*, presided over by Piero Soderini and faithfully served by Machiavelli. Machiavelli had made himself an enemy of the Florentine nobles by, on the one hand, encouraging Soderini to maintain a close domestic alliance with the people assembled in the Consiglio Grande, the Great Council, and on the other by initially proposing the establishment of a large citizen military within the city.[16] In other words, Machiavelli wanted Soderini to bolster the people's position civically and militarily relative both to the Florentine *ottimati* and to external threats like France and Spain.

As we know, opposition by the Florentine nobles compelled Machiavelli to recruit peasants from the *contado* for Florence's militia,[17] and they themselves eventually enlisted a foreign power, the Spanish army, to reinstall the Medici and overthrow the republic, permitting them to oppress the Florentine people.[18] Less discussed among commentators is that Machiavelli's first act upon the Medici's return was to send the new princes "*ai Palleschi*," a subtly impassioned memorandum anticipating the advice of *The Prince*, chapter 9, intimating that the Medici ought to switch sides and make the people rather than the nobles the foundation of their new regime.[19] The Medici responded to Machiavelli's advice by shutting down the popular Consiglio Grande and, in short order, arresting and torturing Machiavelli himself. Moreover, the Medici, unlike the Greek tyrants discussed above, never instituted a civic military in Florence, leaving the city at the mercy of foreign powers—the French, Spanish, and German monarchies.

We should read Machiavelli's account of Clearchus, in the *Discourses*, keeping in mind these Florentine circumstances as well as Machiavelli's advice to civil princes in chapter 9 of *The Prince*. In the *Discourses*, Machiavelli describes how the nobles of ancient Heraclea, under conditions of intense social strife between the *popolo* and the *grandi*, recalled Clearchus from exile to help them crush the people and deprive them of their liberty (D I.16). But once authorized in this capacity, Clearchus realized he could neither fully satisfy the nobles' appetite to oppress the people nor govern a people who so severely resented their loss of liberty. Thus Clearchus took a decidedly un-Medicean course of action: he switched his allegiance to the people and disposed of the nobles. Machiavelli reports how, at a convenient time—presumably while the nobles are gathered in their senate house or in a public assembly—Clearchus "hacks them all to pieces, to the extreme satisfaction of the populace" (D I.16).[20] Apparently Clearchus got the memo that the Medici so cavalierly ignored roughly eighteen centuries later.[21]

The cases of Clearchus and Agathocles are very close, yet subtle differences present themselves. The butchering of the nobles, only mentioned in the Agathocles episode from *The Prince*, is described in gory detail in the account of Clearchus from the *Discourses*. Another difference is the popular responses Machiavelli describes in the respective episodes: the Syracusan people seem merely to passively tolerate Agathocles's antiaristocratic crime, while the Heraclean people discernibly delight in the bloody violence Clearchus deploys against the Heraclean *grandi*. We might think this difference occurs because by the time Machiavelli discusses Clearchus in *discorso* I.16, through the examples of Nabis in chapter 9 of *The Prince* and of Agis and Cleomenes in *discorso* I.9, he has better prepared his audience to understand the actions of Agathocles—actions that Machiavelli ostensibly criticized in chapter 8 of *The Prince*. Ironically, whereas he apparently presents Agathocles as a less than fully laudable example in *The Prince*, by this point in the *Discourses*—his supposedly more "republican" book—Machiavelli explicitly endorses the Agathoclean Clearchus as an example to be followed by any "tyrant" who wishes to win over a hostile people (D I.16).

Furthermore, the example of Clearchus in *discorso* I.16 fulfills the promise of chapter 9 of *The Prince*: Clearchus pleases the people not only by exacting vengeance on their oppressors in a bloody spectacle, but also by defecting to their side amid circumstances of social conflict. Machiavelli confirms that a prince will garner deeper affection from the people precisely by defying their negative expectations regarding individuals the *grandi* elevate to supreme rank. Agathocles, Nabis, and Cleomenes, like Clearchus, all assume their positions of supreme command through the "consent" of their cities' senates. In this light the peoples of Syracuse, Sparta, and Heraclea might all have expected increased oppression from these chief magistrates acting as tyrannical agents for the nobles. What they get, in fact, once these individuals betray their cities' senators, to the people's surprise and pleasure, is both less oppression and the demise of their oppressors. Thus the example of Clearchus helps readers more fully comprehend the Agathoclean model for successfully usurping-cum-reforming republics: both Agathocles and Clearchus exploit high office; both betray the nobility; both eliminate the senatorial order of their cities—even if Agathocles evades the people's hatred in doing so while Clearchus wins their affection (to whatever extent there is a difference between the two).

At the start of both chapters 8 and 9 of *The Prince*, Machiavelli speaks as if a criminal prince differs from a civil prince in this way: the former enlists "criminality and other intolerable violence" (P 9) in his ascent to a principality, while the latter comes to power merely with support from fellow citizens, most preferably support from the common people. But Machiavelli obliterates the neat distinction between criminality and popular support: to gain the latter, a prince may have to resort to the former. The historical details of Nabis's career, along with Machiavelli's account of Greek tyrants like Cleomenes and Clearchus in the *Discourses*, suggest that criminality and violence are in fact the necessary means a civil prince must employ to win the favor and support of the common people. The historical Nabis and Machiavelli's own Cleomenes and Clearchus hence retrospectively exonerate Agathocles from the charge of base criminality; in fact, they elevate him to the status of a civil prince who won the people to himself by killing the senators and the wealthiest citizens of Syracuse. Thus the only action Machiavelli truly deems "intolerable violence" is violence perpetrated against the common people; he clearly does not necessarily consider violence perpetrated against the nobility "intolerable" or excessive.

These considerations suggest that, in a certain sense, chapters 8 and 9 of *The Prince* form one unified chapter. Chapter 8 is overwhelmingly descriptive, replete with historical detail and empirical evidence regarding the careers of Agathocles and Liverotto; and it is notably bereft of theoretical analysis—except for the crucial introduction of "cruelty well used" at the chapter's conclusion. Chapter 9 is overwhelmingly theoretical, with many prescriptions for princely behavior; it invokes a few historical figures, like Nabis, the Gracchi, and Giorgio Scali, but it provides very little historical detail concerning their behavior—a shortcoming Machiavelli explicitly concedes. We might surmise that the details in chapter 8 concerning Agathocles's behavior compensate for whatever details of Nabis's career Machiavelli omits from chapter 9. Conversely, Machiavelli's normative endorsement of Nabis as a civil prince in the second chapter retroactively bestows that attribution on the main figure of the previous chapter, Agathocles.

What were the mistakes of the unsuccessful civil princes Machiavelli invokes in chapter 9 of *The Prince*: the Gracchi in Rome and Scali in Florence? Unlike Nabis and Agathocles, Machiavelli suggests, the Gracchus brothers and Messer Scali do not assume supreme command of a citizen army and enlist the people's aid in violent conflict against their cities'

nobilities. "Founding on" the people, which Machiavelli insists is necessary for a successful civil prince, entails much more than mere popular favor; one must be able to command the people, which means they must be
armed and ordered under one's own charge. The Roman and Florentine
grandi managed to overcome the Gracchi and Scali precisely because the
latter had not formally and militarily enlisted the people in their defense.
Roman tribunes, like the Gracchi, who presided over the plebeians in assemblies but did not command them in legions, were thoroughly crushed
by Rome's senatorial order. Giorgio Scali, who served as the patron of
lower guildsmen during the Ciompi Revolt, was easily outmaneuvered
by Florence's political and economic elites and was executed—his last
words cursing the purported faithlessness of the Florentine people (see
FH III.18). But neither the Brothers Gracchus nor Messer Scali, Machiavelli insists, had anyone but themselves to blame for their inauspicious
demises (see also D I.37).

CIVIL PRINCES IN POLITIES THREATENED
BY IMPERIAL HEGEMONS

The amalgam of these examples of Greek tyrants, drawn from both *The
Prince* and the *Discourses*, illustrates what Machiavelli demands from a new
prince and, in extreme cases, a republican reformer: a tyrant-cum-civil
prince must eliminate the nobility, whose excessive authority and desire to
oppress eventually make healthy civic and economic equality impossible
within republics; and he must deploy a citizen army large enough to keep at
bay expansive military powers like the Macedonian, Carthaginian, and Roman empires. This is essentially Machiavelli's central advice in *The Prince*.
In military affairs princes should rely on nobles as little as they ought to
depend on mercenaries, fortresses, cavalry, or artillery. They ought to rely
exclusively on their heavily armed populaces.

The Medici, by contrast, follow the less preferable examples of earlier,
pro-aristocratic tyrants Machiavelli discusses—all of whom, like the Roman emperors, which the Florentine criticizes, separated the people from
the army and maintained personal bodyguards: Appius Claudius, Cornelius Sulla, Caesar Augustus, and Walter, the so-called Duke of Athens. The
Medici, deeply deficient civil princes, effectively coddle oppressive nobles
("sons of Brutus," as Machiavelli calls them elsewhere) at home, and they
exacerbate continued vulnerability to foreigners like France, Spain, and
Germany—foreign powers that, incidentally, Machiavelli considers vastly
inferior to ancient Macedonia, Carthage, and Rome. The modern military
powers, unlike the ancient ones, fight with large armies comprising professional soldiers rather than citizen-subject militias (e.g., P 13, P 19).[22]

Machiavelli's contemporary readers might not have easily missed the parallels Machiavelli implicitly draws between the ancient city-states ruled by his Greek tyrants—Heraclea, Syracuse, and Sparta—to the modern city-states of Italy. In *The Prince* and the *Discourses*, Machiavelli focuses extensively on small city-states such as Syracuse and Sparta that valiantly held their own against much larger Carthaginian, Macedonian, Greek, or Roman forces precisely because they deployed well-trained and patriotic civil militaries. Machiavelli praises the policies of Agathocles, Nabis, Hiero, and Cleomenes for resisting, over many years, these hegemons' efforts at imperial conquest. The same goes for the Achaean League led by Philopoemen (P 14), which transformed from an imperial hegemon threatening Sparta to an enticing conquerable target of Rome's imperial designs. In Machiavelli's estimation, that these ancient imperial superpowers eventually prevailed over these smaller city-states should not discourage modern city-states from employing citizen militias, precisely because he considers France, Spain, and the German emperor vastly inferior militarily to the ancient hegemons who ultimately conquered these virtuous city-states. As Machiavelli cleverly insinuates, even the second-best of the two Philips of Macedon was superior in virtue to all modern princes (P 24).

If modern, popularly armed Italian city-states cannot decisively defeat massive "barbarian" armies, they nevertheless can—like Hiero's Syracuse and the modern Swiss—make attempted conquest not worth the while of would-be invaders. Prudence and necessity eventually dictate that the latter accept the smaller but well armed city-states as allies rather than as subjects. Put simply, Machiavelli firmly believed that a return to the ancient domestic and military orders Greek tyrants instituted in their city-states would enable modern Italians to beat back contemporary France, Spain, and Germany because these supposed superpowers—no matter the size of their armies—were in fact merely paper tigers. Were the citizens of the Italian cities of Machiavelli's day to become as extensively armed and rigorously trained as their ancient Greek predecessors, the Florentine intimates, they might fare far better against the vastly inferior contemporary hegemons France, Spain, and Germany.

The ultimate geopolitical failure of Machiavelli's Greek tyrants, who crushed domestic nobles and revitalized the popular arms of Sparta and Syracuse, allows readers to observe, as if in a petri dish, how the great founders of chapter 6—Moses, Romulus, and Theseus—in all likelihood consolidated power. But the precise nature of their criminal actions was covered over by the considerable success and longevity of the polities and peoples they founded. Moses, Romulus, and Theseus, we may surmise, acted precisely as did Hiero, Nabis, and Agathocles, but they appear less criminal in retrospect because of the long-term success of the new modes and orders they established. Imperial Rome, named after its founder Romulus, rather late in the game managed to extinguish the living virtue of the polities established by Moses and Theseus but not their enduring reputations. By contrast, Rome quashed the nascent empires of the Greek princes early enough in their development that such leaders are remembered merely as petty tyrants.

By including the "lesser example" of Hiero in his chapter of *The Prince* devoted to the most illustrious founders/legislators in chapter 6, Machiavelli invites a comparison of Moses, Romulus, Theseus, and Cyrus with the Greek tyrants of Syracuse and Sparta. In doing so he suggests that had the "new modes and orders" established by Moses, Romulus, Theseus, and Cyrus been extinguished earlier in their polities' life spans by more powerful empires, as those of the Greek tyrants were (by the Macedonians, the Carthaginians, and especially the Romans), their actions probably would have gone unvenerated by posterity, and they probably would have been entirely condemned by future writers. To the extent that they may have been remembered at all, Moses, Romulus, Theseus, and Cyrus likely would have been posthumously vilified by historians as criminal petty tyrants—just as such writers went on to treat Hiero, Nabis, Clearchus, Cleomenes, and Agathocles—simply because the latter did not establish political orders that endured for centuries.

AGATHOCLES, SCIPIO AFRICANUS, AND "WORLDLY GLORY"

Another potential Roman reformer whom Machiavelli contrasts with Greek tyrants is Publius Cornelius Scipio Africanus. The figure of Scipio necessarily revives the question of glory that I discussed briefly in chapter 1. Recall that Machiavelli seemingly equivocates over Agathocles's virtue, but he much more adamantly declares that the Sicilian failed to win glory. Machiavelli concludes that one can acquire power or "rule" (*imperio*) through Agathocles's methods, "but not glory" (P 8). Many commentators take this remark regarding Agathocles's failure to win glory as proof that Machiavelli's attribution of virtue to the Sicilian is less than robust. However, glory does not operate within *The Prince* as a completely unqualified indication of Machiavelli's praise for individual leaders. More precisely, Machiavelli discusses glory as if it is something he himself is incapable of bestowing upon princes.[23] The "writers," it seems, have already decided who is counted among "the most excellent men" and is worthy of "fame and glory." In other words, Machiavelli argues, those who have not properly apprehended the "effectual truth" of politics—the writers whose opinions Machiavelli so often explicitly departs from—have been the traditional arbiters of excellence, fame, and glory (P 15). One of the most prominent figures in *The Prince* whom Machiavelli suggests won unmerited glory is Scipio Africanus.[24]

We should approach Machiavelli's treatment of Scipio by reviewing what knowledge Machiavelli would have expected any reader of *The Prince* in his day to have. Machiavelli's audience would have been familiar with Scipio from Livy's Roman histories and Petrarch's epic poem *Africa*, and perhaps from excerpts of Polybius and Valerius Maximus as well. They likely would have known at least four salient facts about Scipio: (1) his military career began and accelerated while he was extraordinarily young; specifically, he assumed military command at an unprecedentedly early age after his father and his uncle, incumbent consuls, died fighting the Carthaginians in Spain. (2) Scipio gained great renown for his sexual continence: while commanding Roman forces in Spain, Scipio returned a beautiful local maiden untouched to her noble parents and fiancé after his soldiers presented her to him as a trophy. (3) Scipio earned the agnomen Africanus for invading Africa to draw Hannibal, the scourge of Rome, out of Italy, and for vanquishing Rome's existential enemy, Carthage, in its own backyard. Finally, (4) Scipio voluntarily exiled himself from Rome after prominent senators accused him of wielding excessive political influence over the republic.[25]

On each of these four points Scipio's career contrasts starkly with that of Agathocles: (1) the Sicilian rose to supreme command at a relatively early age solely through his own achievements, without the support of a prominent family legacy. (2) The writers are fond of attributing sexual licentiousness to Agathocles: in his youth, Agathocles was reputed to have rented his beautiful face and body to the most prominent men of Syracuse, and in his adulthood he purportedly lent them promiscuously to many of the latter's wives.[26] (3) Agathocles acquired no glorious title for first devising and then executing the daring military strategy of invading Africa to subdue Carthage. And finally, (4) Agathocles, to put it mildly, exhibits a notable lack of deference to his republic's senators and first citizens.[27]

In *The Prince*, Machiavelli never discusses Scipio's famous accomplishments in any detail; he chooses to emphasize decidedly different aspects of his résumé. He notes that Scipio was indeed a rare example in his own lifetime and in recorded history—but not so much for any positive qualities he exhibited or heroic actions he performed. Rather, Machiavelli finds Scipio remarkable because he managed to gain "fame and glory" despite serious personal deficiencies and notable public failures (P 17). Above all, Scipio serves as the negative example of the fundamental Machiavellian lesson that love is an insufficient bond of obligation for commanding soldiers and ruling subjects. Machiavelli recounts how Scipio's ease and mercy encouraged his soldiers to become impudent and unruly, and even to revolt against his command (P 17; D III.21). Indeed, Scipio's soldiers stage an insurrection based on the mere rumor that their humane commander had taken ill.[28] By contrast, Agathocles's soldiers in both Sicily and Africa remain loyal to him while their captain repeatedly sails back and forth across the Mediterranean (P 8).[29]

Machiavelli provides an additional example of Scipio's pernicious laxity: When Scipio's military emissary unilaterally and excessively punished the Locrians, the Roman commander neither compensated them for their extensive injuries nor reprimanded the official for his egregious offense. As a result of these incidents, Machiavelli reports that the vaunted Fabius Maximus denounced Scipio before the Senate as a corrupter of Roman military discipline and imperial rule; Fabius demanded that Scipio be replaced by other commanders who knew better "how not to err themselves and how to correct the errors of others" (P 17).

Machiavelli not only attributes Scipio's excessively kind and easygoing ways to a fundamentally humane nature, but also notes that this personal disposition was reinforced by a faulty reading of books, especially Xenophon's *Cyropaedia* or *The Education of Cyrus* (P 14). Scipio imitated the qualities of Cyrus accentuated by Xenophon—chastity, affability, humanity, and liberality—and as a result he lost control of his troops and misruled his conquered subjects. By too literally following lessons provided by ancient writers, Machiavelli suggests, Scipio underestimated how necessary for command and rule is the kind of beneficent cruelty employed by other figures invoked throughout *The Prince*, notably Borgia, certainly Agathocles, but perhaps above all by Scipio's ultimate adversary, Hannibal.[30]

Yet Machiavelli points out that despite Scipio's notable early missteps, he manages to pursue a wildly successful military and political career precisely because he lived "under the government of the Senate" (*sotto il governo del senato*) (P 17). Senatorial authority and expertise compensated for Scipio's deficiently permissive approach; it bought Scipio valuable time so he could change his ways before bringing ruin upon either himself or the republic. Ultimately, Scipio's subjection to the tutelage of Roman senators such as Fabius enabled him to recover from his mistakes and win incomparable worldly glory.[31] Without dependence on the Senate, Machiavelli intimates, Scipio's "affable nature" would have irredeemably impaired his reputation, denied him future opportunities to command, and prevented him from gaining glory through the eventual conquest of Carthage. However, Machiavelli claims, not only was Scipio's "harmful quality" of affability "concealed" by his dependence on the Senate, but this dependence "actually better facilitated his glory."

The Roman Senate eventually bestows on Scipio the title Africanus, a title whose renown is spread by subsequent writers—writers very much like those to whom Scipio had displayed the same profound deference he showed to Rome's senators. The writers, who are at least partly to blame for Scipio's early mistakes, posthumously reward him, but not Agathocles, as one of the most glorious military leaders in history. In doing so such writers absolve themselves of their own complicity in the young Scipio's poor command and rule—in fact, Machiavelli suggests, they exacerbate the problem by failing to praise Agathocles's cruel ways, and likewise by failing to instruct readers that Agathocles's methods, like Hannibal's, are generally more effective than those of Scipio (P 17).

If at any moment in his career Agathocles had behaved in the excessively humane fashion of Scipio rather than committing the "cruelty" and "crimes" that writers attribute to him, the Sicilian undoubtedly would have failed to rise from humble origins to become praetor and then prince of Syracuse. Agathocles was a potter's son, not the progeny of Roman nobles. It is therefore very unlikely that the leading men of the Syracusan republic would have granted him any subsequent opportunities to command military forces had the Sicilian committed early blunders comparable to Scipio's. Unlike Scipio, Agathocles, in order to rule and to command successfully, neither requires nor desires the tutelage of his republic's senators—indeed, he proves to be the one who, as it were, teaches them a lesson. Through cruelty well used and the appropriate favor it brought him from his citizen soldiers, Agathocles casts off his senate's authority and defeats Carthage without any senatorial aid other than their initial "consent" to his assuming command (P 8). However, in forsaking dependence on senators in demonstrably refusing to live "under the government of the senate," Agathocles also deprives himself of the formal triumphs and honorifics that senates confer on military victors, whose fame is spread to future generations by obsequious writers (P 17, 68). It is no small injustice, Machiavelli intimates, that Scipio, not Agathocles, is known to posterity as "Africanus" (or that title's Greek equivalent).

To put matters simply, in *The Prince* Machiavelli demonstrates that Agathocles is fully virtuous but not glorious; Scipio is glorious but not fully virtuous. As it happens, the "virtues" Machiavelli attributes to Scipio—chastity, humanity, affability, and liberality (D III.20–21)—are in themselves no virtues at all. In fact, the only "virtues" Scipio seems to exhibit in *The Prince* are the good fortune of having been born into a family of consuls, of having lived under the government of the Roman Senate, and of possessing the—not inconsiderable—ability to learn from his mistakes. Virtue, Machiavelli implies, pertains exclusively to a princely individual's own abilities and actions, while glory is separable from the inherent qualities and observable actions of such individuals. Glory, unlike virtue, entails a substantive form of dependence at odds with the will to autonomy at the heart of Machiavellian *virtù*: to gain glory, at least traditionally, one must exhibit deference to both senators and writers, those who mete out praise and blame in the present and in the eyes of posterity.

Agathocles's superior instincts, intentions, and actions, Machiavelli insinuates, render him a more virtuous political exemplar than the Roman nobleman Scipio, who is lavishly praised by Livy, and especially by Petrarch,[32] for vanquishing Hannibal and the Carthaginian Republic in the Second Punic War.[33] Scipio managed to gain glory despite his deficient virtue, Machiavelli suggests in *The Prince*, because he allowed himself to be coddled, constrained, and eventually even undone by senatorial elites, and also because he exhibited scrupulous concern for the opinion of writers. Agathocles, for his part, cares not a whit for either senates or writers; he cares only for himself and for the great mass of his own citizen soldiers. As a result, Machiavelli suggests, Agathocles wins neither a glorious title, such as Africanus, nor enduring fame, even though he accomplished first and more impressively the feat for which Scipio became eternally renowned: Agathocles invaded Africa to draw a menacing Carthaginian army away from his native city, and he imposed on the Carthaginian Republic a truce that guaranteed the security of his patria.

The opinions of senators and writers notwithstanding, then, the thoroughly plebeian and possibly illiterate Agathocles serves as Machiavelli's preferred example of princely success; by Machiavellian standards, the Sicilian stands as a thoroughly more worthy candidate than Scipio for "worldly glory" (D II.2). Agathocles, scorned or ignored by previous writers, is not merely Machiavelli's model of an enlightened or benevolent tyrant. In the next section, I will suggest that Agathocles serves, more provocatively, as Machiavelli's exemplar of a "civil prince," Machiavelli's radically reformulated version of Cicero's *rector rei publicae*. That is, Agathocles serves as a superior model for the role of defender-cum-reformer of *republics*—a role for which, historically, nobles and writers have rewarded senatorial figures like Furius Camillus, Fabius Maximus, and, most notably, Scipio Africanus, with the highest glory.[34]

AGATHOCLES AND SCIPIO VERSUS "THE GOVERNMENT OF THE SENATE"

Turning to Machiavelli's discussions of Scipio Africanus in the *Discourses*, I suggest that Machiavelli does not necessarily agree with the civic humanist view on the contrast between Scipio and Julius Caesar.[35] What is most pertinent for Machiavelli about the Scipio/Caesar comparison, I argue, is not the difference between the two figures, but their fundamental similarity. Initially, Machiavelli hews closely to classical republican and especially Florentine humanist tropes by praising Scipio as the Roman Republic's consummate hero, and by criticizing Caesar as her consummate usurper (D I.10). Machiavelli declares that leaders like Scipio earn praise for upholding republics, whereas those like Caesar incur censure for corrupting them (D I.10). Scipios, Machiavelli observes, win "worldly glory" for themselves, whereas Caesars suffer "enduring infamy" (D I.10).[36] Despite paying lip service to traditional interpretations, Machiavelli, as I show here and in the next section, considers Scipio and Caesar very much alike: both permitted themselves to be undermined by the Roman Senate in moments when the Roman Republic required socioeconomic and civic-military reforms comparable to those enacted by Machiavelli's Greek tyrants. This criticism applies as well to failed Roman reformers between Scipio and Caesar: the Gracchi and Gaius Marius.

In the *Discourses*, Machiavelli significantly rehabilitates Scipio's virtue, which he seemed to impugn so thoroughly in *The Prince*. Furthermore, he seems quite willing to concede that Scipio may after all be at least somewhat worthy of the glory he eventually attained. However, Machiavelli still demonstrates that the cruel and harsh ways of the arguably less glorious Hannibal are preferable to the more humane ways of Scipio. Hannibal's methods, he suggests, are much more conducive to military and political success than are Scipio's, even though Scipio famously vanquished Hannibal (D III.10).

In the *Discourses*, Machiavelli also discusses Scipio's relationship with the Roman people and not merely, as in *The Prince*, his interactions with soldiers, senators, and writers. Machiavelli notes how Scipio's demonstrations of sexual continence, filial allegiance, and fidelity to the city's defense, along with his military successes, won him the great favor of the Roman people. In fact, in the *Discourses*, Machiavelli recounts how Scipio leveraged his popular favor against the Senate and against his old denunciator, Fabius Maximus, to undertake his invasion of Africa and assault on Carthage (D II.12). When the Senate initially refused to endorse this proposed enterprise, Scipio threatened to put the matter to a vote of the people, an action that would have embarrassed the Senate and compromised its prerogative over the republic's military affairs.[37] Thus Machiavelli demonstrates that Scipio did not, as he himself suggests in *The Prince*, always act so deferentially toward the Roman Senate.

Early in the Second Punic War, the commander Varro, supported by the Roman people, proved disastrously wrong in defying Fabius and the Roman Senate by insisting on directly confronting Hannibal. But at a much later point in the conflict, Scipio and the Roman people correctly surmised that the time was ripe to again go on the offensive against the Carthaginians (D I.53). Had Scipio not, in fact, exploited his popular favor vis-à-vis Fabius and the Senate, Hannibal might never have ceased harassing Rome within Italy; indeed, at some point he may very well have annihilated the city. For our purposes, this episode demonstrates that Scipio adopts an Agathoclean method not only in military affairs—that is, not only in seeking to invade Africa to defeat Carthage—but also, albeit much more mildly, in domestic affairs. Scipio enlists popular favor to manipulate and outmaneuver, if not subdue or crush, his city's senate.

Nevertheless, the Roman Senate would take its revenge on Scipio after the war, despite awarding him the name Africanus for conquering Carthage. Machiavelli recounts how Rome's magistrates, purportedly "wise" and "pious" senators like Cato the Elder, feared Scipio's great reputation and potentially extraordinary authority. Cato charged that no individual had risen to such heights in Rome's civic history, and that "a city could not be called free where the magistrates feared a single citizen" (D I.29). Arousing the Roman people's long-standing antipathy to kingship (D I.58), Machiavelli suggests, Cato turned the people against Scipio (D I.29).[38] Unlike Agathocles, then, Scipio most assuredly was forced to encounter "civil controversies" and contend with "conspiracies" (P 8), during his public career.

As a result of these controversies and denunciations, Scipio leaves as a political exile the very city he saved, thus becoming Machiavelli's chief example of a civic prince who suffered popular ingratitude (D I.29). Yet because Machiavelli himself provides so few details concerning this episode, we must consult Livy for a better sense of the interactions among Cato, Scipio, the Senate, and the people in these circumstances. As in the case of Nabis from *The Prince*, Machiavelli here invites if not demands that readers consult his sources to see what might have really occurred when he appears reluctant to explain as much himself.

Livy, Machiavelli's principal source here, provides no indication that the Roman people wavered at all in their support of Scipio.[39] In fact, he recounts how Scipio interrupts his trial to make a dramatic public show of his popularity just before embarking on his self-imposed exile. In leaving the city, however, Scipio substantively tests neither his popular favor nor the Senate's authority.[40] The people never hear the full case being brought against him, they never publicly deliberate over whatever defense Scipio might have marshaled, and, most important, they never have the opportunity to officially pass judgment on him. Whatever Machiavelli otherwise thinks about Scipio's course of action, it certainly seems to confirm what he declared so authoritatively in *The Prince*: Scipio remained, to the very end, voluntarily subject to "the government of the Roman Senate." At no time, apparently, does Scipio entertain the idea that he *himself* should assume the governing of the Roman Republic.

Scipio enlisted popular support against senators to pursue a military strategy that he believed would ultimately benefit the republic. Yet he clearly refuses to enlist popular support to defend his reputation and authority in ways that—to his own mind, at least—would have harmed the republic. Scipio was willing to risk undermining senatorial authority in the effort to liberate the republic from its greatest external enemy; but he will not do so in any way that jeopardizes the republic's domestic concord. Of course Scipio may harbor selfish as well as public-spirited motivations here: perhaps he knows from his extensive reading of history that writers praise public acts of self-abnegation, especially showing deference toward senatorial authority. By exiling himself, Scipio may hope for greater long-term enhancement of his personal reputation than he could win by remaining in the city, publicly confronting his senatorial accusers, and permitting the people to decide who, Scipio or the senators, is acting correctly or incorrectly.[41]

If Machiavelli, in fact, fully endorses the traditional distinction between Scipio and Caesar, we might surmise that he thinks Cato, the Senate, and especially Scipio, have all acted commendably. This would situate Machiavelli quite comfortably within humanist-republican conventions. On this view, Cato and the Senate prevent a single individual from gaining excessive authority within the republic, and Scipio neutralizes a civic controversy that might have generated intensely dangerous domestic strife. From this perspective, Scipio ought to be glorified for not behaving as Caesar eventually would do (D I.10); that is, Scipio did not use his popular favor against prominent citizens who displayed little gratitude for his previous exemplary service to the republic. Most important, Scipio did not risk becoming a king in vindicating himself against the Roman Senate. Indeed, Machiavelli counts Scipio's accusation among the notable events that brought Rome "back to its beginnings" and so helped extend the republic's life (D III.1).

But we should also consider, in this context, Machiavelli's praise of successful civil princes and his criticism of unsuccessful ones, in chapters 8 and 9 of *The Prince*. Recall that Agathocles and Nabis use the popular support of an armed citizenry against their city's nobles to reform their corrupt republics. In this light we are compelled to consider an especially pressing question: In Machiavelli's estimation, is the Roman Republic sufficiently corrupt at this juncture to suggest that Scipio should have acted more aggressively in seeking to reinvigorate Rome's "free and civil way of life"?

In the *Discourses* Machiavelli notes how the end of the Punic Wars exacerbated long-standing problems in Rome and introduced entirely new ones (D I.16, I.37). The Roman Senate had long used military conflicts as excuses to delay enacting necessary agrarian reforms that would have mitigated increasingly harmful economic inequality within the republic. Without a plausible existential threat to the republic, like Carthage, the Roman Senate would no longer be able to prevent the Roman people from demanding, ever more loudly, economic relief for citizen soldiers who had been impoverished by the republic's continual wars—especially its protracted conflict with Carthage. In fact, with Carthage now out of the way, the Roman nobility hoped to further increase its domestic economic advantages by expanding Rome's empire throughout the Mediterranean and beyond. As Machiavelli insists, the Senate had no intention of adopting measures that would have decreased, let alone halted, its ability to oppress the people at home through economic advantages (D I.37).

These opposing motivations correspond well with the opposing humors of the people and the nobles that Machiavelli describes in chapter 9 of *The Prince* and earlier in the *Discourses*: specifically, the popular humor to avoid and resist domination versus the aristocratic inclination to impose and expand it (D I.3–5). The people seek enactment of agrarian reforms that would minimize senatorial domination at home, while the Senate desires imperial expansion that would intensify its domination of the people, which consequently makes the people even more determined to obtain such reforms. When this kind of conflict between the people and the nobles in a republic becomes irreconcilable, Machiavelli suggests in chapter 9, either the people or the nobles will elevate a civil prince to act on their behalf to crush their sociopolitical antagonists.

As if these two opposing trends, and the vicious cycle they were engendering, were not trouble enough, Rome's imperial expansion after Carthage's defeat would create a new problem: to conquer and maintain ever more distant lands, Machiavelli explains, the Senate began extending the military commands of individual Roman generals, thus greatly inflating the generals' personal authority (D III.24–25). As a result, Rome's increasingly proletarianized citizen soldiers began looking to such commanders, rather than to the republic itself, for their economic well-being and political defense. In short, the Senate was making it possible for individual commanders to grow powerful enough to become civil princes who would usurp the republic as agents of either the people or the nobles.

Scipio was at least partially aware of these problems. According to historical accounts, he persuaded the Roman Senate to grant fresh land to Roman soldiers who served in his successful Spanish and African campaigns.[42] But Scipio would not, or perhaps dared not, advocate extending such agrarian relief to all of Rome's citizen soldiers who had fought against Carthage. By his self-exile, Scipio certainly prevented himself from becoming the first in the long line of military commanders who gained inordinate princely authority within the republic. But he left unresolved the social crisis that would accrue to the benefit of future, perhaps less civically fastidious military champions of the people or the nobles. Not long after Scipio's ill-fated grandsons, the Gracchi, failed to solve these socioeconomic problems themselves, civil war ensued among Rome's unprecedentedly powerful generals—Marius versus Sulla, Pompey versus Caesar, the Triumvirate versus Antony. To all intents and purposes, the republic was finished.

"CAESAR . . . HAD HE LIVED": CAESAR AS SUCCESSFUL TYRANT OR FAILED CIVIL PRINCE?

So did Scipio benefit the republic by defusing civic strife when he exiled himself from the city? Or, by abdicating his position of public authority, did he doom the republic to far more deadly social struggles down the road? These questions invite us to examine more closely the figure of Julius Caesar and Machiavelli's assessment of his career. In the *Discourses*, Machiavelli frequently rehearses and pays homage to traditional civic-humanist criticisms of Caesar and Gaius Marius for seeking to exert undue, even tyrannical, influence over the Roman Republic. However, considering the Agathoclean exemplum constituted by Machiavelli's combined discussions of various Greek tyrants, Machiavelli seems to indicate that what ultimately interests him most about the examples of Scipio and Caesar, from the viewpoint of effectual truth, is how remarkably comparable they are.

Leo Strauss argues persuasively that, throughout the *Discourses*, Machiavelli mitigates most of his otherwise severe criticisms of Caesar's actions.[43] In direct reference to Julius Caesar, Strauss also declares that "Machiavelli is willing to compare his admired Roman nobility to small birds of prey whose natural greed makes them unaware of the big bird which is about to swoop upon them. . . . The qualities and achievements of the Roman nobility . . . prepared the ruin of the Roman nobility and of the Roman [R]epublic by the big bird Caesar."[44]

Certainly Strauss's observation here conforms generally to the overall thrust of Machiavelli's account of the Roman Republic's collapse. However, Strauss's assessment overlooks an important factor in these circumstances. Julius Caesar did not ruin the Roman nobility; they, or rather a notable portion of them, ruined Caesar. This oversight on Strauss's part recalls one of Machiavelli's most significant declarations: "Whoever establishes a tyranny and does not kill Brutus, and whoever establishes a free state and does not kill the sons of Brutus, maintains himself only for a very short time" (D III.3).

Of course, Lucius Junius Brutus originally established the Roman Republic by expelling the Tarquinian royal family from the city; then he assured its survival by overseeing the execution of his own sons, who conspired with other young nobles to overthrow the Republic because they resented the common people's newly won liberty.[45] Marcus Junius Brutus—ostensibly the direct descendant of Lucius, but by some accounts the natural son of Julius Caesar—led the band of young senators who assassinated Caesar, calling him a tyrant who aspired to be king.[46] In view of this account, *pace* the opinions of traditional republicans, Caesar neither fully usurped the Roman Republic nor definitively ruined the Roman nobility.[47] After all, Caesar had pardoned members of the senatorial party, most notably young Brutus, who supported Pompey and fought against Caesar during the Civil Wars.[48] Several of the other young nobles to whom Caesar granted clemency along with Brutus would demonstrate their gratitude by participating in his assassination.

Caesar, then, much like Scipio, the Gracchi, and Marius before him, most certainly did *not* seek the full ruin of the Roman nobility or the elimination of the Roman Senate. He merely wished to reapportion to the Roman people a substantive share of the enormous wealth and political power that the nobility had been amassing for themselves as a result of Rome's imperial expansion. Scipio, the Gracchi, Marius, and Caesar each hoped to diminish, but not destroy, the power of the Roman nobility; and they simultaneously wished to maintain for themselves the esteem of the Roman Senate. In short, like his predecessors among the *populares*, Caesar sought the adoration of both the Senate and the people of Rome. As a result of these divided loyalties, Scipio was exiled, Marius was ruined, the Gracchi and Caesar wound up dead, and the republic remained desperately unreformed.

We will never know if Caesar truly intended, as he claimed, to use his dictatorial authority to institute long-lasting civic, economic, and military reforms that would have reinvigorated the Roman Republic. We will never know if he aspired to be a genuine *rector rei publicae*. Nevertheless, according to the quotation from Machiavelli cited above, if Caesar did intend to become a tyrant, conventionally understood, he should have killed Brutus, the living symbol of republican liberty in Rome (D III.3). If, on the contrary, Caesar intended to be a republican reformer, a civil prince, like Nabis, Cleomenes, Clearchus, and of course Agathocles, then, Machiavelli insists, he should have killed "the sons of Brutus"—in this case, the distant descendants of Brutus *and* his young noble collaborators. These descendants of Brutus's sons murdered Caesar to cancel reforms aimed at improving the lot of the Roman people and to restore and entrench senatorial ascendance in Rome. Whether Caesar intended to be a princely autocrat or a republican reformer determines whether Brutus the Younger should be judged a "Brutus" or a "son of Brutus."

In the ambiguity of Caesar's motivations, therefore, we see the indeterminacy of both Machiavelli's invocation of "the sons of Brutus" as negative exemplars of oppression-craving nobles and his criticisms of Caesar as a usurper of the Roman Republic.[49] If Caesar intended to become king, then young Brutus acted appropriately—in the manner of his family forebear who so illustriously ended the Tarquin monarchy—by assassinating the dictator. If Caesar had intended to reform and restore the Roman Republic, then young Brutus becomes *not* the second coming of the elder Brutus, but rather the second coming of his treasonous and ambitious sons: the leader of a clique of aristocratic obstructers to popular reforms, whom Caesar, in the manner of Agathocles, Nabis, Cleomenes, and Clearchus, should have eliminated rather than spared.

Because Caesar killed neither "Brutus" nor his figurative "sons," the dictator and his reforms lasted "only a very short time," and Rome's disastrous civil wars soon recommenced. Caesar's failure to practice Agathoclean cruelty well used vis-à-vis the Roman Senate wrought longer-term turmoil and misery for all of Rome's citizens. Caesar bequeathed to Rome the following patrimonies: intensification of civil war, the permanent collapse of the republic, and the political emasculation of both the nobles and the people by his nephew Octavian, who would become the emperor Caesar Augustus. These are the consequences for which Machiavelli sarcastically claims that Rome, Italy, and the whole world "owe" such great thanks to Caesar (D I.10). Traditional writers, Machiavelli seems to suggest, were correct to criticize Caesar, but they did so on erroneous grounds.

Indeed, these pernicious outcomes resulting from Caesar's so-called tyranny were generated as much, or more, by sins of omission as by any sins of commission on Caesar's part. Caesar was, in effect, a deeply deficient Caesarist. After all, unlike Cosimo de' Medici, for instance, Caesar does not rise to the principate through support of the people only to set about disarming them militarily. He does not, like the Duke of Athens, Louis XI of France, or the Roman emperors, according to Machiavelli, separate the people from his military forces. He does not, like Augustus, expand the numbers and increase the authority of a personal coterie of satellites, the Praetorian Guard. Unlike many of the Greek tyrants discussed and often praised by Machiavelli, Caesar does not behave very tyrannically at all. In fact, his failure to commit the one act that causes writers to call Agathocles, Nabis, Cleomenes, and Clearchus "tyrants"—eliminating their cities' nobilities—is the chief cause of his failure as a princely reformer.

It is worth noting that Machiavelli is hesitant to declare whether Caesar in fact ever actually became prince of Rome. Indeed, he intimates that

Rome's corruption ultimately spreads from Julius Caesar's failure, *not* from his success at attaining the principate, and that tyranny was effectually taken up under his by his imperial successors. As Machiavelli writes in *The Prince* in a rather extravagantly provisional manner regarding Caesar's relationship to the status of "principality," "Caesar acquired rule through liberality," as it was "necessary" for him to do, because, as an aspiring prince, he was merely "*on the road* to attaining" ("*se' in via* di acquistarlo") the rank of prince (P 16; emphasis added). Furthermore, Machiavelli continues, "Caesar was one of those who *aspired after* the principate of Rome. However, *had he achieved it,* and *had he lived, if* he continued to spend profligately, he *would have* ruined his own imperium" (P 16; emphases added).[50] This passage suggests that Machiavelli largely condones Caesar's rise to power through favor giving—so long as he would not have persisted in such a policy when he eventually attained the principality. But Machiavelli leaves open the question whether he did ever fully acquire the principality by the time of his assassination.

Indeed, in the same chapter of *The Prince*, Machiavelli lists Caesar alongside Cyrus and Alexander as armed, aspiring princes who combined military success with liberality (albeit liberality with conquered peoples' goods rather than those of their own people). These passages make it quite clear that Machiavelli held out the distinct possibility that Caesar would not have adhered to such liberality once he gained the principate. That is, Machiavelli concedes that Caesar may have been participating in Rome's corruption while aspiring to gain the principate by winning over Rome's citizen soldiers with material favors (D I.5, D I.37); but he holds out the possibility that Caesar may very well have stopped or even reversed such corrupt practices once he became prince. Again, we will never know for sure whether he would have actually changed course for one simple reason: Caesar did not, in fact, win that ultimate prize, as Machiavelli intimates with the phrase "had he lived" (*fussi sopravvissuto*), having been assassinated before he could do so.

In the *Discourses*, Machiavelli much more subtly continues this same line of thinking: Julius Caesar did not win the principate, he avers; but his nephew, Octavian, ultimately did so by "calling himself Caesar" (D I.52). Machiavelli intimates that Caesar, the man, did not gain the principality in Rome; it was, in fact, Caesar, the *name*, that did so; a name and principality that were appropriated by Octavian/Augustus to impose complete unfreedom on the Romans: "The glory of that name [Caesar] eliminated its enemies and attained the Roman principate . . . and neither from his heirs nor his agents did anything conducive to the name of freedom ever arise" (D I.52). Caesar the man obviously did not successfully eliminate his enemies; they eliminated him. But his name eventually exacted vengeance on those enemies in the person of Caesar Augustus.

Machiavelli consistently signals in the *Discourses*, just as he did in *The Prince*, that Caesar never successfully solidified his imperium, let alone acquired the principate. As I noted before, Machiavelli seemingly damns Caesar when he states, "If a prince desires worldly glory, he should wish to have a corrupt city that he may reorder like Romulus did rather than endeavor to corrupt one entirely like Caesar did" (D I.10). However, then Machiavelli writes that princes whom "necessity forces to give up their principality such that they do not properly reorder it" deserve "some excuse." Caesar was, of course, forced by "necessity" to give up the principality, or rather his pursuit of it: he was assassinated by Brutus and other young senators before he could "properly order" Rome; therefore he may, in Machiavelli's estimation, merit "some excuse." (In fact, both Caesar and Romulus were murdered by their city's senators—but Romulus had more firmly established his new modes and orders before the ultimate "necessity" of death compelled him no longer to be prince.) Since Caesar left his new orders unimplemented, he could not easily be judged favorably by posterity as a tyrant-cum-civil reformer. Unlike the elder Brutus or, say, Moses, Caesar failed to eliminate "the envy" (P 6; D III.3) of the partisans of the old regime, with the ultimate consequence that he must remain merely a tyrant in the eyes of many writers.[51]

Caesar's failed tyranny ensured that he carried out only the first of the results mentioned above, making clients out of citizen soldiers; but, with respect to the second, Caesar's goal was *never* to disarm the citizens militarily. This is the most likely reason Machiavelli considers Caesar worthy of being called a man of "virtue" (D I.33). That Caesar's tyranny was provisional meant that his incomplete successes remained available for his nephew to appropriate and direct toward more nefarious ends. Augustus used his uncle's practices to disarm a Roman people that Julius Caesar (like the Gracchi and Marius before him) had hoped to arm more extensively. Caesar's economic reforms, which Machiavelli seems to criticize as private favors, were intended to serve military, that is, decidedly public, ends: to reform, sustain, and expand a citizen army—a goal that may be, in terms of policy, the single highest Machiavellian aspiration.

Machiavelli has no problem with a prince's making partisans out of an *armed* populace: in fact, one might say it is the central political lesson of *The Prince* when he implores his addressee to arm the people such that "their arms become your arms ... and they become your partisans" (P 20). Caesar's successors would perpetrate in his name acts of tyranny that he did not commit: disarm Roman citizens, establish a bodyguard, and permit the army to despoil the people. Caesar's rise certainly mimics that of the Medici, but had he lived his rule would *not* have resembled Medici rule. Machiavelli shows how civil princes like Agathocles and Nabis can use private means such as mercenaries early in their rise, but they must eventually dispense with them. Caesar did not permit, and arguably never would have permitted, himself to use his private means to entirely replace public ones.

Thus the single act Julius Caesar committed that rendered Rome unreformable was that he failed to completely destroy the Roman Senate and remake it anew. Instead, unlike the Greek tyrants Machiavelli discusses, Caesar permitted an enviously antagonistic Senate to murder him and obstruct his efforts to reform and revitalize Rome's soldier citizenry (whether he pursued them as a salutary tyrant or as a republican reformer perhaps does not matter much to Machiavelli). Caesar's nephew would set the precedents for subsequent emperors who act like the tyrants Machiavelli unhesitatingly despises: those who separate the soldiers from the people (P 19), those who resort to extensive proscriptions (D I.52), and those who maintain "satellites"—personal bodyguards (D I.40 twice). The emperors retain "the name" Caesar, but they fully act the part of Octavian, not Julius.

Thus the distinction between Scipio and Caesar traditionally set forth by many humanists proves to be no distinction at all for Machiavelli's ultimate purposes. Each, in the end, allowed himself to be undone by the Senate rather than endeavoring to vigorously crush the Senate so as to reform and revitalize the Roman Republic, thus ensuring it would have greater longevity than it actually enjoyed. From this perspective, both Scipio and Caesar deserve to be listed among the failed civil princes Machiavelli names in chapter 9 of *The Prince*. Giorgio Scali and the Gracchi proved to be would-be reformers who, rather than mobilizing an armed citizenry against their republic's corrupt senatorial orders, are themselves consequently crushed—to the ultimate detriment of the entire polity.

The implicit contrast Machiavelli poses between Greek and Roman princely reformers suggests that the Roman reformers—from Scipio, through the Gracchi and Marius, to Caesar—did not wield excessive *authority* over the republic; rather, they exhibited excessive *deference* to the Roman Senate. Consequently Rome's senators, by either exiling or murdering each of these would-be "tyrants," effectively scuttled every attempt by a *popularis* statesman to reform the Roman Republic. The only tyrannies countenanced by the Roman Senate during the life span of the republic were those of Appius Claudius and Lucius Cornelius Sulla—tyrannies that bolstered rather than constrained aristocratic oppression of the people. Like the Medici, they fall into the category of deficient civil princes in chapter 9 of *The Prince*, princes who ultimately base their authority on the nobles rather than on the people.

But in what sense are the Greek reformers who constitute Machiavelli's composite exemplum of the successful tyrant-cum-reformer any more "successful," long term, than the failed Roman ones, whom, I suggest, Machiavelli is criticizing here as failures? None of the Greek tyrants—including those who enjoy considerable short-term military success against superior numbers of foreign enemies, like Agathocles and Nabis—establish modes and orders that last as long as those of Romulus, whom Machiavelli explicitly celebrates, or those of Augustus, whom he implicitly derides. Machiavelli demonstrates clearly how imperial expansion by Macedonia, Carthage, and most decisively Rome eventually (and, to Machiavelli's mind, unfortunately) extinguished the considerable political and military achievements of these Greek tyrants and the civic-military orders that they reinvigorated in Syracuse, Sparta, and Heraclea (P 6, P 8, P 9; D I.9, D I.16).

Machiavelli also subtly suggests that the failure of Rome's reformers, after the Punic Wars, to imitate the actions of precisely these Greek tyrants ensured that a different, more pernicious model of tyranny, that of the Roman emperors, would smother civic liberty in Rome and, more or less, throughout the world for centuries to come. Indeed, perhaps forever, unless sociopolitical trends established across millennia were corrected by radical civic-military measures in Machiavelli's present. Thus it is ultimately the qualitative substance of the Greek princes' socioeconomic and civic-military policies—including eliminating the "sons of Brutus"—rather than the quantitative measure of longevity that matters most in Machiavelli's moral-political assessments of Greek civil princes.

EXCURSUS: "HARDSHIPS AND DANGERS" ENDURED BY AGATHOCLES AND MACHIAVELLI

In his summary of Agathocles's career, Machiavelli repeats that he gained independence from virtually all others. While Agathocles initially depended on the Syracusan Senate's consent to wield supreme command, and on the Carthaginians' complicity to execute his coup, Agathocles's audacity and military skill eventually freed him of such entanglements, domestic and foreign. Machiavelli attributes Agathocles's military success first and foremost to his favor with the Syracusan soldiers, whom he won to himself through many "hardships and dangers" (P 8). These words, *"disagi e periculi,"* echo those with which Machiavelli describes himself in the "Dedicatory Letter" that opens *The Prince* (P dl). Through these words, Machiavelli inserts his own experiences as a political actor into the narrative of *The Prince*, especially concerning oligarchic obstruction to his plans for a Florentine militia and regarding his diplomatic missions to further Florence's security.

Machiavelli, as I mentioned in the previous chapter, attempted to advance his own republic's security against foreign threats through diplomatic and military means: he served as Florence's emissary to the empires that threatened his republic: those of France, Germany, and the Holy See; and, as I said above, he sought to recruit and train a large Florentine civic military force. However, the Florentine aristocracy effectively scuttled Machiavelli's efforts to better serve his patria. Florence's nobles— the *ottimati*, the grandi—blocked Machiavelli's appointment as the republic's ambassador to the German imperial court, and they undermined his efforts to establish a full-scale citizen army within the city. Machiavelli often attributed to his own relatively humble origins the fact that he received so little cooperation, recognition, and reward from his fellow citizens for his difficult and dangerous service to the fatherland.[52]

Curiously, Borgia, or Duke Valentino, is the other figure Machiavelli directly affiliates himself with textually in *The Prince*—both, Machiavelli claims, suffered similar "malignity of fortune" (P DL, VII). Both Borgia's and Machiavelli's political careers were effectively terminated by machinations involving Pope Julius II as Julius attempted to consolidate and extend the church's territorial holdings in Central Italy. On becoming pope, Julius imprisoned Borgia and deprived him of his troops and provinces. (Borgia escaped to resume a military career in Spain, eventually dying in battle fighting for the king of Navarre.) Pope Julius also participated in the plot that overthrew the republic served by Machiavelli and headed by his patron, Piero Soderini. Julius, Florence's nobility, King Ferdinand of Spain, and the Medici family conspired against the republic to restore the Medici as princes within Florence. Consequently Machiavelli was sacked, incarcerated, and tortured.

In contrast to either Borgia or Machiavelli, then, Agathocles remained secure in his state for the duration of his long life. Obviously the hardships and dangers that, in Machiavelli's own words, link him with Agathocles produced greater results for the Sicilian than for the Florentine: after rising to power through Syracuse's civic military and then vigorously removing any aristocratic obstruction to his plans, Agathocles greatly expanded his army's ranks; by contrast, the thoroughly civilian Machiavelli acceded to the objections of his city's nobles and settled for establishing a small militia made up of peasants from Florence's countryside.[53] Agathocles led the heavily armed Syracusans against fearsome Carthage to secure his city's independence on his own terms; the poorly armed Florentines sent emissaries like Machiavelli, basically to beg the great powers who besieged them to—pretty please?—leave them alone. Agathocles died in his bed, king of all Sicily, with dreams of invading Carthage again and adding parts of Africa to his dominion. Machiavelli watched defenselessly as a Spanish army invaded Florentine territory, abolished the democratic republic headed by Soderini, and reinstalled a pro-aristocratic Medici principality in his patria.

Through the phrase "hardships and dangers," Machiavelli signals how desperately he wishes his own arduous efforts in political, military, and diplomatic service to Florence might have benefited his city as much as Agathocles's efforts benefited his "patria," Syracuse: the many "hardships and dangers" Agathocles endured bore fruit through the establishment of the kind of principality Machiavelli hoped would arise within Central Italy: a principality that sharply curbed the ambitions of local nobles (and clerics) and more expansively armed common citizens; a principality that might have unified the Italian peninsula and cast out foreign oppressors (P 26), just as Agathocles's principality did with such startling success in ancient Sicily.

CONCLUSION: SPEAKING WELL OF "EVIL"?

Machiavelli is the most (in)famous expositor of political prescriptions in the history of political thought. *The Prince* is the most frequently cited how-to book on politics ever written. In part 1 I have sought to demonstrate that this is at best a partial characterization of the way Machiavelli imparts political advice. To grasp the full meaning of his political thought, I have shown, an alert reader must pay attention not only to his explicit statements of judgment and injunctions to action but also, just as closely, to the complex web of analogies he constructs through a peculiar manner of storytelling; a narrative approach that highlights slightly different choices made and actions taken by various political actors and their concomitant outcomes in myriad historical circumstances.

Machiavelli, in his most pedagogical mode, presents examples and proceeds from particular case to case without always subsuming those specific examples under a general rule or category. Rather, he invites readers themselves to engage in judicious comparisons/contrasts and reach moral-political conclusions concerning the relation of these particular examples to each other without affording them consistent recourse to definitive statements (or at least without political precepts in the immediate textual vicinity). In this sense Machiavelli is an instructor who guides without always prescribing. This serves as a sketch of Machiavelli's formal method of exemplarity, but what of its content pertaining to exemplary leadership?

As we have observed, Machiavelli's use of exemplarity often turns against themselves traditions within which *exempla* are central; Machiavelli prods readers to draw conclusions often diametrically opposed to standard ideologies, whether pertaining to traditional republicanism, civic humanism, or orthodox Christianity. Machiavelli's exemplary method allows him a comparatively safe space within which (at least temporarily) he can advance political ideas that might be immediately and unreflectively rejected had they been expressed more directly. For instance, from the standpoint of classical philosophy, Roman republicanism, Christian dogma, and Italian humanism, Agathocles was an evil tyrant, a criminal unworthy of being considered virtuous, excellent, or glorious.

To Machiavelli, however, Agathocles—and the various "tyrants" he associates him with—cares not one iota for the preferences and predilections of the generators and expounders of traditional morality who constitute and perpetuate such schools of thought—namely, nobles and writers. The princes who together constitute Machiavelli's Agathoclean exemplum care only for their own ever more widely and heavily armed *popolo*; and they undertake the task of eliminating enemies they share with the people—that is, aristocratic oppressors at home and potential conquerors abroad. Machiavelli's ultimate lesson is that these concerns, and no others, meet the demands of virtue, excellence, and even justice. Such are the Machiavelli-redefined exemplary qualities of a good prince or magistrate.

If Scipio had elected to fully imitate not only Agathocles's military policy, but also his domestic one, then in all probability he would never have become our eternally glorious model of civic virtue. No writers, partial as they are to senatorial authority, would have been willing to speak his praise and spread his fame. Except, that is, for Niccolò Machiavelli. Machiavelli extols figures who decisively side with the people during the intractable social conflicts that inevitably beset republics: figures like Agathocles, Nabis, and, we might add, Cleomenes, Clearchus, and Hiero. Such individuals, to varying degrees, crush the nobles, redistribute their wealth to the people, and greatly expand the ranks of their civic military. The writers often denounce such figures as tyrants, and Machiavelli does not always object to such a designation in name. But tyrants who enrich and arm the people stand superior in his estimation to those who emasculate and, to one degree or another, disarm them; figures such as Appius Claudius, Sulla, Caesar Augustus, the Duke of Athens, and by insinuation the Medici as well.

I conclude part 1 with this thought: The issue of titles presents itself intriguingly throughout *The Prince*. For instance, Cesare Borgia formally acquired the title Duke Valentino as a result of diplomatic negotiations between his father, Pope Alexander VI, and the French throne: from this accord, King Louis XII gained a divorce; his minister, Georges d'Amboise, became cardinal of Rouen; and Cesare Borgia acquired French troops as well as the title Duke of the Valentinois. But Machiavelli makes it a point to say, twice, that he prefers to call Borgia "the duke" because that is what the people call him (P 3, P 7). Because Borgia brought "good government" to the Romagna, because he permitted its inhabitants to "savor well-being" for the first time, the *vulgo*, the common people of that province, choose to call him "Duke Valentino."

Taking his cue from the people, not from a senate, a royal court, or—God forbid—the Holy See, Machiavelli, a new kind of writer, propagates a new kind of glory for princes: princes like Valentino and Agathocles, who are concerned with providing good government to an armed people. It is the opinion of a civically and militarily armed people that, so famously in *discorso* I.58, Machiavelli expressly elevates over the opinion of the writers.

Machiavelli is the writer who, in his own unprecedented way, glorifies the virtuous tyrant who despises senators and disregards writers; the tyrant who cares primarily about empowering the common people against their domestic antagonists and foreign oppressors. Such an individual, in Machiavelli's account, is always both enabled and constrained by his subject citizens. Citizens who are armed and enjoy relatively equal socioeconomic status may rather easily convert a principality into a republic—especially should their tyrant ever fail to observe "cruelty well used" and resort instead to cruelty as such (D II.2). Such an individual, who empowers his people both civically and militarily, is actually no tyrant—except, of course, in the eyes of nobles and writers. Machiavelli and the people understand him to be a civil prince—a republic's reformer, redeemer, or even refounder. More simply, he is merely *il principe*, the prince.

PART 2

CIVIC LEADERSHIP IN *THE PRINCE* AND *DISCOURSES*

3. SEVERE AND PRUDENT CIVIC MAGISTRATES

The Consul, the Dictator, and the
Gonfalonier "for Life"

(LUCIUS BRUTUS, FURIUS CAMILLUS,
AND PIERO SODERINI)

This chapter examines Machiavelli's preeminent examples of effective, public-spirited political leaders from the Roman Republic—Lucius Brutus and Furius Camillus—as well as his vastly inferior Florentine example, Piero Soderini.[1] Through these examples from the *Discourses*, I demonstrate how the influence political leaders exerted and the prerogative they enjoyed at critical moments do not, for Machiavelli, constitute usurpations of popular deliberation; rather, in conjunction with popularly empowering institutions, they serve as necessary complements to democratic politics.[2]

As we will observe, Machiavelli suggests that the closest bonds between leaders and citizens often form after citizens have angrily dismissed leaders from office, or even exiled them from the polity, only to then reappoint them or invite them back. Machiavelli intimates that Camillus, Rome's frequently appointed dictator, gained unprecedented trust and authority from the Roman people by accepting their decision to exile him, faithfully returning to the city when they summoned him home during a crisis, and, on numerous subsequent occasions, eagerly relinquishing supreme command once he'd fulfilled his assignments (D I.29, III.1, III.30). Certainly, Machiavelli demonstrates, Camillus earned much more trust and authority from the Romans than Florence's gonfalonier of justice, Soderini, gained from the Florentine people by obsequiously imploring them to allow him, regardless of circumstances, to hold the republic's highest office in perpetuity (D III.30). Soderini, Machiavelli insinuates, refused to entertain the long-term advantages his own resignation, deposition, or exile might afford him and his republic until it was too late; that is, until his now unavoidable expulsion coincided with his republic's collapse, thus ensuring that no Florentine republic would exist to summon him back and reappoint him.

Willingly resigning office, putting oneself on trial, or permitting the people to judge whether one should suffer exile are not the only ways for a leader to demonstrate devotion to the common good. I will argue that, for Machiavelli, a leader's vigorous defense of the common people against oppressive and avaricious elites also neatly fills the bill. Machiavelli demonstrates how Brutus, Rome's first consul, elicited widespread admiration and respect among the people by eliminating traitorous young nobles, including his own sons, who wished to restore a monarchy, under which they could better oppress Rome's plebeians (D III.3). In contrast, Soderini, Machiavelli's boss and patron, suffers his employee's most severe disapprobation for failing to do the same within the Florentine Republic (D III.3). Soderini, our author suggests, proved too indecisive, reticent, or cowardly to put either himself or the republic's aristocratic enemies on trial for their lives; consequently the republic collapsed, the people lost their liberty, and Soderini lost his authority.

Machiavelli's consideration of these three statesmen boils down to two primary issues: how a leader should endeavor to neutralize envious rivals who seek to supplant his public authority or thwart his policy agenda; and how he should fully demonstrate to the people that his devotion to the common good and civic liberty is greater than to his personal benefit. Machiavelli's answer seems to be that, like Brutus, one must oversee the execution of treasonous and oppressive members of one's own class or family;[3] and one must, like Camillus, frequently abandon supreme command and express no rancor toward citizens for imposing on one political punishments such as exile. Moreover, according to Machiavelli, exhibiting exemplary military virtue while confronting fierce external enemies puts one in an optimal position to accomplish both of these goals. Brutus overcomes envy by executing those near and dear to him after leading Rome in battle to expel the Tarquin royal family (D I.16). Camillus overcomes envy by proving himself indispensable militarily, a fact confirmed by his returning from exile to vanquish the Gauls who occupied Rome (D III.1). In contrast, Soderini's willingness to put himself at the head of a citizen army (proposed at the time by Machiavelli) proved lukewarm, and his agreement to crush the sons of his fellow patricians who wished to overthrow the republic (recommended, again, by Machiavelli himself) proved only halfhearted.

I will begin by discussing Machiavelli's preliminary assessment of Soderini, who lost "his state and reputation" (D III.3) by disregarding Machiavelli's advice regarding the stern actions necessary to deal with enemies both internal and external; consequently, our author places the gonfalonier in Limbo to dwell eternally with other innocent babes.[4] Soderini reemerges later, both in the *Discourses* and in my analysis, as a potent counterexample to, on the one hand, Brutus, whom Machiavelli deems "the father of Roman Liberty" (D III.2–3), and, on the other, Camillus, whom he anoints as "Rome's most prudent captain" (D III.12). Indeed, I will devote most of this chapter to Camillus, Machiavelli's preeminent example of a virtuous and severe leader who suffers the envy of rivals and the resentment of the people during times of peace (D II.22) but who is someone both magistrates and citizens rush to for defense in times of war (D I.29, D III.30).

Machiavelli shows how Camillus initially incurs hatred and mistrust by combining military severity and solicitude with ostentatious self-aggrandizement. However, prudence and patriotism eventually teach him to win popular adoration by displaying his severity and solicitude in tandem with humanity and magnanimity. Camillus bears no discernible grudge against the Romans for exiling him; he frequently exhibits exemplary military skill in defending the republic from fearsome threats; and, as Livy and Plutarch emphasize, he adopts the practice of promptly relinquishing supreme command as soon as he fulfills his appointed tasks (D III.1, III.30). Camillus held the dictatorship, Rome's simultaneously ordinary and extraordinary magistracy, praised by Machiavelli, an unprecedented and unsurpassed number of times.[5] Although the young Camillus carelessly parades his vast personal ambition, he eventually learns to assiduously observe civic decorum and swiftly resign extraordinary authority. As a result of this transformation, in Machiavelli's view it becomes impossible to determine conclusively whether Camillus serves as Rome's ultimate champion of civic liberty, reigns as the city's intermittent king, or both. In any case, the dictator's painfully learned and prudently executed deference to popular judgment makes possible both Rome's renowned civic liberty and his own unprecedented authority.[6]

SODERINI, HIS RIVALS, AND THE FALL
OF THE FLORENTINE REPUBLIC

When evaluating Piero Soderini's leadership throughout the *Discourses*, Machiavelli assumes various perspectives on the gonfalonier of justice and attributes multiple roles to his former employer and patron in the Florentine Republic of 1494–1512: Machiavelli adopts the viewpoints of both Soderini and his enemies; he treats the gonfalonier, on the one hand, as an indecisive civic magistrate and, on the other, as a failed monarch. Moreover, his profound criticisms—both pronounced and subtle—notwithstanding, Machiavelli, as we will observe later, also conceals certain aspects of

Soderini's flawed personality by attributing them to the Florentine people rather than to the gonfalonier himself.

Early in the *Discourses*, Machiavelli primarily examines Soderini's tenure of office from the perspective of his aristocratic adversaries. The Florentine *ottimati* hated the gonfalonier for favoring the people collected in the Great Council; that is, the "multitude," "collectivity," or "universality," who in turn enthusiastically favored Soderini. Machiavelli considers how the nobles might have challenged Soderini's authority without, as they eventually did, destroying the republic altogether. This orientation makes perfect sense, as both of the young *ottimati* to whom Machiavelli dedicates the *Discourses*, Zanobi Buondelmonti and Cosimo Rucellai, were members of families who had been harshly critical of Soderini.[7] And of course the Medici, who ruled Florence both before 1494 and at the time of the book's composition, were staunch enemies of the former gonfalonier. Later in the work, however, Machiavelli flips the script by insisting that Soderini ought to have crushed these aristocratic adversaries through whose eyes he initially evaluated the career of Florence's failed chief magistrate.

Soderini first appears in book I of the *Discourses* as Machiavelli contrasts the conduct of political trials in the ancient Roman Republic and the 1494 Florentine Republic (D I.7). Machiavelli praises Rome for establishing institutions that empower popular judgment over public accusations, and he criticizes Florence for leaving such adjudication to small executive or judicial committees. To highlight Florence's deficiency in this regard, Machiavelli cites incidents in which two individuals who held the republic's chief magistracy, Soderini and Francesco Valori, were respectively exiled and assassinated. Valori, a former gonfalonier of justice, was murdered in a riot after arranging the summary execution of aristocratic conspirators against the republic; and Soderini, who soon thereafter had been appointed gonfalonier for life, was expelled by an aristocratic conspiracy and a foreign invasion that concomitantly overthrew the republic.

The Roman Republic, Machiavelli argues, avoided such personally violent and civically disastrous outcomes because it "institutionalized a mode" through which the people, rather than magistrates gathered in small councils, punished individuals for political crimes (D I.7). Machiavelli emphasizes that, in Rome, citizens accused of corruption, treason, or excessive ambition were prosecuted "ordinarily"—that is, legally, before a large citizen jury such as a popular assembly—hence in a way that avoids and even neutralizes dangerous civic controversies. On the contrary, Machiavelli complains, in Florence distrust or discontent over unfair verdicts rendered by small committees encouraged interested parties to resort to "extraordinary modes" such as homicide or conspiracy to assail or retaliate against prominent citizens suspected of "transgressing the bounds of a civic way of life" (D I.7). These unfortunate incidents from the Florentine Republic will become ever more relevant for Machiavelli's cross-comparisons of Brutus, Camillus, and Soderini as he develops an exemplary model of civic leadership. Political trials, as we will see, play an especially prominent role in Machiavelli's accounts of both Camillus's and Brutus's careers. But first let us examine our author's accounts of the Florentine episodes in greater detail.

Machiavelli writes that Francesco Valori was "almost prince" of the Florentine Republic (D I.7), having served as gonfalonier of justice four times and enjoying considerable prominence as head of the party supporting Friar Girolamo Savonarola, who, to all intents and purposes, founded the 1494 Republic. In August 1497 Valori insisted that the Signoria, the republic's chief executive committee, order the execution of five powerful citizens involved in a conspiracy to overthrow the republic and restore the Medici principality: Lorenzo Tornabuoni, Niccolò Ridolfi, Giannozzo Pucci, Giovanni Cambi, and Bernardo del Nero (hereafter referred to as the Medici Five). In April of the following year, the families of the executed conspirators retaliated by sparking a riot in which Valori, his wife, and several other citizens were murdered.[8]

When the tenure of the gonfalonier of justice was extended from two months to life in 1502, Soderini was elected to the magistracy by the Great Council, Florence's popular assembly. Soderini almost immediately incurred the animosity of many of the same pro-Medici aristocrats who had supported or condoned the murder of Valori and the execution of Savonarola only a few years before. Machiavelli argues that the absence of public accusations, adjudicated by a large popular jury such as the Great Council, caused the republic irreparable harm when these *ottimati*, who wished to challenge Soderini's authority, felt compelled to do so through conspiracy. In 1512 aristocratic animus against Soderini resulted in the summoning of the Spanish army, the overthrow of the republic, and the reestablishment of the Medici principality (D I.7).[9]

Machiavelli harshly criticizes Florence for assigning adjudication over political crimes to small committees of magistrates such as the Signoria or the Eight of Ward, rather than to a popular assembly: "That republic was bereft of a mode by which to properly accuse powerful citizens of ambition. It is insufficient for a republic to accuse a powerful individual before a mere eight judges; rather, very many judges are needed" (D I.7). Small committees, Machiavelli insists, are too easily intimidated or corrupted by external influences so that they rarely issue correct verdicts; moreover, the friends and families of either the accused or the aggrieved do not accept such rulings as valid, often resorting to "extraordinary" acts of vengeance after the fact. The Roman model of assigning public accusations of political crimes to a large citizen jury, Machiavelli argues, would have preserved the republic had it been practiced in Florence, since either Soderini or his aristocratic enemies would have been judged "ordinarily":

> If such a mode had been available, and if Soderini had been conducting himself badly, then citizens would have accused him and vented their animus through such a mode without summoning in the Spanish army. Conversely, if Soderini had been comporting himself appropriately such citizens would have feared accusing him lest they themselves be accused. Thus, the appetites motivating each side to cause a scandal would have been eliminated. (D I.7)

Later in book I, Machiavelli reconsiders how Soderini's aristocratic adversaries, to whom he now ascribes naked "envy" (*invidia*), might have challenged or at least tempered the authority the gonfalonier exerted over Florence without entirely overthrowing the republic. Machiavelli writes:

> Piero Soderini acquired his reputation in the city of Florence exclusively by favoring the collectivity, such that the latter revered him as a lover of the city's liberty. In truth, the citizens who *envied* his greatness could have opposed him much more easily and honestly, and with much less danger and harm for the republic, if they had anticipated the ways through which he acquired greatness; instead, they opposed him in a manner that entirely ruined the republic along with ruining him. If they had taken from Soderini's hands the *arms* with which he made himself great, as it was well within their power to do, they could have challenged him without arousing suspicion and without incurring opposition in all the councils that made public decisions. (D I.52; emphases added)

Contemporary readers would have known that the Florentine *ottimati*, to whom Machiavelli attributes intense envy of Soderini, succeeded in depriving the gonfalonier of military arms by limiting and keeping from his personal command the militia project proposed by Machiavelli himself.[10] Nevertheless, they ultimately failed to take from him the other types of "arms" he wielded, namely, the favor he enjoyed with the Florentine people as a reputed "lover of the city's liberty."[11] Had these *ottimati* themselves, Machiavelli suggests, endeavored to favor the people within the city as Soderini did, rather than favoring the Medici outside it, they could have advanced their own cause without meeting resistance from either the gonfalonier or members of the people gathered either in the Great Council or in other public bodies.

In such circumstances, Machiavelli argues, the nobles would not have felt compelled to call in the Spanish army, which resulted in their effectively swapping their perceived subjection to Soderini (and the people) for their own outright subjection (and that of the entire city) to the Medici. Soderini, for his part, in fearing the *ottimati*'s influence over the people, would have been unable to turn the tables on the nobles by favoring the Medici himself; that is, by attempting to use the family's resources to beat down his enemies as the nobles did in their efforts to ultimately ruin the gonfalonier (and the republic). Had he done so, Soderini would have lost the people's favor—in fact, he likely would have incurred their hatred, always a dangerous disposition among one's subjects or citizens (P 19). Machiavelli explains:

> Piero simply could not have [favored the Medici] honestly or with good reputation because he would have destroyed the very liberty over which he had been made guardian. To have done so surreptitiously and boldly would have been very dangerous for Piero, because had he been exposed as the Medici's friend then the people would have suspected and hated him, thus giving his enemies even greater opportunity to ruin him. (D I.52)

It must be stated that Machiavelli is more than slightly disingenuous regarding both of these Florentine episodes in which Soderini figures so prominently. Machiavelli's tongue may be firmly planted in his cheek when he argues, on the one hand, that the Florentine Republic ought to have instituted popularly judged political trials and, on the other, that the Florentine *ottimati* should have beat Soderini at his own game by favoring the people collected in the Great Council.

As Machiavelli makes patently clear later in the *Discourses*, the 1494 Republic did in fact offer institutional recourse to popular judgment over political trials: specifically, through the law permitting a right of appeals to the Great Council in capital cases (D I.45). But none of the republic's most prominent popular champions—Savonarola, who sponsored the law, Valori, or Soderini—was willing to avail himself of popular judgment in an "ordinary" civic manner, through the law of popular appeal, when it came to adjudicating his own fate or that of his political rivals. As Machiavelli intimates, Valori and Savonarola feared the people might not render judgments personally favorable to them in such circumstances (D I.45). (Moreover, as we will observe, Soderini worried unnecessarily over political consequences resulting from the people's rendering a judgment favorable to him! [D III.3].) Neither Valori nor Savonarola should have denied the Medici Five their right to appeal their death sentences to the Great Council; in denying such appeals—actively in Valori's case and passively in Savonarola's—they basically became complicit in their own subsequent deaths, and furthermore they set the precedent for the republic's collapse. Florence's constitution provided institutional means to conduct popularly judged political trials; but the people's most vociferous champions, Valori and Savonarola, didn't trust the people to—in their view—"properly" exercise such judgment in the Great Council—with dire consequences for themselves and for the republic.

On the second point that Machiavelli seems to treat less than sincerely, he declares earlier in the *Discourses*, and demonstrates throughout the work, that nobles of *all* polities or republics, motivated by a natural humor to oppress the people (D I.5), can feign acts of beneficence only under severely constrained conditions, and only for a limited time. For instance, Machiavelli recounts that the Roman nobles eventually spewed their venom toward the people once the kings were no longer available to prevent them from doing so (D I.3); and that the nobles initially appeared to act magnanimously by paying for extended military service (D II.6), a practice the people later realized served only to intensify their socioeconomic domination by the nobility (D I.37). In short, Machiavelli makes it clear that a republic's nobles can neither long nor consistently refrain from overtly oppressing the people. The full ramifications of these qualifications of Machiavelli's declarations regarding popularly judged political trials, oppressive aristocratic insolence, and Soderini's career will become clearer below.

PRUDENCE, RETURN TO BEGINNINGS, AND REFORM OF CORRUPT REPUBLICS

In the opening chapter of the *Discourses'* final book, Machiavelli sets the stage for his most comprehensive reflections on two of Rome's most illustrious magistrates, Lucius Brutus and Furius Camillus. This lengthy chapter also happens to constitute Machiavelli's elaborate, if nevertheless still perplexing, ruminations over the reform of corrupt republics. I examine how Machiavelli's discussion of Brutus, "the father of Roman liberty," and Camillus, "Rome's most prudent captain," emerge out of his extensive coverage of republican corruption and renewal. Machiavelli subsequently uses both Brutus and Camillus to highlight the poor leadership exhibited by modern civic magistrates, best exemplified by his former employer and patron, Piero Soderini, the ill-fated "gonfalonier for life" of the even worse-fated Florentine Republic.

Machiavelli titles book 3, *discorso* 1, "The Longevity of Sects and Republics Requires Frequent Returns to Their Beginnings." In this chapter—a kind of book within a book (within a book)—Machiavelli reflects on phenomena that promote either the corruption and demise or the renewal and perpetuation of republics. He declares that "mixed bodies, such as republics and sects," may enjoy the full length of life "ordered for them by nature" if they are altered over time in healthy rather than harmful ways (D III.1). If complex, composite social bodies such as religions and polities are to change in salutary rather than deleterious ways, Machiavelli argues, they must continually and frequently be directed back toward their origins. Beneficial changes, reforms that foster "renewal," he insists, are those that lead such mixed bodies "back to their beginnings."[12]

Machiavelli goes on to explain why frequent backward recourse to the original moments that give birth to "mixed bodies" propels religions, republics, and—as he now adds—principalities toward beneficial renewal: "Sects, republics, and kingdoms all have beginnings of some goodness to which their initial reputation and flourishing is attributable. In the course of time such goodness is corrupted, thereby necessitating that something intercede to lead the mixed body back to the mark, or else it will necessarily die" (D III.1). The beginnings of any religion, republic, or principality that lasts for a long time, in Machiavelli's estimation, must be good—or must contain elements that are good—otherwise that entity would never have enjoyed "reputation and expansion" over its early life. Machiavelli identifies two factors that "intercede" to redirect republics, in particular, toward their origins and hence may engender republican renewal going forward: "Republics are returned to the beginnings by either extrinsic accident or intrinsic prudence" (D III.1).

Machiavelli identifies the invasion of the Gauls in 390 BCE as an external accident that returned the Roman Republic to its beginnings. The invasion—and the Romans' ultimate response to it (exemplified by Camillus's civic and military heroism) gave the republic "new birth, life, and virtue" by revitalizing "religion and justice" (D III.1). Before the Gauls invaded, Machiavelli argues, the Romans were deviating from both religious practices and "other good institutions" that Romulus, and subsequent early kings, "had prudently ordered for the free way of life." Machiavelli cites the following as examples of prudent kingly ordering that proved conducive to Rome's liberty: Tullius Hostilius's efforts to restore Roman military virtue and his construction of a senate house (D I.21); Servius Tullius's organization of the people into public assemblies; and Lucius Brutus's vigorous efforts to punish transgressors of the laws. Kings such as Romulus, Tullus, and Servius establish religious, political, and military orders that make *civic liberty* possible (D I.2, I.21, II.3); a civic magistrate like Brutus, as we will observe more clearly below, exhibits *princely virtue* in pursuit of civil justice.

However, Rome's "external beating" by the Gauls, according to Machiavelli, was directly attributable not only to the aforementioned corruption of its civic, religious, and military orders, but also to another form of corruption: the republic's diminishing respect for "good and virtuous citizens" (D III.1). In this regard the French invasion served as an external accident that once again prompted the Romans to "esteem good citizens for their virtue rather than blame them for their defects." Machiavelli declares that after the French invasion the Senate and the people "set aside their envy of the good and virtuous Camillus," permitting him once again "to bear the full weight of the republic." Therefore the invasion may have been an "external accident," but it also inspired exhibitions of such "internal prudence," also mentioned above as an impetus for renewing a republic: certainly this includes the prudence of Camillus, who saved the republic by returning from exile to expel the invaders; but it also entails the renewed prudence of the Senate and the people, who called Camillus back to do so—and who henceforth placed the republic's well-being on his shoulders for as long as he lived (D III.1).

In this *discorso* Machiavelli somewhat imprecisely distinguishes the external and internal factors that prompt republican renewal. As I noted above, it is not clear whether the external "accident" of the Gauls' invasion or Camillus's "prudence" in repelling it constitutes the definitive cause of Rome's salutary return to beginnings. After all, without Camillus's prudence and virtue (and the Romans' renewed prudence in recalling him) the city may well have been entirely destroyed. Moreover, Machiavelli subdivides his classification of the internal factors that generate republican renewal into, on the one hand, "intrinsic orders" or "laws" and, on the other, the personal "prudence" and "virtue" of an individual. More specifically, Machiavelli identifies such intrinsic factors as either "a law that often assesses and renders accountable the men who constitute that body," or "the example of a good man who emerges among them, one whose virtuous deeds produce the same result as the ordered law" (D III.1).

With respect to laws and orders that enable republics to properly appraise men and, when warranted, hold them accountable, Machiavelli shows elsewhere that, not long after the French invasion, Manlius Capitolinus is tried and executed for exhibiting kingly ambition (D III.8). Alternatively, the individual who exemplifies the way personal prudence and virtue may effect republican renewal is Camillus, whom the Romans appoint as dictator an unprecedented number of times after the invasion, granting him absolute authority over the city's institutions, including the Senate and the popular assemblies (D III.30). Moreover, after Camillus's second founding of the city, in which the dictator reaffirmed Rome's commitment to religious and military discipline, the republic would never again suffer foreign invasion—in fact, it would make itself head and defender of the entire Italian peninsula.

Given Machiavelli's imprecision here, we must further examine his claims regarding return to beginnings that renews republics. Again, Machiavelli remarks that "men living in common" frequently require internally generated reforms such as those manifested in laws that surveille and correct citizens "by holding them to account" or reforms initiated by the emergence of "an exemplary and virtuous man" whose actions produce the same salutary results as do laws that facilitate suspicious evaluation and severe correction of wayward citizens (D III.1). This poses a conundrum: Camillus's exile resulted directly from legally aired public accusations and popularly judged political trials that, as we observed above, Machiavelli enthusiastically recommends that republics employ to hold ambitious citizens to account (D I.7–8); and yet Camillus is precisely the kind of good and prudent man whose exemplary virtue sets salutary civic standards for other citizens to follow. It seems that a stark contradiction, or at least a deep tension, potentially plagues Machiavelli's account of the legal as opposed to personal means available for republics to redeem themselves by returning to their beginnings. Perhaps the issue can be resolved in this way: the Camillus who returned to save Rome was substantially transformed in a civically beneficial way by the public indictment that resulted in his exile from the republic. We cannot, however, fully address this question until we examine Camillus's career in more detail below.

Machiavelli concludes this discussion of internally generated republican renewal by again affirming "the virtue" of either "a man" or "an order" that produces "good results in republics" (D III.1). We should not overlook that when the ancient Romans were confronted by a "French" invasion, a prudent and virtuous individual like Camillus was available to rescue and refound that republic. On the contrary, when Florence, the modern republic Machiavelli is writing for, endured a French invasion in 1494, deficiently prudent and deeply unvirtuous individuals emerged to carry out at best partial reforms of the city: Girolamo Savonarola, Francesco Valori, and especially Piero Soderini. All these Florentine "almost" princes, according to Machiavelli, succumbed to the ambitious envy of rival citizens such that before long foreign enemies again invaded the city (the Spanish army in 1512) and the Medici returned from exile to overthrow the republic and reestablish a tyranny (D I.45, D I.7, D III.9).

In the case of ancient Rome, Machiavelli insists, the "accident" of a French invasion, despite threatening the city with near extinction, actually made possible "the revitalization of the city's orders" (D III.1). Rome came very close to being eradicated by the Gauls, except for the virtue of Camillus—and also of Manlius Capitolinus, who initially repelled the French from the Capitol, granting Camillus the occasion to subsequently drive them from the city and its environs (D I.8). Having averted total annihilation, the Romans, Machiavelli observes, again came to acknowledge the necessity of "maintaining religion and justice, of esteeming good citizens, and of assessing the latter according to their virtue rather than any deficiencies that their deeds might otherwise exhibit" (D III.1). Machiavelli notes that after the expulsion of the French, the Romans renewed their ancient religious orders, properly punished the young nobles—the Fabii—who provoked the Gauls to invade, and appropriately put aside their envy to rightly esteem Camillus's goodness.

Moving away from the ostensibly external example of the Gauls' invasion, Machiavelli then enumerates the kinds of orders/laws and exemplary actions that propelled the Roman Republic back to its beginnings. He does so in a way that emphasizes the mutual dependence of good institutions and virtuous individuals and that occasions his ensuing discussion of Lucius Brutus (D III.1). Machiavelli first cites the plebeian tribunate, which was instituted to address the insecurity of the many and to thwart the oppressive appetites of the few; second, he mentions the censors, among other orders and laws, that were established to militate against the insolence and ambition of citizens. "Such orders," Machiavelli insists, "must be invigorated by a virtuous citizen who spiritedly and swiftly directs them against powerful transgressors of the laws" (D III.1).

Brutus, of course, is Machiavelli's quintessential example of a virtuous citizen who used the new republic's laws to punish his treasonous sons (D III.3); and such vindictive virtue was later institutionalized in the orders of the tribunes and the censors, who wielded the powers of public accusations and of public sanctions. The Florentine Republic had instituted orders through which powerful transgressors of laws might be punished—the law of appeals to the Great Council, mentioned above (D I.5)—but it failed to produce virtuous citizens like Brutus who were willing to employ these laws with vigor; moreover, it developed no auxiliary institutions, like the tribunes and censors, to reinforce such orders that hold powerful citizens accountable.

Furthermore, on Machiavelli's view, formal accusations and sanctions, vigorously leveled to deter and correct insolent and ambitious citizens, must spill actual blood to keep civic life uncorrupted. "Notable executions," he asserts, must result from the virtuous deployment of such laws and orders. In this regard, he invokes examples of noteworthy "deaths": Brutus's sons; the tyrannical decemvirs; Maelius the grain seller; Manlius Capitolinus; Manlius Torquatus's son Fabius; and on this list he also cites the indictment of Scipio Africanus (D III.1).

The last example is somewhat puzzling: Scipio was indeed accused by Cato the Censor and indicted by the tribunes, but he was not executed—he chose exile rather than to stand trial (D I.29).[13] In fact, only one of the deaths mentioned above, that of Manlius Capitolinus, resulted from tribunal or censorial prosecutions. Machiavelli could have cited other cases that the tribunes brought and conducted—say, that of Coriolanus near the beginning of the republic, or that of Cicero toward its end. However, as in the case of Scipio—and Camillus, for that matter—these trials resulted merely in exile for the accused rather than execution. It appears then that Machiavelli wishes to make the Roman Republic seem more ferocious than it actually was in punishing transgressors of laws and adversaries of common liberty.

Be that as it may, Machiavelli argues that "extreme and noteworthy" events, such as the execution of prominent Roman citizens, compelled ambitious men to toe the line once again (D III.1). However, as public executions occurred less frequently in Rome, the increasing time between them "afforded corrupt men opportunities for acting in a dangerous and disorderly manner." No more than ten years, Machiavelli insists, should intervene between such executions, "lest men begin diverging from customs and disobeying the laws" (D III.1). Unless "punishment returns to men's memories and fear revives their spirits," he warns, "so many reprobates too quickly band together such that punishment may no longer be meted out safely" (D III.1). The Medici, he notes, insisted on renewing the state every five years (a less virtuous city like Florence apparently requires more frequent reforms—in any case, their rule endured, initially, for only sixty years). The Medici understood renewal to entail "reinstilling within men the terror and fear" that the family aroused in Florentines when they first came to power, presumably by crushing members of the Albizzi oligarchy who preceded their rule. In time, "men recommence venturing new things and saying evil ones," and therefore, Machiavelli insists, they must be brought back to the mark (D III.1).

Machiavelli argues, in line with what he stated before, that good examples provided by exemplary citizens may also encourage adherence to the laws and dissuade violations of them: "The simple virtue of one man may also bring a republic back to beginnings without reliance on laws that lead to executions" (D III.1). Such individuals "are so well-reputed and exemplary that good men naturally imitate them, and evil men prevent themselves from acting contrary to their example." He invokes the examples of Horatius Coclus, Scaevola, the Decii, and Attilius Regulus. Machiavelli ventures the notion that regular public executions, combined with public-spirited actions by such virtuous citizens, occurring within ten-year spans, would have indefinitely staved off corruption in Rome. However, exemplary actions, like public executions, became decreasingly frequent over the republic's history, thus permitting corruption to proliferate. Machiavelli notes that Regulus and the two Catos were separated by too long an interval to keep Rome thoroughly virtuous through their good examples. Machiavelli then returns to the beginnings of the Roman Republic with the example of Brutus—the individual who, through both exemplary public-spiritedness and notable executions, became "the father of Roman liberty" (D III.1)

DEFENDING POPULAR LIBERTY BY KILLING TREASONOUS "SONS"

Machiavelli recalls from Livy's history how Brutus, as a member of the Tarquin royal family, feigned mental deficiency—Machiavelli calls it "insanity," but it appears more like stupidity—to avoid notice, and consequently gain an opportunity to overthrow the monarchy and free his patria (D III.2). The notorious author of *The Prince*, a book dedicated to a Medici prince—and intended to gain employment from him—here emphasizes the following aspect of Brutus's strategy, which he insists ought to be followed by any potential republican founder (or refounder or reformer): an individual who lives discontentedly under a prince must learn to make himself a "friend of the prince" (D III.2). Brutus avoids the middle way between remaining very close to a prince one would like to depose and keeping a distance from him to avoid sharing his ruin once it comes. As Machiavelli explains: "Because I believe that it is impossible to follow such a [middle] path, one must follow one or the other of the two aforementioned modes: either completely keep one's distance from or cleave oneself entirely to him. A man who does otherwise, especially one of notable quality, remains in perpetual danger" (D III.2). In order to stand most safely close to a prince, Machiavelli declares that, like Brutus, one "must act crazy, and make oneself appear quite insane—praising, saying, observing, acting in ways that, in order to please the prince, do not reflect your intentions" (III.2).

By remaining close to Tarquin and by simulating mental deficiency, Brutus was well positioned to overthrow the monarchy at a critical moment. After the infamous rape and suicide of Lucretia, Brutus successfully led his fellow nobles and Rome's armed people in expelling the kings from the city; he then compelled them all to swear the oath that "no one would ever again reign in Rome" (D III.2). Prudently judging that the Roman king, Tarquinius Superbus, was too corrupt to punish his own son, Sextus, for raping Lucretia, Machiavelli reports that Brutus instead "sought retribution with the Roman people" (D III.5). In Machiavelli's estimation, Brutus is "the father of Roman liberty" because he extinguished the monarchy, instituted the republic, and established the principle—invoked frequently throughout the republic's history—that no one should ever rule over the city as king, or at least under "the name" of king (D I.2, D III.2).

Machiavelli declares unequivocally that Brutus exhibited "prudence in establishing Rome's liberty" as well as "severity" in maintaining it (D III.2). Brutus prudently established the consulship in Rome, which maintained important continuity with royal imperium yet departed significantly from it: after the expulsion of Tarquin, supreme authority was henceforth to be shared by two consuls, empowered to veto one another's actions, instead of being wielded by one unassailable individual as under the monarchy. Moreover, the consuls served for only one year, after which they could not be reappointed for several years. Brutus's prudence hence ensured that monarchical power was split in two, and furthermore that it was dramatically limited functionally and temporally. After this discussion of Brutus's prudence, in the next chapter Machiavelli demonstrates Brutus's severity in preserving Rome's liberty during the republic's infancy through an act that, in some sense, repudiated another quasi-monarchical principle, heredity (D III.3).

In this *discorso*, titled "On the Necessity of Killing Brutus's Sons to Maintain Newly Won Liberty," Machiavelli upholds Brutus as "an example most rare among all memory" (D III.3). Brutus demonstrated his severity by personally "presiding over the tribunal that condemned his sons and by overseeing their deaths." Resenting the liberty that Rome's plebeians enjoyed under the newly instituted republic (D I.16), Brutus's sons conspired with other young nobles to restore the Tarquin tyranny. Brutus's behavior is certainly remarkable: he initiated the political trial and oversaw the public executions of his own male offspring for the sake of a greater common, more public good (D III.3), thus rejecting an intimate, personal, merely private good.[14] Hence Brutus asserts paternity over the liberty of his patria rather than over the lives of his progeny. Liberty is the patrimony that Brutus prefers to bequeath to his truly rightful heirs: *citizens* rather than sons.

Although "rare," Brutus's actions illustrate a crucial general rule. According to Machiavelli, "anyone who consults the ancients will learn this timeless lesson: the necessity of executing the enemies of the present state whenever a tyranny has become a republic," as well as the necessity of doing the same whenever the opposite has occurred; that is, when a republic becomes a tyranny (D III.3). To protect the republic he established, Brutus the Elder necessarily killed his sons who sought to reinstate the Tarquin tyrants and revoke Rome's liberty; with similar severity, if for opposite ends, Machiavelli intimates that Julius Caesar, while pursuing a tyranny centuries later, ought to have killed Brutus the Younger. As I noted before, this young noble embodied the memory of his ancestor, the original Brutus—the vanquisher of tyrants who initially made Rome free. As a result of his severity, Lucius Brutus is remembered as the father of Roman liberty; as a result of his clemency, Julius Caesar is remembered as the agent of Rome's ultimate subjection (D I.10). Just as Lucius Brutus kills his sons in the name of liberty, Caesar should have killed Marcus Brutus—who may have been his own natural son,[15] and who nevertheless (or consequently) assassinated *him* in the name of liberty. He might then have secured a principate long enough either to establish a tyranny more firmly, or to demonstrate that he was not in fact a tyrant, but rather a republican reformer.

Machiavelli quickly contrasts ancient knowledge over the proper role of severity in maintaining both republics and tyrannies with ignorance of the same in modern, Christian contexts. "In our own time and in our own patria," Machiavelli recounts from firsthand experience, "Piero Soderini fooled himself" in these matters (D III.3). Unlike Brutus, it seems, Soderini was not merely pretending to be a fool. Machiavelli writes that Soderini—the first and only gonfalonier for life of the reestablished but short-lived Florentine Republic—believed "that patience and goodness would placate the appetite of Brutus's sons to restore the previous government," that is, the young Florentine *ottimati*, who conspired to restore Medici tyranny because they despised the liberty the common people enjoyed under Florence's *governo largo* (D III.3; cf. D I.16).

Machiavelli thinks that Soderini may have shared a certain prudence with Brutus while facing circumstances quite like those confronting the Roman consul, but he insists that the Florentine gonfalonier quite definitively lacked Brutus's severity. Machiavelli suggests that Soderini was prudent enough to know that the young *ottimati* who envied both him and the Florentine people should be punished, and, moreover, that he had the opportunity to do so (D III.3). Presumably Machiavelli is referring to the fact that many young Florentine nobles were committing treason by illegally consorting with the Medici in Rome, arranging marriages with members of the family, and even conspiring to assassinate the gonfalonier—flagrantly treacherous acts that Soderini should have vigorously prosecuted and that the people should have adjudicated in the Great Council.[16] However, according to Machiavelli, Soderini lacked the fortitude, the severity, to do so: "He never set his mind upon doing what his prudence dictated and what their ambition, as if by fate, gave him the opportunity to do" (D III.3). This opportunity is reminiscent of the occasion that, Machiavelli observes, *fortuna* often provides to founders like Romulus and Moses: the *occasio* of encountering a people in need of liberation from oppression (P 6). Indeed, Machiavelli insists that Soderini effectively needed "to strike" and "beat down" Brutus's sons (D III.3) in much the manner that, in *The Prince*, he insists a new prince ought to employ against Lady Fortuna (P 25).

These Florentine sons of Brutus were successors of the young, armed *compagnacci* who hated Savonarola for his populist and puritanical predilections; in order to satisfy their oppressive and licentious desires they wished to institute an oligarchic republic like Venice's within the city or, barring that, to restore a pro-aristocratic Medici principality.[17] These noble youths were effectively "sons" of the biologically childless Soderini; they were the children of the patrician class to which the gonfalonier belonged.[18] Had Soderini truly been the full-scale class traitor Machiavelli wished him to become, the gonfalonier would have had to kill his own figurative sons. Like that virtuous traitor to class and clan, Brutus, he should have severely and stoically overseen their trials and executions—capital trials that would have been "ordinary" in a legal sense, but that in their severity appeared to the gonfalonier to be inappropriately "extraordinary" (D III.3).

Perhaps Soderini's hesitation was motivated by his memory of the summary execution of the Medici Five earlier in the revived republic's history. As Machiavelli intimates, their execution led to the murder of an earlier gonfalonier of justice, Francesco Valori, as well as to the burning of his influential ally outside the government, Friar Savonarola (D I.7–8, D I.45). However, Valori's execution of these *ottimati* was *literally* extraordinary because he and Savonarola denied them their legal right to have their capital sentences put to the ultimate decision of the people, assembled in the Great Council. Soderini, for his part, could have followed a course that, if extraordinary in its sternness, was nevertheless entirely ordinary in a procedural sense. Since the people favored Soderini and distrusted the Medici partisans, Machiavelli indicates that they likely would have upheld the latter's capital convictions on the gonfalonier's word that the sons of Brutus were traitors who wished either to replace the popular government with a *governo stretto* or to restore the Medici's hereditary tyranny in the city. Moreover, as Machiavelli explains earlier in book I, Soderini could have permitted his enemies to put *him* on trial for excessive ambition to either popularly validate or repudiate his behavior in these circumstances (D I.7).[19]

Machiavelli discusses in detail Soderini's misunderstanding of what constitutes extraordinary versus ordinary recourse against sons of Brutus. On the one hand, Soderini incorrectly "believed that patience would quell their bad humor" and that "rewards would mitigate their animosity for him" (D III.3). On the other, his prudence dictated to him the necessity of eliminating them. However, the gonfalonier confessed to "friends"— among them, quite plausibly, his trusted counselor Machiavelli—"his fear that extraordinary means would violate civil and legal equality." Unlike Brutus, whose ties to traitors among the nobility were even more intimate than Soderini's, the latter refused to act as a thoroughgoing class traitor, demurring from treating the sons of his fellow patrician friends and relatives in, as he understood it, an uncivil manner.

Moreover, the gonfalonier was even less inclined to behave outside the bounds of legality as did Romulus and Moses: Machiavelli points out that Romulus murdered his own kin (his brother, Remus) and a colleague in rule (his coregent Titus Tatius) (D I.9); and, furthermore, that Moses killed "infinite numbers" of men to establish his laws and orders (D III.30). Although extraordinary from a legal standpoint, Machiavelli exonerates both Romulus and Moses since they engaged in these killings for the benefit of their own prominence (to eliminate the "envy" of adversaries); for the longevity of the institutions (the "modes and orders") they had established; and for the security (or "happiness") of the people they had liberated and were protecting (P 6).

According to Machiavelli, Soderini worried that wide-scale executions of traitorous young nobles, whether conducted ordinarily or extraordinarily, would "terrify the collectivity," even if he would not again resort to such means "tyrannically" in the future (D III.3). Yet Soderini, on Machiavelli's view, ought not to have been excessively concerned that the people's terror would turn to hatred and thus endanger either his person or the republic. There is no indication in Machiavelli's account that the people would have turned on the gonfalonier for eliminating their enemies among the nobility—to truly incur such hatred Soderini would have had to deny the Great Council its authority, as Savonarola and Valori previously did (D I.7, D I.45), completely shut it down, as the Medici eventually would, or betray the people by favoring the Medici himself (D I.52).

In any case, "terror," recall, is precisely the emotion a refounder/reformer is supposed to arouse in the people when he returns a republic to its beginnings (D III.1). Machiavelli suggests that Soderini actually worried that the people might offend *him* after his death; specifically, he feared they would decline to renew the office of lifetime gonfalonier, which he was the first to hold (D III.3). In other words, Soderini demurs from necessary recourse to severity because he wants in some sense to live forever through his office, a lifetime magistracy that survives him for eternity. Brutus, by contrast, employs severity and gains eternal life as the father of Roman liberty even though he held an office with a fixed temporal limit (D III.3). I will revisit these themes in subsequent sections: whether Soderini should have acted extraordinarily, not only by deploying severe means to eliminate obdurate adversaries, as Brutus did, but even with recourse to illegal, kingly—in fact, tyrannical—means as Romulus and Moses did, to accomplish this end. Furthermore, when more fully discussing the example of Camillus below, I suggest that Soderini misunderstands what it really takes for a founder or reformer to win eternal life in the memory of his people.

For now, Machiavelli insists that besides worrying that future generations of Florentines would abandon a life-termed chief magistrate,

Soderini feared that aggressive recourse against the republic's enemies would leave a bad example that others would subsequently use for nefarious ends. Machiavelli argues, on the contrary, that Soderini should have left it to others—specifically, to the people—to judge whether "his works and intentions" had been tyrannical, based on their *ends* (D III.3). As Machiavelli avers in *The Prince*, in the world there are none but "the vulgar"; the common people are the ultimate arbiters of right and wrong, good and bad (P 15). The people, Machiavelli insists, must themselves judge whether they enjoyed more freedom from internal and external oppression as a result of Soderini's actions: if he had crushed the sons of Brutus within the city and prevented their enlisting Spain to reinstall the Medici, then the answer would likely have been a resounding yes.

Regarding the course of action his patron should have pursued, Machiavelli remarks: Soderini "should have believed that, good fortune and long life permitting, everyone would affirm that he acted for the sake of the patria's security and not his own ambition" (D III.3). But he did not. In other words, Soderini, like Savonarola and Valori not long before him, ultimately distrusted the very popular judgment his legitimacy depended on; if one claims to trust the many over the few, as all three did, then one must in fact let them decide. Again, these good Christian leaders ultimately exhibit little faith in the people's ability to see clearly their good intentions and the good effects of their potentially severe actions against the people's (and their own) adversaries. Certainly, as Machiavelli details elsewhere, they exhibit far less faith than did their Hebrew antecedent Moses; the grave pagan magistrate Brutus; and even the cruel pagan tyrant Agathocles. All these pre-Christian leaders build lasting domestic peace through the mutual security that they themselves and their armed peoples enjoyed with and from each other (P 6, P 8).

Machiavelli argues that Soderini "could have arranged matters such that no successor could endeavor for evil what he had endeavored for good" (D III.3). If he is thinking of Brutus here, then perhaps the following considerations are relevant: Brutus avoided a bad precedent by following "ordinary" law; what was "extraordinary" in his case was the *target* of those laws: his own sons, who happen to be young, rich and powerful nobles— that is, those who conventionally assume themselves to be exempt from punishment. It is extraordinary to execute a group of young *ottimati* "ordinarily" through legal procedures that apply to them de jure, but seldom do de facto.[20] How did Brutus "arrange matters" such that his successors did not use his example tyrannically? Through Brutus's example none themselves could depart from established legal procedures, since he himself did not. As Machiavelli laments in the first chapter of book III, discussed above, would that the Romans had more often used these ordinary laws to eliminate extraordinarily prominent transgressors; then the republic would have lasted much longer than it did.

Machiavelli judges Soderini's "respect" for freedom, equality, and the rule of law to be "good"; but he quickly adds that "one should never permit evil to run rampant due to respect for the good, especially when this evil can eliminate entirely that very good which is so esteemed" (D III.3). In Florence's past, as we will see Machiavelli demonstrate in the *Florentine Histories*, Giano della Bella's strict adherence to "the good" literally permitted "the evil" of noble oppression to run rampant in the person of Corso Donati; furthermore, it allowed nearly perpetual civil war between the nobles and the *popolani* to persist (FH II.13). More immediately, Soderini's fastidious adherence to the goods of civil-legal freedom and equality permitted such principles to be entirely extinguished by greater evils: the collapse of the republic that guaranteed them; Spanish invasion; the return of the Medici; and Soderini's exile (not to mention Machiavelli's consequent personal and professional misfortunes). The oppressive appetites of Florence's young nobles, Machiavelli seems to suggest here, would be satisfied by nothing less than the abolition of both the lifetime gonfaloniership and the Great Council; and to achieve this end they resorted to colluding with exiled traitors like the Medici and with foreign enemies like the papacy and Spain. Circumstances dictated that Florence's sons of Brutus be confronted with a spirit as obdurate as their own to prevent such disastrous outcomes for the republic.

As we saw Machiavelli emphasize in the first chapter of book III, republics must invigorate and revitalize orders and laws that indict and convict powerful and ambitious citizens who would corrupt and usurp them (D III.1). Yet the neo-Roman order of popularly judged capital trials that Savonarola instituted in Florence was circumvented by Valori and by the friar himself when, shortly thereafter, they feared that the people would not uphold the death sentences of their political adversaries among the *ottimati* (D I.7, I.45). Soderini, in failing even to level indictments for treason—let alone prosecute such cases in the Great Council—misjudged the people's favor for him and their animosity for the *ottimati*, or at least he proved too timid to test either.

Thus Soderini followed his first impulse, his inclination toward patience and gifts, rather than his second one, his intuition motivated by prudence. In this, Machiavelli insists, the gonfalonier "was deceived": Soderini "did not understand that malignity may neither be subdued by time nor be appeased by gifts of any kind" (D III.3). Put simply, "Soderini did not know how to be Brutus." (Later Machiavelli indicates that he was no Camillus either [D III.30].) And precisely because he was no Brutus, Soderini "lost his patria, as well as his status, and reputation" (D III.3). Foreigners invaded his republic, young nobles usurped it in favor of tyrannical dynasts, and thus Soderini enjoyed no successors whatever in the office of gonfalonier for life. Indeed, he did not even serve out his own life term, and (in no small part thanks to Machiavelli) his name is forever associated with impotent and ineffectual leadership and statesmanship.[21]

SODERINI, ROMULUS, AND OTHER EARLY ROMAN KINGS

The preceding reflections follow Machiavelli's suggestions that Soderini should have pursued civil means—ordinary in their legality, extraordinary in their severity—to eliminate the sons of Brutus who were threatening the Florentine Republic; specifically, civil means such as public accusations and popularly judged political trials. Subsequent chapters of book III, however, offer alternative courses of action. In short, they raise the question whether Soderini should have become a prince in order to save the republic. Machiavelli seemingly insinuates that the gonfalonier ought to have pursued violent, extralegal, and even tyrannical means as well.

As I said before, Machiavelli implicitly compares Soderini to Rome's ancient kings. I argue here that he does so to amplify mistakes the gonfalonier should have avoided and to accentuate courses of action he might have taken to have more securely preserved his reputation and maintained his state. Machiavelli first links Soderini with Romulus, Rome's founding monarch, who overcame crimes (murdering both his brother, Remus, and his coregent, Titus Tatius) by "ordering things" or "arranging matters" such that both his subjects and posterity came to recognize that he committed extraordinary violence for civic purposes, not primarily for his own benefit. Machiavelli declares that Romulus's intention was to establish a long-lasting monarchy that was compatible with a "civic and free way of life" (D I.9); Soderini too wished to establish an executive office that would endure far into the future—the magistracy of the gonfalonier for life—but his actions precluded the perpetuation of both that office and civic liberty within his own patria (D III.3).

Machiavelli uses similar phrases to describe how Romulus succeeded, but Soderini failed, in setting forth appropriate examples that demonstrated the commitments of each to the common good and dissuaded any of their "successors" from acting tyrannically. This common phraseology indicates Machiavelli's belief that the gonfalonier, once he appropriately killed the sons of Brutus, should have imitated Romulus to relieve the Florentine people of their "terror" that he would govern tyrannically (D III.3). I will further demonstrate how Machiavelli then suggests, through an intriguing segue between chapters, that Soderini in fact enjoyed formal authority comparable to that of other early Roman monarchs—but that, like

Rome's final kings, he comported himself so as to cause outrage among the nobility and disaffection among the people, and then he usurped his own quasi-monarchical form of government.

Machiavelli famously argues that founders or reformers such as Romulus often must enlist "extraordinary" authority initially in order to fully renew principalities or republics (D I.9). One who does so ought to follow Romulus's example in clearly demonstrating through subsequent behavior that whatever crimes or violence he initially committed would eventually be absolved by his subjects; he should act so that they would subsequently judge the founder's or reformer's actions to have been motivated by public spirit, not personal ambition. Machiavelli writes: "He should be sufficiently prudent and virtuous to prevent someone else from inheriting the authority that he wielded himself . . . *such that no successor could use ambitiously the authority that he had used virtuously*" (potrebbe il suo successore usare ambiziosamente quello che virtuosamente da lui fusse stato usato) (D I.9; emphasis added).

Later in the *Discourses*, when Machiavelli insists that Soderini should have endeavored, perhaps extraordinarily, to eliminate the aristocratic enemies of the Florentine Republic—"to kill the sons of Brutus"—he suggests, in strikingly similar language, that the gonfalonier's subsequent comportment ought to have convinced the people that he had resorted to drastic measures for the republic's sake and not his own. Since Soderini's "intentions and actions would be judged by their ends," Machiavelli argues, "he should have believed that, good fortune and long life permitting, everyone would affirm that he acted for the sake of the patria's security and not his own ambition" (D III.3). Moreover, he insists, echoing his remarks on Romulus, that Soderini "*could have arranged matters such that no successor could endeavor for evil what he had endeavored for good*" (e poteva regolare le cose in modo, che uno suo successore non potesse fare per male quello che elli avessi fatto per bene) (D III.3; emphasis added).

What did Romulus, in Machiavelli's estimation, do to prevent a "successor" from using "extraordinary" means such as homicide ambitiously and, furthermore, to signal to the Romans that he had acted on behalf "of the patria" and "the common good" and not "his own ambition" (D I.9)? According to Machiavelli, Romulus "immediately established a senate with whom he consulted and whose opinion he followed," and he "reserved for himself nothing more than command of the army during war and convocation of the senate" (D I.9). In this way Romulus ensured that his city was ordered in a manner "conducive to a civic and free way of life rather than to an absolute and tyrannical one" (D I.9). Considering Romulus's example, one might therefore surmise that Soderini should have killed the sons of Brutus—perhaps even summarily—but then created a senate and armed the plebs. The surviving Florentine nobles, who no doubt would have been outraged by Soderini's unilateral execution of pro-Medici and antirepublican *ottimati* within their ranks, would have been assuaged if Soderini had proceeded to establish a substantively powerful senatorial council, an institution they had been clamoring for since the ouster of the Medici in 1494.[22]

Moreover, the militia Soderini did establish in Florence, which very much pleased the people, would have been even more wildly popular had the gonfalonier expanded its numbers to include citizens in the city, not merely subjects from the countryside. He might have persuaded the nobles to accept this wider-scale militia had he, as Romulus did, entrusted consultation over its deployment to the simultaneously established aristocratic senate. However, rather than placating the nobility by deferring to them by establishing a genuinely collaborative legislative process and maximizing the people's favor by enlisting them more extensively in military affairs, Machiavelli suggests, Soderini proceeded to offend both parties.

Indeed, Machiavelli's later implicit comparison of Soderini with ancient Roman kings suggests that the gonfalonier's behavior was less like that of Rome's founding monarch, Romulus, than that of its last several kings, including the corrupt and arrogant Tarquinius Superbus. Machiavelli declares that the transition from chapter 3 of book III, where he contrasts Brutus and Soderini, to chapters 4 and 5, which deal with the Roman kings, constitutes a shift in discussion from republics to principalities. Yet in each of the latter two chapters, ostensibly devoted to princes, Machiavelli subtly indicates that he is still, to a significant extent, talking about the Florentine gonfalonier as he analyzes the careers of Rome's last three kings. These two chapters depart from Machiavelli's usual mode of offering no explicit modern or Florentine counterparts to Machiavelli's ancient examples, and so they invite readers to speculate in this regard. Machiavelli's descriptions of the late Roman kings contain elements that could easily apply to several Florentine figures, such as Maso and Rinaldo degli Albizzi; to Lorenzo, Piero, and Lorenzo II de' Medici; and, quite plausibly, to Piero Soderini as well.

Initially, when discussing the reign of Tarquinius Priscus, Machiavelli reminds readers that Roman monarchs were elected in Rome's popular assembly, just as, his contemporary readers would recall, the gonfalonier for life was elected in Florence's Great Council. Machiavelli declares that Priscus's crown "was granted to him by the people and confirmed by the senate" (D III.4). In this respect Soderini is at least half a Roman king: while he may have been elected by Florence's Great Council, the Florentine Republic, as I noted before, had no authoritative senatorial council within which the nobles might confirm his election.[23] Be that as it may,

Soderini shares with Priscus an inflated estimation of their constitutional legitimacy. Machiavelli declares, with a phrase he'd just applied to Soderini in the previous chapter (D III.3), that the Roman king "deceived himself" into believing that the formal legality of his principality ensured his security. Much like Machiavelli's Soderini, in fact, Priscus overestimated how far his legal, popularly acclaimed legitimacy would temper the animosity Rome's young nobles harbored toward him.

According to Livy, in pursuit of the Roman throne, Priscus convinced the people that he should be king rather than any of the sons of his predecessor, Ancus Marcius.[24] In some respects this foreshadows Soderini's ascent to the office of gonfalonier: Soderini defied expectations among young nobles that he might govern to the benefit of the *ottimati* rather than the popolo once he was elected gonfalonier for life.[25] Machiavelli also describes Priscus's mindset in a manner that recalls the naïveté our author often ascribes to the gonfalonier: "He did not believe that so much indignation could consume the sons of Ancus that they would refuse to live contentedly with what contented all of Rome" (D III.4). Ancus's sons eventually kill Priscus, but they fail to secure the throne for one of themselves, as Servius Tullius quickly outmaneuvers them for the crown.[26]

Machiavelli then reports how Servius too was undone by a fatal Soderinian misapprehension: he overrated the extent to which his kind treatment would appease the sons of Tarquinius Priscus, who, like Ancus's sons before them, thought they should reign. Machiavelli remarks, in tones that echo his indictment of Soderini's generous and humane treatment of the Florentine sons of Brutus (D III.3): "One cannot win over a dispossessed prince with gifts or good examples" (D III.4). Patience and gifts, Machiavelli avers, are insufficient to appease the resentful envy of either the actual sons of Ancus or Priscus in Rome or the figurative sons of Brutus in Florence (D III.3–4). As Machiavelli writes, "Servius Tullius was undoubtedly less than prudent in believing that Tarquin's sons would be content to live as sons-in-law of one over whom they deemed themselves worthy of ruling as king" (D III.4).

In the very next *discorso*, chapter 5, Machiavelli recalls, without naming them, the figures of Romulus and Soderini, who used extraordinary authority to found a principality (Romulus) and should have used extraordinary measures to reform a republic (Soderini)—and who proceeded such that their violence possibly could be forgiven in the future. Machiavelli writes how Tarquin the Proud gained the kingship through "extraordinary and hateful means," killing Servius Tullius; but he observes, Tarquin could have maintained his reign securely thereafter "had he followed the previous kings' ancient orders" (D III.5). Instead, effectively reversing Romulus's policies toward them, Tarquin incited both the Senate and the plebs against him: Tarquin conducted within his private palace public matters that previously had been held in civic forums, thus displeasing senators and arousing their envy; moreover, he employed the plebs in demeaning, nonmartial work, hence incurring their hatred (D III.5):

> Tarquin violated the kingdom's laws and ruled it tyrannically, accruing to himself the entirety of the senate's authority. Affairs that previously, to the Roman senate's pleasure, had been conducted in public, he administered within his palace, eliciting their censure and envy. Thus, very quickly he deprived Rome of all the liberty that it had enjoyed under previous kings. Not enough was it for him to incur the enmity of the city's fathers, he also inflamed the animosity of the plebs, wearing them out in menial tasks most unlike those in which his predecessors had employed them. (D III.5)

The implication for Soderini's tenure of office is this: The gonfalonier could have acted extraordinarily, outside the bounds of legality, and still have survived in power had he subsequently returned to faithful observance of such legality. The Florentine *ottimati* accused Soderini of dishonoring them and of circumventing civil norms by conducting deliberations in whatever small councils he controlled at any particular moment, where they were either absent or outnumbered.[27] Soderini, very much like Tarquin and thoroughly unlike Romulus, refused to take counsel from the *ottimati*, thus enraging them and inflaming their envy. As for the plebs, Soderini capitulated to aristocratic pressure and relented from enlisting the city's guildsmen, let alone the urban *ciompi*, in the republic's militia—instead confining military recruitment to the countryside, the *contado*.

Hence Soderini's militia never boasted the number of soldiers formerly armed in the guilds' military companies at Florence's geopolitical height before the Ciompi Revolt of 1378. And the militia project never remedied the grave mistakes the city made in crushing its armed plebs at the conclusion of the revolt, in subsequently disarming the guilds, and in increasing the city's reliance on foreign mercenaries. Much like Tarquin, who ordered the Roman people to dig sewers rather than fight enemies, Soderini—despite the marginal success of Machiavelli's limited militia project—continued to allow Florence's *popolani* to concern themselves exclusively with trade, and its *plebe* to toil in arduous labor with minimal recompense. I will examine Machiavelli's criticisms of these developments in chapter 7.

Let us return to the transition from chapters 3 to 4 and 5 of *Discourses*, book III, to consider other ways Machiavelli's discussion of Roman kings applies to Florentine princes both civic and monarchic. Machiavelli titles chapter 4 "A New Prince Does Not Live Securely While Those Whom He Has Despoiled Remain Alive" (D III.4). Soderini, of course, never enjoyed

full security in his office because the Medici, whom his republic had despoiled of power, still lived; moreover, the Medici, at the time Machiavelli
composed the *Discourses*, were not entirely secure because they had permitted Soderini to live on in exile once they reassumed power in Florence.
This lesson also applies perhaps most obviously to Julius Caesar vis-à-vis
the senators he had despoiled of power but let live—only to have them conspire against and assassinate him. As Machiavelli states, "it is dangerous
and difficult to despoil an individual of their kingdom and let them live"
(D III.4).

Indeed, the Medici could have learned from the very next *discorso*, chapter 5, which I read in consideration of Soderini's example above. Recall that
Machiavelli writes how Tarquin the Proud gained the kingship through
"extraordinary and hateful means," and yet, he asserts, could have maintained it securely thereafter had he reverted to "the previous kings' ancient
orders" (D III.5). Likewise, the Medici, who resumed power extraordinarily
in 1512 through an internal coup and external invasion, would have been
more secure had they subsequently conducted themselves in a more civic
and less courtly manner (D III.5). The Medici, by implication, could have
enjoyed a second chance for a long-lasting principality had they not broken the ancient modes, laws, and customs the Florentines had been living
under for most of the city's history—that is, had they returned to the quasi-
civil modes of Cosimo rather than adopting, as they did, the ostentatiously
tyrannical modes of Lorenzo the Magnificent. Going further than even Cosimo had, while pretending merely to be "first citizen," the Medici could
have better preserved their reign had they adopted the following policies:
maintaining the Great Council to satisfy the people; establishing a senate
to please the *ottimati*; and perhaps even adopting and expanding Machiavelli's and Soderini's citizen militia project.[28]

The Medici, as I said before, were very likely the unnamed civil princes
who came to power through the nobles rather than the people, described
in chapter 9 of *The Prince*; but, Machiavelli suggests that, despite this
disadvantaged position, they could have gained enthusiastic favor from
the common people had they at least partially betrayed the nobles and
empowered the universality. Here, in the *Discourses*, Machiavelli suggests
that the Medici, had they adopted more civil modes, could have become
like Timoleon of Corinth and Aratus of Sicyon: their peoples compelled
them to continue as princes even though they feigned the desire to return to private life, because of the security, satisfaction, and even freedom their reigns had afforded the people (D III.5). The same might have
applied to Soderini had he put his own abdication or exile to the people's
vote before internal conspiracy and external invasion compelled both
eventualities.

EXCURSUS: A REVERSAL IN MACHIAVELLI'S
CHARACTER STUDY OF SODERINI?

Recall how Machiavelli previously equivocated over the existence of popularly judged political trials in the 1494 Florentine Republic and the ability of nobles to consistently and enduringly favor the common people in republics generally. Machiavelli is similarly slippery when addressing Florence's handling of the Spanish invasion, which, as I already noted, precipitated the fall of the republic in 1512. In his discussion of this crisis, Machiavelli attributes to the Florentine people poor judgment that, given Soderini's prerogative over diplomatic affairs, could plausibly be attributed to the gonfalonier himself.

In a chapter titled "Conquest Should Be Sufficient for Prudent Princes or Republics, Because Defeat Often Ensues When It Is Not" (D II.27), Machiavelli blames the Florentine people for the mistake of overreaching in favorable circumstances; a mistake that may have been equally or largely attributable to Soderini, who as gonfalonier was principally responsible for the republic's foreign policy. One might plausibly surmise that Machiavelli misapplies culpability in these circumstances because the rashness or audacity he describes here contradicts the character portrait of the gonfalonier that he paints throughout the *Discourses*.

Machiavelli often attributes patience, goodness, humanity, hesitation, humility, timidity, and even cowardice to Soderini (D I.52, D III.3, D III.9, D.III 30). Yet in this chapter it is impudence that characterizes the unnamed gonfalonier when Machiavelli wishes to substantiate his claim that "either victory or false hope thereof often generates insolence" (D II.27). As Machiavelli famously writes elsewhere of the gonfalonier, "Piero Soderini conducted himself in *all* his affairs with *humanity and patience*. Both he and his patria thrived while the times conformed to of his way of proceeding; but later when he needed to forsake *patience and humility*, he knew not how to do so, such that both he and his patria were ruined" (D III.9; emphases added). Perhaps, consistent with his implied affiliation of Soderini with Tarquin the Proud, discussed above, Machiavelli really thought that more than a small dose of temerity underlies Soderini's ostensible timidity.

Returning to the claim that political actors often unwisely fail to settle for sufficient victories in foolhardy anticipation of more comprehensive triumphs, Machiavelli observes that both princes and republics frequently "lose the opportunity to secure an obtainable good by aspiring after a dubiously obtainable better" (D II.27). Machiavelli notes, for instance, that the Carthaginian senate imprudently failed to secure a favorable truce after Hannibal's armies defeated the Romans at Cannae; moreover, he notes how the Republic of Tyre declined an advantageous peace in similar circumstance vis-à-vis Alexander the Great—in both cases, rather than accepting moderate victories, these foolhardy republics instead suffered complete conquest by their more powerful adversaries. Likewise, Machiavelli writes, the Florentines unwisely refused an accord with the Spanish army that would have preserved their republic, a refusal that thereby brought about their destruction (D II.27).

The Spanish army had entered Tuscany at the direction of a conspiracy against the republic forged among Florence's nobles, the Medici family, Pope Julius II, and the Spanish king. According to Machiavelli, the army initially intended to reinstall the Medici within the city, change the Florentine state, sever the city's alliance with the French monarchy, and extract lavish payments. However, when the Florentine *ottimati* failed to provoke the armed insurrection against the republic that they promised the Spanish army would occur when it invaded, the army was left in dire want of provisions in the field. Consequently, Machiavelli writes, "they pursued an accord" with the republic, according to which the army would accept payments and a revocation of the French alliance in exchange for evacuating Florentine territories. Machiavelli reports that "the now prideful Florentine people" rejected the terms of the peace, "thus causing the Spanish conquest of Prato and the collapse of the Florentine state" (D II.27).

Machiavelli insists that the people—or perhaps, Soderini—should have accepted these terms, since they kept the republic intact; instead, the people or Soderini or both obstinately and unwisely refused the offer: "The Florentine people should have considered itself sufficiently victorious in gaining certain concessions from the Spanish army and in granting to the latter certain others" (D II.27). Machiavelli insists that had the army been given what it most wanted (the ability to feed itself and a diplomatic shift pleasing to the Spanish king), and had the Florentine people retained what was most important for itself (the republic's security), then "each party would have earned some honor and satisfaction." However, after incurring good fortune in both withstanding the aristocratic coup and observing the Spanish army starving in the fields, the Florentines wrongly assumed that fortune would remain with them if they refused to grant the Spanish any concessions whatever. As Machiavelli chides them:

> Having survived the invasion, the people should have concerned themselves not at all regarding either the alliance or the money. They should not have left to fortune's discretion, in any degree whatsoever, a supposedly greater, perhaps even attainable, victory. In doing so, they imprudently encouraged the Spanish army to take recourse in last resorts without the necessity of doing so. (D II.27)

In retaliation for this diplomatic rebuff, the desperate and infuriated Spanish army sacked Prato with much killing, rape, and pillage, easily defeating Machiavelli's militia there.[29] This military disaster in turn gave the Florentine *ottimati* the leverage they previously lacked to oust Soderini, overthrow the republic, and reinstall the Medici.

In his concluding remarks on these episodes where republics suffer catastrophic defeats by spurning moderate victories, Machiavelli moves away from blaming peoples generally or even the Florentine people particularly for the error of overreaching. He writes in a way that blames individual princes or captains, thus reinforcing the possibility that it is in fact Soderini he has in mind regarding the crisis of 1512. For instance, Machiavelli declares: "There is no greater mistake to be committed by *princes* who are assaulted by more powerful forces than this: to summarily reject an accord offered to them by the latter. Such an offer never obnoxiously lacks some benefit and often generally entails at least a partial victory for him who accepts it" (D II.27; emphasis added). Moreover, Machiavelli invokes Hannibal, whom he perhaps considers the greatest captain in all history, as a commander who was willing to accept a partial victory that would have left his republic intact rather than pursuing a total victory he might not actually achieve—a decision that might cost his city its independence or even its very existence. Machiavelli's words, in fact, conjure the image of the far less virtuous, less fully armed, and less experienced Piero Soderini:

> If Hannibal, who was of such virtue and in command of his entire army, pursued peace over combat because he recognized that defeat would render his patria servile, what should someone of lesser virtue and lesser experience do? But men err in this way when they fail to limit their hopes; consequently, often motivated by such hopes rather than by an appropriate assessment of themselves, they are ruined. (D II.27)

Invoking here the moment when Hannibal sought a truce with Scipio before the battle of Zama that the Carthaginians were likely, but by no means certain, to lose,[30] Machiavelli implies that the deficiently armed Florentine Republic—led by the hardly Hannibal-like Soderini—should certainly have been at least as humble, not to say as prudent, as the supremely virtuous Carthaginian captain.

The historical evidence suggests that the alternatives facing the Florentine Republic in the summer of 1512 were perhaps not quite so clear-cut as Machiavelli presents them; in fact they entail further possibilities that point to Soderini rather than the Florentine people as the decisive judge of these circumstances. Soderini, often referred to as "Pier," was personally committed to the alliance with France and so may have been less inclined to break it than the people were.[31] Moreover, there is some evidence that, as part of the agreement to leave the republic intact, the Spanish may have also insisted either that Soderini step down as gonfalonier, or that the Medici be permitted to reenter the city as private citizens, or both.[32] In either case Soderini's especially intense personal investment in remaining gonfalonier for the length of his life, discussed further below, combined with his personal animosity toward the Medici family, may have accounted for some of his obstinacy about coming to any accord with the Spanish army.

If this was indeed the case, then the gonfalonier's intransigence served only to bring about the very outcomes he himself most feared—along with the additionally disastrous result the republic's collapse spelled for the city. If Soderini cared more about keeping his job than about preserving the republic, this proved to be a rather perverse choice. He accelerated the elimination of the very republic to which, like Camillus, he might have been reappointed chief magistrate—had he enabled it to survive. Thus Soderini may not have been the "lover of the city's liberty" (D I.52) that the people thought he was; rather, like other deficient Florentine popular champions such as Savonarola and Valori, he may have been primarily out for his own benefit.

Conversely, if Machiavelli is sincerely critical of the Florentine people in these passages, perhaps he reproves them for more than their prideful obstinacy toward the Spanish, which may or may not have been Soderini's. Rather, it may be their own intransigence in failing to depose and perhaps even exile the gonfalonier for his blatant lack of prudence in risking the republic's existence—"the people's survival" as Machiavelli puts it.[33] In order to save the republic, the people should have compelled Soderini to resign, and perhaps even to exit the city—leaving open the possibility that he might return to serve them in some future crisis, much as Camillus returned from exile when the Gauls invaded. Note that in one of these cases foreign invasion prompted the exile of a chief magistrate and the collapse of a republic, while in the other it prompted the recall of a magistrate and the salvation of a republic. Whoever Machiavelli primarily blames for the collapse of the Florentine Republic, Soderini or the people, the crisis of 1512 provides a negative object lesson on how leaders and citizens should share power and accountability in democratic republics.

4. ROME'S MOST PRUDENT CAPTAIN AND FLORENCE'S UNARMED PROPHETS

Envy, Exile, and Willingly Leaving Office

(CAMILLUS, MOSES, SODERINI, AND SAVONAROLA)

I now delve more deeply into Machiavelli's depiction of Furius Camillus's career,[1] exploring further why he deems the dictator to be "Rome's most prudent captain." As he continues his analysis of envy, *invidia*, among political rivals, the entwinement of civic and military affairs, and the question of ordinary versus extraordinary political action, Lucius Brutus somewhat recedes from Machiavelli's consideration of Camillus, while the example of Moses comes more prominently to the fore. Machiavelli's paradigmatic failed Florentine civic princes—Piero Soderini and Girolamo Savonarola—remain, whether explicitly or implicitly, close to the renowned Roman dictator.

ELIMINATING ENVY, MILITARY NECESSITY, AND EXPEDITIOUS ABDICATION

Late in book III of the *Discourses*, Machiavelli revisits his analysis of Soderini in reflections where Camillus, the frequently appointed Roman dictator, becomes Machiavelli's ancient foil for his former patron, the Florentine gonfalonier "for life" (D III.30). This *discorso* seems to be devoted to two distinct themes: first, the way the Romans abandoned the envy they previously directed toward exemplary citizens, such as Camillus, and second, a reaffirmation of the Roman Republic's virtuous military ordering. Its lengthy title comprises two parts: "One Citizen Wishing to Benefit His Republic with His Authority Must Eliminate Envy; and How One Must Order a City's Defense against Enemies" (D III.30). However, the whole chapter turns out to be a thoroughgoing indictment of the incessantly envious and woefully unarmed Florentines: the "enemies" in the title prove to be not merely external armies, but also, and more pointedly, the envious citizens whom Soderini, in particular, failed to manage or eliminate, and who in turn expelled him and overthrew the republic. Thus, although *discorso* 30 seems to combine two distinct *discorsi* in one, the two parts prove intimately related: good citizens may more readily eliminate the envy of domestic rivals when they prove especially adept at defeating external enemies.

Machiavelli begins the chapter by recounting how the Roman Republic confronted a dangerously powerful alliance of Latin, Hernici, and Volscian armies moving against them (D III.30). Camillus, one of the five recently elected consular tribunes, thought that appointing a dictator was unnecessary—perhaps because he already held consular authority and thus would have been legally ineligible to serve as dictator himself. Camillus declares that if his consular colleagues would grant him supreme command informally, in these dire circumstances, then there would be no formal need to resort to the dictatorship. Camillus's colleagues readily grant him supreme authority over themselves and the city, Machiavelli claims, because they did not interpret any increase in his authority, whether formal or informal, "to be a diminution of their own majesty" (D III.30).

Machiavelli previously recounted in great detail how, early in his career, Camillus had incurred the envy and suspicion of the Roman Senate and people (D III.1). Yet at this later point in his life and in the republic's history, Camillus is granted absolute authority over the city without formal recourse to the dictatorship, the ordinary magistracy that the Romans often relied on to address extraordinary circumstances (D I.34). The full extent of both Camillus's authority and the trust his fellow Romans placed in him is exemplified by Machiavelli's description of how Camillus prepared the city's defense: most notably, "for the patria's security," he placed armed guards on both the senate house and the popular assembly. In other words, Camillus takes measures similar to those that Machiavelli says notable Greek tyrants exploited in trying to usurp republics and establish principalities: figures such as Agathocles and Nabis in *The Prince*, Cleomenes and Clearchus in the *Discourses*, and more ambiguously, as we will observe in chapter 6, Pacuvius Calanus in Capua (D I.47). Yet for his part Camillus does not on this occasion, despite the opportunity, forcibly seize formal princely authority (D III.30).

Machiavelli claims Camillus managed to eliminate envy in these circumstances because the dangerous "accident" of this unprecedentedly powerful military league threatening the republic made the Romans fear for their security. As a result, they individually set aside their personal pride and collectively pledged obedience to "a good and wise" man of "virtue" like Camillus. Again, Camillus does not technically abrogate constitutional norms by insisting, in an unprecedented manner, that the Senate appoint him, a formally sitting magistrate, as dictator (D III.30); instead, in consultation with his consular colleagues, he assumes the role of an informal dictator, or a dictator without the official title.

This outcome is possible, Machiavelli insists, only because of Camillus's previous exhibitions of virtue during his three earlier terms as dictator, terms in which he had always used his considerable authority "for the public and not for his personal utility" (D III.30).[2] Camillus was, of course, historically renowned for holding the dictatorship an unprecedented number of times, and for renouncing such authority each time as soon as he accomplished the tasks he was appointed to perform. Hence, in present circumstances, Machiavelli writes, "no one either felt ashamed or feared his greatness" in granting Camillus supreme authority (D III.30).

Besides the external accident of a foreign invasion, which obtained in this Roman episode, Machiavelli suggests that envy of a good and virtuous citizen may be eliminated "when those who are envious die either through violence or natural causes" (D III.30). In a corrupt city, "one lacking in good education" like Florence, however, "a dangerous accident such as an invasion will not prove sufficient to induce the envious to forsake their pertinacious spirit—even if it will result in the patria's ruin." The Florentine nobles did not forswear their envy for Soderini when the Spanish invaded in 1512; actually, their envy in no small part *caused* that invasion—they invited the Spanish in!—which therefore was no "accident" in a conventional sense. To overcome such especially intense envy, Machiavelli declares, "the only remedy is the death of those who are consumed by it." He ruminates further: When the envious rivals of a good man who wishes to employ his authority to benefit his city die "ordinarily," then he "attains glory without controversy" (D III.30).

However, it is not clear whether such an "ordinary" death may be attributed to either the natural or the violent causes that Machiavelli mentions above—or to both. Of course, if someone dies in bed, without foul play, then this death may be deemed ordinary. But so too, according to Machiavelli, may a violent death that results from a legally conducted, popularly judged capital trial, be deemed "ordinary" (D I.7–8). In any case, our author insists that "absent such luck" in having rivals die "ordinarily," a virtuous man who wishes to benefit his patria while confronting extraordinary accidents "must consider every means of removing such envious obstruction and of holding firmly to whatever means will do so" (D III.30). This applies perhaps less directly to Camillus in these circumstances, and more appropriately to the figures of Moses, Savonarola, and Soderini, whom Machiavelli treats later in the chapter—examples I will discuss below.

The figure of an envious rival who suffers an ordinary if violent death calls to mind Manlius Capitolinus, whom Machiavelli invokes early in the

Discourses (D I.8). In fact, the very first mention of *invidia* in the entire work occurs in book I, where Machiavelli describes how Manlius, "laden with envy" of none other than Furius Camillus, attempted to usurp the Roman Republic. Although he was granted the illustrious title of "Capitolinus" for heroically defending the Roman Capitol from the invading Gauls, Manlius deeply resented the glory bestowed on Camillus as "second founder of Rome" for definitively expelling the enemy forces.[3] Notably, in neither Machiavelli's nor Livy's account does Camillus himself eliminate Manlius and his "blinding envy" (D III.8): initially, the Senate and a dictator imprison Manlius for stirring up dangerous tumult among the plebs, and then, after he redoubles his efforts to become king, the plebeian tribunes and the people themselves eliminate him through a public accusation and a capital trial (D I.8, III.8).

Much like the killing of Brutus's sons, Machiavelli suggests that Manlius's execution was both ordinary and extraordinary. It was perfectly ordinary in a procedural sense and yet quite extraordinary in its severity: the people legally condemned Manlius to be hurled to his death from the very Capitoline hill that his valor had saved during the invasion of the Gauls. Machiavelli's somewhat vague remarks concerning the various ways an envious adversary may be eliminated—naturally, violently, ordinarily, extraordinarily—invite readers to consider whether he is retroactively implying that Camillus played some decisive yet unacknowledged role in eliminating his intensely envious rival, Manlius.[4] Or, in line with Machiavelli's remarks on reforming a republic through exemplary civic examples (D III.1), is our author content with the conclusion that Camillus's exemplary behavior—returning from exile to defeat the Gauls—was sufficient to encourage his fellow citizens to eliminate his adversary's envy on Camillus's behalf?

Without settling this issue, Machiavelli turns from Camillus to the cases where neither natural causes nor legal proceedings work to eliminate the envious rivals of individuals who wish to benefit both the patria and themselves: Moses, Savonarola, and Soderini. The envious adversaries opposing these Hebrew and Christian prophets as well as the Florentine gonfalonier neither died of natural causes nor were executed after a capital trial. Moses serves as Machiavelli's exemplary figure who successfully vanquished envy through extraordinary violence: "Judicious readers of the Bible know that Moses, so as to ensure longevity for his laws and orders, was compelled to *kill infinite numbers of men, motivated entirely by envy*, who opposed him" (D III.30; emphasis added). Machiavelli here alludes to the episode of the Golden Calf, in which Moses commanded his most loyal partisans, the Levites, to slaughter thousands of unfaithful Hebrews to reestablish his authority over the people of Israel.[5]

Reprising the famous juxtaposition of Moses and Savonarola in *The Prince* (P 6) as the quintessential armed and unarmed prophets, Machiavelli remarks here in the *Discourses* that "Savonarola also recognized quite clearly the necessity" of eliminating envious rivals. But Machiavelli reminds readers that Brother Girolamo could not overcome the envy of others, as did Moses, "because as a friar he lacked the requisite authority to eliminate it himself"; moreover, "he could not clearly communicate this necessity to his followers in authority," in particular, Francesco Valori (D III.30; see D I.7). Savonarola's sermons vividly displayed his knowledge of the danger posed to his new orders, to the institutions of the newly established *governo largo*, by those envious of him, whom he vilified as the sinfully ambitious, "worldly wise." But "accusations" hurled from the pulpit often prove too vague to be understood by the devoted; and in any case such invective does not have the legal force of a formal indictment, let alone constitutionally enacted executions.[6]

This discussion of Savonarola naturally recalls the example of Soderini, whom Machiavelli reintroduces here. The Florentine gonfalonier, Machiavelli insists again, also understood the necessity of eliminating the envy of those who opposed him and sought to undermine his orders and authority (D III.30), as Machiavelli's earlier reference to his prudence attests (D III.3). Unlike Moses, however, Soderini "believed that patience, goodness, kind fortune and gifts would eliminate such envy" (D III.30). He presumed that the relatively young age at which he was elected gonfalonier for life, and the widespread popular support he won by conducting himself as a defender of the Great Council within the new republic, would "enable him to conquer any number of envious adversaries without any controversy, violence, or tumult" (D III.30). Yet, Machiavelli insists, the gonfalonier was unaware that "one cannot outwait the envious with patience, overcome their evil with good, rely on the constancy of fortune, or appease the malicious with gifts" (D III.30). Thus both Savonarola and Soderini, "through either ignorance or incompetence, were ruined in the face of envy" (D III.30). As Machiavelli emphasizes when discussing the examples of the Gracchi and Giorgio Scali in *The Prince*, *popular favor* is not sufficient to eliminate envy and secure one's rule; *popular arms* summoned at one's command are necessary (P 9).[7]

Machiavelli concludes this long, multifocused chapter by returning to the example of Camillus, emphasizing how meticulously the commander ordered the army he left in charge of the city during the unprecedented military assault confronting Rome—in particular, how he set armed guards at the Senate and the popular assembly (D III.30). The Romans were certainly accustomed to preparations for war, Machiavelli notes; nevertheless, Camillus would not risk the possibility that the people might arm themselves "tumultuously" in these emergency circumstances and that chaos might ensue—or, perhaps, better conforming to the main theme of the chapter, he refused to take the chance that envious usurpers might exploit such tumult for their own nefariously ambitious ends. Machiavelli declares that those who are arming a people during a crisis should avoid, like a ship must avoid "a shoal" (D III.30), doing so in a disorganized manner. Implicitly juxtaposing Camillus with Soderini, who did not, in fact, allow himself to become the commander of armed men in the city of Florence, Machiavelli writes:

> An individual charged with guarding a city ought to avoid as if a shoal allowing men to arm tumultuously. Rather, he must first enroll those whom he wishes to arm, appoint those whom they must obey, indicate where they should meet, and direct where they should go. Then, those he does not enroll should be commanded to remain in their own homes to guard them. He who maintains such order in a city that confronts an assault will readily defend himself; he who does otherwise fails to imitate Camillus, and hence fails to defend himself. (D III.30)[8]

Machiavelli's insinuation that Soderini "failed to imitate Camillus" by neglecting to assume military command of Machiavelli's proposed citizen militia stands as one of his most monumental understatements.

The other ancient figure mentioned in the chapter, Moses, had also carefully arranged with his most devoted followers the military procedures through which they might crush unfaithful members of the Israelites should circumstances call for it.[9] Of course, since Camillus had evidently overcome envy much more than even Moses had, he did not need to command soldiers to slaughter unfaithful citizens or subjects. Nevertheless, despite the differences between the examples of Camillus and Moses, together they serve as reminders that neither Savonarola nor Soderini commanded men at arms ready to preserve the laws and orders they established or championed in the city. These modern Florentines therefore could not "imitate Camillus" and thus did not "defend themselves with ease" (D III.30)—in fact, they were unable to defend themselves at all. Machiavelli, of course, in his role as civil servant and adviser to Soderini, had previously offered the gonfalonier the opportunity to command an extensive citizen militia. Yet the gonfalonier yielded to the charges of envious Florentine *ottimati* who insisted that Soderini wished to become a tyrant; again, they succeeded in constraining Machiavelli's militia project and preventing Soderini from exerting command over it.[10]

Returning to Camillus's ordering of Rome's military, especially his guarding of the Senate and popular assembly when facing an impending foreign invasion: in an earlier chapter of the *Discourses*, Machiavelli describes the way Camillus's grandson—unidentified as such—treated conquered Latin cities (D II.23), an account that sheds curious light on his forebear's domestic ordering of Rome during wartime. Machiavelli's description of the younger Camillus's dealings with subject cities eerily presages his account in book III, just discussed, of the elder Camillus's treatment of Rome itself during frightful circumstances when the city confronted multiple foreign enemies. Machiavelli writes here that the dictator's grandson Camillus, "after compelling the Latins to surrender and place themselves in the Romans' hands, and having *put guards [avendo messo la guardia]* upon every town in Latium, took hostages from each of them and, upon his return to Rome, reported to the senate that all Latium was now in the hands of the Roman people" (D II.23; emphasis added).

The conjunction of these two chapters (D III.30 and D II.23) seems to suggest the following regarding Machiavelli's view of the elder Camillus's leadership, in light of that of the younger: in a moment when an unprecedented number of foreign enemies marched on Rome, Camillus's consular colleagues readily surrendered all their authority to him; moreover, Rome's senators and people unhesitatingly permitted him to place them under armed guard, effectively making themselves his hostages. In short, Rome's magistrates learned to defer to Camillus's military virtue, and all its citizens trusted his goodness to the extent that they were willing to let him treat them as conquered subjects. Machiavelli makes a commander named Camillus declare on each of these occasions that Rome's subject cities and the republic itself are in the collective hands of Rome—when, in fact, the effectual truth is that they are under the direct control of no one but a Camillus.

CAMILLUS AROUSES ENVY, HATRED, AND SUSPICION

I now range more widely through the *Discourses* to examine the circumstances and the conduct through which Camillus, over the course of his career, first aroused such envy, hatred, and suspicion among the Roman people that they felt justified in exiling him; and second, how he rehabilitated his reputation to the extent that he eliminated the envy of other Roman citizens. Indeed, in the examples discussed above, Machiavelli shows how Rome's magistrates were willing to bestow on him informal dictatorial authority, and Rome's Senate and people were willing to let him treat them as conquered subjects (D III.30).

Machiavelli endorses Livy's characterization of Camillus as "an excellent man," one who maintained "the same spirit and dignity" in both good and ill fortune; an individual of "firm spirit" who neither departed from his "moderate mode of living" nor exhibited "drunken vanity" in success, such that others would consider him "intolerably hateful" (D III.31). To substantiate this assessment, Machiavelli directly quotes the words Livy attributes to Camillus: "Neither did I ever permit the dictatorship to inflate my spirit nor allow my exile to extinguish it entirely."[11] The first part of this statement proves to be a considerable exaggeration. As Machiavelli's account of Camillus's early career demonstrates, the dictator did in fact permit a significant military victory to alter his spirit and comportment in such a vainglorious and extravagant manner that he very much aroused the Roman people's envy, hatred, and suspicion.

Despite frequently invoking the fact, Machiavelli takes an exceedingly long time to address exactly *why* Camillus was exiled to Ardea, and thus why the former dictator was absent from Rome at the moment when the republic needed him most: when the Gauls routed Rome's armies, invaded and pillaged the city, and besieged the Capitol. Camillus, Machiavelli writes, "was the one alone who would have remedied such an evil" (D II.29). And yet he waits until the middle of the third and final book of the *Discourses* to offer a specific explanation for why Camillus was exiled in the first place. While evaluating which mode of treating citizen soldiers is more beneficial for a republic—Manlius Torquatus's severity or Valerius Corvinus's humanity—Machiavelli endorses the severe modes of Torquatus, which, he suggests, Camillus himself also employed early in his career (D III.22). The severity practiced by Torquatus, Machiavelli avers, "rarely offends" citizens and moreover arouses "little hatred" among them. However, he explains, Camillus's severity brought him greater hatred than did Torquatus's because it also aroused "suspicion" among citizens. Camillus possessed "additional virtues" not exhibited by the virtuously severe Torquatus—virtues that enabled him to gain a "reputation" far greater than the dyspeptic and poor-spoken Torquatus could ever acquire. To clarify the relationship of severity and hatred, reputation and suspicion in the case of Camillus, Machiavelli then embarks on an entire *discorso* devoted to "The Causes of Camillus's Exile from Rome" (D III.23).

Machiavelli begins the chapter by explaining why Camillus's severity caused offense and aroused hatred to an extent that Manlius Torquatus's did not. He relies on Livy to emphasize that the Romans never unequivocally hated Camillus: the people's hatred for him, however intense, was always accompanied by deep admiration (D III.23). Machiavelli and Livy agree that the Romans found Camillus's virtue "both marvelous and hateful." They marveled at "how solicitously, prudently, with what great spirit and good order, he managed and commanded the army." However, the soldiers also hated "the greater severity" with which Camillus punished them for their failings more than "the liberality" he showed in rewarding them for their successes. And yet, of the three examples Machiavelli draws from Livy to validate this claim, only two pertain to disproportionate displays of severity and liberality; moreover, these two examples do not fully address the issues of reputation and suspicion that Machiavelli raises at the end of the previous chapter. Let us examine them more closely.

Both instances pertaining to Camillus's excessive severity—or what Machiavelli claims can be reduced to insufficient liberality—occur immediately following Camillus's conquest of Veii: the dictator, on two occasions, denies his soldiers the spoils they believe they have rightfully earned in prosecuting and ending Rome's ten-year siege of the city. First Machiavelli notes that Camillus assigns to public funds—which formally belong to the Roman people but that effectively fall under the custodial care of the Roman Senate (D I.37)—booty that the soldiers wanted distributed directly to themselves (D III.23). Skipping for a moment the second reason why, according to Machiavelli, the people began to hate Camillus, and moving on to the third, during his victory the dictator also mistakenly failed (or conveniently forgot) to immediately set aside the tenth of the spoils he'd vowed to devote to Apollo in exchange for victory. He therefore proposed that the soldiers, after the fact, individually give up a tenth of the spoils they had secured for themselves (which, remember, was already much less than they thought they deserved) to satisfy his pledge to the god.

In the first instance, Camillus prevents the soldiers from acquiring plunder that they believed they had fully earned; in the second, he proposes "removing from their hands" spoils that they already possessed (D III.23)—which in Machiavelli's estimation amounts to a much greater offense than the first. Machiavelli here reprises an observation regarding hatred and property that he offered in *The Prince*: nothing, aside from molesting one's subjects' women, arouses more hatred in them than economically overtaxing what they already own (P 19). At this juncture in the *Discourses*, Machiavelli again declares that "a prince," even a prince in a republic, should never take from the hands of his citizen soldiers things that they deem "useful" for meeting "the necessities" of life. Since these necessities confront them daily, they never forget such an overt act of deprivation, and thus they forever maintain—perhaps ever intensify—their hatred for the agent of this harmful dispossession (D III.23).

Sandwiched between these two examples in which severity takes the form of insufficient liberality—that is, occasions where Camillus seems to severely punish his soldiers *not* for their failure but rather for their obvious success—Machiavelli addresses this issue of hatred deriving from popular suspicion—specifically, suspicion for a citizen who acquires a great reputation while exercising his virtue. He describes how, in the triumph the Senate granted to Camillus for his victory at Veii, the dictator elected to have his chariot drawn by "four white horses" (D III.23). Machiavelli suggests that this unprecedented, grandiose display implied that Camillus was so "prideful" as to "equate himself with the sun." Appearing to be so "sodden with pride" before the people, "especially a free people," Machiavelli insists, is certain to incur their hatred, even if such "prideful and pompous" behavior causes them no tangible harm.

Conversely, since such ostentatious displays afford no genuine "profit" to princes of republics, such as Camillus, Machiavelli sternly advises them to avoid this "reckless and imprudent" behavior much as a ship should avoid "a shoal" (D III.23). Note that Machiavelli again employs the nautical metaphor of avoiding a shoal in reference to Camillus: in a *discorso*, examined before, Machiavelli affirms Camillus as a positive exemplar who successfully avoids the "shoal" of preparing the people for war in a disorderly fashion (D III.30); here the dictator serves as a negative exemplar who *failed* to avoid the shoal of grandiosely aggrandizing himself before a free people. The implication is that Camillus eventually learned to accentuate those aspects of his own person that citizen soldiers genuinely admire (military prudence and solicitude) rather than those they deeply resent (vanity and pride).

Indeed, as the example of Veii illustrates, Camillus was fully capable of conducting himself with solicitude and prudence in *securing* a military victory, but in Machiavelli's estimation he was not yet capable of doing so while *celebrating* it. In meting out the spoils and the honors of victory, Camillus deprived his citizen soldiers materially and reputationally. To the dictator (and not his men), Camillus imprudently assumes, go both the spoils and the glory of victory. Even more, during his triumph Camillus exalts himself to the status of the very god for whose veneration he sought to impoverish his soldiers economically.[12] Thus the Roman people came to hate Camillus's actions, suspect his intentions for the future, and feel inclined to exile him not long after his ostentatious triumph.

However, perhaps owing to the admiration for Camillus's military virtue that, according to both Machiavelli and Livy, prevented the Roman people from ever fully hating the dictator,[13] they do not sentence him to death for his offenses; they decide merely to fine and exile him. Thus, although distant from Rome in the hour of the republic's greatest need, Camillus was still available to be recalled. The Roman people show they are prudent enough *not* to consider Camillus's offenses equivalent to the crime for which they eventually execute Manlius Capitolinus: harboring "an unseemly greed for rule," that is, greed for kingship (D III.8)—at least not as overtly as Manlius did. Moreover, Camillus shows he is wise enough to neither spitefully take vengeance on the Roman people for exiling him, as Coriolanus previously sought to do during his exile (D I.29), nor aloofly ignore their plea when they call him back to save the city.

CAMILLUS REHABILITATES (AND EXPANDS) HIS
REPUTATION FOR PRUDENCE, GOODNESS, AND VIRTUE

In an especially crucial chapter of the *Discourses*, Machiavelli refuses to count Camillus's exile from Rome as an example of unjustified ingratitude on the part of the Roman people (D I.29): Machiavelli suggests that it was not necessarily inappropriate for them to have exiled Camillus "for behavior injurious to the plebs"; and in any case he notes that the Roman people nevertheless recalled Camillus from exile and thereafter "for the entirety of his life adored him as a prince" (D I.29). Certainly Camillus, by exhibiting no resentment toward the Roman people and by rushing to rescue them from the Gauls, garnered their gratitude and adoration. However, what other aspects of Camillus's character and comportment, exhibited both before and especially after his exile, according to Machiavelli, induced the Romans to set aside their envy, hatred, and suspicion of the dictator and revere him as a prince in perpetuity?

Throughout the *Discourses*, Machiavelli accentuates the qualities and conduct that earn Camillus the praise and admiration of fellow citizens and even foreign enemies. Machiavelli emphasizes in particular Camillus's use of religion to inspire his soldiers and increase the spoils of war (D I.13); his resort to manipulation and magnanimity in securing nearly bloodless military victories (III.20); and also his exemplification of the Roman way, on the one hand, of conducting war through arms rather than through money (D III.30–31) and, on the other, of training for battle during both wartime and peacetime (D III.31). Finally, as we have already observed, in the lengthy chapter that commences book III, Machiavelli identifies Camillus's expulsion of the Gauls, and the concomitant abatement of envy for the dictator among Rome's citizens, as one of the acts that returned the city to its beginnings and hence renewed the republic.

Machiavelli deems Camillus a "wise" and "prudent" individual who maintained veneration for religion among the Romans, especially by exploiting piety when it proved salutary to the republic (D I.12). Machiavelli attributes to Camillus the reverence with which his soldiers entered Juno's temple during the conquest of Veii, and he praises the dictator for validating their belief that the goddess's statue discernibly assented to being transported to Rome. However, as I said before, it is Camillus's own piety, whether sincere or feigned, that contributed to his growing unpopularity with the plebeians. Camillus had vowed, should he successfully end Rome's decade-long siege of Veii, to dedicate a tenth of the spoils to Apollo (D I.55). Yet during the city's capture he failed to set aside the requisite amount of booty, and the plebs steadfastly defied the Senate's decree that they voluntarily give up a tenth of their spoils to fulfill the dictator's personal pledge to the god. Machiavelli perhaps ironically takes the plebs' indignant refusal to be tithed—rather than resort to any duplicity by defrauding Camillus, the Senate, and even Apollo during the collection of spoils—as an indication of the people's "goodness and religiosity." One could reasonably justify the plebs' defiance here as an act of "decency" (P 9), but not very plausibly as an act of "piety" (D I.55).

In any case, Machiavelli uses the example of Veii's conquest to establish his claim that Camillus was unequivocally "Rome's most prudent captain" (D III.12). To expedite his victory, Camillus shouts to his soldiers within earshot of the Veientes that no one lacking arms should be harmed; he thereby induced the enemy soldiers to cast away all their weapons, thus enabling the Romans to earn a "nearly bloodless" victory. How far Camillus's prudence was entwined with an inclination toward humanity is exemplified by another episode Machiavelli discusses. While Camillus's troops besieged the Falisci, a tutor of their city's noblest children spirited them outside the walls and offered them to Camillus so he could use them to obtain the Falisci's surrender (D III.20). Camillus not only rejects "this gift," he immediately strips the schoolmaster naked and instructs the children to flog their tutor with rods as they safely march him back into the city. Having witnessed Camillus's act of "humanity and integrity"—through which he empowered young pupils to school their treasonous schoolmaster—the Falisci eagerly surrendered to the Romans, encouraging several other hostile cities to sue for peace with Rome. Machiavelli takes this incident to confirm that "sometimes" men can be influenced more by "humanity and charity than by ferocity and violence."

No Machiavellian exemplar worth imitating should, of course, rely more on love than on fear or more on conciliation than on force, especially one like Camillus, to whom Machiavelli attributes the virtuous quality of military severity. In this respect he endorses Livy's view that Camillus exemplifies Rome's commitment to the principle that virtue rather than money was the source of the republic's liberty and greatness (D II.30; cf. D III.10): When the starving Romans, besieged by the Gauls, were preparing to purchase their liberty in a servile manner, Camillus burst into the negotiations, threw his sword on the scales, and exclaimed that steel, not gold, would win Rome's salvation.[14] Camillus and his forces then went on to rout the French and liberate the city—again, earning the dictator the title "second founder of Rome."[15]

Camillus also figures prominently at a moment in the *Discourses* when Machiavelli reaffirms one of his preeminent principles concerning military and civic virtue: Where there are good arms there are always good laws (and vice versa) (P 12; D III.30). Machiavelli, apologizing for what readers might deem "superfluous repetition," again insists that "good laws are nonexistent where good arms are lacking" (D III.31). He then goes much further in this regard than he does anywhere else in his writings by insisting that "nothing good whatsoever" obtains in the absence of good military orders. Building on arguments from the *Art of War*, Machiavelli re-affirms why an army made up of citizens or subjects is potentially the great-est of all military forces.[16] The best armies, Machiavelli argues, are those that continually train for battle; since it is impossible to be constantly at war, training must necessarily be conducted during times of peace. More-over, it is simply too expensive, he insists, to constantly train any kind of military—certainly not a mercenary or auxiliary military—other than one made up of a city's own people during peacetime.[17] For Machiavelli, Camil-lus exemplifies this principle. For when his soldiers feared an enormous Tuscan army amassed before them, Camillus marched through his camp calmly but firmly enjoining his soldiers to simply "do whatever they have been taught or trained to do"; he thus restored their confidence in "the or-dering that they had received *in both peace and war*" and "dispelled from their minds" any fears that the Tuscan force was in any way their superior (D III.31; emphasis added).

So important, Machiavelli insists, is the constant training afforded citizens and subjects in peacetime that no captain—not even a "new Hannibal"—could succeed without it (D III.31). The peacetime ordering for war characteristic of the Roman Republic, he claims, instills within every soldier the virtuous modes of commanders like Camillus, qualities that manifest themselves in battle whether or not that captain is in their immediate presence. Since "in every day of their lives," both individually and collectively, such citizens have "tested their own virtue against for-tune's power" through military discipline and exercises, they have learned to maintain "the same dignity under any circumstance." Machiavelli in-sists that modern republics like that of the Venetians—and presumably of the Florentines as well—consistently fail in battle because they rely on fortune's vagaries rather than on well-ordered military virtue, instilled not only occasionally during times of war, but continually in times of peace.[18]

THE SHORT-LIVED LIFETIME GONFALONIER AND THE RECURRENTLY REAPPOINTED KING OF ROME

I return to Machiavelli's assertion that Soderini worried whether the Flo-rentine people would maintain the office of gonfalonier for life beyond his tenure in office (D III.3). Soderini hesitated to employ "extraordi-nary authority" against the 1494 Republic's enemies because he fretted over the longevity of his magistracy at least as much as over his own life term within it. Machiavelli writes that Soderini was apprehensive about "terrifying the collectivity such that *after his death* it would never again *gather together* (*non sarebbe mai poi concorso*) to make a lifetime gonfalonier, an order he judged good to keep and perpetuate" (D III.3; emphases added). This statement seems to be a direct gloss on the Gospel of Matthew, in which Christ declares that, after *his* death, "wherever two or three are *gathered together* in my name, there am I in their midst."[19] The parallel of these two passages may signal Machiavelli's sharp criticism of Soderini's understanding of an afterlife. For whatever reason, Soderini associates the perpetuation of his name (his soul?) with the permanent maintenance of the office of chief executive that he was the very first citizen to hold—gonfalonier for life. In Soderini's own mind, he would live forever only so long as this office endured within his republic. In this respect, Machiavelli seems to substantively, if subtly, contrast Soderini with Camillus. Machiavelli insists that Camillus was invisibly present with his soldiers, even when he was not there physically, through training and ordering them militarily (D III.31).

Bracketing the most obvious differences between the two magistrates that I noted before—that Camillus, unlike Soderini, withstands both internal conspiracies and foreign invasions—another perhaps not superficial contrast is this: the Roman captain exercised greater, indeed "extraordinary," political authority and wider historical renown than Soderini did precisely because Camillus *did not* aspire to a life-tenured office. Camillus held dictatorial and consular authority multiple times, often renouncing such authority as quickly as he could; he consented to exile so that the Romans might call him back in their urgent need; and consequently he earned eternal fame as "father of his country" and "the second founder of Rome." Soderini enjoys greater formal authority than Camillus—authority, Machiavelli intimates, comparable to that of a Roman king (D III.3-4)—but he fails to either exercise or maintain it effectively because he attempts obstinately, even desperately, to hold it in perpetuity. Camillus consistently and expeditiously gives up supreme authority over the Roman people, as they repeatedly place themselves under his authority like ransomed hostages or conquered subjects (D III.1, D III.30).

This bespeaks poor thinking or impoverished imagination on Soderini's part. Not only does Soderini lack the capacity to act cruelly or severely, he also does not understand civic government institutionally. It is not entirely clear whether Machiavelli thinks a life-termed supreme magistracy is at all compatible with a healthy republic: the Roman kings were elected for life—indeed, like Soderini, they were elected by the people, as Machiavelli emphasizes in a chapter following his discussion of the gonfalonier (D III.4)—and consequently they perhaps rather rapidly succumbed to corruption. Moreover, the Venetian doge, the institutional model for Florence's life-termed gonfalonier, is part of a constitutional model that Machiavelli famously expresses serious reservations about (D I.36).

Returning to the Christological aspects of Machiavelli's treatment of Soderini,[20] Machiavelli intimates here that, like Giano della Bella in the Florentine Republic's early years, Piero Soderini has in his head Christ's model of good behavior rather than the behavioral model of either Brutus or—in closer theological proximity—Moses. Christ's deference to political power results in his death; not insignificantly, like the exiled Giano and Piero, Jesus "left the city" but is remembered well by the people for submitting to humiliation and for suffering rather than committing evil acts. Jesus, John, and Peter each want to achieve good ends only through good means; that is, without themselves directly causing harm to anyone else—even those who most deserve it. Moses, on the contrary, knows that good ends can be achieved only through occasional but definitive recourse to evil means—that is, harm to those who deserve it, individuals who are motivated by jealousy of the legislator/founder and those who would scuttle the enactment of his laws that are intended to benefit his people more generally.

Furthermore, there seems to be deeper theological—or antitheological—significance surrounding the issue of immortality that Machiavelli explores through his contrast of Soderini, on the one hand, and Brutus and Camillus on the other. Soderini declares that he wants to be remembered and to live on after his death through the institution of the gonfalonier for life; in Machiavelli's rendering, Soderini wants eternal life, but he doesn't know the proper way to attain it (D III.3). One best lives on eternally through the laws and orders one establishes precisely through the "extraordinary" letting of blood that invigorates those institutions (D III.1). Brutus killed his sons, as did the Christian God; Soderini should have killed his city's "first sons" as Moses did to the first sons of Egypt and, later, even to many of Israel's. Romulus kills his brother, as did, allegedly, Cesare Borgia;[21] and Agathocles kills the Senate, the fathers of his city. If Soderini is Christian, then he is Christian in the wrong way: even the Christian God was prudent enough to act as Brutus did. The "good" at the start of Christianity that accompanies all long-lasting sects and republics (D III.1) is the principle that someone must die in a spectacularly bloody way to expiate human sin; what God the Father did to his son (or God the Son did to himself), Machiavelli insinuates at the start of book III, subsequent Christians ought to do regularly—at least every ten years. They must conduct spectacular executions of those who commit sins against the city, the envious, powerful, and ambitious: the *grandi*, the *ottimati*, the sons of Brutus.

EXCURSUS: THE ROMAN REPUBLIC'S "MOST PRUDENT CAPTAIN" OR ITS ORIGINAL CORRUPTER?

When discussing Manlius Capitolinus's failed attempt to become king of Rome, Machiavelli invokes the issue of corruption (D III.8). Manlius, whose considerable virtue of body and spirit, our author insists, would have made him a great prince had he usurped a corrupt republic, failed to realize that Rome was not yet sufficiently corrupt for him to fulfill his royal ambitions and satisfy his "unseemly" or "blinding greed for rule" (D III.8). In this respect Manlius's envy, as Machiavelli declares, may have been "blinding" indeed. After all, Machiavelli argues, republics cannot be corrupted overnight, certainly not in one lifetime. Manlius's rival, Camillus—intense envy of whose "honor and glory" drove Capitolinus's pursuit of the principate (D I.8)—exhibits considerably greater powers of discernment and adaptation. Camillus, whom Machiavelli strongly intimates was Rome's uncrowned, intermittent king, once he'd experienced the disapprobation of the Senate and the people over his ostentatiously proud and potentially impious military triumph (D III.23), may have become cognizant that Rome was still civically vibrant and as yet uncorrupted. Camillus correctly anticipated (or perhaps confidently hoped) that humbly acceding to his own exile and quickly forsaking his subsequent dictatorships would make the Romans comfortable with placing absolute power in his hands on successive occasions until the very end of his life—to the benefit of both the Roman Republic and the reputation of its most prudent captain.

But what if an unintended consequence of Camillus's successful effort to become de facto king of an uncorrupt polity initiated the corruption that would eventually destroy the Roman Republic? Machiavelli may indicate that Camillus sows the seeds of the corruption that Manlius could not use in his own time to become a Roman king but that Octavian would eventually exploit to become the first Roman emperor. There are indications in Machiavelli's narrative that Camillus is the original founder of the imperial principate that permanently supplanted the Roman Republic (D III.24). I am not suggesting in this excursus that Camillus's possible contribution to the Roman Republic's eventual corruption and ultimate collapse is conclusive. I merely suggest that Machiavelli gestures toward an alluring possibility concerning the historical ramifications of Camillus's career that even he is not entirely sure about.

There is something perhaps more than merely prophetic in Manlius's charge, which Machiavelli recounts early in the Discourses, that Rome's senators were keeping for themselves war-related riches that belonged to, or at least ought to have been shared with, the republic's plebeians. Manlius insisted that "private citizens had appropriated the unused treasure collected to pay the Gauls; riches that, if recovered, could serve public purposes such as relieving the plebs of their tax burdens or their private debts" (D I.8). Manlius could not, when interrogated by the Senate-appointed dictator, identify the precise location of this treasure; yet this does not mean such funds had not in fact been misappropriated. Manlius's response to the dictator and the senators surrounding him—that "it was unnecessary to inform them of what they already knew"—was certainly no definitive indication of deceit or deflection.

Intriguingly, Manlius's allegation basically conforms to what Machiavelli identifies as the mode of corruption through which the Roman Republic was eventually destroyed—indeed, it serves as a concise allegory for it. As I discussed in chapter 2, according to Machiavelli the Roman Senate exacerbated socioeconomic inequality over time precisely through such means, inaugurating the kind of political inequality that destroys civic liberty and popular government. Throughout the *Discourses*, Machiavelli details how the Senate encouraged further imperial expansion not for geopolitical security but out of sheer avarice: they pursued the conquest of lands farther from Rome initially and farther from Italy eventually, lands that only they and not the plebeians could render productive and profitable (D I.37). These spoils were in some sense "hidden" because the Senate, and Rome's richest citizens disproportionately benefited from what were ostensibly public lands held in their custodial care.[22]

As a result of the growing economic inequality caused by the Senate's imperial policy, Machiavelli delineates how two intertwined developments ensued: the Senate prolonged terms of office for military commanders so that few additional individuals gained military expertise and renown, and Rome's soldiers, away from the city for years at a time, came to depend on these ever fewer commanders for their economic well-being. They no longer pledged loyalty to Rome but rather to their generals, who effectively became warrior princes. As Machiavelli argues, the Senate's greed set in motion a process through which, ironically, Rome's citizen soldiers entirely "forgot the Senate" and became more soldier clients than citizen soldiers (D III.24). This disequilibrium abroad came to affect Rome's domestic politics as even the republic's most virtuous citizens fearfully demurred from running for office against the richest and most powerful citizens, and they refrained from opposing the self-aggrandizing laws that such overbearing citizens increasingly proposed in Rome's assemblies (D I.18).

Machiavelli may very well have noticed that Livy clearly describes the early seeds of these developments in passages between Camillus's expulsion of the Gauls and Manlius's execution. The Roman historian recounts how the tribunes alerted the people that senators were appropriating lands conquered from the Volsci; but since the plebs could not transport their

livestock to provinces at such a distance from the city and were preoccupied with rebuilding their homes that had been destroyed by the Gauls,
they did not immediately react to the tribunes' entreaties.[23] When the tribunes finally aroused the plebs' indignation, the Senate conveniently decided that war with Etruria had become necessary and, as would become
the norm, the protests ceased. Moreover, Manlius's speech accusing the
Senate of hoarding the gold meant to ransom Rome from the Gauls explicitly invokes the body's increasing tendency to appropriate both public
lands *and* public funds: "No longer satisfied with merely seizing public
lands," Manlius exclaims, "the Senate now seeks to hoard public moneys
as well."[24] Thus the senatorial practice of exacerbating economic inequality through misappropriation of public wealth, which would engender civic
corruption, was already operating after Camillus's return from exile and
the expulsion of the Gauls.

But how can Camillus be held even remotely responsible for developments that he was not directly affiliated with during his lifetime and that
would not culminate until centuries after his death? Perhaps because both
Machiavelli and his sources at least indirectly associate him with these developments. Machiavelli accentuates certain aspects of Camillus's early
career described by Livy, Plutarch, and Dionysius of Halicarnassus, incidents where Camillus's management or apparent mismanagement of war
booty disproportionately harms the plebs and arouses significant animosity among them. On more than one occasion Camillus causes scandal by
handling war spoils in a manner detrimental to the plebs: as we observed,
Machiavelli invokes the spoils from Veii that Camillus placed under public
and religious auspices rather than distributing to his soldiers (D III.23); and
he airs Manlius's charge that the Senate had perhaps misappropriated the
gold collected to ransom Rome from the Gauls during Camillus's liberation
of the city (D I.8). Moreover, Livy mentions two other occasions when the
dictator consigns war spoils to public (that is, senatorial) authority rather
than to his plebeian soldiers;[25] and Plutarch further notes that Camillus ex-
tracted tribute for Rome but no spoils for its soldiers in the bloodless victory over the Falisci.[26]

Were these merely isolated incidents in Camillus's career that have no
relation to the Senate's avaricious motivation? Or did Camillus collude
with senators in what was in fact a skimming of public funds and war booty
for senatorial advantage? Plutarch and Livy report that Camillus worried about incurring the animosity of the Senate at least as much as that
of the people on matters pertaining to the spoils of war.[27] Did the dictator overcome this potential hostility on the part of senators by diverting
undeserved spoils their way? That is, did he do so intentionally to benefit
the Senate economically, *not* because he was motivated by piety or was

forgetful? Could the individual Machiavelli deems "Rome's most prudent captain" be both so genuinely pious as to seek to satisfy Apollo and so woefully incompetent that he would forget to collect the spoils to do so? Machiavelli provides no explicit answer, yet both Livy and Plutarch describe Camillus's full complicity in the Senate's desire to maintain and increase economic inequality in the city: for instance, the strategy of sending the plebs on unnecessary military missions so they would not be susceptible to tribunes' calls for land redistribution[28]—policies Machiavelli insists Rome should have adopted early in the republic's history to stave off the political corruption generated by economic inequality (D I.37).

Moreover, Plutarch repeats the tribunes' charges that Camillus had personally appropriated spoils from Veii;[29] and Livy presents Camillus as a staunch defender of the veto, by which senators could induce individual tribunes to block the redistributive initiatives of their colleagues.[30] Finally, both sources confirm that Camillus plays a decisive role in brokering the compromise by which the plebs would share consular offices with the nobles.[31] In his chapter devoted to the agrarian laws, Machiavelli notes how the Senate would ultimately relent in its opposition to sharing offices with the plebs but would hold out obstinately against any initiatives requiring them to share wealth with them (D I.37). Both concessions, Machiavelli insists, would have been necessary to keep the republic from succumbing to economic-cum-civic corruption (D I.37). In short, Camillus seems deeply implicated in the Senate's political and economic policies that would eventually lead to the collapse of the republic.

As for the corrupting practice of prolonging commands: Machiavelli places his chapter on the topic (D III.24) immediately after his chapter devoted to Camillus's exile. By doing so, he may be accentuating the fact that virtuous republics send their prominent commanders abroad *alone* as political punishment rather than placing them at the head of legions as a political reward. Prominent citizens such as the exiled Camillus should feel shame for such treatment and long for a return to their patria; they ought not, as later proconsuls and praetors, be regaled with magisterial titles and luxuriate as petty potentates in distant foreign lands. Moreover, Camillus's most famous personal attribute—giving up authority before his formal tenure of office has ended—seems diametrically opposed to the comportment of later commanders who ambitiously sought the offices of proconsul or military governor, extending their magisterial tenures years and even decades beyond their original terms.

However, only a few chapters after those devoted to Camillus's exile and the prolongation of commands (D III.23-24), Machiavelli discusses in great depth the episode, examined above, where Camillus's consular colleagues accede to his request to be appointed dictator informally because he is legally ineligible to assume such authority formally. This is a far cry from the Camillus who, according to Machiavelli's sources, on being recalled from exile, refused to accept the dictatorship unless all the proper religiolegal niceties were painstakingly observed—even if the requisite delay jeopardized Rome's very existence.[32] It seems that Camillus is procedurally fastidious while attempting to rehabilitate his reputation for civic integrity, but perhaps much less so once he has successfully reestablished it. In gaining informal dictatorial authority, Camillus effectively undermines—by circumventing the spirit, if not the letter—Rome's procedures for appointing magistrates. Machiavelli may be suggesting that Camillus sets the precedent for Rome's corrupting practice later in its history of altering its terms of office by prolonging commands, which was necessary to maintain and expand its empire—an empire that disproportionately enriched its senators and wealthiest citizens, corrupted its citizen soldiers, and caused the republic's collapse.

To contrast the civic health of the early Roman Republic with the corruption of its last days, Machiavelli remarks that the elder Brutus could found the republic with an oath, but the younger Brutus could not reform it even with the support of all Rome's eastern legions (D I.17). The deeper question is why Rome had eastern legions. That it eventually deployed them may itself be a mark of the republic's irredeemable corruption.

CONCLUSION

Through Camillus's interaction with the Roman people, Machiavelli demonstrates the mutual dependence of civic liberty and successful leadership within popular government—as well as the entwining of liberty and leadership with indeterminacy, or one might say with fortune. When accepting his exile, Camillus risks the possibility that the Roman people will never recall him to the patria; for their part, the Roman people later hazard that Camillus, after his return, might use his ever increasing civic-military authority to usurp their liberty and overthrow the republic. Camillus repeatedly exhibits deference to the Roman people's "internal prudence," to their renewed ability to set aside envy and suspicion and "esteem good citizens for their virtue" (D III.1). Likewise, the people increasingly defer to Camillus's virtue, assuming that the dictator will continue to place "the patria's security" over his own pride when exercising his vast authority (D I.34).

Of course, these instances of deference need not have paid off for either the people's liberty or the dictator's majesty. Had the Romans not recalled Camillus from exile, and had they not placed unprecedented authority in his hands, they very likely would have been vanquished by their enemies, with the names of both Camillus and Rome disappearing from history. Had Camillus fully availed himself of the tantalizing opportunity to imprison the Roman Senate and people and formally declare himself king, then he would have become one among a long list of petty if virtuous tyrants in the history of the ancient Mediterranean—certainly not the "most prudent" statesman, the "second founder" of history's most free and virtuous republic.

5. CIVIC CORRUPTION, CAPITAL TRIALS, AND THE ASSEMBLED PEOPLE

(MARCUS MENENIUS AND PIERO SODERINI)

Two seemingly minor figures from the *Discourses*, Marcus Menenius and Pacuvius Calanus, play fundamental roles in Machiavelli's lessons on political leadership.[1] Through these examples, whom I discuss in this chapter and the next, Machiavelli instructs leaders on the proper role that capital trials should play within republics beset by class conflict, aristocratic conspiracies, geopolitical rivalries, and imperially exacerbated civic corruption. In particular, he refines his view that leaders must find suitable opportunities to prosecute oppressive elites before the common people in capital trials; moreover, he affirms that such leaders must demonstrate their own deference to the people by encouraging them, at appropriate moments, to pass legal judgment on themselves.

Menenius and Pacuvius appear in episodes involving Capua, a subject city of Rome, thus enabling Machiavelli to explore the interaction of leaderly prudence, domestic class conflict, and imperial rule. Machiavelli suggests that Capua's extravagant wealth encourages conspiracies that destabilize Rome's domestic politics and generates corruption that undermines its imperium. Capua's riches—in the form of either tribute or bribes—provide the Roman nobility with massive resources that, Machiavelli intimates, they consistently use to undermine the republic's elections and to smear potential reformers.

Machiavelli demonstrates that this imperially generated and intensified civic corruption eventually culminates in the collapse of the Roman Republic. As I discussed previously, he illustrates this explicitly through his own reconstruction of Roman history.[2] Moreover, as I suggest here, he onomastically demonstrates this through episodes of class conflict involving figures who bear names quite similar to his Marcus Menenius. Machiavelli's Menenius is a plebeian who has risen through the ranks of Rome's military to attain the republic's most powerful office, dictator. When his investigation into conspiracies *against* Rome occurring in Capua leads him to inquire into conspiracies involving prominent citizens *within* Rome, the republic's nobility slanders Menenius so that he feels compelled to resign his office and suspend his investigation of civic corruption. Ultimately, Machiavelli's Menenius and Pacuvius, whom I discuss in chapter 6, demonstrate how public-spirited civic leaders can properly mobilize the people to expose, combat, or resolve instances of foreign conspiracy, domestic tumult, and aristocratic corruption for the benefit of their polities.

MARCUS MENENIUS: CORRUPTION, CALUMNIES, AND POPULAR JUDGMENT

Book I, chapter 5 of the *Discourses* is renowned both for reinforcing Machiavelli's claim that conflict between the people and nobles is beneficial to civic liberty, and for introducing Machiavelli's argument that the people, rather than the nobles, should be constitutionally empowered as "liberty's guardians" within republics—two assertions that contravene traditional wisdom on well-ordered government.[3] In the *discorso*'s main section, Machiavelli stages a debate between himself, acting as a tribunician advocate for the people, and hypothetical partisans for the nobility. The debate quickly devolves into an irresolvable dispute over which class motivation, popular or aristocratic, is more dangerous to a republic.[4] Machiavelli eventually concedes that he cannot persuade his aristocratic interlocutors with words or with reason of the civic value of either class conflict or the popular guardianship of liberty. Machiavelli consequently changes the terms of the debate so that his noble audience must now consider whether republics should expand imperially, as did Rome's *governo largo*—popular government—or remain mostly self-contained, as did Venice's or Sparta's more *stretto*—restricted or narrow—republics. Perhaps, Machiavelli wagers, geopolitical necessity or enlightened self-interest rather than reason or morality will induce his aristocratic audience to forsake a Venetian-Spartan republican model in favor of a Roman-style democratic republic.[5] He declares that he will comprehensively discuss republican expansion in the next chapter, *discorso* 6.

Given the gravity of such a topic, readers may be forgiven for jumping ahead to that chapter, where Machiavelli takes up in earnest his promised disquisition over the necessity of imperial republicanism. And yet the often-ignored postscript that concludes chapter 5 provides valuable insights into Machiavelli's analysis of tumult, liberty's guardian, and the relative dangers posed to republics by popular versus noble humors. Furthermore, the coda offers a tantalizing foretaste of Machiavelli's treatments of republican empire and popularly judged political trials—topics explored at greater length in the following chapters (D I.6 and D I.7–8). In this curious addendum to *discorso* 5, Machiavelli recounts an episode involving two plebeian magistrates, the dictator Marcus Menenius and his master of horse Marcus Fulvius, whose popularly endorsed investigation into electoral corruption was stymied by calumnies spread against them by the Roman nobility.

Machiavelli thus introduces problems endemic to republics that both, on the one hand, exhibit the otherwise salutary conflicts between socioeconomic classes, which Machiavelli insists are conducive to liberty, and, on the other, pursue the kind of military expansion he also deems necessary for geopolitical security. Among these problems, according to Machiavelli, are the need for tumultuous/imperial republics to identify and punish aristocratic citizens who invariably attempt to corrupt public institutions, especially elections, and who degrade its civic culture by launching anonymous smear campaigns against magistrates seeking to expose and prosecute such acts of corruption.

Machiavelli initially introduces the postscript to *discorso* 5 as a "further discourse" on the question of who poses more serious harm to a republic, the people or the nobles; or, as Machiavelli recasts these alternatives, "either those who desire to acquire, or those who fear the loss of what they already possess" (D I.5). This reformulation complicates his earlier attribution of humors "to oppress" and "not to be oppressed," respectively, to the nobles and the people (D I.3–4): while naturally distinct in isolation—especially in philosophical or rhetorical debates over class politics—the popular and aristocratic humors become less distinguishable in the contestatory realm of political practice. Machiavelli demonstrates in the coda that the more naturally acquisitive nobles perceive popular efforts to thwart their oppressive behavior as potentially devastating deprivations of the offices and wealth that they already possess; and that the people, although naturally content with what they have, increasingly desire to obtain offices and wealth so they can avoid, resist, or overcome oligarchic domination.

In practice, therefore, both the nobles and the people want to acquire more wealth and offices, albeit for different reasons: the former to increase oppression, the latter to halt it—although the nobility invariably interpret the people's defensive efforts as constituting aggressive acts against the nobles. Moreover, both classes of citizens also want to maintain what they have, to satisfy their desires for either more or less oppression. Both social classes consequently can be shown, in a certain sense, to want to acquire more as well as to maintain what they already have.[6]

Turning to the details of the incident Machiavelli narrates in the postscript to *discorso* 5: The Senate and consuls appoint Menenius, a plebeian, as dictator to investigate conspiracies against Rome in Capua, her sumptuously wealthy and militarily indolent subject city.[7] Machiavelli reports that the Roman people subsequently extend to Menenius—and to his fellow plebeian aide-de-camp Fulvius—the authority to investigate *Roman* citizens who were scheming to acquire the highest magistracies of their own republic "ambitiously and extraordinarily" (D I.5). In effect, the people instruct the dictator to follow the money from external to internal conspiracies: as Machiavelli verifies later in the *Discourses*, prominent Roman citizens were using revenue accumulated through imperial conquest of cities like Capua to fund their efforts either to buy magistracies for themselves or to overstep the authority of offices they already held (D I.18, D I.37, D III.24).

In the general terms that Machiavelli establishes for the controversy in the chapter: The nobles want expanded empire abroad to bring them additional wealth so they can exert more oppressive authority over the plebs at home; the plebeians, originally ineligible to hold magistracies such as the consulship or dictatorship, eventually acquire them by demonstrating military virtue in expanding the empire. Ultimately the plebs broaden a plebeian dictator's jurisdiction so they can diminish the nobility's capacity to oppress them and undermine civic liberty. Thus, both the nobles and the plebeians benefit from military expansion: the nobles gain more of the wealth and power they already possess, while the plebeians acquire entirely new access to high office and institutional protection of their security. Whether each class benefits equally in these respects, Machiavelli answers more definitively later in the *Discourses* (D I.18, D I.37, D III.24).

Not surprisingly, Menenius's widened investigation elicits an invidious response from the Roman nobility. Machiavelli declares that the dictator targeted "whoever" might be ambitiously or extraordinarily seeking "to attain the consulship and other high magistracies"; however, the nobles seem to expose themselves as the actual transgressors, given that, as Machiavelli writes, it "appeared to them" that they were the specific objects of the dictator's expanded investigation (D I.5). Why would the nobles respond so defensively to the inquiry, without being named specifically as its targets, unless they were in fact "scheming" in the fashion described? As Machiavelli confirms elsewhere, the nobles unvaryingly perceive popular empowerment consistent with civic liberty as constituting hostile diminutions of aristocratic authority—even as efforts to render the nobles entirely servile (e.g., D I.16, D III.3).

The nobles react to the dictator's investigation into electoral corruption by turning the tables on Menenius and on the plebs, alleging that the dictator in particular and the people in general were actually the ones seeking offices with ambitious intent and through illegitimate means. Machiavelli reports that the nobles "spread word throughout Rome that it was not the nobles who were pursuing honors ambitiously and extraordinarily, but rather the ignobles, lacking in blood and virtue, who were pursuing extraordinary paths to such ranks" (D I.5). The patricians spread the rumor that the plebeians and Menenius are too deficient in "blood and virtue"—which in their estimation correspond with birth and wealth—to ascend to magistracies through legitimate means and thus they stoop to using corrupt ones.[8]

In terms that conform fairly closely to the way, earlier in the same chapter, Machiavelli had cast the nobility's reaction to *his own* charge that they are motivated above all by a desire to oppress,[9] here the nobles refuse to engage with the accusation and instead launch a countercharge: however much nobles may resort to extralegal means to further their attempts to oppress the people, the people will do so even more readily and energetically because *their* desire to oppress the nobles is both less justifiable and more extreme. As Machiavelli has the nobles exclaim here, It is not *we* the nobles but *they* the ignobles, and the men they raise up against us, who are motivated by excessive ambition and who resort to usurpation to satisfy it.

Of course, when the investigation was focused exclusively on Capua and Capuans, Roman senators thought Menenius virtuous enough to hold the dictatorship; but now that Roman citizens, including Roman nobles, are the targets of his judicial inquiry into conspiracies, they charge him with acting "extraordinarily." But this raises the further question, by what means are the *plebeians* extraordinarily or illegitimately seizing high magistracies? The nobles, more plausibly, are deploying the spoils of empire—by expropriating or colluding with wealthy citizens of Capua—to engage in electoral corruption to gain or to monopolize high magistracies. What comparable resources are available to the plebs to perpetrate any alleged electoral fraud?

The nobles provide no evidence to support such claims; they simply resort to well-financed, widely disseminated gossip. In chapters soon to follow (D I.7-8), Machiavelli distinguishes between accusations, which are leveled formally and supported with evidence, and calumnies, which are spread anonymously through the considerable if elusive force of hearsay. In the incident here, Menenius, the dictator, launches formal accusations against certain nobles, the veracity of which the people will legally adjudicate in assembly; the nobles, for their part, spread unverifiable calumnies against the dictator and the plebeians. The mere fact that plebeians hold the dictatorship, which Machiavelli describes as a kind of ordinary/extraordinary office (D I.34), may, in the nobility's view at this juncture, constitute an "extraordinary" or illegitimate exercise of plebeian authority—even though they themselves had initially consented to Menenius's appointment.[10]

Machiavelli notes that the "accusations"—or, as he quickly clarifies, the "calumnies"—the nobles spread against both the people and Menenius prove so pervasive and forceful that the dictator resigns his post, calls an assembly (*concione*), and "submits himself to the people's judgment" (D I.5). He asks the people to decide whether the nobility's claims against him and his master of horse are truthful accusations or slanderous calumnies. During the proceedings, Machiavelli reports, "there were extensive debates about who was more ambitious, one who desires to maintain or one who wishes to acquire." In terms that match or exceed in sophistication the debate Machiavelli stages between himself and noble partisans earlier in the chapter, he describes how the people debate the respective humors of the plebs and the nobility. The people ultimately conclude that the nobles, those who already possess wealth and power, are the more dangerous source of disturbance because "men seldom perceive that they hold securely what they already have without acquiring more."

However, by *resigning* an office of supreme authority, does Menenius, a plebeian magistrate, actually prove Machiavelli's original point that plebeians do *not* seek, at all costs, to maintain what they have or even to acquire more? And, further, does he prove that the plebs may actually be more willing than the nobles to *give up* valuable possessions? The dictator, and by extension the people, neither maintains nor acquires in the episode—indeed, Menenius forswears something quite desirable: dictatorial authority. Alternatively, the episode may in fact suggest that, for Machiavelli, the people should acquire (as well as maintain and expand) something valuable: the authority of ultimate judgment over political praise and blame.

To a significant extent, the people's judgment corresponds with what has in fact occurred in this episode: The nobles have undoubtedly conspired to use their wealth and power, through the fruits of empire, to acquire even more riches and authority; and, once confronted with obstruction to these endeavors by the people and their magisterial agents, they use this wealth and authority to spread calumnies that spawn civil controversies. Notwithstanding what conventional republican wisdom maintains (as definitively affirmed by Machiavelli's aristocratic interlocutors in the body of the chapter), the people, pointedly, are *not* the social class that initiates upheavals—or even the class that causes the greatest harm in doing so. Indeed, as Machiavelli's people observe here, "Since those who already possess, possess much, they can more swiftly and forcefully undertake an alteration" (D I.5)—*alterazione*, a word in Florentine parlance that connotes political maneuvers ranging from sparking a scandal to launching a full-scale coup d'état.[11]

Machiavelli's plebeians concede, however, that even if they do not naturally wish to acquire more than they have, in the rough-and-tumble world of class interactions, they are incited to do so by the nobles: they contend that the nobility's "incorrect and ambitious behavior inflames in the breasts of those who do not already possess things, the desire to in fact possess them; either so as to wreak vengeance upon those who do possess such things by expropriating them, or by attaining for themselves the wealth and offices that they observe being used incorrectly by those who already possess them" (D I.5).

Based on such deliberations, the people absolve the plebeian dictator of the charges of exhibiting excessive ambition and of employing extraordinary measures to satisfy it. Having put himself on trial before the people, Menenius is duly acquitted. Nevertheless, the nobility's calumnies have induced the dictator to resign his post, and thus they have effectively put a halt to his inquiry into their conspiracies to corrupt the republic (D I.5). What is Machiavelli trying to tell readers by having this plebeian magistrate absolved by a judgment of the people and the nobles thereby explicitly censured—if not concretely punished—by the same? The popular deliberations in the *concione*, according to Machiavelli, confirm the more harmfully ambitious motives of the nobles, even if their conspiratorial efforts to act on such motives go unpunished by the dictator. Indeed, Livy, for his part, reports that the dictator's investigations into corruption were "finally suppressed by the cliques and factions" against whom they had been directed, and that the people eventually lost interest in the case.[12] The nobles wind up successfully ending the dictator's tenure and litigating the people into political exhaustion.

Among the many issues the brief Menenius episode raises is the question of popular judgment. Should the people be allowed to render a verdict in a case where they are an interested party? They too were conspired and calumniated against by the nobility alongside Menenius and Fulvius. Should we therefore be surprised that the people exonerate their partisans, who were making a case on *their* behalf? However, as we observed in the Manlius Capitolinus episode, Machiavelli declares that the people are capable of deciding *against* a popular champion when that individual clearly exhibits excessive ambition (D III.8). Thus an unfairly biased, popularly partisan outcome in such cases is by no means a foregone conclusion. Moreover, recall Machiavelli's intimations (discussed in the context of the figures Lucius Brutus and Piero Soderini in chapter 3) that the people, acting as a whole and institutionally empowered to pass final judgment, are incapable of acting extraordinarily—such decisions are always "ordinarily" correct. So in this sense too the Menenius episode validates popular judgment.[13]

The episode in the coda of *discorso* 5 also takes to extremes Machiavelli's later argument regarding the domestic consequences of republican expansion: extensive inclusion of the people in a martial republic will result in their attaining significant political authority—not only the plebeian tribunate, which the nobles detest despite its limited power—but also the dictatorship, a magistracy that wields unappealable authority over the life and death of citizens outside the bounds of the city and, unlike the consulship, even within them. As Machiavelli shows on numerous occasions, a militarily robust republic that pursues empire will afford men of virtue, whether noble or ignoble, the opportunity to rise to the ranks of the most supreme magistracies (P 8; D I.31, D I.60).

Nobles who, as Machiavelli has already demonstrated, steadfastly resist the establishment of a plebeian tribunate in his own day should be horrified at the prospect of plebeians' attaining the dictatorship—an institution typically thought to be the nobility's most effective instrument of class suppression.[14] However, the nobles might take more than a small bit of solace from the following facts: in this episode at least, their vast economic advantages afford the nobles the opportunity to effectively libel plebeian magistrates, even dictators, and hence to neutralize their efforts, however legally formidable, to expose and to punish oligarchs conspiring to oppress the people. Calumnies are the consummate weapons of the wealthy within republican politics. In short, republican empire, again, enables both expanded civic authority for plebeians *and* acquisition of greater material resources for the nobility, with which the latter can neutralize the effect of enhanced popular empowerment.[15]

CAIUS MENENIUS AND OTHER POSSIBLE COUNTERPARTS TO MACHIAVELLI'S "MARCUS MENENIUS"

Most editions of Livy available to Machiavelli call the plebeian dictator Caius Menenius and his master of horse, Marcus Follium.[16] Machiavelli either mistranscribes their names or purposely changes them to Marcus Menenius and Marcus Fulvius. Moreover, Machiavelli makes the master of horse a plebeian, when in fact he is a patrician in Livy's account. "Menenius" and "Fulvius" are especially significant names in the history of class conflict within a Roman Republic acquiring an ever-larger empire. What light do the careers of such figures shed on the magistrates whom Machiavelli makes their namesakes in our episode involving imperial rule, civic corruption, class conflict, and the adjudication of accusations/calumnies within popularly judged political trials?

Let us first examine a few points of divergence between Machiavelli's and Livy's accounts of the episode.[17] According to the Roman historian, the Senate itself, not the people, expands the scope of the dictator's investigation to include potential conspirators in Rome and not merely in Capua.

This is our first indication that Machiavelli makes the nobles and, to a lesser extent, the people more aggressively partisan than they are in his source: Livy's senators are perfectly willing to see fellow nobles tried for political corruption, and his people do not endeavor to inflate the plebeian dictator's authority, whether or not nobles are primarily the target of his investigation.

Moreover, in Livy's account the nobles collectively turn against the plebeian dictator only once the tribunes refuse to acknowledge the appeals of individual nobles against the dictator's indictments. This is perfectly appropriate on constitutional grounds, as there is no right of appeal against a dictator while he holds office—hence the tribunes may very well be motivated by fear of the dictator's authority rather than by any hatred of the nobles in denying the latter's appeals. Furthermore, according to Livy, as punishment for the magistrates' impudent behavior, the nobles threaten to put the dictator and the master of horse on trial for political corruption as soon as they leave office.[18]

Livy's dictator—Maenius in the original, Menenius in Machiavelli's sources—a prominent plebeian, speaks to the assembly, attesting to his innocence and to the treachery of certain nobles who defied his authority through specious appeals to the tribunes, egregious slanders against him, and inappropriate threats to prosecute him. Once Maenius resigns, Livy reports no ensuing deliberation on the part of the people regarding the general question either of noble versus popular motivations or of the desire to maintain wealth and offices versus the desire to acquire them. Moreover, the *concione* does not function, as Machiavelli implies, as a formal political jury but serves only as a deliberative assembly—in Livy, the Senate assigns the consuls the task of legally judging the dictator's case. Furthermore, after they hear testimony against Maenius by members of the nobility, the consuls definitively acquit him and his master of horse, Marcus Follium—who again according to Livy is not, like Maenius, a plebeian as Machiavelli insists.

Livy reports that in the assembly the dictator earnestly addressed the people and admirably resigned his post "thinking more of his reputation than his office."[19] Maenius expressly declares that he will "use his office" neither to explicitly impugn the motives of those who oppose him (he will let the people form their own opinion about why certain nobles attempted to sabotage his investigation), nor to influence those who would ultimately try him (he will let the consuls decide for themselves both his own and his aide-de-camp's manifest innocence independent of the exalted ranks they had held). Maenius implies that the nobles had already absolved him of their subsequent charges and also had already confirmed that he was above petty partisanship when they conferred the dictatorship on him. "Gods and men," he exclaims, should recognize the implications of the fact that "I will allow myself to be legally judged, putting myself before my enemies for trial, while they, for their part, avoid such judgment at all costs."[20]

Again, Machiavelli makes the episode more emblematic of intense class conflict than it really is. He may wish to imply that Livy understates the intensity of class conflict in Rome's early history. Perhaps he alters Livy's account to accentuate how far Machiavelli himself thinks popular champions can expect favorable judgment from the people in popular assemblies. Alternatively, he may do so to assure nobles that their calumnies will successfully enable them to evade popular punishment in assemblies. Or perhaps he wishes to encourage popular champions to be more confident and assertive in pursuing antiaristocratic agendas within such assemblies. Ultimately, I believe, Machiavelli wants to instruct republics how to put on trial not only public-spirited whistle-blowers and reformers, but *also* anonymous members of the nobility who commit crimes in the shadows. This, I will argue further below, is the fundamental reason for Machiavelli's departures from Livy in the Menenius episode.

We first turn to the question, Why does Machiavelli change the dictator's name from Gaius to Marcus Menenius and the master of horse's name from Marcus Follium to Fulvius? Additionally, Why does he make the dictator's lieutenant a plebeian? As I mentioned above, Menenius and Fulvius are especially significant names in the history of class conflict as the Roman Republic acquires an ever-expanding empire. What light do the careers of such similarly named figures shed on the magistrates whom Machiavelli, in an onomastic fashion, places in our episode involving imperial rule, civic corruption, class conflict, and the adjudication of accusations/calumnies in popularly judged political trials?

Chronologically speaking, the first Menenius who might be pertinent to our concerns is the consul Menenius Agrippa, who ends the first secession of the plebs in 493 BCE by narrating the famous parable of the limbs and the stomach.[21] Menenius Agrippa, who Livy suggests may have been born to a family of plebeian origins, convinces the plebs that they, like the limbs in the tale, may underestimate how much they rely on the Senate, the republic's stomach, to distribute back to them nourishment that they initially provide to the stomach.[22] Machiavelli may consider the lesson of the parable specious despite its fame, since he fails to mention it in the *Discourses* and also intimates that the nobles are the far more parasitical part of the republic—something several of the episodes we consider here confirm. In any case, Livy's Menenius Agrippa, the consul, and Machiavelli's dictator, Marcus Menenius, are both effectively conciliatory figures.

In Livy's account of the secession, Menenius Agrippa persuades the plebs to be satisfied with the concessions, including the plebeian tribunate, that the nobles have granted in response to their mass evacuation, and not to deny the Senate anything further that might eventually deprive the plebeians themselves of sustenance. The nexus of military affairs (if not yet imperial conquest) and domestic discord is apparent here as Livy reports that the Senate fears that the armed plebs, who have seceded from the city to protest economic exploitation by the nobles, will either attack the city or stand by should an enemy city do so.[23]

The plebeians demonstrate their gratitude to Menenius Agrippa for ending the secession when, after he dies, they individually contribute to pay his burial, which the former consul's family could not afford to fund.[24] Both the Livian and the Machiavellian Menenius characters, therefore, acquire popular favor for acknowledging the legitimacy of plebeian grievances but also for ending a tense civic conflict with the nobles. Menenius Agrippa's son, Titus Menenius, according to Livy, did not fare so well with the people: in the midst of subsequent conflicts over land redistribution, the tribunes indict the younger Menenius for losing a military outpost while consul; and although the people vote merely to fine rather than to execute him as charged, soon thereafter Menenius dies from shame.[25] The two earliest appearances of the name Menenius in Livy therefore correspond with, first, a magistrate who reconciles the Senate and the people and thereby gains popular favor, and second, his son, whom the people treat more leniently than perhaps they should have been simply because of his name.

A public figure with a name *identical* to that of Machiavelli's dictator is Marcus Menenius, a plebeian tribune who, in 410 BCE, while demanding land redistribution to the plebs, refused to permit plebeians to be enrolled for military service despite fierce opposition from the Senate, the consuls, and also his nine tribune colleagues—a refusal he maintained in the name of justice even after Rome incurred a serious military defeat.[26] Eventually, Livy reports, once the consuls and the other tribunes collude to override appeals to Menenius by individual plebeians, and then to arrest any pleb refusing to enlist for service, the army is fully mobilized and Rome achieves a decisive victory. However, when the consul refuses to distribute booty among the previously recalcitrant soldiers, the soldiers—already ill-tempered at being compelled to enroll for service—disrupt the consul's triumph by shouting the name of Menenius in the procession rather than that of their commander. They effectively give the triumph to the tribune, not the consul.

The Senate retaliates against both the plebs and the plebeian tribune for this impertinence by preventing Menenius from being elected as the city's chief magistrate; they schedule elections of consuls rather than consular tribunes, so that Menenius, a plebeian, would be ineligible to run for the office. This episode contains several instances of aristocratic corruption:

efforts to prevent redistribution (refusal to enact agrarian laws), to mis-use funds (failure to distribute spoils to victorious soldiers), and efforts to engage in electoral corruption (preventing the popular former tribune from assuming consular authority). However, it also confirms that, from the years 410 to 320 BCE—that is, from the time of Livy's tribune, Marcus Menenius, to that of Machiavelli's identically named dictator—inclusion of plebeians in military service leads to their gaining not only consular au-thority but, eventually, even the dictatorship. It also demonstrates that the earlier Menenius, the tribune, pursued policies that addressed the root of the problem of which the later Menenius, the dictator, can address only symptoms: namely, the fraught relationship of military expansion and eco-nomic redistribution.

Although not precisely a "Menenius," the comparably named Gaius Memmius shares similar characteristics and especially circumstances with Machiavelli's plebeian dictator. He confronts domestic corruption trace-able to imperial expansion—expansion now extending far beyond the Ital-ian peninsula: beyond Capua in Campania to Numidia in Africa. Sallust reports that Memmius, as tribune of the plebs in 111 BCE, exposed exten-sive corruption among Roman senators, who were accepting bribes from Jugurtha, the king of Numidia, to secure the king's geopolitical interests rather than those of Rome.[27] Memmius, whom Sallust calls "a staunch en-emy of aristocratic power," mobilized the people's indignation over the Senate's conspiracies with the king, which resulted in the resumption of Rome's Jugurthian War. However, it eventually became clear that the con-sul assigned to again prosecute war in Africa, Lucius Calpurnius Bestia, had been bribed to settle for a peace favorable to Jugurtha, and that the Senate was hesitant to denounce him because of their own connivance with the king.[28] In response to this situation, Memmius gives one of the most withering anti-oligarchic orations in all classical sources. Indeed, Machiavelli would draw on it extensively for the infamous speech of the nameless *ciompo* in the *Florentine Histories*.[29]

For our purposes, Memmius's speech, imploring the people to defend "their republic and their liberty,"[30] illuminates the example of Machiavel-li's Menenius in several respects: it shows how the rampant evils of impe-rially generated political corruption have grown since the Capua episode two hundred years earlier; it demonstrates how Roman history definitively confirms which of the two humors is more dangerous to a republic; and it indicates that the cost of investigating oligarchic corruption may entail not merely the unseating of plebeian magistrates, but their murder at the hands of nobles.

In Sallust's rendering, Memmius hesitates over addressing the people, given their general submissiveness, the nobility's power, the absence of justice in the city, and the obvious danger he faces in doing so. The tribune makes it immediately apparent that he is just as perturbed by popular quiescence as by aristocratic corruption. Memmius laments that the people, whether through "apathy," "exhaustion," or even "cowardice,"[31] have allowed themselves to become "playthings of the insolent few"; that they have failed to "avenge their slain champions," such as Tiberius Gracchus, Gaius Gracchus, and Marcus Fulvius; and that they have permitted countless numbers of their own to "perish in dungeons" for resisting aristocratic oppression.[32]

When assessing the nobility, Memmius astutely confirms what Machiavelli has already illustrated for us: the nobles will invariably attribute extraordinary ambition, royal or otherwise, to leaders seeking to uphold "the rights of the plebeians";[33] they consistently cast their charges as cynical pretexts to undermine or eliminate popular champions, and as camouflage for their own recidivist expropriations of the public weal. Memmius decries the nexus of domestic corruption and external conquest foreshadowed in Machiavelli's Menenius/Capua example: specifically, how powerful Roman nobles collude with elites abroad to oppress the plebs at home:

> For many years you have been quietly indignant over aristocratic pillaging of the treasury, over tribute paid by kings and free peoples to a few nobles, over the latter's hoarding of both the highest glory and the greatest wealth. And yet, not satisfied with having committed these crimes with impunity, they have handed over your laws, your sovereignty—all things human and divine—to your enemies. These perpetrators exhibit neither shame nor sorrow, grandly strutting themselves about before your eyes; flaunting priesthoods, consulships, and triumphs as if they were well-earned honors rather than what they are: stolen goods. . . . Who are these men who have usurped the republic? Criminals with bloody hands, as arrogant as they are avaricious, men who convert loyalty, dignity, propriety—everything honorable or dishonorable—into sources of naked gain. . . . They have betrayed to the fiercest of our enemies the Senate's authority and your imperium; they have prostituted the republic both at home and in the field.[34]

We are here a long way from the terms of Machiavelli's somewhat tense debate with his nameless noble interlocutors (D I.5), from the comparatively sterile popular deliberations over the motivations of those seeking to maintain versus those seeking to acquire (D I.5), and even from the reservedly passionate speech of Livy's dictator, Gaius Menenius. The upshot of all those public exchanges or speeches was that the nobility's aspirations were more morally reprehensible and their actions more civically transgressive than the people's were. However, here Sallust has Memmius go much further in his unsparing assault on the nobility's intentions and behavior. Two centuries of the nobility's benefiting disproportionately from the spoils of empire, of aristocratic corruption of elections, of senatorially sanctioned assassinations of multiple plebeian magistrates, of slaughter and incarceration of hundreds of plebs, of incessant oligarchic scuttling of economic redistribution and political reforms—in Sallust's estimation—justify the ferocity of Memmius's denunciatory rhetoric.

However, it must be reemphasized that Memmius's conclusion that the nobles are more avaricious and ruthless than the people is not an unqualified compliment to the people; popular "goodness," as Machiavelli himself often intimates, can be a civic deficiency, not an asset.[35] As Memmius harangues the people here, "If you cared as much for liberty as they lust for domination, the republic would be ravaged less thoroughly than it presently is; then you would consequently bestow favor upon the truly best men and not merely the most brazen."[36] No, the people's humor not to be dominated, however "decent" or "just," to use Machiavelli's designation (P 9), is no positive attribute when it either accompanies or fosters a docility that ensures rather than repels domination. As the tribune continues:

> I myself consider it quite disgraceful to permit those who commit injustice to go unpunished. I would nevertheless countenance you to pardon, out of equanimity, criminals because they are your fellow citizens—*if* it were not for the fact that such compassion will certainly result in your utter destruction. For such is the extent of their insolence that, beyond behaving badly with impunity, they desire to wrest from your hands the ability to prevent them from engaging in further wrongdoing. . . . Therefore, how can you hope for trust or harmony? They want to dominate; you to be free. They desire to inflict injuries; you to prevent them.[37]

Not only does Sallust here presage Machiavelli's account of the aristocratic and popular humors to, respectively, dominate and not be dominated; he also prefigures the Machiavellian question of maintenance versus acquisition. Memmius declares that the nobles have deprived the people of power they had necessarily gained to keep the nobles from maintaining their advantages by acquiring more. From his point of view, the plebeians have lost civil rights that must now be reacquired: "Your ancestors twice seceded in arms and occupied the Aventine in order to secure justice and establish their sovereignty. Will you not struggle with the most strenuous efforts to win back the liberty that you received from them? Ought you not do so all the more vigorously because it is a greater disgrace to lose an acquisition than not to have acquired it at all?"[38]

Memmius declares that a third plebeian secession will not be necessary to punish "those who have betrayed the republic"; rather, he recommends convening a political trial in which King Jugurtha should testify against his Roman coconspirators; only then could they bring to justice those who "have caused their republic such grievous damage and disgrace."[39] Thoroughly persuaded by Memmius, the people dispatch a praetor, Lucius Cassius, to bring Jugurtha to Rome, under public protection, to testify to precisely which Roman nobles had taken bribes from him.[40] Yet, just as Jugurtha appeared before the people in assembly and Memmius stepped forward to interrogate him regarding his Roman coconspirators, Gaius Baebius, a tribune the king had bribed, interceded to put an end to the proceedings.

Despite wild popular demonstrations of outrage, the trial concluded before any senators who colluded with Jugurtha could be identified, and before guilty verdicts could be leveled against any obvious wrongdoers—not against Bestia, the consul under suspicion, Baebius, the corrupted tribune, or King Jugurtha himself.[41] Moreover, Memmius's intuition that he was putting himself in grave danger by endeavoring to punish Rome's nobility for corruption and treason was confirmed a decade later: in 100 BCE, as he was about to be elected consul by the Roman people, Memmius's enemies among the nobility directed a mob of clients to club him to death in the middle of the assembly.[42]

We must fully consider the ramifications of possible connections between these Roman leaders also named Menenius, or similarly named Memmius, and Machiavelli's plebeian dictator. Additionally, we must consider this: Machiavelli also changes the name of Livy's master of horse in the Menenius/Capua episode to that of a famous *popolare* politician who, like Memmius, met a bad end at the hands of the Roman nobility. While Livy identifies the master of horse as Marcus Folius (or Follium), Machiavelli's invention, Marcus Fulvius, shares the name of the historical Marcus Fulvius Flaccus, about whom a few facts are pertinent: a great military strategist, Flaccus was the only former consul to serve as tribune of the plebs; an ally of the Gracchi, with a reputation for personal immorality—especially among the nobles—he helped the brothers promote citizenship for Latin allies and administer pro-plebeian land reforms throughout Italy. Consequently, he was murdered by senators, as were other supporters of Gaius Gracchus in 121 BCE.[43]

ALTERNATIVE COURSES OF ACTION
AVAILABLE TO MENENIUS?

To reiterate, a surface reading of book I, *discorso* 5, suggests that plebeian magistrates and the people themselves are willing to settle for less, to abandon their attempts to acquire more, in political contests with the nobility. The nobility, however, never cease in their ambitious and extraordinary efforts to acquire more, externally and domestically, in the service of their jealous desire to maintain what they have, resorting to smear campaigns to do so—and ultimately they get away with it. At this early stage of the *Discourses*, popular partisans might be satisfied by the episode's validation of the people's moral purity; aristocratic partisans might gleefully applaud Machiavelli's perhaps admiring account of how deceitfully the nobles get what they want without recourse to overt violence. Menenius the plebeian behaves honorably; the nobles behave ignobly—but no one really gets hurt.

However, Machiavelli's conversion of Livy's "Caius Menenius" into his own "Marcus Menenius," and the history of expanding empire, intensifying civic corruption, and proliferating violence that such a renaming invokes, renders the episode not quite so innocuous. Perhaps, in retrospect, Machiavelli actually thought that leaders like Menenius ought to have acted more vigorously early in the republic's history to combat the civic corruption promoted by access to subject cities like Capua; that is, long before matters deteriorated in the egregious manner typified by senatorial collusion with imperial clients like Jugurtha—an example that manifests far more rampant civic corruption and adds the especially pernicious and increasingly frequent element of extraordinary, lethal violence.

The Menenius/Capua episode demonstrates just how successfully the resources of the nobles, even at a relatively early juncture of the republic's imperial history, could be converted into an anonymous slander campaign against a populist magistrate—smears that undermine his integrity, scuttle his reform efforts, and chase him from office. Popular governments, of course, provide freedoms that enable some individuals to accumulate more resources and privileges than other citizens. These few then maximize such advantages (by spreading disinformation, acquiring clients, etc.) to exploit republican freedom of speech even further in ways that subvert efforts by the general citizenry to ameliorate disparities of political and socioeconomic power. Machiavelli knew firsthand, through "hardship and dangers," what our own contemporary politics (from "fake news" to even worse) makes obvious: within republics, powerful citizens, maintaining plausible deniability (often with the assistance of foreign entities), disseminate anonymous smears or spread slanders via third parties against reformers as effectively as autocratic regimes deploy brute force.[44] Therefore the question arises, Does freedom itself impose a glass ceiling on political accountability and reform initiatives in a republic? In the context of the *Discourses* as a whole, Machiavelli answers, yes, quite often, but not invariably.

Read in light of the quickly succeeding chapters on accusations and calumnies and the later discourses devoted to political trials, the coda to *discorso* 5 seems to beg for Menenius to have adopted some alternative course of action. Granted, the case is difficult because the dictator does not know exactly who among the nobility sponsored the calumnies spread against him. But a class inversion of the confrontation between Manlius Capitolinus and the unnamed dictator Machiavelli describes soon thereafter (D I.8) suggests a possibility. Just as *that* dictator, acting on behalf of the Senate, demands evidence from Manlius to support his antipatrician charges, Menenius, before resigning his office, could have used *his* dictatorial authority to demand that the Senate either produce evidence against him or pass a proclamation clearing his name. Alternatively, in the spirit of the early chapters on accusations and calumnies, where only one individual suffers punishment, Menenius could have singled out the most likely culprit among the patricians and ordered him to stand trial as a calumniator before an assembly of the people. Having done that, the dictator could have *then* resigned his office and subsequently asked the people to decide who is the true calumniator, the indicted senator or Menenius himself.

Each of these options would have been an improvement on Menenius's actual course of action; they would have either formally implicated the Senate as a whole or punished a particular patrician, synecdochical of the entire nobility, rather than letting that whole class and each of its members go unpunished. Nevertheless, both alternatives still share the deficiency inherent in the plebeian dictator's original strategy: they do not sustain the inquiry into the ways the nobles use their resources, increasingly accumulated from empire, to stack the political system of the republic even further in their favor. Without the continuation of that investigation, the nobility will have successfully converted an issue of sociopolitical equality, and therefore invariably liberty, into what we now call personality politics. Whether the nobles smear the whistle-blowing upstart who brings charges against them or sacrifice the life of one especially compromised individual from their own ranks, in either case the authority of "the senatorial order" (D I.35, D I.53) prevails, and its constant conspiracies against the people's liberty persist. If this were Machiavelli's ultimate intention, then the young *ottimati* to whom he dedicates the *Discourses* might be reconciled with the popularly inclusive institutions that he proposes in the book. In such case, political philosophers—who still today as in ancient times ally with the interests of the *ottimati*—would be correct in promoting such an elite-friendly interpretation of Machiavelli's presentation of political trials.

Both, however, should only cautiously draw premature conclusions along these lines. Machiavelli later offers alternative means a plebeian magistrate might use in such circumstances to protect himself and pursue a populist reform agenda: one way that Menenius might have kept the issue framed in terms of popular liberty rather than personality politics would have been to use his dictatorial authority over life and death to prosecute more than just one conspirator against whom he had the best evidence—as in the cases, discussed before, of the sons of Brutus or the Medici Five.[45] Accusing more than one patrician allows class politics to prevail over the politics of individual personality. Few know the names of the nobles (save perhaps Bernardo del Nero) engaged in these antirepublican conspiracies, ancient and modern. What *is* remembered are their motives, their schemes, and their ultimate fates. Convicting one noble may indeed dispose of a single bad apple, but discovering a half dozen or so suggests that an entire bushel has turned rotten. Of course, if he were so inclined, Menenius could have behaved toward the *entire* Senate as did several of Machiavelli's other notable examples we've observed: Clearchus (D I.16), Agathocles (P 8), and the Corcyran demos (D II.2). But such senatocide points down the path of tyranny rather than toward "the way of freedom" that, as we have observed in previous chapters, Machiavelli associates with Lucius Brutus, with Furius Camillus, and with republics.

Within a republican context, once Menenius sees to it that the nobles accused of conspiracy and calumny have been convicted, he could have resigned his office and permitted their friends and family to put *him* on trial—but only after the fact. As I discussed previously, Machiavelli intimates that Piero Soderini could have done this once he had prosecuted the Florentine "sons of Brutus," that is, the young *ottimati* conspiring to overthrow the 1494 Republic and restore the Medici principate. Vindication in a kind of popularly judged trial did neither Menenius nor Soderini—nor their republic—any good: on August 27, 1512, the gonfalonier won a resounding vote of confidence in the Great Council. Less than a week later, four sons of Brutus, whom he should have previously tried for treason, stormed the palace, threatened to assault him, compelled his exile, and ended the Florentine Republic.[46] By submitting themselves to popular judgment only *after* executing noble conspirators, Soderini or Menenius would have reformed their republics while also allowing dissenters to "vent their animus," thus deterring future magistrates from using such measures against elites either frivolously or nefariously.

More cunningly, Menenius and Soderini certainly should have allowed the people to judge the legitimacy of their actions *after* the people themselves had already participated in the judgment and in the execution of nobles engaged in corruption-serving slander campaigns. The two supreme magistrates would have thereby put the people in the position of retroactively judging their own judgment. However, to put oneself on trial, as Menenius and Soderini do, without first prosecuting and eliminating their patrician adversaries, and before enlisting the people as compatriots in doing so, is a colossal waste of a fortuitous opportunity to punish the usurpers of popular liberty and to enhance one's own reputation with the people. This is only confirmed by the assembly sessions Menenius and Soderini convene, in which the people enthusiastically affirm that the nobles, and not their own magistrates, are guilty of acting in a corrupt and ambitious manner. Would that Menenius and Soderini, Machiavelli seems to intimate, had given the people the opportunity on such occasions to act more robustly on this disposition and to definitively punish their mutual adversaries.

CONCLUSION

At first blush Menenius seems to be a civically responsible figure: in the manner of Camillus or Scipio, he chooses exile or resignation to preserve his civic reputation and avoid an escalation of social strife. However, considering Machiavelli's discussion of Soderini later in the *Discourses*, he seems imprudent: his antipatrician policies fail because he allows aristocratic calumnies and conspiracies to force him from from office. Both Menenius and Soderini effectively put themselves on trial without first vigorously prosecuting their adversaries among the *ottimati*. If Menenius does in fact stand for Soderini in this respect, then who, in Machiavelli's account, might be the dictator's plebeian master of horse, his aide-de-camp, his military arm? The master of horse, Fulvius, also lost his post as a result of patrician conspiracies against the republic and owing to calumnies asserting he was unworthy to hold high public office. Furthermore, he too must somehow be implicated in his boss's failure to use supreme authority and popular support to proceed more aggressively against the nobles (see D III.3).

Niccolò Machiavelli's famous militia plan was intended to provide Gonfalonier Soderini with the means to break a corrupt civic-military nexus, similar if not identical to the one that confronted Menenius and Fulvius; specifically, an interconnection between aristocratic power and foreign mercenary troops that crippled Florence both domestically and geopolitically.[47] Machiavelli, whose career advancement was often blocked by aristocratic denunciations of his civic worth,[48] ultimately envisioned a citizen and subject army that would not only improve the republic's military position vis-à-vis foreign powers but also stem civic corruption.[49] A citizen militia would have decreased the republic's need to grant lucrative financial rewards to wealthy Florentine citizens for hiring mercenaries, a practice that had inflated the *ottimati*'s economic and political prominence in the city. Moreover, the Menenius/Fulvius episode replays, in an altered context, circumstances where Soderini and Machiavelli were trying to reacquire a subject city, Pisa, which Florence lost because of the French invasion in 1494—much as Rome would eventually lose Capua through a Carthaginian invasion of Italy.

Soderini, although a Florentine patrician, can nevertheless, like Menenius, be considered "a plebeian magistrate" owing to the favor he enjoyed "with the collectivity" (D III.3; cf. D I.52). But why does Machiavelli even bother to mention Menenius's master of horse, Fulvius, in the episode? He seems to serve no purpose except to enable Machiavelli to transform Menenius's military assistant into a plebeian and, like the dictator, a popular champion who was decisively undermined by corrupt, treasonous nobles. Perhaps Machiavelli includes Fulvius, with both altered name and modified class status, precisely because it permits Machiavelli to insert himself into the narrative of the *Discourses*: that is, to invoke Machiavelli as the gonfalonier's primary military adviser—as it were, Soderini's likewise ill-fated "master of horse."

6. OPENING THE PEOPLE'S EYES (AT LEAST PARTIALLY)

Civic versus Princely Leadership

(PACUVIUS CALANUS AND CESARE BORGIA)

Pacuvius Calanus is Machiavelli's second figure to appear in an episode involving Capua. Like Marcus Menenius, Pacuvius allows Machiavelli to explore the interaction of statesmanly prudence, class conflict, and foreign policy.[1] He shows that an astute magistrate like Pacuvius can use popularly judged capital trials to combat aristocratic oppression and to reform a republic—even a corrupt city like Capua. This strategy, Machiavelli suggests, proves especially effective in republics caught between warring imperial hegemons such as Rome and Carthage or, in Machiavelli's time, France and Spain.

This chapter also offers a modest contribution to the exploration of a perennial question in the history of political thought: What is the relation between Machiavelli's *The Prince* and his *Discourses on Livy's History of Rome*? A traditional view, perhaps originated by Rousseau, casts the two books as fundamentally different: In *The Prince*, Machiavelli endeavored (whether ironically or sincerely) to advise tyrants how to seize and hold power, whereas in the *Discourses* he encouraged the establishment and maintenance of republics. The former book provided historically unprecedented guidance to tyrannical autocrats; the latter work called for a revival of ancient civic virtue. This view culminated in a classic article by Hans Baron on the supposedly contradictory relationship of the books—a purported puzzle that he tried, admirably but unsatisfactorily, to solve by pinpointing the precise dating of each work's composition.[2] This perspective was supplanted in the late twentieth century by the view that *The Prince* and the *Discourses* were more similar than different. Scholars with such diverse views on Machiavelli as Leo Strauss and Quentin Skinner nevertheless agreed that, in Skinner's words, "the underlying political morality of the two books is the same."[3]

I entirely concur with this this view, even though, as both Strauss and Skinner were aware, subtle differences between the two books manifest themselves. For instance, Machiavelli attributes Girolamo Savonarola's political downfall to different causes in each book. In *The Prince*, Machiavelli calls the friar a prophet who lacked an armed populace he might militarily command to his advantage during a political crisis (P 6). In the *Discourses* he blames Savonarola for disarming the Florentine people *civically*, losing their support by denying them the very opportunity to decide political trials that he had fought so hard to secure for them constitutionally (D I.45).

In *The Prince*, Machiavelli extols Nabis's reign in Sparta as an exemplary *civile principato*, a principality so "civil"—one that enjoys so much popular support—that it is practically a republic (P 9). In the *Discourses*, Machiavelli describes Nabis as a usurper of the Spartan republic, albeit a "tyrant" who enjoyed the friendship of the Spartan people (D I.40). Moreover, Machiavelli presents Cesare Borgia's career differently in the two books: in *The Prince*, Machiavelli casts Borgia as the would-be uniter of Italy (P 7), whereas in the *Discourses* he ultimately demotes Borgia to the mere instrument of Pope Alexander VI's geopolitical strategy on the peninsula (D III.29). It is the Borgia of *The Prince* who figures prominently in what follows.

This chapter investigates the proper role that Machiavelli assigns to leadership in, respectively, a principality and a popular government. Through the example of Pacuvius Calanus (D I.37), I argue, Machiavelli teaches that civic leaders must establish procedures that allow common citizens to prioritize their own political preferences and to render autonomous judgment over important matters of public policy such as the status of elite citizens. I contrast Machiavelli's standards of democratic leadership with what he considers salutary monocratic leadership, typified by Borgia, in a principality. A princely leader like Borgia, Machiavelli suggests, must obscure the manipulation he practices on the people, while a civic leader like Pacuvius encourages the people to "open their eyes" (D I.47)—that is, to fully enlighten themselves about their political priorities. Machiavelli insists that the common people, serving as the "guardian of liberty" (D I.4-5), directly decide over officeholding, lawmaking, and capital trials. Moreover, we will observe how Machiavelli's Pacuvius invites the Capuan people to decide the tenures in office—and even the very lives—of their republic's senators, such that the people may prioritize their preferences regarding domestic and geopolitical policies.

PACUVIUS CALANUS: REFORMING REPUBLICS
THROUGH CAPITAL TRIALS

In *discorso* 47 of book I, Machiavelli introduces Pacuvius Calanus, chief magistrate of the Capuan Republic.[4] Machiavelli deems Pacuvius a "prudent man" who endorses, in an unprecedented way, popular judgment over political trials. He calls Pacuvius a man of superior "quality" (*grado*) who serves a fabulously wealthy, civically tumultuous, and militarily weak republic—much like Machiavelli's Florence—one that exists under the constant threat of invasion by imperial foreign hegemons. Like the 1494–1512 Florentine Republic, which is constantly beset by intense class conflict and frequently threatened by French and Spanish invasions, Capua is on the verge of civil war and trapped between Rome and Carthage during the Second Punic War (216 BCE). The Capuan people are considering deposing the Capuan Senate at the very moment that the city's senior ally, Rome, has suffered an unprecedented defeat by Hannibal at Cannae.

Should he have chosen to do so, Pacuvius could have exploited civil strife and foreign menace to usurp civic authority and become Capua's sole ruler—much like Machiavelli's tyrannical examples of Agathocles, Nabis, and Clearchus (P 8–9; D I.16). Yet, despite Machiavelli's ostensible reputation for advising leaders to maximize their personal power at all costs,[5] he praises Pacuvius for disdaining the opportunity to become a tyrant. Indeed, Pacuvius is one of Machiavelli's principal exemplars for defending a republic's liberty against conquest, tyranny, and license in times of dire crisis.

Pacuvius holds the supreme magistracy while Hannibal's Carthaginian army marches in Capua's vicinity and the common people are poised to take up arms against the senate within the city's walls (D I.47). Invoking the "dangers" of invasion and insurrection, Pacuvius informs the senators that he will empower the people "to punish them so as to save them"—specifically, to save them from "the danger of being killed [by] the collectivity." Indeed, deftly manipulating their greatest fear, he persuades the Capuan senators to permit him to "govern the situation" by "locking them up in their palace." Readers already acquainted with Machiavelli's accounts of, say, Agathocles or Clearchus might find this scenario eerily familiar. Surely Pacuvius, having confined the nobles to the senate house, will now cut them to pieces, gain the support of the people they had previously oppressed, and establish himself as prince. However, Pacuvius adopts a decidedly different approach—one more conducive to maintaining republics than to instituting principalities.

With the senators confined in their chamber, Pacuvius calls an assembly of the people—indeed, like Marcus Menenius, he holds a *concione*. Unlike Menenius, however, Pacuvius aggressively stokes the people's indignation:

he announces that the time is ripe for them to "tame the nobility's pride," enjoining the people "to take vengeance for the harms inflicted on them" by the senate (D I.47). Also, unlike Menenius, Pacuvius puts the nobles rather than himself on trial before the people. He could have, of course, incited the people to storm the senate and murder the incarcerated nobles, as Machiavelli describes the outcome of similar events in Corcyra (D II.2). Instead, radicalizing Machiavelli's previously prescribed procedures for popularly judged political trials (D I.7–8), Pacuvius gives the people the opportunity to eliminate the entire nobility in a formally legal fashion (D I.47).[6]

Pacuvius bids the people to decide, case by case, whether each senator should be executed or exonerated. However, Pacuvius adds a decisive twist: he further suggests that the people should replace each "old senator" they condemn to death with a "new senator" elevated from their own ranks (D I.47). He surmises publicly that the people do not wish to live "without a government," and the people, riled up though they are, do not contest this notion.

As Pacuvius draws and announces the first name, the people erupt, loudly denouncing the particular noble's pride, arrogance, and cruelty; but they fall silent when the magistrate requests the name of a suitable replacement (D I.47). As possible plebeian candidates are eventually voiced, the people engage in noisy debates over the individuals' worthiness for "senatorial status," shouting, whistling, and ridiculing one another over the proposed substitutes. Ultimately, Machiavelli informs us, the people decide to replace *not even one* senator with a citizen from their own ranks, and therefore *not a single* senator suffers execution.

In a speech that Machiavelli attributes to Pacuvius, which does not appear in Livy, the magistrate concludes that the people must, in fact, think the present government is the best available. Moreover, he predicts that the fear the senate has just experienced about being killed by the people will make the nobles "humble and humane" going forward (D I.47). Both classes, Pacuvius announces, are now sufficiently chastened as to be "reconciled with each other": the nobles no longer incorrectly believe they can abuse the people without incurring severe consequences, and the people have been disabused of the erroneous notion that a better government is currently available.

CAN THE PEOPLE RULE? AND EVEN IF THEY CAN, SHOULD THEY?

Machiavelli does not spell out all the implications the Pacuvius/Capua episode has for the relation of leadership to popular government. Commentators often interpret this incident somewhat cynically, and from a rather elitist perspective. The Capuan people, some scholars suggest, are bamboozled by Pacuvius into accepting government generally and this previously abusive senate in particular.[7] Such interpreters understand Machiavelli's lessons to be that the people need to be tricked into accepting government, because they would actually prefer not to be ruled at all; and furthermore that Machiavelli actually approves of government exclusively by nobles—that is, he favors oligarchic rule legitimated by the sham of popular ratification.

The first point is obviously incorrect: Machiavelli never suggests that the people desire not to be *ruled*, or not to be *governed*, as such. On the contrary, time and again he demonstrates that the people want to "taste the well-being" provided by good government, "*buon governo*," as he calls Cesare Borgia's new rule in the Romagna (P 7). In *The Prince*, Machiavelli may declare that the people want to be neither oppressed nor commanded by the *grandi*, but he strongly suggests that they are more than willing to be ruled and commanded by a virtuous prince. In the *Discourses*, Machiavelli abandons altogether the notion that the people resist command by the nobles. In fact, he explicitly enjoins the nobles of republics to command an armed citizenry in military exploits abroad rather than oppress an unarmed populace within their own city's confines. In short, Machiavelli clearly distinguishes between oppression, which the people rightfully resist, and government or command, which they tolerate and even welcome when conducted appropriately.

The second point, that Machiavelli does not really want the common people to participate in ruling, is just as easily refuted: as we have observed, Machiavelli endorses the rise of plebeians to the ranks of supreme command, and he prescribes institutions through which the plebeians collectively and directly exercise rule. As he states, "It was fitting that the plebs had hope of gaining the consulship and then that they actually attained it" (D I.60). Opening the consulship, and later even the dictatorship, to plebeians allowed republics like Rome, in Machiavelli's eyes, to avail themselves of virtue wherever it resides, among both "the nobles and the ignobles" (D I.30). Republics like Sparta, Venice, and even Florence, that fail to arm the plebeians and to elevate them to high command, can never fully tap into popular virtue, whether military or civic.

Ironically, many contemporary self-styled "radical" democrats also suggest that Machiavelli was opposed to the people themselves collectively exercising rule.[8] Inspired by Hannah Arendt, Sheldon Wolin, and Jacques Rancière, adherents of this view are hostile to the notion of "rule" by the people or to institutional approaches to democracy.[9] The people, such scholars aver, should act as agents of contestation against the forces of "rule" (i.e., powerful economic and state actors) but should not themselves rule; doing so renders their actions somehow ethically impure and practically self-defeating. In fact, it signals a co-optation of the people into the matrices of power, a neutralizing of their primordially good, spontaneously expressed political vitality. Moreover, institutional or constitutional analyses—even reform proposals that empower direct popular judgment and rule—are woefully insufficient or downright counterproductive: institutions and laws, on this "radical" view, inevitably serve oligarchic and almost never democratic ends. Democratic moments are simply too rare and uncontainable to be formally regularized in law.[10]

As I have demonstrated more extensively elsewhere, Machiavelli did not adhere to "no-rule" as the normative standard of popular government.[11] In the *Discourses*, Machiavelli not only recommends that the people wield negative claims on rule, accentuated by so-called radical interpreters (including publicly and collectively protesting the senatorial order and wielding veto power on public policy through the tribunes of the plebs), he also endorses the people's positive, constructive, collective participation in government. Departing from the opinion of "all" previous writers (D I.58), Machiavelli argues that well-ordered republics structure themselves so that common people contain, contest, and control the behavior of political and economic elites, *and* that they place the ultimate judgment over legislation and political punishment in the hands of the many and not the few.[12]

Machiavelli explicitly endorses widely participatory, substantively deliberative procedures through which the people refine their judgments over political prosecutions and lawmaking. In historically unprecedented fashion, Machiavelli insists that republics permit common citizens to *initiate* proceedings pertaining to political trials, *propose* new legislation, formally *discuss* among themselves all the matters pertaining to political punishment and lawmaking, and *render* ultimate judgment over each sphere (D I.18). Small committees and councils, according to Machiavelli, prove more susceptible to corruption by or collusion with those partisanly interested in legislation or accused of political crimes. Therefore Machiavelli recommends bodies of "very many judges"—preferably, as in Rome, the whole citizenry—formally assembled, to decide on law and public trials (D I.7-8). In fact, Machiavelli thoroughly *Athenianizes* actual Roman practice when he praises lawmaking in Rome's assemblies:

A tribune, or *any citizen whatsoever*, could propose a law to the people, against or in favor of which every citizen was entitled to speak before a decision was reached. . . . It was good that *anyone* who cared for the public good could propose laws, and that *everyone* could speak their mind on it so that *the assembled people* could subsequently choose what was best. (D I.18; emphases added)

In a famous chapter of the *Discourses* devoted to the "wisdom of the multitude" (D I.58), Machiavelli notes how historians and philosophers often fault the people for inconstancy: for favoring an individual one day, then condemning him another; for pledging alliance to a prince one minute, then cheering for liberty the next. But Machiavelli insists that the standards by which "all the writers" judge the people are unfairly skewed: they consistently compare examples of multitudes "unshackled" by laws with those especially rare examples of law-abiding, and hence "good and wise," princes. The proper comparison, Machiavelli avers, is "a multitude regulated by laws," like the Roman people, with likewise "bridled" princes like those who ruled ancient Egypt, Macedonia, and the France of his day. From this more apposite analysis peoples emerge not merely the equals but the superiors of princes:

> A well-organized people that commands is just as stable, prudent, and grateful as a prince, in fact, *more so* than a prince, even one considered wise; conversely, a prince unshackled by laws will be *more* ungrateful, inconstant and imprudent than a people. . . . [Therefore], I declare that a people is more prudent, more stable and is capable of *better judgment* than a prince. (D I.58; emphases added)

In short, flouting the Spartan-Venetian preferences of the aristocratic republicans of his day, Machiavelli insists that the people both freely discuss and directly decide legislative and judicial matters in their assemblies (D I.18, D I.58, and D III.34).

Thus many contemporary interpreters of Machiavelli fail to capture the full significance of the Pacuvius episode. Machiavelli's point is neither that the people need to be fooled into accepting government per se, nor that they should always submit, wittingly or unwittingly, to exclusive rule by patrician magistrates. Such interpretations of the Pacuvius incident underestimate (1) Machiavelli's ultimate validation of collective popular judgment; (2) the genuine indeterminacy surrounding the people's impending decision over the nobility's lives; (3) the impact of a potential Carthaginian siege of Capua upon the deliberations; and (4) the authentic fear experienced by the Capuan senators.

VALIDATION OF POPULAR JUDGMENT

Machiavelli argues that previous writers, who criticize the people for allowing their passions to interfere with their political evaluations (D I.58), confuse popular *opinion* with popular *judgment*. In the title of 1.47, he seems to associate the former with false general ideas but the latter with more correct particular notions: "Men May be deceived in Generalities but not in Particulars." He admits that the people may claim to want one thing or another—in taverns, in their homes, on the street—but they often choose something quite different when they are formally empowered to deliberate and decide within assemblies. As I will elaborate further below, in *discorso* I.47, Machiavelli insists that formal procedures of judgment compel the people to descend from the "generalities" of their opinions to the "particulars" of their true preferences (D I.47). Under such conditions, the people, according to Machiavelli, will decide matters correctly; they will make good decisions much more often than any similarly empowered prince or group of elites (D I.58).

Institutions that formally empower the people to make decisions themselves, Machiavelli insists, allow them to clarify their preferences and moderate their impulses. On the contrary, circumstances when the people are completely disempowered, or when their only recourse is to ask intermediaries to act for them, are the occasions when they allow themselves to succumb to uncontrolled passions and irrational fancy.[13] Republicans from Cicero to James Madison and beyond empower the people's representatives to serve as the filter through which the people's views are "refined and enlarged." Machiavelli, I argue, insists on institutional arrangements through which the people themselves refine and enlarge their views. Civic leadership, in his estimation, should not substitute for direct popular judgment; rather, it should interact with such judgment to encourage peoples to make civically salutary choices through such arrangements. But the ultimate decision must remain with the people themselves.[14]

For instance, when Coriolanus proposed that the Roman nobility starve the plebs into submission, Machiavelli concedes that the people wanted to tear him to pieces on the Senate steps—an outcome that might have precipitated a civil war (D I.7). However, he insists that the people would have judged Coriolanus's case objectively once the tribunes summoned him to stand before them, formally collected in assembly. Furthermore, Machiavelli admits that the people might have considered following their champion, Manlius Capitolinus, in violent revolt against the Senate (D I.8). But as I mentioned above, when Manlius was tried before a popular assembly for launching unsubstantiated charges against the nobility, the people found him guilty and sentenced him to death (D III.8). Even if the people are party to a political controversy, Machiavelli insists, when formally empowered to render ultimate judgment—when "shackled by laws"—the people decide more objectively than would a prince or the nobles (D I.58).

In the Capua episode, Machiavelli credits Pacuvius with "devising a mode through which the people's eyes could be opened by compelling them to descend from generalities to particulars" (D I.47). The people may think, in general, that some number of nobles should be executed or that members of the common people should replace certain senators in government. But when asked which particular individuals should govern, they come to an altogether different conclusion. Consequently, Machiavelli declares, magistrates ought to follow the example of "a prudent man" (*un uomo prudente*) like Pacuvius and "never evade the people's judgment over particular matters."

In the simplest sense, Pacuvius has motivated the people to descend from the "general" notion that they would like to get rid of their present senators by asking them to choose which "particular" citizen would serve as a superior replacement for any senator they want to depose/execute. To put the people's decision in game-theoretical terms: The extent to which the people can provide "new" replacements for the "old" senators is roughly proportionate to how much they really want to dispense with the present senate. Since the people can provide no "particular" replacements, they have revealed to themselves that their "general" preference was erroneous—or at the very least, much more qualified than they had initially thought. In fact, Pacuvius implicitly asks the people to make *two* intertwined "particular" judgments: (1) which plebeian, particularly, would serve as a better senator than noble X or Y given the (2) "particular" situation in which the city now finds itself. The game-theoretical frame invites the people to add the immediate foreign policy dimension to their calculations of optimal utility.

Along these lines, Pacuvius himself seems to conclude the following about the situation in Capua: If the plebeians are willing to put aside their mortal hatred for the nobles and allow them to continue in office, then they must desire good government more than they desire vengeance. Within the formal confines of what begins as a rather raucous assembly—Machiavelli recounts no Habermasian "ideal speech situation" here—the people eventually, in a more sober fashion, weigh the trade-offs entailed by their various desires: Do they want to govern themselves to the complete exclusion of the nobility, or do they want to benefit from the most optimal form of government viable at the moment? Do they really want to kill senators or merely not be oppressed by them? Moreover, what effect does the proximity of a Carthaginian army, which had just killed 71,000 Roman troops at Cannae, have on the Capuan people's calculations?[15]

GENUINE RISK OF ELITE EXECUTION
OR GUARANTEE OF ELITE EXONERATION?

Nevertheless, a legitimate question must be asked: Has Pacuvius intervened into the people's decision making such that exoneration of the Capuan nobles is a foregone conclusion? It is rather startling that the people choose not to execute even a single especially insufferable senator, if only to make an example of him. This is even more astonishing when one considers that popular revolt was impending before the trial, and that Pacuvius made rhetorical efforts to exacerbate popular indignation at the trial's outset. Does Pacuvius somehow stack the deck in favor of a complete acquittal of the senate by asking the people to replace each sitting senator they condemn with a new plebeian senator? Does Machiavelli think that the senate's security is automatically ensured by this "kill but replace" procedure? If this outcome is guaranteed, then Pacuvius may be said to have denied the people an opportunity to make a genuine choice—to exercise authentic judgment—in these circumstances.

I would address these questions in the following way. Pacuvius might wager that, when faced with the choice he presents to them, the plebeians may defer to the grandeur of individual nobles or demure from voting to have them executed—but there is no way he can be certain of this outcome. Given the intense animosity prevailing between the plebs and the nobles at the moment, the situation is rife with indeterminacy. The situation, I submit, poses a genuine risk to the senators. That Pacuvius himself inflames the people's anger toward the nobles may suggest he thinks it quite possible that they may choose to execute some small number of senators—an outcome he has no great concern about—but, I suspect, he also predicts that they will *not* vote to execute all, or even most, of the sitting senators, for reasons discussed below.

A final note on the risk/determinacy issue: Pacuvius is in no position to unilaterally exonerate the nobles once he grants the people judgment over their fates. If, in fact, the Capuan people had voted to elevate some number of themselves and eliminate some number of senators, he would have had no choice but to enroll the people and execute the senators. Otherwise the people would have surely turned their rage from the nobles to Pacuvius himself. Machiavelli famously faults Savonarola for denying the Great Council its legal authority to serve as ultimate judge over the lives of political criminals (D I.45). Savonarola gained great favor with the Florentine people by securing them such formal authority of capital judgment, but he subsequently lost that favor—and ultimately his life—for denying them the same. Ultimately, legally bound, popular judgment over the lives of *ottimati* is not necessarily, in Machiavelli's estimation, a surefire assurance of their security, let alone their tenure of office.

HANNIBAL AND THE NECESSITY OF ELITE EXPERTISE?

This brings us to the presence of a fearsome Carthaginian army—commanded by Hannibal, no less—in Capua's vicinity (D I.47). This may be the decisive factor that inclines the Capuan plebeians to continue relying on the political experience of their present senators. At the outset, Pacuvius may have wished to persuade the people to temporarily set aside their anger at the overbearing senate and rely on the senators' diplomatic and military expertise in dealing with Hannibal. Yet he prudently realized that the people were simply too furious with the city's domineering elites to entertain such an explicit appeal.

But how does Pacuvius *"aprire gli occhi a' popoli"* such that the people come to see as their biggest problem *not* their own senate, but rather Hannibal—especially without even invoking the terrifying Carthaginian's name? Perhaps each individual plebeian, when faced with the necessity of replacing a sitting senator with either himself or one his neighbors, begins to doubt whether new, inexperienced senators are best equipped to decide an urgently pressing situation: whether Capua should maintain its alliance with Rome and endure a Carthaginian siege, or whether the city should break with Rome, succor Hannibal's troops, and risk incurring merciless Roman retribution in the future. As Machiavelli observes regarding the first secession of the Roman plebs, in dangerous situations that temper an excited people's anger, individuals begin to consider their personal safety, and if flight is not an option they seek reconciliation with those who can best protect them:

> When men's spirits are sufficiently cooled and each one realizes that he must return to his own home, they begin to doubt themselves and to think about their security, either by fleeing or by reaching an accord. Thus, an excited multitude, hoping to avoid these dangers, immediately makes a head from among itself so as to correct it, to unite it, and to consider how best to defend it, as Rome's plebeians did when they exited Rome . . . and created twenty tribunes from among themselves to save themselves. (DI.57)

Pacuvius's "kill but replace" stricture prompts the Capuan people to think less about exploiting the senators' present insecurity about the people and more about their own imminent insecurity in the face of Hannibal. As isolated individuals, they begin doubting their own ability to protect their persons and homes, and they reevaluate the senate's ability to afford them such protection. Despite their anger, then, the fear of Hannibal allows the people to see the (relative) virtues of the senators compared with their own or those of their fellows. The Capuan people do not locate the "head" necessary to defend them within their own ranks, as Rome's plebs do on the Mons Sacer; rather, the Capuan plebeians decide that the "head" best suited to "save them" is at present incarcerated in the senate house.

The interaction of Hannibal's proximity and Pacuvius's injunction that the people provide "new senators" induces the people to think about both pressing geopolitical circumstances and the experience required to address them. It is unlikely that the prospective new plebeian senators fear that they themselves would be put on trial for their lives at some future point under these revised constitutional arrangements; rather, they now worry about the very existence of a senate, a republic, or a Capua should they mishandle the threat of Hannibal.

Pacuvius asks the people, in this urgent geopolitical moment, to provide an alternative yes—an affirmative substitute—if they say no to the life of an individual noble. In so doing, he encourages them to think about government and what it entails rather than simply about vengeance. Had Pacuvius not insisted that the people supply a replacement for any senator they chose to eliminate, it is far more likely that they would have voted to execute one, a few, or some significant number of senators. In Pacuvius's estimation, and presumably in Machiavelli's as well, this would have constituted a shortsighted choice motivated by anger and revenge rather than by concern for prevailing political circumstances.[16] The consequences of eliminating more than a few senators might leave the people decidedly disadvantaged regarding Hannibal. Faced with what is in fact a genuine choice, the people decide to absolve the senators (for the time being) and to avail themselves of their expertise in addressing the Carthaginian threat. In short, fear of Hannibal sharpens the people's minds in the direction of prudence, enhancing their internal deliberations by tempering the hotter, more irrational emotion of hatred that they had previously felt for the nobles.[17]

Machiavelli highlights how, on the one hand, Pacuvius's subtle, indeed silent, explication of political alternatives and, on the other, his deference to popular judgment produced a salutary political outcome—a better outcome than had he attempted to cajole or harangue the people through speech or had used force to achieve his objectives. The senators have been compelled to accept the precedent that they should endure popular judgment over their offices (and lives), and the people have enlightened themselves regarding their own political priorities. Perhaps putting too fine a point on it, in giving the people the opportunity to both execute and replace individual nobles, Machiavelli's Pacuvius effectively asks them to consider which they desire more: freedom from foreign conquest or vengeance against arrogant elites. The choice is entirely their own.

However, lacking such an imminent, dire foreign threat, it is certainly conceivable that the people might have decided that one, some, or many from their ranks should replace individual nobles—if only to eliminate the most egregiously oppressive members of the senate. Machiavelli never suggests that nobles will *always* be exonerated in political trials judged by the people—in fact, quite the opposite. Besides the notable Roman examples where Machiavelli shows that the Roman people would have or in fact did vote to execute Coriolanus and Manlius Capitolinus (D I.7, D I.24, D I.58, D III.1, D III.8), Machiavelli repeatedly laments that Girolamo Savonarola and Piero Soderini failed to try treasonous Florentine nobles for their lives before the Great Council (D I.45, D I.52, D III.3, D III.30). In fact, Machiavelli insists that if Brother Savonarola or Gonfalonier Soderini had mustered the temerity to indict the aristocratic enemies of the Florentine Republic in the Great Council, the assembled people would have readily and appropriately condemned them to death (D I.45, D III.3). Deference, it seems, has its limits.

With this in mind, that the people absolve *all* of Capua's senators is, in my view, something of a red herring. Objectively, it is hardly likely that the republic's ability to deal diplomatically with Hannibal would have been much impaired if a few plebeians had replaced a few dead nobles as senators (even if, subjectively, not one plebeian thought it worth the risk to elect themselves or one of their compatriots to the senate). Machiavelli's more significant point, I believe, is that even under conditions of intense antiaristocratic animosity, a prudent magistrate can encourage the people to think more clearly about, and to prudently reprioritize, what the common good requires at that particular moment. Depending on the circumstances, this will entail either the execution or the exoneration of nobles charged with oppression, treason, or corruption. In the Capuan episode, if Hannibal had not been an immediate threat, then likely several noble heads would have rolled; and even if *all* their heads had rolled, the city would not have suffered terribly, precisely because there was no Hannibal to test and potentially expose the inexperience of the new plebeian senators.

AUTHENTIC ARISTOCRATIC FEAR

This leads us to a final, often underestimated dimension of the Pacuvius episode: stark aristocratic fear. While locking the Capuan senators in their palace, Pacuvius tells them only that they would be "punished" once they were confined, punished to save them from "being killed." But he never informs them that this punishment entails the possibility of them actually being killed—that the punishment he has in mind might in fact be *capital*. Hence Pacuvius's proposal to the people must have come as something of a shock to the nobles. I submit that Machiavelli invites his readers to visualize the following: How many senators soiled their togas when they heard Pacuvius put their lives in the people's hands?

This, I think, is another lesson that Machiavelli's Pacuvius example imparts: He suggests that a republic can endure only when its magistrates and wealthy citizens fear mortal retribution from common citizens. This retribution must be decided collectively through formalized procedures, not exacted through mob violence, and certainly not ordered through unilateral action by a would-be prince. Such outcomes usually spell the end of what Machiavelli calls a free and civil way of life.

Recall how carefully Pacuvius proceeds here: he combines elements from episodes where tyrants like Agathocles and Clearchus (with, respectively, Machiavelli's implicit and explicit approval) eliminate senates in their entirety with elements of electoral politics in popular governments. The Capuan magistrate combines and formalizes the prospect of killing the nobles and popular judgment; in doing so he creates a novel combination of capital trial and general election.[18] The alternative outcomes are not, as is usual for candidates seeking (re)election, public versus civilian rank. Rather, under Pacuvius's procedural innovation, elites confront the dire alternatives of office or death.

In the Capuan civic example, as opposed to the Syracusan and Heraclean tyrannical cases, no armed prince unilaterally decides to kill elites on the people's behalf; rather, the common people themselves decide this question by procedural means. In the Agathoclean/Clearchan model, the nobles face certain death at the hands of an aspiring tyrant; in the Capuan model the outcome could go either way. Whether senators rule or die depends on several factors: the extent of the nobility's previous oppression of the people, the people's level of indignation, and prevailing geopolitical circumstances such as a foreign threat.

Moreover, and this is equally germane, Pacuvius employs popular judgment to prevent himself from becoming a tyrant: even if the people choose to kill some number of nobles, Pacuvius, true to his word, will have "saved" the senate. Because he has called for appointing replacement senators, Pacuvius would find himself confronted by a new senate—albeit one comprising noble senators and plebeian senators: first-generation magistrates, who in both ancient Roman and contemporary Florentine contexts were called "new men" (*uomini nuovi*). Tyrants, Machiavelli intimates in his discussion of the "civil principality," aspire to be "alone" with the people (P 9). Pacuvius, on the contrary, governs in the company of both the assembled people, formally exercising judgment, *and* a senate—old, new, or mixed—whose continued function would be to advise and oversee magistrates such as Pacuvius himself.

Who then is really tricked, fooled, deceived by the Pacuvius episode? It seems to me that readers who complacently take its lesson to be an ironclad guarantee of aristocratic security must be counted among the bamboozled. The appearance of noble advantage in the episode may successfully induce contemporary *ottimati* and their partisans to accept practices enshrining popular judgment—judgment that may not on every occasion yield an outcome favorable to them. Anyone who extols the Pacuvius example based simply on the particular outcome in this instance—aristocratic exoneration—rather than the principles underlying it—popular judgment and elite accountability—would seem to have been captivated by mere appearances. According to the categories Machiavelli establishes in *The Prince*, those who are captivated by mere appearances—whatever their aristocratic pretensions—ought to be counted among "the vulgar" (P 18).

CESARE BORGIA, PRINCELY LEADERSHIP, AND PARTIAL POPULAR ENLIGHTENMENT

As I discussed in previous chapters, in *The Prince* Machiavelli presents Cesare Borgia as Machiavelli's paradigmatic "new prince," whose "ferocity and virtue" nearly enable him to overcome his initial detrimental reliance on fortune (P 7).[19] Machiavelli declares that he can give "no better example" than Borgia, who deceives, bribes, poisons, strangles, and outmaneuvers virtually all those who obstruct his "high intentions" to become the undisputed arbiter of Italy.[20] He considers Cesare a "prudent and virtuous" prince, whom he prefers to call by the exalted title "Duke Valentino," because that's what the common people, "the vulgar," call him (P 3, P 7). Machiavelli famously declares that the people, the vulgar, are impressed above all by "results and appearances" (P 18). Borgia indeed proves to be a master of delivering good results to the people *and* of manipulating appearances for them; that is, he both provides the people with good government and avoids their censure for using unpleasant means to bring about such a salutary outcome. Cesare both benefits the people and confuses them about the modes of his beneficence.

To repeat important aspects of Borgia's career: Machiavelli introduces Cesare as the natural son of Pope Alexander VI (P 3, P 7). The pope provides Cesare with French and mercenary troops that enable him to conquer the Romagna, a province that Borgia finds badly disordered: the local lords prefer "to expropriate rather than correct their subjects," and Machiavelli invokes the crimes, feuds, and insolence that plague the people there (P 7). To help him bring "good government" to the Romagna, Cesare resorts to a "kingly arm": he promotes the "cruel and able" Remirro d'Orco, who almost immediately eliminates the corrupt, petty lords of the region and renders the people "peaceful and united."

It is important to emphasize again that, in Machiavelli's account, before Borgia came to the Romagna, the "*signori impotenti*" had endeavored to rob rather than rule the people. By eliminating these petty yet rapacious lords, Remirro thus gains the "greatest reputation" relieving the people of a considerable inconvenience; but he also imposes on them a rigorous form of rule to which they are entirely unaccustomed (P 7). It seems that the people cannot fully appreciate the welfare they have begun to "savor" under Borgia's rule, Machiavelli avers, because the "rigors" Remirro has put the province through have aroused "some hatred" among them.

Machiavelli explicitly declares that Cesare worries that the malevolent "spirit," the "hatred," that Remirro's "excessive authority" has generated in the people will be directed toward Cesare himself (P 7). Thus Borgia ruminates about what means he might use to show the people who truly ordered the cruelty that oppressed the Romagna: *not* Cesare, but his minister, Remirro (P 7). However, it is plausible to surmise that Cesare is just as concerned about the great reputation that Remirro has acquired for himself as a potential rival to Borgia as he is by the people's hatred for Remirro. Earlier in *The Prince*, Machiavelli insists that anyone who helps another come to power, as Cesare has occasioned Remirro's rise to greatness here, will himself come to ruin (P 3).

Thus Machiavelli prompts readers to consider Borgia's present dilemma: How can he ensure that the people's hatred is directed solely toward Remirro yet guarantee that any great reputation for providing the people with good government accrues exclusively to himself? At this point in Machiavelli's narrative, Borgia is effectively sharing both hatred and greatness with Remirro. To resolve this equivocal situation, Cesare must project onto Remirro not simply "some" of the people's hatred, "*qualche odio*," but *all* of it, *tutto l'odio*. In doing so he can acquire the "greatest reputation" exclusively for himself and gain, as Machiavelli mentions twice, "all the people . . . entirely to himself."

Cesare establishes a court with a respected presiding officer and representatives from all parts of the Romagna (P 7). Initially it seems that the founding of legal and representative institutions will lessen the people's anger over being rendered peaceful and united via Remirro's cruel but effective measures. However, Borgia recognizes that formally rational institutions will prove insufficient to "purge" the people's hateful "spirit." (And certainly Borgia does not want the people to hear any testimony Remirro might give were the duke to put his lieutenant on trial before such a court.) No, he discerns that an extralegal, affectively gripping exhibition is necessary both to purge the people's ill spirit and to definitively settle for them the perplexing dilemmas of hatred and greatness, blame and praise.

Machiavelli unforgettably recounts the subsequent event staged by Borgia: One morning in the town square of Cesena, the people find Remirro in two pieces, *in dua pezzi*, with a bloody knife and a piece of wood beside him (P 7). Machiavelli reports: "This ferocious spectacle at once *satisfied* and *stupefied* the people." How should we interpret this bloody scene, this simultaneously satisfying and stupefying *spettacolo*?

By so spectacularly murdering his minister, Borgia exonerates himself, in the eyes of his subjects, of responsibility for the cruelty that Remirro committed at Borgia's behest; and through meticulous stagecraft he acquires for himself, in their eyes, *all* of the great illustrious reputation he previously shared with Remirro. The people of the Romagna are satisfied with the notion that Borgia alone brought good government, *buon governo*, to the Romagna, but they are also confused over which individual, Borgia or Remirro, was ultimately responsible for the cruelty necessary to establish such good government. As we observed earlier in this chapter, Pacuvius Calanus asks the Capuan people to weigh the consequences of killing nobles they deeply despise. By providing the Romagnol people with the spectacular fait accompli of Remirro's bisected corpse, Cesare himself settles matters for the *vulgo*: Remirro is a hateful, justly mutilated thug; Borgia is the people's deeply revered "Duke Valentino."

Such is the essence of princely leadership for Machiavelli: a prince should take credit for providing tangibly good outcomes to the people; but he should maintain the appearance that someone else is entirely responsible for the unsavory means necessary to deliver such salutary results.[21] This is not to say there are no similarities between Borgia and Pacuvius. Each (in their respectively masterful ways) either purges or aids the purging of the people's hatred. Borgia theatrically redirects the Romagnol people's hatred entirely toward the dead Remirro; Pacuvius procedurally induces the Capuan people to transform their blind hatred for the nobles into prudent fear of Hannibal—precisely by raising the prospect of dead nobles.

Unlike Pacuvius, who effectively asks the Capuan people to choose between Hannibal and their own senators, Borgia makes a crucial decision on behalf of the Romagnol people. He compels them to conclude the following: *Borgia himself* beat down the nobility who misruled the people for so long; *he* ended the arbitrary violence that continually plagued them; and *he* established judicial and representative institutions for them. *Borgia* provided "good government" and allowed them to "savor well-being" (P 7). Moreover, Borgia's bloody execution of Remirro stuns the people into accepting the appearance that Cesare is less than fully complicit in the cruel policies Remirro employed to help deliver good government and well-being. The people know the good ends provided by "Duke Valentino"; they do not know—or choose not to know—that Borgia himself employed evil means to bring them these good results.

CONCLUSION

From Machiavelli's rhetorical efforts in the examples discussed in this chapter we may draw an implicit distinction between tyrants and magistrates: Would-be tyrants like Agathocles and Clearchus order soldiers to kill senators; the soldiers cannot contest these orders, and the senators certainly cannot appeal them. Prudent magistrates like Pacuvius—unlike perhaps imprudent ones like Marcus Menenius, discussed in the previous chapter—ask common citizens to decide whether they want elites to maintain their positions of political prominence or to die. Moreover, such magistrates are obliged to abide by the people's decision, lest they themselves, like Savonarola, become targets of popular rage for denying the people their appropriate role as ultimate judges of political crimes. In this sense an astute leader like Pacuvius seems to practice what Machiavelli preaches throughout the *Discourses*, especially at the start of book III: Pacuvius imitates Brutus's "extraordinary" acts of indicting his sons and their fellow aristocratic conspirators and of presiding over their executions. And in fact he makes these acts "ordinary"; that is, he regularizes political trials of the nobles who threaten popular liberty, trials that may result in executions that, in a most felicitous fashion, bring republics back "to their beginnings" (D III.1–3).

In Machiavelli's view, then, the kind of leadership that is most compatible with popular liberty requires strict and faithful adherence to the principles of formal popular judgment: magistrates must assign more, not fewer, matters—especially those concerning the oppressive behavior of elites—to be decided by the formally assembled people. This applies even or especially to cases where the people may be clamoring to settle matters by violence, outside formal judicial channels. A virtuous leader must remind the people that they make better and more just decisions when they gather, deliberate, and decide in assembly than when they scream and lash out as a disorganized mob in the street. Where such institutional avenues for popular judgment exist, as in Rome and Florence, Machiavelli insists, prudent magistrates should use them; where these procedures do not exist, as in Capua, he implores leaders to introduce them. In most instances, institutions of direct popular judgment produce decisions that are less corrupt, fairer, and more conducive to the health of republics than are either unilateral decisions of princes or collegial-cum-collusive decisions of the few (D I.7–8, D I.58).

Against those who fear that such procedures foster tyrannical rule by demagogues who cynically flatter the people and exploit their anger against the nobility, Machiavelli suggests the following: certainly institutions of collective popular judgment provide opportunities for leaders who consistently indict the nobles to increase their own favor with the people. But they also may serve as powerful checks on such leaders. Machiavelli insists that in republican contexts nobles who survive political trials (as well as friends and family of those who have been executed) may seek formal redress by indicting their erstwhile prosecutors before the people for abuse of power (D I.7–8). Magistrates must then keep this in mind before engaging in frivolous and potentially deadly litigation before the people against the nobles.[22]

To be sure, Machiavelli illuminates the fine line between tyranny and statesmanship that an astute civic magistrate such as Pacuvius must walk when negotiating conflicts between elites and the people: such magistrates must spontaneously satisfy the raw, unrefined appetites of *neither* the nobles *nor* the people. Unlike tyrants like Agathocles or Appius Claudius, who, on their own initiative, either liquidate or accommodate politically obnoxious elites, Pacuvius instead enlists the assembled people as ultimate judges in political trials of overweening elites.

These moderating strains of his analysis notwithstanding, Machiavelli emphatically upholds office or death as the political alternatives that must confront elites if common citizens are to enjoy the liberty promised by republics, and if free regimes are to endure. In Machiavelli's model of popular government only these alternatives will keep the nobles, a social class driven and defined by their humor to dominate, from threatening the liberty of others—and eventually destroying the regime as a whole.

In this sense Machiavelli's examples of senate houses suggest that such structures may prove as conducive to maintaining popular liberty as to celebrating aristocratic privilege and status. In republics like Florence that lack a senate chamber, the plebeians must hunt down the nobles house to house during insurrections such as the Ciompi Revolt. As Machiavelli recounts in the *Florentine Histories*, discussed in subsequent chapters, such behavior results in much physical destruction for the city and few lasting political gains for the people. On the contrary, Machiavelli seems to suggest, common citizens—as well as their civically minded champions—in republics that feature senate houses know exactly where to find wealthy and prominent individuals when aristocratic oppression reaches intolerable levels.[23]

By any reasonable criterion, elites ought to prefer punitive detention within public palaces in republics to the certain fate that awaits the *grandi* under "populist" tyrannies. Machiavelli's imagery conveys the surer and more extreme outcomes they can expect from well-executed tyranny: tyrants will cut to pieces the few—in other words, they will dismember, unmember the few from their exalted status; furthermore, they will partition, divvy up, and distribute the nobility's great wealth among the people. In other words, prudent tyrants like Agathocles and Clearchus will endeavor to make the *grandi piccoli*.

Machiavelli's example of Pacuvius offers readers an instructive metaphor for the appropriate place of elites within republics: The nobles must be confined within their official chamber—that is, their oppressive behavior must be publicly contained, restricted, circumscribed. Whether the nobles continue to enjoy the relatively safe incarceration of office or ultimately lose their lives is a question that virtuous magistrates are prudent enough to put to the formal judgment of the people. But the people themselves, Machiavelli insists, should ultimately decide whether a senate house is to serve as a rather comfortable penitentiary or something approximating an abattoir.

PART 3

IMPRUDENT LEADERSHIP
IN THE *FLORENTINE HISTORIES*

7. FAULTY FOUNDINGS AND FAILED REFORMERS

The Civic Ills of Goodness, Patriotism, and Concord

(GIANO DELLA BELLA, CORSO DONATI,
AND MICHELE DI LANDO)

The *Florentine Histories* is arguably Niccolò Machiavelli's most difficult work. Machiavelli seldom makes entirely clear how he views the conduct of individuals he discusses in the book; he rarely declares unequivocally what political lessons he expects readers to draw from episodes he describes; and he never directly invokes *The Prince* or the *Discourses* to clarify the relation between the relatively straightforward analysis and advice set forth in those works and the more oblique, often contradictory, analyses and lessons offered in the *Histories*.[1] Machiavelli, of course, is renowned for presenting throughout his political writings pertinent information and quasi-historical facts that often qualify or even contravene his own explicit judgments concerning episodes, individuals, social groups, polities, and such.[2] Nevertheless, I venture to say that Machiavelli deploys this often confounding rhetorical strategy much more extensively and subterraneously throughout the *Histories*, making it an even more demanding text to interpret than the already notoriously elusive *Prince* and *Discourses*.[3]

This chapter explores two cases that I believe exemplify the more opaque mode of argumentation Machiavelli pursues in the *Histories*; specifically, his less than transparent presentations of Giano della Bella and Michele di Lando, political leaders who encountered opportunities to become successful founders or reformers of the early Florentine Republic. In the "Dedicatory Letter" of the *Histories*, Machiavelli declares that he assiduously avoids both gratuitous flattery and severe condemnation when assessing the behavior of individual Florentines. Readers will note, he asserts, "how far from adulation [*adulazioni*]" he proceeds, and how diligently he avoids "hateful words [*vocaboli odiosi*]." This turns out to be only partially true: throughout the *Histories*, Machiavelli does indeed eschew overt denunciation when evaluating Florentine political actors, but he quite often indulges in false praise when summing up their careers. In what follows I argue that Machiavelli conceals his profound criticism of Giano and Michele beneath disingenuous expressions of admiration for these two less than successful gonfaloniers of justice.

Machiavelli subtly communicates that, at crucial moments in Florence's history, Giano and Michele were favorably positioned to imitate the modes and orders of Moses, Romulus, and Brutus, ancient founders/reformers whom Machiavelli celebrates in *The Prince* and the *Discourses*. Machiavelli declares in the *Histories* that intense class conflict in his native city could have afforded "a wise legislator" the opportunity "to easily reorder the city in any form of government whatsoever" (FH III.1); and he clearly shows that Giano and Michele stood poised to avail themselves of certain dangerous but advantageous circumstances that they could have exploited for the benefit of their own authority and their city's civic health. Giano and Michele find themselves caught between, as Machiavelli describes such situations in the *Discourses*, "the insolence of the aristocrats . . . and the rage of the people" (D I.16; see P 9). Yet, despite the opportunities afforded them by the extreme social conflicts afflicting Florence, both fail to act in the manner of Machiavelli's previously discussed ancient legislators or reorderers: they fail to spiritedly invigorate new laws and orders with necessary and salutary violence; they neglect to properly manage the "envy" of rival peers; they pursue a harmful "middle way" between elites and the people; and they fail to militarily organize or mobilize all their city's common people (D III.3, D III.30; FH II.13).

According to Machiavelli, the most virtuous princes and magistrates of the ancient world understood that new laws and orders—especially those promulgated to ensure the people's liberty—must be secured in at least two ways: by shedding the blood of "the sons of Brutus," aristocratic abusers of the people and intransigent opponents of founders/reformers (P 6; D III.3, III.30), and by unifying the people in an extensive civic military as Moses and Romulus did, to the great detriment of their cities' external enemies (P 6; D I.9, D III.30).[4] In the *Histories*, Machiavelli suggests that naive or undifferentiated notions of goodness or patriotism prompt Giano and Michele to spurn the common people, to exhibit deference to rapacious elites, and eventually to abandon the city, leaving it worse off than before (FH III, chaps. 13, 17, 22). By shunning recourse to the force necessary to effectively enact their own laws and ensure the enduring welfare of their patria, Machiavelli intimates, Giano and Michele fatefully demur from imitating Romulus, Moses, or Brutus.

If space permitted, I would argue that Machiavelli intends his description of every major Florentine figure in the *Histories* to invite a parallel or contrast with an ancient exemplar from *The Prince* or the *Discourses*. For instance, Corso Donati and Walter Brienne (the Duke of Athens) also enjoy, in Machiavelli's retelling, the possibility of assuming the role of Florentine founder or reformer. However, unlike successful ancient antecedents, each fails to avoid arousing harmful popular hatred rather than productive popular fear, each neglects to organize civic rather than merely sectarian military forces, and each relies too extensively on foreign (French or papal or both) support for his defectively established authority. Moreover, in the cases of Walter and Corso, Machiavelli insinuates that—unlike Giano and Michele, who were naively "good"—a defective notion of self-interested "evil" prevents these tyrannical figures from acting in ways that in the long run might ultimately benefit the city (FH II.21, 33–34).

Throughout the *Histories*, Machiavelli demonstrates how successive Florentine individuals encountered the opportunity to assume the role of a founder like Romulus or a reformer like Brutus: princes or magistrates who confronted, simultaneously, aristocratic insolence and popular rage. Yet each would-be civil prince ultimately declined to adopt the modes deployed by their ancient counterparts; that is, they balked at decisively crushing the nobles and fully arming the people civically and militarily. As a result of such negligence, ignorance, or cupidity on the part of would-be Florentine princes, social conflicts (not only between classes but especially among families, factions, cliques, and parties) continued to persist in more periodically destructive, rather than constructive, ways than they did in ancient republics (P 6, P 8–9, D I.9, I.17, I.40, I.58, II.2, II.12–13). Machiavelli's *Histories* meticulously registers how Florence's faulty orders and flawed leadership result in the city's continued degeneration, measured by rapid geopolitical decline and extensive civic corruption that robust ancient republics managed to correct or forestall.

CONTINUITY THROUGHOUT *THE PRINCE*, THE *DISCOURSES*, AND THE *HISTORIES*

The notion that the *Histories* ought to be read in light of *The Prince* and the *Discourses* is an increasingly controversial position within Machiavelli scholarship. Accepted wisdom dictates that the *Histories* manifests a decisive break in Machiavelli's intellectual corpus; that it represents a dramatic shift over several fundamental aspects of his political theory.[5] Here I wish to challenge one crucial strand of this now hegemonic interpretation: specifically, the insistence that the *Histories* largely abandons the emphasis on individual political actors that so pervades Machiavelli's earlier writings.

I will show that the *Histories* still delineates, albeit less overtly, the ways Machiavelli, in *The Prince* and the *Discourses*, advises potential founders or reformers to take advantage of the opportunities that fortune always presents to political actors—especially opportunities generated by conflicting social forces that Machiavelli, in previous works, insisted were characteristic of "every polity" (P 9; D I.4).

In an important article, John Najemy established a then novel and today ever more influential approach to comprehending Machiavelli's *Histories* and addressing the hermeneutic challenges the book poses.[6] Najemy observed, quite rightly, that no founders, lawgivers, or princely redeemers emerge from the pages of the *Histories*—certainly no successful ones. Furthermore, Najemy argued that Machiavelli indicates within the work that he harbors neither hopes nor expectations (retrospectively applied to the events and actions he conveys) that a princely or civic reformer could have emerged in Florence to reorder the city in anything approaching a successful and salutary way.[7] According to the new understanding of power, politics, and history that Machiavelli purportedly evinces in the *Histories*, any and all effective refounding or reforming of the Florentine Republic, in our author's estimation, supposedly remained far beyond the capabilities of any particular individual.[8]

I will challenge the thesis that the *Histories* exhibits a significant change in Machiavelli's expectations regarding the political capacities of individual actors, while also taking into account the broader interpretive difficulties the work poses. I argue that just because in the *Histories* Machiavelli never shows any individual Florentine to have successfully assumed the role of founder or reformer, this does not imply that he thinks no such figures could or should have energetically endeavored to do so. In fact, as quoted above, Machiavelli explicitly declares that a wise legislator *could* have reordered Florence in a beneficial manner—whether as a principality or as a republic (FH III.1). On my reading, Machiavelli indicates that Giano della Bella and Michele di Lando enjoyed ample opportunities to proceed in the mode of the ancient founders and reformers discussed in *The Prince* and the *Discourses*; and he precisely if subtly delineates how the two Florentine would-be civic princes each failed to successfully imitate his ancient exemplars.

It is worth noting that Machiavelli never declares in the *Histories* that he has changed his mind about how he thinks princes, founders, reformers, and magistrates ought to behave generally, or about how he thinks they ought to act toward elites and peoples, whose conflicts, he insists, characterize all political regimes. Indeed, given that Machiavelli seriously intimates that a comprehensive conceptual unity undergirds his entire intellectual oeuvre, I will argue that the political prescriptions that so dominate *The Prince* and the *Discourses* must be taken just as seriously in the

Histories as are certain statements in the latter book that may seem to contradict them.[9]

With this in mind, Najemy's assertion that the *Histories* signals Machiavelli's abandonment of the leadership lessons presented in *The Prince* and the *Discourses* is suspect for this reason: the failures of the Florentine protofounders Machiavelli discusses in the *Histories*, especially Giano and Michele, correspond so closely to the failures of more recent Florentine figures, such as Girolamo Savonarola and Piero Soderini, whom Machiavelli has already criticized in his earlier writings. In *The Prince* and the *Discourses*, Machiavelli insists that the potential Florentine founders and reformers Savonarola and Soderini could and should have attained political success by recourse to modes more prudent and virtuous—that is, modes more ruthlessly violent, conventionally immoral, and antiaristocratic—than those they actually pursued.

Therefore, without explicit instructions from Machiavelli, I contend that contemporary readers of the *Histories* ought not assume, as so many now do, that Machiavelli came to believe that failed founders or reformers like Giano and Michele had no other option, no other choice, than to act in the unwisely good (or, in the case of Corso Donati, imprudently evil) ways that they actually did historically. Or, for that matter, that Machiavelli had fundamentally changed his morally unconventional notions either of how new princes or reforming magistrates ought to secure their rule or of "good and evil" as such. The primary difference between Machiavelli's famous treatments of failed Florentine founders/reformers like Savonarola and Soderini in *The Prince* and the *Discourses* and his less renowned depictions of Florentine figures like Giano and Michele in the *Histories* is this: in the earlier works Machiavelli readily supplies ancient examples as explicit interpretive counterpoints, and in the later book he omits such ancient/modern comparisons/contrasts. But this does not mean such parallels and contrasts are not still very much implied in the *Histories*.

I suggest that Najemy and those who share his assumptions concerning the *Histories* confuse the descriptive and normative levels of Machiavelli's narrative in the work; that is, they mistakenly interpret Machiavelli's historical descriptions and, more understandably, his evaluative statements as if they always tightly corresponded with each other, and as if they were identical with Machiavelli's actual, more fundamental normative aspirations or intended political prescriptions. This is to some extent comprehensible, given the hermeneutic difficulties posed by the *Histories* that I mentioned above. However, as I will demonstrate, Machiavelli's aspirations and prescriptions are deeply entrenched within his historical narrative, and they unfold, without explicit editorializing on Machiavelli's part, within his account of long-term historical trends.

Indeed, I will show that Machiavelli's ultimate judgments of individual political actors like Giano and Michele cannot easily be equated with the laudatory declarations that accompany his accounts of their political careers in the *Histories*. Rather, his definitive evaluations of Giano and Michele are communicated with greater veracity in the following ways: first, through minute, seemingly incidental details that Machiavelli provides as he recounts their conduct—details whose full significance he leaves readers to divine. (For instance, Why does Michele appoint himself rector of Empoli during his term as Florentine gonfalonier?). And, second, through Machiavelli's descriptions of the deleterious political circumstances that ensued as a direct result of each figure's actions (or lack thereof), which he expects readers to notice and reflect on. (For instance, What do the tyrannical exploits of Corso Donati say about Giano's political choices, which immediately preceded them?)

Readers, I contend, must consider the specific details and concrete outcomes of Giano's and Michele's political efforts, which substantively undermine Machiavelli's own declared, largely admiring assessments of their careers. Machiavelli employs the very opposite of "hateful words" when assessing their actions, but on careful reflection a denunciatory narrative of their behavior eventually emerges. Machiavelli's narrative ultimately undermines his ostensible praise of their leadership. In short, to ascertain his definitive evaluations of individual leaders and his actual normative prescriptions for political leadership in the *Histories*, readers must accentuate within Machiavelli's narrative facts over opinion, deeds over words, and verbs over adjectives. I proceed by privileging his descriptions of actions and outcomes over his declared judgments, revealing important discrepancies between word and deed in the *Histories*. Furthermore, my comparisons/contrasts to Machiavelli's examples of ancient founders/ reformers sharpen his critique, illuminating precisely how far short Giano and Michele fall of Machiavellian standards of leadership. Ultimately, I insist, one must cross-reference the outcomes of Machiavelli's narration of facts, deeds, and concrete results—effectual truths, if you will—with his more explicit declarations regarding political leadership in *The Prince* and the *Discourses*.[10]

MOSES, BRUTUS, AND ROMULUS: EXEMPLARY ANCIENT FOUNDERS/REFORMERS

To establish the framework through which I believe Machiavelli wishes readers of the *Histories* to assess the individual actors he describes between its covers, let me briefly recapitulate his accounts of the ancient founders/reformers, discussed in parts 1 and 2 of this book, to whom he devotes the most time and space in *The Prince* and the *Discourses*: Moses, Brutus, and Romulus. Moses serves as one example of Machiavelli's most virtuous princes, an individual who made himself "happy" and his patria "very happy" by eliminating the "envy" of rivals who sought to thwart the enactment of his new laws and orders; in fact, Machiavelli stresses that Moses kills "an infinite number" of envious men in order to bring about such felicitous outcomes for himself and his people (P 6; D III.30).[11] Brutus, Machiavelli notes, led the aristocratic revolt that expelled the Tarquin kings from Rome, established the civic magistracy of the consuls to take up kingly imperium within the republic, then oversaw the prosecution and execution of his own sons and their fellow conspirators among young nobles, who sought to overturn the republic, reinstitute the monarchy, and intensify their own oppression of the Roman people (D I.16, III.1, III.3, III.5–6).

Machiavelli unhesitatingly apologizes for the crimes of Romulus, who murdered both his brother and his coregent so that he could more efficiently rule alone and enact laws and orders conducive to "the collectivity's benefit" and "the civic way of life" (D I.2, I.9). Specifically, Romulus prudently ordered the natural antagonism between the great and the people as it manifested itself in Rome. He assembled members of the wealthiest and most prominent Roman families in the Senate and collected all of Rome's poor citizens into a unified public army. The institutionalized competition between an aristocratic Senate and a plebeian army, Machiavelli intimates, kept the nobles and the people more unified among themselves, so that each group did not split into the "unnatural" antagonisms, such as the Guelf/Ghibelline, Black/White Guelf, *popolo/plebe* oppositions, that perpetually plagued Florentine politics. Furthermore, these arrangements encouraged the institutionalized class competition or "tumult" between the nobles and the people that, after the reigns of Romulus's royal successors, resulted in the establishment of a magistracy that made Rome "more perfect": the plebian tribunate.

In short, all three of these ancient princes, in one way or another, kill or contain "the sons of Brutus," Machiavelli's generalized term for the aristocratic common enemy of founders/reformers and poor subjects and citizens. Moreover, all three either expand or maintain a robust civil military comprising a widely armed citizenry. These are not the only steps that, Machiavelli suggests, a founder/reformer must take in ordering or renewing a city. Were this the case, the *Discourses* would be a much shorter work, and the already brief *Prince* even briefer. Nevertheless, his accounts of the actions of Moses, Romulus, and Brutus provide the basic blueprint. Crucially for our purposes, none of the Florentine leaders Machiavelli discusses in the *Histories* proceed fully in the modes of these ancient princes or establish comparable orders when presented with manifest opportunities to do so. As I will demonstrate, the sociohistorical circumstances that confront Giano and Michele very much recall the opportunities seized by Moses, Romulus, and Brutus—opportunities that, again, resulted in the "happiness" of these founders/reformers and their people. As we will observe, Machiavelli often praises the patriotism and goodness of the failed Florentine founders/reformers in demurring from fully taking up the violent modes of Moses, Romulus, and Brutus.[12] But because Machiavelli never repudiates his earlier resoundingly explicit endorsements of the conduct of such ancient founders and reformers, I judge the *Histories* to function as an implicit but nevertheless severe criticism of Florence's excessively "good" would-be princes.

GIANO DELLA BELLA: FOUNDER OF NEW ORDERS? FATHER OF FLORENCE'S FREEDOM?

The first figure to emerge in the *Histories* with the prospect of acting as a Florentine founder or reformer is Giano della Bella. Giano appears during a period of rapid institutional innovation inspired by intensifying social conflict between the Guelf and Ghibelline nobles and by egregious acts of oppression on the part of the entire nobility toward members of the people—especially toward common citizens enrolled in commercial and artisan guilds (FH II.12–13). By standards set forth by Machiavelli in the *Discourses*, the institutions the Florentines devised to address these tumultuous circumstances are very imperfect: Florence adopts neither an aristocratic senate nor a plebeian tribunate; it observes no popularly judged political trials; and its terms of office are a meager two months rather than a full calendar year.

Nevertheless, imperfection does not pose the gravest problem for the various institutions auditioned by the Florentine people in these circumstances; such innovations may have proved relatively workable had only a Florentine individual of virtue stepped forward to "invigorate" them in the manner that, as Machiavelli insists in the *Discourses*, all "new modes and orders" require (D I.17, D III.1). He declares that in corrupt cities "even well-ordered laws are useless lest they be *invigorated with extreme force* by one individual who ensures compliance such that those who are corrupt become *good*" (D I.17; emphases added). Furthermore, Machiavelli reemphasizes this warning later in the work when he insists that laws neither institute themselves nor automatically become effective: orders and laws that "oppose men's *ambition and insolence* must be invigorated by a *virtuous citizen* who runs *spiritedly* to enforce them against the power of their transgressors" (D III.1; emphases added). Giano, notwithstanding Machiavelli's apparent praise, will prove to be woefully ill-adapted to the kind of spirited institutional invigoration that makes ambitious and insolent men good citizens.

Machiavelli begins book II, chapter 11 of the *Histories* by reporting how the Guelf nobles, after exiling many Ghibelline nobles in about 1291, became "insolent" toward the people (FH II.11). Much as the Roman nobles began "to spit their poison" on the Roman people once the Tarquin kings were expelled (D I.3), the Guelf nobles, in the absence of their Ghibelline foes, return to expressing their natural desire to dominate the common people. The powerful institution of the Guelf Party, a kind of shadow government in Florence, rendered the republic's civic institutions impotent, so that the nobles "felt no fear of the magistrates" (FH II.11). Machiavelli recounts numerous acts of murder and physical intimidation perpetrated by the great at this time, offenses that went unpunished because the perpetrators were "favorites" (family, friends, clients) of powerful nobles (FH II.11).

In these circumstances of revived and intensified aristocratic oppression, the people eventually entrusted the guilds with the task of reordering the city's government to the nobles' disadvantage. The nobles, Machiavelli suggests, at first acquiesced to the creation of a new chief executive magistracy, the Signoria, which included only the common people and a few aristocrats enlisted in guilds, because most of the nobles were preoccupied by the Guelf/Ghibelline conflicts still raging among themselves (FH II.11). However, Machiavelli reports that the Signoria failed to prevent individual noblemen from continuing "to injure someone from the people daily" (FH II.12). Retribution for such offenses, let alone deterrence, was unavailable to the Florentine people under the new government of the Signoria because "every noble managed to defend himself through family and friends" against the authority of the priors and the captain of the people (a foreign judge imported to the city annually), "such that neither laws nor magistrates provided redress" (FH II.12). In short, abuse by the nobles and collusion among them prevented the institutions of the republic—specifically, its executive committee and its preeminent judicial official—from upholding freedom and justice.

To rectify this situation, the guilds created, as head of the Signoria, the gonfalonier of justice, a guildsman armed with a thousand soldiers, an office that, Machiavelli recounts, initially terrified the nobles (FH II.12). But he then reports that the nobles' natural insolence returned when they realized how easily any noblemen enrolled in a guild who happened to be sitting as a prior in the Signoria could, at any moment, block the gonfalonier from acting against one of their own. Moreover, the nobles soon learned they could readily intimidate the witnesses who were necessary to substantiate the charge of an accuser from testifying against a member of the great. Thus, Machiavelli reports, the nobles quickly returned to disorderly conduct among themselves and abusive behavior toward the people because the republic's judges proved excessively slow and lenient in imposing judicial sentences (FH II.12).

The figure of Giano della Bella arose, according to Machiavelli, amid the popular despair resulting from these circumstances in which the nobles, with continued impunity, increased their oppression of the people. Giano is elected Florence's chief magistrate, the gonfalonier of justice, at the very moment when the republic's new institutions, the gonfalonier and the Signoria, much like its traditional judicial magistracies, the podestà and the people's captain, proved excessively susceptible to intimidation and corruption by the city's nobility (FH II.12–13). Machiavelli writes that although Giano himself descended from a "very noble" family, he was nevertheless a "lover of the city's freedom" (FH II.13). Giano encouraged the guild leaders to yet again reform the city's government, now in this way: the gonfalonier of justice would live with the members of the Signoria during their concurrent terms of office, and the number of soldiers at his command would be increased from one thousand to four thousand; the nobles would be declared entirely ineligible to serve within the Signoria as priors; the accomplices of any individual accused of criminal acts would be subject to exactly the same punishment as the indicted offender; and a public report of a crime, unsupported by witnesses, would henceforth be sufficient for imposing a criminal sentence on any accused individual.

Once this collection of laws, known as the "Ordinances of Justice," was passed, Machiavelli writes, the people gained greater authority in the city and Giano incurred the intense animosity "of the powerful citizens and the richest guildsmen"—that is, the hatred of both the Guelf nobles and the wealthiest of the people (FH II.13). The former despised Giano for diminishing their political influence and capacity to oppress; the rich *popolani* envied him as one among themselves who had gained inordinate authority. Giano and the common people hence become the objects of the "envy" that Machiavelli previously attributed to the sons of Brutus and to elite adversaries of the founders of new modes and orders (P 6; D I.40, I.52, III.3, III.30). The sons of Brutus, Machiavelli explains, resent institutions that guarantee popular liberty, understanding that they diminish their own freedom; and the partisans of old orders invariably become jealous of an individual who acquires the authority to introduce new laws (P 6). These partisans will generally enlist "the magistrates" in their efforts to block or roll back such reforms. In the words Machiavelli deployed in the *Discourses* (D I.16), the new guild republic certainly has "partisan enemies": first, the nobles who, like Brutus's sons, wish to continue molesting the people without institutional restrictions; and second, the envious rivals of a founder/reformer like Moses or Giano, who seek to halt enactment of new laws and orders.

However, perhaps unlike the early Roman Republic, the guild republic most decidedly *does* enjoy what Machiavelli calls "partisan friends" (D I.16): as Machiavelli will show, the Florentine people, perhaps more virtuously than the Hebrews or the Romans, rush to defend themselves and Giano, their champion, as well as his new laws. As we will observe in Machiavelli's account, the Florentine people spontaneously, and even before any figurative sons of Brutus are executed, rush to Giano's defense. In fact, Giano will have the opportunity to become a Moses or a Brutus with even more overt popular support than those two figures initially enjoyed—but he ultimately elects not to avail himself of this opportunity. As Machiavelli declares in the *Discourses*: "He who governs a multitude either through the way of freedom or through a principality, who does not secure himself against the enemies of the new order, establishes a very short-lived state" (D I.16). In those passages and others, Machiavelli insists that the founders and reformers of, most especially, republics must secure themselves and their new laws by killing the sons of Brutus at the first opportunity; and, as if on cue, the enemies of Giano's orders give him the opportunity to eliminate them almost immediately.

Soon after the Ordinances of Justice are established and, unfortunately, soon after Giano's requisitely short two-month term as gonfalonier, Machiavelli recounts how a gang of nobles, among whom was Corso Donati, murdered a guildsman in a street fight (FH II.13). Corso, as the boldest among the nobles present, took the blame for the entire incident and was arrested by the captain of the people. But Corso was soon freed, Machiavelli explains, either because he was innocent or because the captain was afraid to convict him. (Machiavelli's subsequent recounting of Corso's career suggests he was more than capable both of committing such a murder and of threatening the captain.) The people were outraged at Corso's acquittal: yet again, no matter what institutional reforms the city undertakes, the nobles, in the people's estimation, continue to—literally—get away with murder. The people spontaneously arm themselves and rush to Giano's house, entreating him—in terms that recall the *uno solo* whom Machiavelli insists must resort to violence to enforce his new modes and order—"to be *the one* to ensure that the laws that he authored be followed" (FH II.13; emphasis added).

Machiavelli calls Giano a lover of liberty; moreover, he shows that he is spirited enough to propose the Ordinances of Justice and to carry them out during his term as gonfalonier. Presumably then, Giano, like the people, wanted the laws he initiated to gain force and longevity. Machiavelli also notes that Giano "desired the punishment of Messer Corso"—but he does not say whether this is because Giano believed such punishment would serve justice or because he wished to eliminate a rival to his authority in the republic. The more pressing question is, Will Giano act as Florence's Romulus or Moses—each of whom, Machiavelli has previously told readers, famously killed rivals, with felicitous results for themselves and their own authority, to benefit their peoples and to ensure that their new laws and orders would endure in perpetuity (P 6; D I.9, D III.30)?

Whatever his motivations, Giano proves indecisive; furthermore, he sends the people a mixed message. He encourages them to pursue the proper legal course by proceeding to the Signoria and pleading for a reconsideration of the case; but he does *not* insist that the people disarm themselves before doing so, as his adversaries thought he should have done (FH II.13). No doubt the nobles and the wealthy *popolani* who feared and resented Giano's reputation with the people are alarmed to see the people assembled at Giano's house bearing arms.

Giano's behavior here, Machiavelli writes, only inflamed the people's indignation: they thought the captain's "offense" against them had now been compounded by Giano's "abandonment" of their cause (FH II.13). They therefore disobey Giano, abjuring the procedurally legal route he recommended; instead, they exact vengeance on the captain by ransacking his *palazzo*. Giano's enemies, who already desire his ruin, quickly blame him for the incident and set in motion the events that lead to his exile.

One might conclude that here Giano seems to take one of Machiavelli's dreaded "middle ways." As Machiavelli observes in the *Discourses*, "men often take very harmful middle ways, not knowing how to be completely wicked or completely good; too often they know not how to be evil in an honorable way or good in a perfect way. Thus, they demure from the former even when evil portends true greatness or at least partial generosity" (D I.26-27). By acting in an honorably evil fashion, Giano could have acquired "true greatness" for himself as Florence's Romulus, Moses, or Brutus—as something like "the father of Florence's liberty." Moreover, he could have exhibited more than "partial generosity" to the people by punishing or perhaps eliminating their aristocratic oppressors. Both Giano and the people would have benefited immensely had he given vitality to the already established laws that would have substantively protected the people well into the indefinite future. Recall Machiavelli's declarations: "Well-ordered laws are useless lest they be invigorated with extreme force by one individual who ensures compliance" such that insolent and corrupt individuals "become good" (D I.17); and orders and laws that "oppose men's ambition and insolence are invigorated by a virtuous citizen who runs spiritedly to enforce them against the power of their transgressors" (D III.1).

Thinking back to both Machiavelli's earlier praise of successful ancient founders and reformers (Romulus, Moses, and Brutus) and his previous criticisms of failed Florentine princes (especially Savonarola, Valori, and Soderini) in *The Prince* and the *Discourses*, exactly what should Giano have done in these circumstances? Several alternatives to Giano's "middle way" are available to the former gonfalonier. Giano could have led the armed people to the Signoria or to the captain's palace and insisted that either of them arrest Corso and prosecute him anew. Moreover, recall that under the Ordinances of Justice, *all* the nobles who were in Corso's company on the night of the murder were eligible to be indicted and punished on the same charge—without need for witnesses. Therefore Giano could have taken this opportunity to indict and try *all* the offending parties among the nobility—not just Corso but perhaps even all those who were outspoken opponents of the Ordinances of Justice as well.

These alternative modes of proceeding conform in spirit to the actions of Brutus, who followed legal channels in prosecuting and overseeing the execution of his treasonous sons and their fellow young aristocrat conspirators, who sought to overthrow the Roman Republic (D III.3). Of course, Brutus enjoyed the luxury of still serving as consul at the very moment when he pursued the prosecution of his sons. Giano, because of Florence's excessively short terms of office, is no longer gonfalonier, so he must necessarily act somewhat extralegally in pursuing the retrial and prospective execution of Corso (and perhaps of his noble accomplices as well).

But Machiavelli does not rule out such quasi-legal or extralegal measures when strictly legal ones prove unavailable. Recall from chapters 3 and 4 his thoughts on the legal and extralegal options open to Soderini as he faced the necessity of eliminating the envy of the sons of Brutus—literally, the young pro-Medici nobles who opposed the 1494 Republic. In the *Discourses* Machiavelli concedes that it would have been convenient if Soderini could have dealt with them through ordinary modes; but if that was not a genuine possibility, then he should have explored extraordinary means (D III.1).

Alternatively, Giano could have pursued the "perfectly good," as opposed to "honorably evil," course of action—an entirely different approach that still would have enabled him to avoid taking a "harmful middle way" in these circumstances. He could have insisted that the people, in his presence and at his house, immediately disarm and then peaceably proceed to the Palazzo della Signoria and entreat the priors to revisit Corso's case. Machiavelli is in general not particularly sympathetic to leaders who disarm their people, as his judgments of the Roman emperors (P 19), Louis XI (P 13), and Cosimo de' Medici (FH IV.27, FH VII.6) bear out. But at least Giano, in this case, would have freed himself of the suspicion of harboring tyrannical intentions—raised by his enemies and rivals among Florence's elite—as well as depriving them of the opportunity to falsely charge him with starting a riot.

More radically, though, Giano might have led the armed people to the Signoria and demanded that the present gonfalonier resign so that Giano, the author of the magistracy in its present form, could reassume the office under the present emergency circumstances, then call to arms the four thousand soldiers under his command as gonfalonier. He could then have pursued whatever course he deemed necessary to "invigorate" the magistracy of the gonfalonier and the "Ordinances of Justice," as well as to ensure the security of the people against the "sons of Brutus": that is, any of the oppressive nobles and rich *popolani* who opposed both the magistracy and the laws. By Machiavelli's ancient standards this very likely would have entailed killing not only Corso, but also whichever nobles and *popolani* vehemently envied Giano's authority. This is reminiscent of the mode through which Moses eliminated "infinite" envious competitors for his authority, in the process making himself "happy" and his patria "very happy" (P 6; D III.30). It is also akin to the extraordinary means that Machiavelli hints his former boss Soderini should have deployed against the "sons of Brutus" who envied his authority and despised "the collectivity" with whom Soderini held so much favor (D III.3). Had he taken these actions, Giano would have become prince or first citizen, one who is "alone" at the head of an enlarged armed citizenry, the *uno solo* who could remake the Florentine constitution in any mode he saw fit.

Returning to Machiavelli's account of Giano's short, ineffective, but still noteworthy political career: soon after the incident at Giano's house, one of his detractors is appointed prior and formally accuses Giano as a rabble-rouser to the captain (whose house, recall, had been sacked in the recent popular riot) (FH II.13). The people may have initially resented what they interpreted as Giano's abandonment of their cause, but they seem completely disposed to forgive him. On hearing news of Giano's indictment, the people again arm themselves and rush to his house to defend him against not only the Signoria or the captain, but also, Machiavelli emphasizes, against all of his "enemies" more generally—that is, against the nobles and rich *popolani*. Fortune, the saying goes, knocks only once; the people, Machiavelli seems to suggest, are more than willing to ring twice.

In Machiavelli's account, the Florentine people spontaneously pledge to support Giano against his rich and powerful accusers, but Giano demurs. Machiavelli writes, "Giano wished neither to test his popular favor nor entrust his life to the magistrates, fearing the former's instability and the latter's malice" (FH II.13). Like many flawed, especially modern, popular champions whom Machiavelli criticizes in *The Prince* and the

Discourses—such as Virginius, Savonarola, Valori, and Soderini—Giano reveals that he does not fully trust the people, whose cause he supposedly promotes (D I.44, I.45, III.3, III.30). All popular champions who signal distrust of the people's judgment and fidelity this way wind up as catastrophic political failures. The Roman centurion Virginius refused to let the people judge the capital trial of the deposed tyrant Appius Claudius (D I.45); Savonarola and Valori refused to permit the people to decide the judicial cases against the pro-Medici enemies of the 1494 Republic (D I.45; I.7). Likewise, Soderini, Machiavelli explains, did not trust the people to properly evaluate whatever extraordinary actions he might have been compelled by necessity to take against the Florentine "sons of Brutus" (D I.52, III.3, III.30).

As we saw Machiavelli stress in the *Discourses*, unlike the Romans, the Florentines did not have (or did not consistently employ) popularly judged trials, which, he argues, rendered more objective and effective sentences than did Florentine judicial institutions, whether foreign rectors like the Podestà and the Capitano, or small councils like the Signoria or the Eight of Ward (D I.7–8). Machiavelli suggests that Valori and Soderini should have been tried for ambition or abuse of power by their aristocratic enemies before the people assembled in the Great Council, rather than suffering aristocratic conspiracies that resulted in their murder or exile and the collapse of the entire republic.

Here in the *Histories*, Giano fears that his enemies among the nobles and rich *popolani* in the guilds will sway either the captain or the Signoria against him, and that the people—despite two vivid examples to the contrary—will prove to be merely an inconstant source of support. Yet in *The Prince* Machiavelli claims that only those individuals who depend on a disorganized and unarmed people, as did Giorgio Scali or the Gracchi, "build on mud" when anticipating promised popular support (P 9). On the contrary, individuals like Giano who enjoy an armed, enthusiastic people at their backs are afforded many intriguing possibilities should they decide to take up the vocation of founder or reformer.

In his final estimation of Giano, Machiavelli does not merely intimate that the former gonfalonier was a hypocrite and a coward. He certainly emphasizes Giano's fear of injury at the hands of his enemies; but he also invokes Giano's seemingly sincere desire to keep his supporters/friends, presumably the people, from "harming their patria" (FH II.13). Such fears, of course, never inhibited the likes of Moses, Romulus, and Brutus. The more reserved Giano believes that leaving the republic improperly or incompletely ordered is more "patriotic" than is risking greater disorder in the effort to decisively set its affairs in order. So Giano capitulated to his enemies' "envy," unlike Romulus, Brutus, or Moses and very much like Savonarola and Soderini, hoping to ameliorate their "fear" of him.

Like Soderini after him, Giano "departs" from the city, voluntarily opting for exile. Machiavelli seems to praise Giano, deeming his efforts effective and his motivations good; he writes that Giano "left the city" a polity that "he freed from subjection to the powerful through careful and dangerous actions" (FH II.13). However, entirely different conclusions are in order given, on the one hand, Machiavelli's previous advice to would-be princes throughout *The Prince* and the *Discourses*, and, on the other hand, his description, in the *Histories*, of subsequent rampant oppression of the Florentine people by the city's *potenti*, including Corso Donati. Giano did not prudently or effectively "free" Florence from aristocratic oppression, nor were his modest actions either sufficiently prudent or audacious. Giano's actions, in fact, left Florence worse off than before. What Machiavelli writes of Soderini in the *Discourses* applies equally to Giano, his predecessor as gonfalonier of justice: "one ought never permit an evil to run wild by adhering to a good, when precisely such a good could be so readily destroyed by that very evil" (D III.4).[13] As Machiavelli's *Histories* makes painfully evident, Corso Donati and his noble confederates, whom Giano failed to see effectively punished, will soon become the personification of evil run wild.

In the *Histories*, Corso becomes the chief agent of virtually every one of the many civil disturbances, political controversies, foreign interventions, exiles, and deaths that ensue between Giano's peaceful departure and the violent end of Corso's even more violent life (FH II.13–23). Eventually, after fourteen years of Corso's wreaking havoc on the republic, the same magistracies that in 1294 failed to convict him for murder, the Signoria and the people's captain, in 1308 finally sentence him to death for conspiring to become tyrant of the city (FH II.23). Machiavelli seems to suggest that if only, at Giano's and the people's insistence, these magistracies had originally sentenced Corso to death, the city would have been spared countless convulsions and copious blood and tears. The failure to use cruelty "well," that is, "at a stroke," Machiavelli explains in *The Prince*, often ensures that even greater cruelty will proliferate in ever more ugly and unpleasant ways for years to come (P 8, P 17). Machiavelli intimates the following in his accounts of both Giano's and Corso's careers in the *Histories*: if only Giano, who loved liberty and his patria, were slightly more like Corso—a man of rare "virtue" and a "restless," if "indecent," spirit—the city would have been better off. The reverse also appears to be true: if only Corso had been motivated by a bit more of the goodness that inhered within Giano, Florence would have been a more stable and freer republic.

Ultimately, Giano winds up like Scipio Africanus, an illustrious statesman who, Machiavelli reports, voluntarily exiled himself because elite citizens suspected him of tyrannical motivations, rather than availing himself of his favor with the common people in an effort to repudiate or destroy his (and their) aristocratic rivals (D I.29). Giano is the quintessential "good man" who will not take up the ways of a "bad man" in the effort to reorder his republic in a necessary and beneficial way (D I.17). The unpunished Corso, as Machiavelli shows in subsequent chapters, becomes the classic bad man who, despite a certain "virtue," does not know how to do the good things that bring security to his patria and reputation to himself; who instead continues to maraud among the people and instigate civil discord until the very end of his very "restless" life (FH II.13–23).

Machiavelli reasoned that Roman liberty depended on "the elimination of the Tarquins and the killing of Brutus's sons" so that "all its modes and orders" could maintain that freedom (D I.16). Florence may, in some sense, have performed the first task by throwing off the authority of the German emperor early in its history, but Giano, like subsequent Florentine would-be founders, decidedly failed, repeatedly, to do the second: to kill the sons of Brutus so that its laws and orders might effectively maintain its liberty.

MICHELE DI LANDO: SAVIOR OF THE REPUBLIC OR LACKEY OF THE "POPULAR NOBLES"?

Few if any individuals are praised more fulsomely within the pages of the *Florentine Histories* than Michele di Lando. The barefoot, rag-clad Michele leads the plebeian mob that overthrows the Signoria during the Ciompi Revolt; becomes the first gonfalonier of justice in the fledgling popular republic; then militarily suppresses the woolworkers barely a month after they had acclaimed him as their champion. Machiavelli's compliments for Michele are effusive:

> This victory that ended the tumults was entirely attributable to the Gonfalonier's virtue. His spirit, prudence, and goodness exceeded those of all the other citizens in his time, and he merits being counted among the very few to have benefitted their patria. If he had been motivated by a spirit either malign or ambitious, the republic would have lost its liberty completely and would have succumbed entirely to a tyranny even greater than that imposed by the Duke of Athens. His goodness never permitted a thought to enter his mind that ran counter to the universal benefit, and his prudence was such that those whom he could not overwhelm with arms he gained to his party through his mode of conduct. (FH III.17)

Later, in his political epitaph for Michele, Machiavelli expresses dismay over the ingratitude shown to the former gonfalonier by fellow citizens upon his exile from the city: "Michele di Lando could not be saved from the rage of the parties despite all the goods that his authority had provided while the unbridled multitude were licentiously ruining the city. For his good deeds his patria paid him poor recompense" (FH III.22).

Most interpreters take Machiavelli's lavish praise of Michele largely at face value.[14] However, Machiavelli's assessment looks quite different once one evaluates his judgment of Michele's virtue, spirit, prudence, modest ambition, and, especially, goodness while bearing in mind Machiavelli's analyses of new princes or civic reformers in *The Prince* and the *Discourses*. Michele's initial behavior substantially heeds the advice that Machiavelli offers founders and reformers in previous works. Ultimately, however, Michele does not go nearly far enough in behaving as Machiavelli advises new princes to act—indeed, Machiavelli demonstrates, without expounding on the fact, that Michele blatantly violates central tenets of Machiavelli's most fundamental political lessons.

Machiavelli's introduction of Michele in the *Histories* is unforgettable. Leading the insurrectionist woolworkers into the Palazzo, up the stairs and to the threshold of the Signoria's chamber, Michele presents an enticingly contradictory image. Although "shoeless and barely clothed," Michele held in his hands the banner of the gonfalonier of justice, the emblem of the republic's highest magistracy (FH III.16). A vision conjoining poverty and majesty, Michele turns to face his compatriots, addressing them with these words: "You see, the palace is yours, and the city is in your hands. What do you now propose to do?" According to Machiavelli, "the multitude" answered that Michele should assume authority as "their gonfalonier and lord" and should govern them and the city "however he saw fit" (FH III.16).

It is not clear whether the *ciompi* take the easy way out here by bestowing the authority of gonfalonier on the person already carrying the banner of that office, or whether they judged Michele worthy of such status because of his courage in leading them to the republic's seat of power. Machiavelli endorses the latter view as he calls Michele "by nature rather than fortune a sagacious and prudent man"; that is, it was no accident that Michele was the singular individual who took up the gonfalonier's standard and led the plebeians to seize the palace (FH III.16). Moreover, this natural rather than accidental prudence and sagacity is borne out in Machiavelli's account of how Michele initially set about "quieting the city and ending the tumults."

Machiavelli recounts how, in the effort "to preoccupy the people, and acquire the necessary time to order affairs," Michele, in his first act as gonfalonier, demanded the arrest of a certain Ser Nuto, who was serving as warden of the Bargello (FH III.16). Nuto presumably had incarcerated numerous *ciompi* after the many burnings and lootings committed during the early days of the woolworker's revolt; no doubt the plebs would have been deliriously happy to see him punished. However, Machiavelli indicates that Michele also sends a clear message that any further acts of retribution would be pursued through expressly if severely lawful means: "To commence with justice the rule that he had acquired through favor, he had it declared publicly that all arson and robbery must cease; and to terrify anyone who would disobey these orders, he set up a gallows in the Piazza" (FH III.16). In other words, Michele makes it clear that just because he gained authority through popular favor, he will tolerate neither license nor disobedience, and that, should the people resort to either, he will not hesitate to punish with death even those to whom he owed his authority. Justice, not anarchy, will purportedly characterize Michele's new rule.

Nevertheless, Michele does countenance one wanton act of vengeance by his plebeian constituency: Machiavelli describes how, after locating Ser Nuto, "the multitude" dragged him into the Piazza and "hanged him from the gallows by one foot, whereupon every one nearby tore pieces from his body, such that at a stroke nothing was left of him but the lone extremity from which he had hung" (FH III.16). Michele is off to a commendable start by standards previously set by Machiavelli for a founder: a new prince ought to found authority on the people and purge their vindictive spirits with a spectacular execution, as Lucius Brutus and Cesare Borgia did in different contexts (P 7, P 9; D III.1). Michele manages to fix the attentions of the formerly oppressed woolworkers, for the moment, on a single object of vengeance, and in doing so he buys himself time to better secure his rule.

But what about the content of Michele's rule? With what modes and orders will he refound the Florentine Republic? Machiavelli reports that Michele immediately fired all the syndics of the guilds and appointed new ones; dismissed all the members of the Signoria, the Colleges, and the Eight of the War; and burned the existing bags containing names of those eligible for office (FH III.16). Hence the republic would enjoy a fresh start with entirely new magistrates within the most prominent social and civic institutions.

In the meantime, however, not everyone accepted the new authority that the plebs conferred on Michele as "signore." Machiavelli recounts how the Eight of the War, the Guelf Party's primary agents in government, interpreted the dismissal of the priors to mean that they were now undisputed princes of the city, so they proceeded to appoint a new set of priors to make up the Signoria (FH III.16). On hearing this, Michele ordered the Eight to leave the palace immediately, so that he could "demonstrate to everyone that he knew how to govern Florence without such counsel." Again, Michele indicates that he comprehends instinctively many of the lessons

Machiavelli offers new princes in *The Prince* and the *Discourses*: in this case he shows that he understands that a founder must rule alone and eliminate rivals, especially those already holding magistracies (P 6; D I.9).

Michele then convened his new, hand-picked syndics of the guilds and created a new Signoria, made up of four priors from the lower plebs (the *plebe minuta*), and two each from the major and the minor guilds (FH III.16). Moreover, he established a new scrutiny (*squittino*) and divided the state into three parts: one for the new plebeian guilds, one for the minor guilds, and one for the major guilds. The new Signoria and new bags of office constitute the very first inclusion of the *ciompi*, now finally organized in their own guilds, within Florence's government.

Notably, this new arrangement doubles the number of seats in the Signoria that the plebs themselves had demanded during the revolt: Machiavelli previously reported that the woolworkers wanted only two priors of their own (FH III.15), which would have left them, a majority of the newly constituted citizenry, with a minority of seats in the magistracy. Michele instead grants them *four* seats, making it much easier for them to achieve a voting majority within the Signoria. Beyond doubt, Michele has established laws that formally grant the Florentine plebs immense power. But, as we asked concerning Giano della Bella and his Ordinances of Justice: Does Michele use sufficiently "spirited" action to "invigorate" these new laws and give them appropriate substance, force, and longevity?

Machiavelli implies an answer to this question. He reports that Michele then takes several steps that immediately compromise his standing with the *ciompi* and that will eventually undermine his own authority vis-à-vis the city's elite citizens from the richest guildsmen, *popolani* whom Machiavelli calls the "popular nobles": Machiavelli reports that Michele granted to Salvestro de' Medici the exceedingly valuable proceeds from the shops along the Ponte Vecchio; and that he assigned to himself the rectorship (*la podesteria*) of a subject city, Empoli—a traditionally Ghibelline city (FH III.15). Moreover, Machiavelli writes, Michele conferred on numerous other prominent citizens, who were supposedly favorable to the plebs, "many other benefits" so that such citizens "might defend him in the future against envy."

By trying to please both the plebs and the richest guildsmen, Michele is pursuing a middle way here that violates, both in general and in particular, crucial Machiavellian maxims for princely success. Machiavelli insists that a successful new prince, whether Cesare Borgia, Agathocles, Nabis, or Cleomenes, must establish his authority on popular and not aristocratic support: he cannot found on both the people and the nobles because of the conflicting humors motivating these adversarial classes; and he certainly cannot found his state mostly with the support of the nobles, because they will inevitably depose such a prince when he invariably fails to satisfy their unquenchable appetite to oppress (P 9; D I.9).

Recall how Machiavelli declares, If a prince comes to power through the support of the great he should switch sides to the people at the first opportune moment (P 9), as did Clearchus of Heraclea (D I.16); he should *never* do the reverse—throwing off popular for elite support, as Appius Claudius did (D I.40), a course of action Michele is precariously close to replicating here. Machiavelli also insists that a prince who has come to power through the people's support should never exhibit any loss of confidence in their judgment, lest the people lose faith in his good intentions, thus jeopardizing his authority—as happened, again, to both Savonarola and Virginius, when each signaled a loss of faith in the people (P 6; D I.45).

And then there is the issue of "envy" and how a new prince should deal with it, which Machiavelli raises in his description of Michele's interactions with popular nobles like Salvestro de' Medici and other prominent citizens. In both *The Prince* and the *Discourses* Machiavelli is adamant that a new prince should worry, first and foremost, about the envy of the nobles, the "sons of Brutus"; an envy that Brutus and Camillus successfully managed in a republican context, but that Friar Savonarola and Piero Soderini quite spectacularly did not (P 6; D III.30). Indeed, Michele seems to be following here almost precisely the course of action for which Machiavelli, in the *Discourses*, excoriated Savonarola, but especially Soderini, Michele's eventual heir in the office of gonfalonier of justice.

As I noted previously, Machiavelli traced Soderini's failed attempt to eliminate the envy directed toward him by the "sons of Brutus"—the young nobles who despised the popular government over which Soderini, much like Michele here, presided as gonfalonier. Machiavelli describes how Soderini thought "patience and *gifts*" would overcome such envy, but warns that "he did not understand that such malignity can be . . . neither subdued by time nor appeased by *gifts* of any kind" (D III.3; emphases added). More specifically, Machiavelli declares that Soderini believed that "patience, *goodness*, kind fortune, and the dispensing of *benefits* would eliminate envy" (D III.30; emphases added).

Soderini, Machiavelli observes, failed to appreciate a singularly brutal fact: "To overcome such envy the only remedy is the death of those consumed by it" (D III.30). In short, Machiavelli declares unequivocally that the nobles' envy cannot be placated by goodness, the quality he most frequently attributes to Michele. Furthermore, he insists, the only "gift" that ultimately satisfies the sons of Brutus is "death." The gifts that Michele awards the likes of Salvestro de' Medici and other very rich *popolani* will not satiate their envy—not even the gift of real estate, however lucrative. Michele, by implication, is foolish to think otherwise. Again, Michele intuitively knows some Machiavellian lessons but clearly not all of them: in the case of Ser Nuto, he successfully scapegoats an individual in order to redirect the people's ill spirit; but he himself has not yet spiritedly invigorated the modes and orders through which the people, including the plebs, have been empowered to rule. Brutus secured the fledgling Roman Republic by overseeing the trial and execution of his sons and their aristocratic coconspirators against the new regime; and Cesare Borgia secured his new principality, and the popularly beneficial judicial institutions undergirding it, by eliminating the corrupt signori who had previously misruled the Romagna (D I.16, D III.3; P 7). But Michele has thus far eliminated no comparably serious threats from the sons of Brutus to his new modes and orders. Just as crucially, he has not followed the example of Romulus, who founded Rome by arming the entire people under his own command (P 6, P 20; D I.9-10). Michele has made no effort to integrate the armed plebs, the majority of the able-bodied free men in the city, into a unified Florentine civic-military order.

One might begin to ponder whether Michele understands how to gain the support of the people but not how to maintain it. This is borne out by his pursuit of an ill-advised middle way: Michele pleases the plebs by giving them unprecedented formal, political authority in government, a move that no doubt raises the ire of the popular nobles; then, to placate the nobles, Michele grants them expanded economic authority within the city, which naturally compromises his relationship with the plebs. By Machiavellian standards, Michele moves quite half-heartedly regarding the sons of Brutus, that is, rival elites or enemies of the new order: he dismisses some of them from their previous positions of guild and civic authority, but he attempts to win over others with precious offerings to earn their future support. As we will see, by leaving the people's adversaries and his own rivals alive, not only does Michele permit them to persist in mischief directed against the newly enfranchised plebs, but he also puts them in a position to use their still considerable power to undermine his own authority.[15]

Finally, besides perhaps unwisely believing that his inherent goodness and outward beneficence will mollify dangerous adversaries among Florence's elites, why does Michele assign himself such prominent and profitable authority over a foreign city like Empoli? What message does this send to his supporters among the plebs? They might reasonably ponder, Does Michele plan to continue selling out the *ciompi* to the wealthiest guildsmen and then move on to enjoy a luxurious retirement in Empoli? Or, more alarmingly, does he intend for this foreign city to serve as a source of military power from which he will draw forces to establish a tyranny over the plebs? Machiavelli previously noted in the *Histories* how the tyrannical Duke of Athens used French troops, in combination with the armed Florentine plebs, to oppress Florence's guild community (FH II.36). Conversely, does Michele here intend to use the richest *popolani* among the guilds, combined with foreign forces from Empoli, to suppress the *plebs*?[16]

Unsurprisingly, Machiavelli records that the plebs immediately start to worry that Michele's "excessive partisanship" for the upper guildsmen has jeopardized their own status within the new republic; they fear they do not in fact possess a role in government sufficient "to preserve and protect themselves" (FH III.17). Before Machiavelli began his account of the Ciompi Revolt, he elaborated on the extent to which oppression and exploitation of the plebs by the *popolani* of the major guilds—who had been steadily co-opted and corrupted by the city's ancient nobility—were the underlying causes of the woolworkers' insurrection (FH III.12). Given this recent history, the plebs have good cause for anxiety over Michele's cultivating favor with the popular nobles and his grasping for power outside the city. Machiavelli seems to take Michele's side in describing their response, condemning, as he often does in the *Histories*, the plebs' supposedly immoderate desires and behavior: the *ciompi*, he writes, "motivated by their usual audacity," took up arms, and tumultuously marched on the Palazzo, demanding that the Signoria pass further measures "for their security and well-being" (FH III.17).

Michele, Machiavelli writes, was quite perturbed by the plebs' "arrogance" in this instance (FH III.17). But because he did not wish to provoke them further, he suggested that whatever the merits of their demands, the *ciompi* ought not express them in such a tumultuous manner; he insisted that the plebs lay down their arms so that the priors might address their concerns "with dignity rather than through compulsion" (FH III.17). In response, the insulted multitude, Machiavelli writes, left the palace and retired to Santa Maria Novella, where they appointed eight of themselves to serve as their own heads, with ministerial trappings and other orders that might lend them "reputation and reverence."

The behavior of the *ciompi* here subtly recalls the two secessions of the Roman plebs, praised by Machiavelli in the *Discourses* (D I.3-4, D I.40, D I.44): secessions that resulted in an institution of "eminence and reputation," the plebeian tribunate. Like their Roman antecedents protesting the republic's refusal to address their grievances, the Florentine plebs in this instance retire from the public seat of power and set about establishing their own tribunician institution with veto authority over the workings of government: "The heads of the plebs decided that eight members elected from their own guilds should always reside with the priors in the Palace, and that all of the Signoria's decisions must meet their approval" (FH III.17). When the Roman plebs complained that senatorial and consular authority was biased and self-serving, Machiavelli endorsed their effort to create their own magistracy, the plebeian tribunate, with veto power over senators and consuls—which, he claimed, made Rome "more perfect" (D I.3). Does Machiavelli really believe, as he declares here, that the Florentine people are behaving with excessive arrogance and audacity by pursuing a similar course of action? If such institutional innovations succeeded in making Rome nearly perfect, according to the *Discourses*, then why aren't they appropriate for Florence here in the *Histories*? Especially when Machiavelli, while composing the *Histories*, proposed a new constitution for Florence including a tribunician magistracy very much like the one the plebs demanded here.[17]

The plebs, according to Machiavelli, sought to validate these tribunician reforms by sending two delegates to the Signoria, insisting that the measures be ratified by the Council of the People and the Council of the Commune, and threatening to use force, if necessary, to ensure such an outcome (FH III.17). In apparently derogatory terms, Machiavelli declares that the plebs acted with "great audacity" by approaching the priors in such a manner, and with "even greater presumptuousness" by chastising Michele for "the ingratitude and disrespect" he'd shown them in return for "the dignity and honor" they'd conferred on him. Again, how audacious and presumptuous, really, is this behavior? The plebs, at this point, have merely sent emissaries to address the Signoria; they are not assaulting it with military force. Moreover, they expected Michele to serve the *ciompi* cause and subdue their adversaries among the *popolani*, not to make himself rich and the *popolani* even richer. Furthermore, as Machiavelli declares in the *Discourses*, such displays of popular indignation ought to be alarming "only to those who merely read about them in books" (D I.4).

At this moment Michele could have taken the opportunity to reaffirm his commitment to the *ciompi*. He could have assuaged the plebs' fears of the popular nobles' increasing power and influence by accepting the plebeian reform proposal and by allowing their representatives tribunician veto authority over the Signoria's decisions. Instead, Machiavelli reports that when "their rebukes turned to threats," Michele could no longer endure the "arrogance" of the plebeian delegates; thinking more of "the high rank that he held than of his abject origins, he decided to use extraordinary modes to check such extraordinary insolence" (FH III.17). Michele's immediate actions demonstrate that he now thinks of himself as a *signore* and no longer as a *ciompo*. Resorting to physical violence, Michele struck the plebeian delegates with his sword and ordered them arrested and imprisoned. In response, the enraged multitude decided "to gain with arms what they had failed to win without them," and then "furiously and tumultuously" attacked the Signoria.

Machiavelli reports how Michele resolved that it would "redound to his glory" if he preemptively engaged his opponents rather than "wait behind walls," only to be compelled to flee like his predecessors, "much to the palace's dishonor and to his own shame" (FH III.17). He therefore mobilized a large number of citizens, many of whom now believed they had erred in challenging Michele's authority; mounting a horse at the head of these armed men, Michele marched on Santa Maria Novella to commence hostilities with the rest of the *ciompi*. But he failed to engage this group, which had taken a different route to the piazza. When Michele returned with his forces, he found the palace under siege, at which moment he assailed and routed the plebs, driving many from the city and "compelling the rest to give up their arms and go searching for places to hide" (FH III.17).

Let us pause to examine Michele's motivations and actions here. Machiavelli writes that Michele is concerned with his own glory, with the dignity of his office, and with the honor of the palace (FH III.17); in defense of these, he uses favors to garner support from the city's nobles, and he uses force to disperse and disarm the plebeians. This course of action defies the main lessons of *The Prince*, which insists that a new prince—like Cesare Borgia, Agathocles, or Nabis—to guarantee longevity and success, first must found his authority on the people, whose motivations for security can be satisfied, rather than on the nobles, whose envy and desire for oppression cannot (P 6, P 9). Second, he must arm as many citizen subjects as he can rather than, like Roman emperors, French monarchs, and later Medici princes, disarm the populace (P 6-8, P 13, P 19-20). Furthermore, in the *Discourses*, Machiavelli provides the examples of Romulus and Cleomenes, who, on the one hand, arm all of their peoples and, on the other, if the nobles are not yet fully corrupt, collect them in a senate—or if they are irredeemably corrupt, kill them and distribute their wealth to the common people (D I.9-10).

Indeed, the figure from previous works perhaps most reminiscent of Michele is Agathocles the Sicilian. Agathocles, like Michele, is an individual of abject origins; he is a common potter's son who nevertheless rises through the ranks of Syracuse's civic military to become chief magistrate of the city (P 8). Machiavelli describes Agathocles, like Michele, as one who possesses extraordinary virtue of spirit and body, who comes to power through the support of fellow armed citizens and through crimes (we must not forget that Michele himself participated in much arson and looting on his path to authority). Both are lowborn, virtuous, and sufficiently ambitious to secure the supreme magistracies of their cities. The similarities, however, end there.

Agathocles's ambition is not satisfied by attaining high office—Machiavelli notes that he is not content with the praetorship that Syracuse's elites consented to grant him; and he is not so respectful of the latter that he forsakes his close relations with fellow lowborn, armed citizen subjects (P 8). In contrast, Machiavelli suggests, Michele is quite proud of the high "rank" of gonfalonier, he seeks to distinguish himself from those of similar common origins at a critical moment, and he cultivates intimate relations with his city's elites. Agathocles betrays and murders his city's magistrates and richest citizens; he then leads his large citizen army in conflict with Carthage, freeing Sicily of foreign occupation (P 8). Michele, rather than conquering a foreign city, seeks political support abroad, then violently betrays the Florentine people, not the nobles (FH III.16–17). In doing so, he squanders Florence's last and greatest chance to amass an army comprising both the traditional guildsmen and the multitude of able-bodied men previously excluded from the guild-dominated republic—a civic military that would have rivaled, within contemporary Europe, those of the vaunted Swiss and German city-states (P 10, P 12, P 25–26; D II.12, D II.16).

Agathocles, Machiavelli points out, does not win glory despite his prodigious achievements because he liquidated his city's political and economic elites (P 8); Michele does win the glory he desired, being celebrated long after the Ciompi Revolt for saving Florence (or, more specifically, for saving the city's elites from the wrath of the plebs).[18] But does each figure deserve the relationship to glory attributed to him by posterity? Whose behavior results in more tangible good for his city, and therefore who is more truthfully deserving of glory? Machiavelli attributes selfish ambition to Agathocles and, for the most part, selfless public-spiritedness to Michele; but his descriptions of facts on the ground raise serious questions concerning these assessments. Agathocles secured his citizen subjects from oppression by both domestic elites and foreign conquerors, employed cruelty only "for the utility of his subjects," died in his bed at the end of a long reign, and established the conditions for restoring a sturdy civic-military republic in Syracuse (P 8; D II.2). We need to look more closely at Michele's legacy before passing a considered, definitive judgment on his career.

Recall from the passage I quoted at the start of this section the innumerable admirable qualities that Machiavelli attributes to Michele: virtue, spirit, prudence, and especially goodness (FH III.17). Moreover, Machiavelli declares that Michele's goodness "never permitted a thought to enter his mind that ran counter to the universal benefit." We will have to assess whether Michele actually lives up to this wildly laudatory litany of qualities. In particular, we must question whether the "goodness" that sets the boundaries of Michele's political imagination conforms to what Machiavelli means by the term. After all, a consistent political good that he exalts in *The Prince* and the *Discourses* is the military empowerment of "the universality"—that is, *all* the people inhabiting a polity, and certainly not the wholesale disarming of the vast majority of them. Michele violently divides, suppresses, and disarms the *ciompi*, resulting in the immediate "demoralization of the plebs" (FH III.17). In this sense Michele has certainly not, as Machiavelli asserts, benefited "the universality"—a word, like the "multitude," that Machiavelli often uses interchangeably with "the people" or even, more specifically, "the plebeians" (e.g., P 17, P 19; D I.2, D I.16–17).

And there was more harm to come. Machiavelli then reports that Michele's military victory over the plebs "encouraged the upper guildsmen to reflect upon the ignominy of the fact that they, who had subdued the pride of the nobles, should now have to endure the stench of the plebs in the magistracies" (FH III.17). The *popolani* begin to ask themselves, "Why should they who triumphed over the ancient nobility of the city in earlier armed conflicts now have to sit among the unwashed plebs within the city's highest offices, especially since the latter too have now been vanquished militarily?" The envy of the sons of Brutus, the insolence of the popular nobles, who have not been eradicated by Michele, is now becoming inflamed. Michele, wittingly or not, has encouraged the richest guildsmen to disarm the plebs not only militarily but *civically*.

Machiavelli then reports that when the next Signoria was to be filled with new priors, armed men swelled the piazza, insisting that they would suffer no "lesser men" (*popolo minuto*) to serve as signori (FH III.18). This armed mob—presumably organized by the rich *popolani*—demanded the immediate removal of two "notoriously vile" men from the magistracy and the appointment of more worthy ones, Messer Giorgio Scali and Francesco di Michele. They go even further in rolling back the constitutional reforms through which Michele had so daringly empowered the plebs in government: the antiplebeian mob then disbanded the lesser people's guild, and expelled from office and barred from further eligibility all its members—except Michele di Lando and a few others of "superior quality" (FH III.18).

The popular nobles then insisted that the magistracies be divided into two parts, so that the Signoria would contain five priors from the minor guilds and four from the major ones (FH III.18). Most of the plebs Michele had enfranchised for the first time in the republic's history were once again, and now permanently, excluded from Florence's government. Machiavelli fails to tell readers or even speculate aloud whether Michele was complicit in the armed demonstration that led to the plebs' expulsion from the Signoria, their disenfranchisement (with the notable exception of Michele himself), and the elevation of popular nobles like Giorgio Scali to the Signoria. He certainly does intimate that by previously crushing the plebs militarily, Michele ensured that his new constitutional orders would be gutted—the *ciompi* were now disenfranchised again, and perhaps worse, they were now completely disarmed for the first time since the reign of the

Duke of Athens. Florence's opportunity to boast more able-bodied free men at arms—plebs and *popolani* alike—than any other city in Europe was gone for good.

Whether or not Michele colluded in this counterrevolutionary scaling back of the popular republic that he himself had founded, he clearly did nothing to stop it. Yet even readers considerably less cynical than the notorious Machiavelli might pause to wonder: Perhaps Giorgio Scali, Salvestro de' Medici, and other of the richest guildsmen were pulling Michele's strings all along—or at least had been doing so for some time. Ultimately, Machiavelli leaves readers to guess at the veracity and the extent of what other chroniclers of the Ciompi Revolt explicitly assert: Michele had been bought.[19]

When Machiavelli surveys Florence's political landscape in the aftermath of Michele's suppression of the *ciompi* and their disenfranchisement by the popular nobles, he notes that although the republic had been removed from the hands of the plebs, the minor guildsmen were nevertheless still formally more powerful than the popular nobles under present arrangements (FH III.18). He claimed that the noble guildsmen temporarily yielded to the minor guildsmen out of necessity: they allied with them and tolerated their continued political ascendance, for the time being, merely for the dual purpose of depriving the *ciompi* or lesser people of their recently won social-political status and of suppressing members of the Guelf Party (FH III.18).

Machiavelli names the men who stood as "almost princes of the city" within this new form of government: Messer Giorgio Scali, Messer Benedetto Alberti, Messer Salvestro de' Medici, and Messer Tommaso Strozzi (FH III.18). On this list of quasi-princes—all of them notably "sirs"— Michele di Lando's name is nowhere to be found. His term of office as gonfalonier completed and his power base among the plebeians disarmed and dispersed, whatever Michele may have been promised by the popular nobles, Machiavelli suggests that he has been consigned to irrelevance. His own motivations notwithstanding, the elimination of the plebs' power, Machiavelli shows, definitively results in the evaporation of Michele's own power as well. He does not appear again in Machiavelli's narrative until the moment of his exile, several chapters later, when Machiavelli recounts the ascension to power of the "harmful and offensive" Albizzi oligarchy (FH III.20–22)—which in effect ends republican government in Florence for generations to come.

Despite all the Sturm und Drang of the Ciompi Revolt, Machiavelli indicates that very little has changed in the city's sociopolitical situation: the division between the Guelf nobles and the middle/lower guildsmen, which Machiavelli declares had originated before the recent tumult in the competing ambitions of the Albizzi and Ricci families, was merely deepened after the conflict. It has now simply solidified into intense, and still quite bloody, party competition between what he will henceforth call the more conservative "popular party" and the more broadly based "plebeian party" (FH III.18). The popular nobles comprising the former party will eventually outmaneuver those, like Giorgio, Benedetto, Salvestro, and Strozzi, who serve as leaders of the latter party, for control of the city. As for the *ciompi*, Machiavelli had already made it clear before his account of their revolt that they, the most numerous freeborn men in the city, returned to their disenfranchised and exploited conditions—conditions, Machiavelli noted, that persisted into the time when he was writing the *Histories* (FH III.12).

The "plebian republic" that emerged after the Ciompi Revolt endured for only three years, Machiavelli writes, because its leaders among the *popolani* were compelled to enact "many executions and exiles" resulting from their suspicions of "so many malcontents" residing both within and outside the city (FH III.18). He recounts the executions of over half a dozen prominent popular nobles of the conservative party and the exile of many Guelf Party members. Moreover, he reports that the republic paid an exorbitant sum to the mercenary captain John Hawkwood to accomplish nothing in pursuit of the city's foreign policy agenda (FH III.18-19).

The discerning reader of *The Prince* and the *Discourses* might ask at this point in the *Histories*: What benefit would Michele di Lando have bestowed on the republic if, like Moses or Brutus, he himself had rid the city of its many "malcontents"—many nobles of both the popular and conservative parties—during his tenure as gonfalonier and lord? And would the republic have needed any further recourse to mercenaries like Hawkwood if Michele had imitated Romulus and fully integrated the armed plebs into a unified civic military force instead of dividing, humiliating, and disarming them? But Machiavelli does not explicitly raise such questions. Instead, he then recounts the fall from power and execution of Giorgio Scali, whom, as I mentioned above, Machiavelli identified in *The Prince* as the true founder and leader of the popular republic that emerged out of the Ciompi Revolt, not Michele di Lando (P 9). There Machiavelli blames Scali, like the Gracchi in Rome, for trying to make himself head of a republic based on popular favor rather than on full-scale popular arms. The oligarchic opponents of both Scali and the Gracchi easily outmaneuvered them, primarily because they lacked extensive armed popular support.

One must therefore wonder whether Scali effectually slit his own throat by abetting Michele's efforts to crush the plebs rather than encouraging their full civic-military integration into the republic. In fact, since we do not know the full extent of Michele's collusion with popular nobles like Scali and Salvestro de' Medici, it is entirely possible that Scali instructed Michele to destroy the plebs at the first opportunity—in which case the "victory that ended the tumults" would not have been, as Machiavelli claims, "entirely" attributable to "the gonfalonier's virtue" after all. Was Scali, to a significant extent, the master of Michele's virtue in much the same way that Machiavelli eventually reveals Vitellozzo Vitelli to have been the "master" of Liverotto da Fermo's "virtue" in *The Prince?*—a fact that becomes apparent only after the nasty conclusion of each figure's political career (P 8). Perhaps Giorgio was orchestrating Michele's movements all along or, at least, once Michele had become gonfalonier.

When Machiavelli narrates Michele's exile, he laments that the former gonfalonier was treated with regrettable "ingratitude" despite "all the goods that his authority had provided to his patria" (FH III.22). However, as with Giano della Bella, the empirical facts and historical details Machiavelli provides, cross-referenced with the lessons of *The Prince* and the *Discourses*, suggest that Michele provided no goods at all. Indeed, he may be accused of helping to make conditions in the republic demonstrably worse. Under the Albizzi oligarchy and the subsequent Medici principate, Machiavelli later indicates, Florence's civic culture would succumb to unprecedented corruption; and its reliance on mercenary arms rather than a wide-scale popular army would leave it hopelessly vulnerable to a procession of foreign invaders.[20]

CHRISTIANITY AS INSUPERABLE OBSTACLE FOR MODERN FOUNDERS/REFORMERS?

In the *Histories*, Machiavelli continues, as he did in *The Prince* and the *Discourses*, to draw readers' attention to historically novel constraints, both psychological and structural, that seriously inhibit modern political actors like Giano della Bella and Michele di Lando—more so than did the otherwise serious impediments confronting ancient founders and reformers like Moses, Romulus, and Brutus. Prominent among these are three interrelated obstacles pertaining to the prominence of Christianity in modern Europe: the impact of Christian morality on individual political actors; the pervasiveness of unnatural sectarian conflicts, such as the Guelf/Ghibelline divide, that plague modern polities in addition to the "natural" class divisions that characterize them; and—although less pertinent to Giano and Michele—the negative effect of papal politics on modern principalities and republics.

Among these potential obstacles that might hinder Machiavelli's modern protofounders/reformers from fully imitating their ancient predecessors, there are reasons to think that the first one is potentially the most insurmountable: the pervasive and deleterious influence of Christian morality. At certain moments, Machiavelli implies that Christianity has thoroughly mystified modern political actors, inhibiting them from behaving in civically salutary ways: most chillingly, perhaps, when Machiavelli asserts, in his discussion of ecclesiastical principalities in *The Prince*, that *all* subjects of modernity, allegorized as a comprehensive Christian principality—both subjects and political leaders—can imagine no ultimate authority other than the church (P 11).[21]

Within the pages of the *Histories*, Christian morality certainly seems to inhibit "good" men like Giano and Michele from acting in "bad" ways that would serve the well-being of their patria; likewise, it seems to induce "bad" men, like Corso Donati and the Duke of Athens (discussed in chapter 8), to disregard certain prudentially "good" modes that might result in beneficial outcomes for their polities and, just as important, for themselves.[22] However, if Machiavelli truly believed that Christianity's effect on modern minds was as totalizing and incapacitating as such passages suggest, this would necessarily render futile his own explicitly declared efforts to overcome Christianity in the service of worldly liberty and greatness (see P 15, the prefaces to D I and D II, and D III.1).

However formidable Machiavelli thought such constraints on individual initiative and prospective political success to be, the *Histories* shows, I have argued, that he had not abandoned the hope that Florentine would-be princes could and would overcome them. Perhaps modern Christians could not fully, in every respect, imitate the modes pursued and orders enacted by Moses, Romulus, and Brutus; but they certainly could go much further than Giano and Michele did. This may be one important reason Machiavelli provides the less exalted example of Hiero in chapter 6 of *The Prince* as a model for modern imitation. While he is surely no Moses, Romulus, or Brutus, Machiavelli demonstrates that Hiero at least reformed Syracuse's military by eliminating mercenary arms and expanding its citizen foundations. In this sense Machiavelli suggests that potential founders/reformers from Florence's early history could have at least partially imitated Moses, Romulus, and Brutus, instituting portions of their programs and earning praise equal to the kind he bestows on Hiero for modestly benefiting his patria civically and militarily. Presumably, in the future founders/reformers, whether Florentine or other, having availed themselves of Machiavelli's writings, might be expected to more fully imitate his greatest ancient exemplars of political leadership.

Put simply, in Machiavelli's estimation Christianity makes prudent and virtuous foundings and reorderings difficult; it does not render them impossible. Indeed, I argue that Machiavelli intends the *Histories* to illuminate these historically novel structural and psychological constraints, which so seriously inhibit modern political actors, so that these actors might more readily surmount them. Machiavelli certainly does not accentuate these impediments, I contend, with the goal of providing political leaders, such as Giano or Michele, with excuses for why they no longer ought to emulate exemplary ancient princes, whom Machiavelli previously lionized—especially those like Moses, Romulus, and Brutus, who practiced and instituted wholly new modes and orders or radically revised and reformed established ones. Machiavelli demonstrates, subtly but definitively, that Giano and Michele could have successfully capitalized on the eternally recurring sociopolitical opportunities, emerging from inevitable social conflict, that Machiavelli still considers potentially advantageous for both founders/reformers and their polities.

CONCLUSION

In the dedicatory letters of both *The Prince* and the *Discourses*, Machiavelli declares that each work contains "everything" that he knew or that he had learned. Machiavelli never explicitly repudiates these claims anywhere in subsequent writings, nor does he assert that later works such as the *Florentine Histories* deserve to occupy a similarly comprehensive epistemological status within his oeuvre. Therefore I have operated with the assumption that the two earlier works continue to serve as authoritative guides for attempts to understand the arguments of *all* of Machiavelli's political writings, including the *Histories*.

Furthermore, Machiavelli indicates that *The Prince* and the *Discourses* are meant both for a specific audience within the author's immediate context and for a much broader audience posited far beyond it; in contrast, it seems that the *Histories* is meant—at the surface level, at least—exclusively for a more local audience. In *The Prince* and the *Discourses*, Machiavelli identifies two sets of readers the books are intended for, and therefore two sets of persons through whose eyes they are meant to be interpreted: the primary audiences of *The Prince* are a Medici prince, Lorenzo, and readers characterized as "whoever understands" the book (P 15); the audiences of the *Discourses* are the two aristocratic friends to whom Machiavelli dedicates the work and "young" readers more broadly who will "come after" Machiavelli to build upon the foundations he establishes in the book (D I and D II, prefaces). In the *Histories* and accompanying works, Machiavelli explicitly gestures to no comparably specific audience beyond the Medici prelates who commissioned the work and the patrician circle of *amici* (friends) and *ottimati* (aristocrats) through whom the Medici family rules Florence.[23]

The differences between the intended audiences of these two sets of books—enlightened versus parochial, transhistorical versus proximate, combined with Machiavelli's epistemological elevation of *The Prince* and the *Discourses*—suggest that the earlier works hold a comprehensive status in his corpus that the *Histories* does not, and therefore that the *Histories* should be considered hermeneutically subordinate. In other words, readers ought to enlist the authoritative knowledge or learning contained in *The Prince* and the *Discourses* when endeavoring to comprehend the, to some extent, inferior or insufficient *Histories*.

By keeping the lessons of *The Prince* and the *Discourses* firmly within the interpretive frame of the *Histories*, as opposed to dismissing them as irrelevant to the concerns of that book—as many recent interpreters do—I have shown that the *Histories* demonstrates how modern political actors such as Giano and Michele could and should have behaved in ways consistent with Machiavelli's examples of ancient virtue; that is, in ways that make the vigorous reordering of modern polities like Florence a genuine possibility.

8. FAILED TYRANTS

Bad Men Who Know Not How to Appear Good

(APPIUS CLAUDIUS, WALTER BRIENNE, AND SEPTIMIUS SEVERUS)

I previously mentioned the similarity of Machiavelli's depictions of Corso Donati and Walter Brienne (the Duke of Athens) in the *Florentine Histories*. Both are tyrannical leaders who contribute nothing of civic value to the city of Florence. In this chapter I argue that Machiavelli's account of Walter in the *Histories* reproduces central elements of his analysis of Appius Claudius in the *Discourses*. I suggest that the unspoken links between Walter and Appius draw on and reinforce Machiavelli's crucial advice to new princes and political founders offered in *Discourses* and *The Prince*.[1] These links further demonstrate that the *Histories* delineates, in a way that is remarkably consistent (if somewhat oblique), Machiavelli's instructions for political leaders set out more programmatically in the earlier works.

Moreover, the chapter contributes to a somewhat iconoclastic strand of Machiavelli scholarship that distinguishes between forms of tyranny Machiavelli condones—or even advocates—and those he proscribes: I suggest that in the *Discourses*, *The Prince*, and the *Histories*, Machiavelli does not reject tyranny per se, but rather redefines the concept in ways that, if operationalized, he believes will mutually benefit a new prince, the majority of his subject citizens, and their patria.[2] To accomplish this, I will furthermore consider, on the one hand, how much Machiavelli's portrait of Walter offers an implicit critique of Medici rule in the Florence of his day and, on the other, how much Machiavelli's account of the Roman emperor Septimius Severus, in *The Prince*, offers a corrective to the example of Appius's failed tyranny. I argue that Machiavelli's depictions of the bungled tyrannies of Appius in ancient Rome and Walter in medieval Florence instruct potential founders to assiduously avoid the conventional evil employed by failed usurpers of republics and instead to spiritedly pursue the more "honorable evil" exhibited by successful new princes, especially tyrannical reformers of republics (D I.27, D I.16-17).

Machiavelli criticizes Walter and Appius—and by implication, the *Histories*' addressees, the Medici—for failing to follow the exemplary behavior exhibited by the ancient founders/reformers discussed in *The Prince* and the *Discourses*: both Walter and Appius refuse to unequivocally found their principalities on the people as a whole, instead favoring the nobles (or some especially oppressive subset of them); they neglect to avoid the "middle way" between difficult political choices; they fail to pursue "cruelty well used," and thus provoke dangerous hatred rather than salutary fear among subjects; they either dishonor their subjects' women or encourage their molestation; and they fail to militarily mobilize all of their polity's common people.[3] Moreover, the religious or foreign trappings of Walter's and Appius's reigns also call to mind certain salient aspects of Medici rule in Florence. Finally, Machiavelli's example of Severus seemingly offers a viable model for tyrants like Walter and Appius, who wanted to maintain their principalities without relying on the people's friendship.

THE DECEMVIR AND THE DUKE

Walter Brienne, the so-called Duke of Athens, whom Machiavelli discusses extensively in book II of the *Histories*, invites direct comparison with an ancient figure whose career Machiavelli minutely analyzed in the *Discourses*: Appius Claudius, the leader of the Decemvirate, which ruled tyrannically during the early Roman Republic (D I.35, D I.40-42, D I.45). Machiavelli uses Appius's career as an example both republics and tyrants can learn from; the former to avoid the circumstances that bolstered Appius's rise to power, and the latter to avoid "the mistakes" he committed that cost him his reign (D I.40). When discussing Giano della Bella and Michele di Lando in the *Histories*, Machiavelli establishes a sharp if implicit contrast between these Florentine failures and successful ancient founders/reformers in *The Prince* and the *Discourses*, such as Moses, Romulus, and Brutus. However, in the respective modern and ancient cases of Walter and Appius, the behaviors of the leaders, and hence their respective failures, are virtually identical. Again, simply because Machiavelli does not explicitly invoke an ancient counterpart to the modern example of Walter in the *Histories* does not mean he does not intend readers familiar with his other works to undertake a comparative analysis of the examples themselves.

Before turning to the details of Walter's career, allow me to review Machiavelli's account of Appius Claudius from the *Discourses*. Appius fulfills some but not of all of the criteria for a successful new prince that Machiavelli sets out in *The Prince* and the *Discourses*. Appius uses high civic office as a springboard to princely power (P 6, P 9): he heads the Ten (the Decemvirate), a committee authorized to revise and codify Roman law (D I.40). But instead of fully subjugating or altogether eliminating the nobility, so as to be "alone" with the people as Machiavelli recommends "civil princes" do (P 6–9), Appius merely abolishes competing magistrates, the consuls and tribunes, and leaves Rome's "senatorial order" intact. Indeed, he allows senators' sons to gratuitously satisfy their desire to oppress the people, rather than—as do the examples of civil princes and successful tyrants whom Machiavelli extols (Agathocles, Nabis, Cleomenes, and Clearchus)—defending the people from the nobles by pursuing economic redistribution and the expansion of civil militaries.

At this point in Machiavelli's account of Rome's history in the *Discourses*, the people had become exasperated with the Senate's persistent use of religious strictures and unnecessary wars to divert them from pursuing domestic reforms (D I.13); thus the people began to associate the religious trappings and military functions of the consulship with oppression itself (D I.40). While the plebs felt subjugated by the consulship, the nobles considered themselves harassed by the plebeian tribunate, a magistracy specifically designed to keep them in check and reserved exclusively for members of the common people. In this context of "disputations and contestations" between the nobles and the people, the Romans tried to reduce social conflict by imitating the legislative clarity of Athenian law; thus they elected a ten-member committee, the Decemvirate, with Appius as its head, to revise and codify Roman law in a similar manner (D I.40). While the Romans' intention was to "better secure the state's liberty," the outcome was diametrically opposite.

From the outset, Appius and Walter have two things in common: both are foreigners in the cities they would tyrannize, and both have links to the Greek city of Athens. Appius descended from a wealthy Sabine family that had recently emigrated to Rome and gained immediate prominence in the Roman Senate; Walter was a French noble who served as a vassal to Robert, king of Naples. Appius headed a magistracy charged with codifying laws that were brought back to Rome from Athens by a fact-finding commission that had closely studied Solon's constitution. Walter earned his title, the Duke of Athens, while attempting (unsuccessfully) to reclaim Athens for the papacy during his military campaigns in Greece. There may be more than a little irony implied by the fact that both vicious tyrants would have links to Athens, the city known as perhaps history's greatest expositor of the principles of liberty and equality. Moreover, their aristocratically based tyrannies contravene the model of populist "Greek tyranny" that we have observed Machiavelli recommend throughout his writings. Additionally, the "Athenian" origins of Appius's and Walter's tyrannies may reinforce "orientalist" intimations, scattered throughout Machiavelli's writings, suggesting that despotism and servitude initially came to the free and virtuous Italian peninsula from "the East."[4]

Appius, whom Machiavelli deems "a man of sagacity and restlessness," ascended to the leadership of the Ten by "lavishing humanity" upon the people, though he had formerly treated them with condescension and cruelty (D I.40). While drafting the Twelve Tables, Appius successfully exploited the hatred of the Senate and the plebs for, respectively, the consulship and the tribunate, to entirely suspend the operation of each magistracy; the decemvirs then governed in place of both offices and deauthorized the people's judgment in political trials (D I.35, D I.40). Having thus removed crucial institutional obstacles to the Ten's power, Machiavelli notes—with more than a little admiration—how deftly Appius, with a "transformed nature and sharpened ingenuity," converted a special agency charged with legal reforms into the "unequivocal prince of Rome" (D I.40, cf. D I.41).

For their first year in office the Decemvirate, according to Machiavelli, "governed civilly": despite formally stripping the people of this authority, as a courtesy the Ten continued to leave judgment over capital trials to the assembled people (D I.40). Thus, when Appius spread rumors throughout Rome that the new law code could be perfected if the Ten were permitted to reign for another year, the people, eager to do without consuls and assuming that continued judicial appeals to the people's judgment made the tribunes superfluous, eagerly acceded to his wishes. If the people were deceived by Appius's false humanity, Machiavelli writes, the nobles were deceived by their belief that the leading decemvirs could be shamed into forsaking office for an additional year and would give way to an entirely new committee that would replace them: the nobles gave Appius the authority to propose new candidates to serve in the Ten's second term, assuming that he would never be so arrogant as to transgress prevailing norms and submit his own name; thus they were "stunned and dismayed" to witness him nominate himself and nine other nobles subservient to him.

Dispensing with the civil "mask" that had concealed his "innate pride," Appius initiated his second term by expanding the number of bodyguards accompanying the Ten from twelve lictors to one hundred and twenty, thus instilling "terror" in the people and the nobles (D I.40). However, the two groups suffered disparately from Appius's tyranny as he began to cultivate the Senate and abuse the plebs. Rather than honor appeals to the people, as they did in their first term, the Ten now redoubled the punishments of plebeians who appealed the excessive verdicts of individual decemvirs. When the people "realized that they had erred" in first favoring and then reelecting Appius, Machiavelli reports that the Senate haughtily rebuffed their entreaties for relief, since the nobles "found their suffering satisfying." When Appius's second year of office concluded, he maintained the magistracy through violence and with support from young nobles, whom Appius had made "clients" (*satelliti*) with property expropriated from citizens convicted by the Decemvirate.

Hence, rather than turning against the nobles to favor the people, as other tyrants praised by Machiavelli, such as Agathocles, Cleomenes, Clearchus, and Nabis (the last of whom Machiavelli again invokes here), did so successfully, Appius follows the opposite path: once in power, despite having gained authority with the people's consent, he partners with the nobles to tyrannize the plebeians. Far from liquidating the senatorial order in the manner of Machiavelli's examples of successful Greek tyrants, Appius encourages the nobility, especially young nobles, to oppress the people. Indeed, Machiavelli sets up the following contrast within the pages of the *Discourses*: whereas Brutus, "the father of Roman liberty" (D III.1), gained eternal fame for severely punishing young nobles, including his own sons, for aspiring to deprive the people of their liberty (D I.16, D III.3), Appius gains historical infamy as the chief agent of the Roman Republic's first "tyranny" (D I.40) by actively encouraging oppression of the common people at the hands of "the sons of Brutus."

As for the more senior nobles who constituted the Senate during the Decemvirate's reign, Machiavelli suggests that they could have deposed Appius and eliminated the Ten at any time (D I.40); instead, they decided to tolerate Appius's tyranny out of "envy" for the people's former liberty and in hopes of indefinitely preventing reappointment of plebeian tribunes. More than that, as Machiavelli observes, senators were content to see the Ten's tyranny persist so long as the plebeians suffered disproportionately from the abuses committed by Appius and by their own sons, whose favor he cultivated as the principal base of his continued authority (D I.40).

There are other important differences between Appius and Machiavelli's more astute and more accomplished tyrants, some of which will apply to Walter as well: Rather than, as Agathocles and Nabis did, using successful military command to consolidate power, Appius remained dependent both on the Senate "to order for war" and on a popular army to prosecute it (D I.40). Moreover, the decemvir allows others to command Rome's army while he remains in the city. When the Volsci and Sabines attacked Rome and the Ten were compelled to convene the Senate, Appius elects to stay in the city rather than lead any of the levied soldiers. Oblivious to the wisdom Machiavelli offers in *The Prince*, that princes must always personally command their troops (P 14), Appius—like other imprudent tyrants, biblical and classical—succumbs to erotic enticements at home when he ought to have been leading soldiers in the field. Appius infamously attempts to dishonor and ravish Virginia, the daughter of the centurion Virginius, a plebeian soldier. As Machiavelli declares unequivocally in *The Prince*, princes are sure to arouse popular hatred when they molest their subjects' women (P 17, P 19).

Indeed, readers are prompted to wonder whether Machiavelli's advice regarding leading one's troops in the field and avoiding mischief at home are mutually reinforcing. In this instance, Appius's attempt to degrade and defile Virginia provokes her desperate father into "killing her so as to save her," and the outraged people, mobilized collectively for war, secede from the city and overthrow the Decemvirate's tyranny, which culminates in Appius's arrest and suicide (D I.40). The people and the Senate, who through "excessive desires" for, respectively, liberty and rule, had "erred greatly" by eliminating the consulship and the tribunate, reinstitute these magistracies and thus restore "Roman liberty to its ancient form"—with severe social strife forestalled in the city for a considerable time. However, as we will observe, after the Florentine nobles and people collaborate to overthrow Walter's tyranny, their interclass coalition almost immediately collapses, and Florence falls back into violent social conflict (FH II.39–42).[5]

THE SOCIAL FOUNDATIONS OF WALTER'S TYRANNY

Walter's tyranny emerges out of circumstances not entirely unlike those that enabled Appius to become tyrant of Rome: Florence suffered not only from intense discord between the nobles and the people, but from violent splits among the nobles (FH III.12). Moreover, the people were divided between guildsmen (*popolani*) and the *popolo minuto* (the plebs or *sottoposti*), who were not enrolled in guilds of their own but were subject to arbitrary and exploitative governance by the guilds (FH III.12). Adding to Florence's domestic turmoil, losses to the city's Tuscan territorial holdings immediately before Walter's ascension to power increased popular discontent in the city.

Machiavelli reports how, in 1340, the city's most powerful citizens (*cittadini potenti*)—a dominant clique comprising nobles, magistrates, and wealthy guildsmen—were abusing their authority in the republic. In particular, the nobles strictly supervised the selection of the foreigners who served as the city's "rectors," the *Capitano* and the *Podestà*, to ensure that these judicial magistrates consistently rendered judgments favorable to themselves in criminal and civil proceedings (FH II.32). So pleased were the nobles with the corrupt and abusive functioning of these foreign judges that they established a new, extraordinary rectorship, the captain of the guard, which exerted full authority over the entire Florentine citizenry. Machiavelli's emphatic endorsement, in the *Discourses*, of practices through which popular assemblies rather than foreign arbitrators render judgments in domestic trials no doubt derives from such corrupt use of foreign judges throughout Florence's history (D I.7–8).

Machiavelli reports that the new captain of the guard, Jacopo da Gubbioto, continually injured as many individuals as pleased the city's most powerful faction; but when he offended two nobles of the Bardi and Frescobaldi families, these "naturally arrogant" nobles conspired to take vengeance on the captain through a conspiracy, including many other noble families and also some *popolani* "who disliked the tyranny of the ruling clique" (FH II.32). Armed conflict was avoided only when the Podestà permitted the Bardi and Frescobaldi factions to retire to the countryside (*contado*) with the promise that they would henceforth be left alone. Yet the ruling clique of *potenti* quickly broke the accord by establishing yet another rector, with jurisdiction over the countryside, to further punish the Bardi and Frescobaldi families, who had in good faith laid down arms and retired from the city (FH II.32). Looking ahead to the tyranny of the Duke of Athens, Machiavelli remarks of the Bardi-Frescobaldi faction: when they eventually "met the opportunity to gain vengeance" for this grievous offense, "they used it well" (FH II.32).

As a result of these upheavals in the republic, Florence lost an important subject city, Lucca, to its Tuscan rival, Pisa (FH II.33). The efforts to win it back, according to Machiavelli, cost Florence a great amount in money and even more in reputation. As "always happens" in the loss of a war, he declares, the people were furious with the government, publicly accusing the magistrates throughout the piazzas of greed and malfeasance. Machiavelli suggests in the *Discourses* that this kind of popular indignation can be ameliorated in republics like Rome, where the people are free to air such accusations in large public assemblies, which were lacking in Florence throughout most of its history (D I.7–8). In any case, when the war to keep Lucca began, the Florentines, as they often did, appointed a special commission—in this case comprising twenty citizens—to oversee its prosecution (FH II.33). Unlike the Roman consuls, Florence's chief magistrates, the priors or *signori*, held authority for too short a time to conduct military campaigns, let alone lead troops in the field.

After the first captain appointed by the Twenty of War proceeded, according to Machiavelli, with neither spirit nor prudence, the Florentines asked King Robert of Naples for aid (FH II.33). Robert, as he had done in 1326, sent to Florence as his vicar Walter, the Duke of Athens. The duke arrived just when the war he had been sent to oversee ended in disaster with the loss of Lucca. The Twenty, in Machiavelli's estimation, compounded their initial mistake of choosing a bad first captain by giving their new one, Walter, complete authority to help them subdue the now fully indignant people, to halt the denunciations many were hurling against them, and to protect them unreservedly. Thus the Twenty appointed the duke as their protector—specifically as captain of the magistracy's armed companies (FH II.33).

The Bardi-Frescobaldi nobles, Machiavelli reminds us, were already enraged by the appointments, instigated by rival nobles, of hostile rectors in both the city and the countryside. Since they were familiar with Walter from his earlier tenure in Florence, "they judged that now was the time to quench the fire burning within themselves by ruining the city" (FH II.33). So, much like Appius Claudius, Walter is empowered by two sets of political actors, each thinking the prince will serve *them*, not their adversaries. However, in Florence the two actors are not, initially, the "natural" humors embodied by the nobles and the people, as in Rome; rather, on the one hand are the fearful magistrates of the Twenty and, on the other, an especially disaffected subset of nobles. Machiavelli writes that the nobles of the Bardi-Frescobaldi faction sought to gain vengeance "by subjecting themselves to a prince whose virtue was known to them, and whose insolence would shortly be known to their adversaries. Thus they hoped that he might reward the one and crush the other" (FH II.33).

In this light Walter, at the start of his reign, seems to be the less preferred form of a "civil prince" whom Machiavelli describes in chapter 9 of *The Prince*: one who assumes the rank of prince within a republic through support from the nobles (or of some part of them) rather than from the people. But the situation becomes more complicated as Walter, in support of his tyranny, soon enlists the plebs, who in Florence, unlike ancient republics, stand fully separated from and subordinated to the people. Machiavelli reports that the disaffected nobles often met Walter secretly, entreating him to seize complete lordship over the city, pledging their full support (FH II.33). Several debt-laden families from the upper guilds also supported this growing conspiracy: according to Machiavelli, they "hoped that others would pay the debts that they themselves could not; and that their patria's enslavement would lead to their own freedom from their creditors" (FH II.33). Florence's discredited magistrates, disaffected nobles, and dissolute *popolani*, Machiavelli suggests, aroused the duke's already "ambitious spirit to even greater greed for rule."

To demonstrate his "severity and justice" and enhance his favor with the plebs (FH II.33), Machiavelli reports, besides fining and exiling many citizens, Walter executed the individuals the Twenty had commissioned to carry out the failed reacquisition of Lucca, including Giovanni de' Medici. While Machiavelli often casts Walter as an enemy of the Medici family, as he clearly does here, his account of the duke's reign will highlight many affinities with Medici rule in his own lifetime (here he accentuates how, in the city's past, the Medici had served as bulwarks against tyranny, but he will proceed to highlight the nature of their present tyranny within Florence). The city's middling citizens, Machiavelli recounts, were frightened by these executions, which pleased only the nobles and the plebs: "the former out of a vengeful spirit against the people and the latter because they naturally revel in evil" (FH II.34). But if the plebs "naturally" exult in evil, as Machiavelli claims here, why must Walter give the appearance of being "a severe and just man" to win them over? As I argued in chapter 7, readers must always ask such questions whenever Machiavelli seems to repudiate his previous favorable views of the *popolo* and the *plebe* in the *Histories*.

Be that as it may, whereas Appius had to manage merely two classes in subjugating an ancient republic like Rome, Walter must take account of six different sets of social actors to secure his rule in Florence: the magistrates of the Twenty, who were seeking to deflect blame for their failure to retake Lucca; the nobles and their allies in the magistracies and rectorships who had been dominating the politics of the city; the Bardi-Frescobaldi nobles who are seeking vengeance against these nobles; the four treacherous, profligate *popolani* families seeking debt relief; the plebs who resent being exploited and oppressed by the richest guildsmen; and the majority of citizens who make up the middle and lower guilds. Only the last group, at this point, opposes Walter.

As Walter paraded in the streets, Machiavelli describes how he was praised and encouraged by many parties to investigate and punish corruption among the magistrates (FH II.34). Consequently, and contrary to their expectations, the Twenty's authority diminished and the duke's greatness increased—so much so that out of fear many families began painting his coat of arms on their doorways to demonstrate their "friendship" with Walter. As Machiavelli remarks elsewhere on Hiero of Syracuse (P 6; D dl), Walter was now prince in all but name. However, unlike Hiero, the duke will not free his city of reliance on mercenary forces and then broaden and strengthen its civic military. Instead of unifying the Florentine nobles, *popolani*, and plebs into one military force, the duke will combine only the plebs with foreign forces he calls into the city to serve as his base of military power. Moreover, perhaps to emphasize how "effeminate" Walter's reign would ultimately prove to be, Machiavelli describes how the duke, to give himself an air of religiosity and humanity, took up residence in a convent.

THE SPEECH OF THE UNNAMED PRIOR, OR MACHIAVELLI'S PLEA TO THE MEDICI TYRANTS

Machiavelli recounts how Walter next informed the Signoria, the republic's chief executive committee, that he should be given full lordship for the greater good of the city, since supposedly all its parties desired such an outcome (FH II.34). The priors, Machiavelli notes, were afraid to refuse the duke for their own safety; but since they felt loyal to their patria, they "spiritedly declined" the duke's offer. To put his "evil designs" in motion, Walter publicly called for "the whole people" to gather before him the next morning at the Piazza della Santa Croce. This practice was known in Florence as a *Balìa*: a gathering of the multitude where general acclamation reigned, rather than a formal assembly within which the people discuss matters before issuing a formal judgment by a head count. The Signoria, given that the duke's armed forces were larger than their own, decided their only recourse was to "pray" that Walter desist from this endeavor, or at least consider taking up a more limited form of lordship over the city. Machiavelli attributes to one of the priors who approached Walter one of the most memorable speeches from the *Histories*: an address that echoes important observations on liberty that Machiavelli already made in *The Prince* and the *Discourses*.

Three themes run through the speech of the unnamed prior: the unreliability and insufficiency of the duke's base of support; the depth of Florence's love for liberty; and dire predictions concerning the outcome of the duke's efforts to impose tyranny upon the city. Regarding Walter's unsteady allies, the prior points out that the nobles do not seek the duke's benefit but merely want "to spew their poison" on their rivals (FH II.34). Once these "present friends" use Walter's tyranny "to combat their adversaries with your authority," the prior avers, they will eventually "seek to eliminate you and establish themselves as princes." These remarks call to mind two important passages from Machiavelli's previous works: in the *Discourses*, he speaks of the venom that the insolent Roman nobility spewed on the people after the expulsion of the Tarquins (D I.3). They also recall Machiavelli's suggestion in *The Prince* that the nobles who empower a prince to oppress others are quite likely to turn on him eventually (P 9).

Proceeding further, Machiavelli has the nameless prior claim that the duke's military support is too weak "to keep this city enslaved" (FH II.34): the external arms available to Walter "are insufficient" to the task, and his internal forces, the plebs, are "untrustworthy," for they "will change their minds at the slightest accident" (FH II.34). The prior proves prescient in both these regards, as the duke's French forces are too few, and the plebs—as well as most of the disaffected nobles—do turn against Walter as his fortunes begin to sour.

In heralding the Florentines' love of liberty, the prior insists that Walter's tyranny is bound to fail because "here, the name of freedom is infused with a vigor that no force can conquer, no duration extinguish, no effort countermand" (FH II.34). This claim resonates with Machiavelli's remarks in *The Prince* concerning the persistence of "the name of liberty" in cities that have once been republics (P 5). Even if the duke managed to establish a principality that endured for generations, the prior insists, it would never be fully secure, since "no span of time diminishes the appetite for freedom, not only among those who have experienced it, but also among those for whom it remains a civic memory."

The prior suggests that there are two ways the civic memory of liberty persists in former republics: in the first place, "memories of freedom passed on to sons by their fathers" have often proved sufficient to inspire the overthrow of tyrannies in free cities like Florence (FH II.34). The second enduring source of memories of freedom emanates from the physical structure of the city itself: the Signoria's spokesman insists that even if fathers prove remiss in passing along their own experiences of liberty to their children, "the civic buildings, the seat of government, and the symbols of free orders" will continue to remind future generations of the city's legacy of liberty. The implication is that even if Walter killed all the adult citizens, to eradicate the memory of liberty he would have to raze the city as Machiavelli, in *The Prince* (P 5), advises tyrants to do with former republics.

The prior warns that at some point he and his colleagues will surely say "I told you so" to Walter, should they survive the "ruin" that will inevitably result from his tyranny: he remarks, sardonically, "You will well remember that we advised you wisely" (FH II.34). Again, Machiavelli constructs his narrative so that the unnamed prior is prophetic. Walter will, in fact, confront "the whole city as an enemy," a circumstance in which he must "fear everyone and enjoy no recourse against anyone." Evoking strains of Machiavelli's admonitions in *The Prince* against incurring hatred, especially among the collectivity of the people (P 9), the prior insists: "No remedy will be available for this evil, for only those lords are safe who have few enemies whom they can either kill or exile. But those who have aroused universal animosity are never secure, for evil comes from all directions.... Only those dominions endure that subjects voluntarily accept" (cf. P 9; D I.16–18).

The prior concludes by insisting that Walter will wind up with less power, not more, than he already enjoys, and that he will cause more damage to himself and to the city in the effort to expand and extend his lordship. He implores the duke to avoid an inevitably perverse course of action: "Do not be blinded by shortsighted ambition to pursue a position in which you can neither be secure nor from which you can ascend any further; you must inevitably fall from such a status with great harm ensuing both for yourself and for us" (FH II.34).

Given the political context in which Machiavelli composed the *Histories*—specifically that it was commissioned by Medici prelates who continued to rule the city as tyrannical princes—it is not difficult to imagine that this *laudatio*, which Machiavelli places in the mouth of the unnamed prior, functions as an exhortation to the Medici. Their reign shares many commonalities with Walter's: both were installed in Florence by collusion between disaffected nobles and a foreign prince (Walter by Robert of Naples, the Medici by Ferdinand of Spain); both take to ruling with religious airs (Walter governs from a convent, the Medici from the Vatican); both replace the people's coats of arms with their own throughout the city; and both rule with foreign aristocratic and nonnative, noncivic honorific titles (Walter is a duke, and the Medici are prelates). Given these similarities, Machiavelli seems to be imploring the Medici to either completely destroy the memory of liberty in Florence or fully restore its status within the city. Walter's impending fate, of which they are fully aware, should encourage the Medici (if they are paying attention) to depart from his mode of ruling.

Nevertheless, Machiavelli writes that the duke's "obstinate spirit" remained unmoved by the words of the Signoria's anonymous representative (FH II.35)—no more than Appius could he be shamed by senatorial appeals to civic decorum. Like Appius, who professed he wanted to improve Rome's liberty by perfecting its legal code, Walter claims he intends not to remove but to restore freedom by uniting the city. He responds to the prior that "only disunited and never united cities are truly slaves." Most sinisterly, Walter uses a certain Machiavellian logic in claiming he gave no thought to any perils he might suffer by pursuing lordship over Florence, for "only a man who is not good would forsake pursuit of the good out of a fear of evil; and only a coward would avoid a glorious enterprise because of an uncertain outcome" (FH II.35; cf. P 26; D I.18, D III.4).

The priors agreed that the next morning, in their piazza and not in the duke's, and by their own authority, not by his, they would bestow on him in front of all the people the one-year lordship that they agreed upon with King Robert (FH II.35). Machiavelli then recounts how, on September 8, 1342, Walter, accompanied by all his friends and many citizens, came to the piazza, then ascended the steps of the Palazzo della Signoria with all the priors (FH II.35). During the announcement that conferred on the duke a one-year lordship over the city, someone in the crowd shouted, "For life!," which caused a tumult that one of the priors tried to quell, only to be shouted down.

"Thus," Machiavelli writes, "the people consented that the duke be appointed lord not only for one year, but perpetually; and then his name sounded forth throughout the *piazza* from the shouting multitude" (FH II.35). The Florentines apparently do not love liberty as much as the anonymous prior suggested the previous evening—or at least not as much as they will once they realize the grave costs of having it taken away from them. Is this, in Machiavellian terms, an example of the people desiring their own ruin (D I.55)? Or does it set the stage for them to later express greater ferocity in reclaiming rather than maintaining their liberty (D II.2)? Or does Machiavelli really blame the Florentine people as sharply in acclaiming Walter as he surely does the Roman people in electing Appius? The Florentine episode does have the air of a sham: likely the individual who nominated Walter for a lifetime lordship, and some large number of the audience who subsequently acclaimed him, were plants.[6]

Whatever the truth, Machiavelli then describes how the head of the Signoria's guard, who—perhaps tellingly—had been bribed by Walter's "friends," admitted the duke, but not the signori, into the palace. And so the priors, "fearful and dishonored," slinked back to their homes while the duke's family ransacked their quarters, tore to pieces the ensign of the people, and raised the duke's banner above the palace. This outcome, Machiavelli remarks, deeply saddened good men and pleased those who, either ignorantly or maliciously, had acquiesced to bring it about (FH II.35).

THE DUKE OF ATHENS'S DISHONORABLE EVIL

Having attained lordship, the duke, Machiavelli writes, sought to deprive the republic's traditional defenders of liberty of authority by banning the priors from ever returning to the palace (FH II.36). Walter then seized the banners from the gonfaloniers of the companies of the people (thus ensuring that the people could not be formally called to arms beneath them); revoked the Ordinances of Justice against the nobles (so that they could now hold magistracies without having to enroll in guilds); freed many prisoners (presumably political allies of his clients); called back from the countryside the exiled Bardi and Frescobaldi families (whose friends and relatives had initially hatched the plot to make Walter prince); and banned the private holding of arms throughout the city. In the effort to intimidate residents within the city, he cultivated friendship with many foreigners outside its confines (making allies of both former subjects like the Aretines and stalwart enemies like the Pisans, whom he was hired to vanquish); and finally he manipulated debts and taxes to benefit his supporters and harass those he distrusted.

With respect to the government of the city, Machiavelli describes how Walter stripped the magistrates of all authority and relied exclusively on the judgments of foreign rectors (FH II.36). Through these rectors from Perugia and Assisi (the latter, ironically, the home of Christendom's gentlest saint) the duke despoiled and oppressed the citizenry via excessive assessments and unjust sentences. This is of course precisely the mode of ruling pursued by the clique of *potenti* that initially prompted the Bardi-Frescobaldi faction of nobles to revolt and eventually resulted in Walter's elevation to prince. In effect, nothing has changed but the targets and intensity of the prevailing injustice. Machiavelli notes that Walter's humane and severe posture—much like Appius's, we should note—quickly gave way to his arrogant and cruel nature, both in and out of the city: he tortured, exiled, or killed many "great citizens and popular nobles." Machiavelli reports that the duke began to spy on the nobles within the city, despite their initial support of him, and restored those outside to the patria, fearing that their continued exile would excite their "generous spirit" and result in their attacking him militarily (FH II.36).

Within the city, Machiavelli writes, Walter benefited only two groups, based on whose favor he sought to secure his tyranny: the plebs and the foreign men of arms (FH II.36). In May, during the season of popular festivals, the duke established "new companies of the plebs and lesser people, to whom he gave titles of honor, banners, and money" (FH II.36). The duke hence endeared himself to the plebs: before Walter's tyranny they had no right to carry arms and bear standards in their own companies, since they were not organized in any guilds of their own; rather, as Machiavelli later explains, they suffered subjection to the arbitrary jurisdiction of other established guilds (FH III.12).

As for the foreign soldiers, Machiavelli describes how large numbers of Frenchmen came to Florence—either invited by the duke or seeking his favor on their own initiative—and were promptly rewarded with Walter's personal trust and with prominent positions. Soon Florence was subjected not only to French military forces, Machiavelli observes, but also to their feudal and courtly customs, "as men and women began imitating them in manner and dress, affronting both civil life and common decency" (FH II.36). Contemporary readers might find this reminiscent of the way Lorenzo de' Medici's followers corrupted Florentine nobles through decadent and debauched courtly ways.[7] In the *Discourses*, perhaps Machiavelli also had in mind Walter and Lorenzo, not just Appius, when he described how easily the decemvir managed to corrupt so many young Roman nobles, despite their "good upbringings," as well as the honorable senator Quintus Fabius, despite his "good manners" (D I.42). Even the slightest "ambitious appetite," Machiavelli observes, can be fanned into the flame of corruption by the "malignity" of a tyrant such as Appius in Rome or Walter and Lorenzo in Florence.

What most offended Florentines about Walter's rule, according to Machiavelli, was the wanton and disrespectful violence with which the duke and his Frenchmen treated Florentine women (FH II.36). Like Appius, Walter breaks one of the principal rules set forth in *The Prince*: Do not molest your subjects' women, lest fear, which benefits a prince, be converted into hatred, which invariably precipitates his downfall (P 17, 19). A son may forget the death of a father, Machiavelli infamously muses (especially if it accelerates his inheritance of a patrimony), but a man will avenge, at any cost to himself, the rape of a wife, mother, sister, or daughter. Like Appius the decemvir, Walter the duke would pay with his principate for such shameless abuse of his subjects' women.[8]

The Florentines' indignation grew, Machiavelli claims, as they witnessed the majesty of the city degraded, its orders destroyed, its laws revoked, its decency corrupted, and its civic comportment eviscerated (FH II.36). Those who were unaccustomed to bowing before pompous displays of regality could not encounter Walter in the streets without despair, compelled as they now were to shamefully honor someone who paraded about in the company of numerous armed soldiers and horsemen—the French equivalents of Roman lictors. Moreover, much as the Ten secured their tyranny by expropriating the property of imprisoned, dead, or exiled enemies and sharing the proceeds with their clients, Machiavelli emphasizes how the duke increasingly intimidated and destroyed individuals and families through excessive assessments and arbitrary executions.

To demonstrate that he was universally loved when in fact the opposite was true, according to Machiavelli, Walter did this: When Matteo di Morozzo attempted to ingratiate himself with the duke by exposing a purported Medici plot against him, Walter had Matteo executed rather than any of the Medici (FH II.36). Whether he acted with heedless cruelty in this instance or seeking to regain the affection of the Medici, whom he had previously offended, here, Machiavelli avers, the duke acted stupidly: it completely discouraged others who might warn him of future conspiracies. Perhaps the duke's most singularly despicable act, conveyed by Machiavelli, occurs when Walter violently removes the tongue of someone who protested his assessments.

Machiavelli sarcastically claims that even a people more servile than the Florentines, who themselves know not how to be either freemen nor slaves, would have risen up to reclaim their liberty from a tyrant such as Walter (FH II.36). Soon, therefore, citizens of "every quality" decided to either lose their lives or win back their freedom: and so three separate conspiracies emerged among the *grandi* (the nobles), the *popolani* (the popular nobles and upper guildsmen), and the *popolo* (the artisans of the middling and lower guilds). The first group realized that they had not gained the city for themselves as they had hoped; the second recognized that they had lost it entirely; and the third were growing increasingly impoverished under the duke's yoke (FH II.36).

Florence's archbishop, Agnolo Acciaioli, who had previously praised the duke in his sermons and encouraged the people to favor him, Machiavelli reports, now decided to make amends by leading the strongest conspiracy, that of the Bardi-Frescobaldi nobles (FH II.36). The Donati served as "princes" of the second conspiracy, primarily comprising former noble and traditionally high *popolani* families. Antonio Adimari led the people's conspiracy, with the support of the Medici and other popular families. As Walter begins to catch wind of the conspiracies forming against him, he has Adimari arrested, but he rejects the advice of his minions, who advised him to immediately execute any citizens who might oppose him.

Machiavelli recounts that Walter instead adopted an alternative plan that posed some likelihood of successfully securing his rule: since he had on previous occasions summoned citizens for consultation over particular policies, the duke announced the names of three hundred men who should appear before him for such a conference, while simultaneously sending abroad for additional foreign forces (FH II.36). Walter planned to arrest the three hundred citizens once they appeared. However, Adimari's detention and the call for outside forces alarmed the conspirators, and thus significant numbers refused to accept the duke's summons. Contrary to Walter's intention, the list of three hundred now served as a public roster of the disaffected citizens for all the conspirators to observe, even those who previously were unaware of each other. Consequently, all the conspirators quickly began conferring with one another, encouraging themselves to die like armed men rather than be led like heifers to the slaughter. Thus Walter's plan backfired. In a matter of hours, Machiavelli recounts, all three conspiracies were mindful of each other, and they agreed to meet armed at the Mercato Vecchio the next day, July 26, 1343, and "call the people to liberty."

In some sense Walter did unintentionally and unwisely what, according to Machiavelli, Romulus had done intentionally and prudently; that is, collect three hundred leading citizens into a kind of senate (D I.9). But Romulus did so long before he became hated by Rome's leading citizens. Given these different circumstances, Walter, like Agathocles or Clearchus, might then have used the assembly of such senatorial figures as an occasion to eliminate them all as threats to his rule (P 9). But Walter, unlike Machiavelli's Agathocles, did not keep his appeal for outside support a secret; hence he could not avoid alerting his potential victims among "the senators and the richest of the people" to his deadly intentions (P 9). Unlike Agathocles, the duke actively fosters collaboration against himself among the city's elite.

NEITHER LOVE NOR FEAR, ONLY HATRED

At noon on July 26, according to Machiavelli, the armed conspirators assembled at the old market, while "the entire people," as they often do early the *Histories*, "arrived with arms, shouting for liberty" (FH II.37).

The heads of all the families, both noble and popular, Machiavelli reports, gathered and pledged unity for their mutual defense and to achieve the death of the duke, save for half a dozen pro-Walter families. The latter, along with "the basest among the plebs," including the butchers, came running to the piazza to defend the duke. Walter himself armed the palace and called his horsemen from many parts of the city, who, having suffered numerous casualties along the way, arrived at the piazza in numbers only approaching several hundred. While the duke dithered over defending the palazzo or attacking the piazza, Machiavelli relates that the most aggrieved of the conspirators, the Medici, Ruccellai, and Cavicciuli, among others, worried that, should the duke appear, many who now stood against him might change their allegiance in his favor (FH II.37). Thus they attacked the palace aggressively, prompting the pro-Walter *popolani* and plebs, now fully cognizant of the duke's drastic change of fortune, to switch sides against him.

The combat between the duke's forces and what was now the entire *popolo* proved fierce, and Machiavelli notes that the palace could not hold out long (FH II.37). Large numbers of the duke's forces either surrendered or fled. In response, the duke attempted to sway the people by a desperate act of humanity: he freed the detained conspirators "with love and grace," including Adimari, whom, much to the man's consternation, he made a knight. Walter also restored the people's ensigns to the palace and removed his own. But none of these gestures served him well, performed as they were, in Machiavelli's words, "so late and passed season," and "through compulsion rather than dignity." Now desperate in the palace, knowing that he faced either starvation or the sword in just a few days' time, Walter realized that in aspiring to too much—precisely as the nameless prior had earlier predicted—he was now on the verge of possessing nothing (FH II.37).

The Sienese sent forces to support the *popolo* and ambassadors to negotiate between the duke and the people, but the people would agree to nothing until the rector from Assisi, Guglielmo, and his son were handed over to them (FH II.37). Walter, recall, had used such foreign magistrates to perpetrate his most cruel and unjust acts of oppression in both the city and the countryside. The duke was compelled by his men within the palace to comply with this demand. Thus, in Machiavelli's terrifying account, the father and son from Assisi, delivered over to thousands of their former victims, suffered the fury of the multitude: the crowd stabbed, tore, and even chewed the two in a cannibalistic orgy that persisted long after they were dead. Not even the boy's youth, beauty, and innocence, Machiavelli observes in a seemingly sympathetic tone, could save him from the ferocious wrath of the multitude. Yet one is prompted to ask, If the son was so innocent, why did the crowd ask for him, and not only his father, to be turned over to them? One must query whether the son of Guglielmo had in any way behaved like either the "sons of Brutus" or the sons of senators whom Appius Claudius had permitted to rampantly oppress the Roman people.

In what may, in fact, be a clear warning to the Medici, Machiavelli describes what happens to usurpers-cum-tyrants of republics, their henchmen, and their most intimate relations as well: The people sought to satisfy all their bodily senses in the acts of vengeance they inflicted on the rector and his son—the people were enraptured by hearing their cries, observing their wounds, and ripping their flesh (FH II.37). Only the sense of taste was left to be satisfied, and, as if in some unholy mass, the people devoured the father and son alive. Repeating what he declares elsewhere, Machiavelli observes, "Undoubtedly, the people vent more indignation and inflict graver harm in recovering as opposed to defending their liberty" (FH II.37; cf. D II.2).

Once the multitude purged its vengeful spirit by consuming the body and blood of the rector from Assisi and his son, an accord was possible: Machiavelli describes how the duke was then permitted to leave the city safely with his men and his possessions (FH II.37). Before departing, Walter renounced all claims on Florence, a pledge he reluctantly ratified once he reached the security of Casentino—he would have retracted this renunciation but for his armed escort's threat to take him back to the city as a prisoner. After ten months (evoking Appius's ten-man tyranny), Florence was freed from the rule of a man whom Machiavelli describes as avaricious and cruel; one who desired others' enslavement rather than their goodwill; an impatient addressee and overbearing speaker. Machiavelli surmises that Walter may have wanted to be feared rather than loved, but he insists that the duke proceeded in a way that brought him only hatred. Our author finally judges that Walter's "own wicked deeds" cost him the lordship that "the wicked counsel of others" had granted him (FH II.37).

After the duke's expulsion, all parties of the city, popular and noble, reconcile and, like their Roman forebears, reinstitute the orders of their republic; in particular, the guildsmen revoke the Ordinances of Justice so that previously banned nobles can once again hold office. However, the nobles immediately attempt to expel the guildsmen from the government, sparking a full-scale civil war far more violent and destructive than the revolt that expelled Walter (FH II.39–42).[9]

DOES A PRINCE OR TYRANT ALWAYS NEED THE PEOPLE?

In his concluding reflections on Appius Claudius in book I, chapters 40 and 41, Machiavelli departs from the advice he gives civil princes-cum-tyrants in The Prince (P 9), and elsewhere in the Discourses (D I.16); namely, to favor the people consistently and energetically. In considering the demise of Appius's tyranny, Machiavelli ponders circumstances when a prince might successfully forsake reliance on the people's support—indeed, when he might turn to oppressing them outright. He writes that a tyrant who has come to power with the people's favor

> should never begin oppressing the people until he has eliminated the nobles, at which time, once the people realize that they have become servile, they can find protection nowhere else. All of those who have established tyrannies in republics have followed this mode. If Appius had maintained this mode, he would have established a tyranny more vital and enduring; but he did exactly the opposite, and in so doing, he acted most imprudently. (D I.40)

Two odd aspects of this passage are immediately apparent. First, it is not as if Appius's failure to eliminate the Roman nobility enabled the people to enlist the nobles' aid in alleviating their oppression or in overthrowing the decemvirs. Machiavelli makes it patently clear that the nobles refused to help accomplish either. To be sure, the senators Valerius and Horatius later aided the plebeian cause, but only after the plebs had seceded from Rome and hence made the demise of Appius inevitable (D I.44). Second, Machiavelli's claim that *all* tyrants who emerged in republics with the support of the people eventually became their oppressors seems overstated. After all, several princes who inspire Machiavelli's model of the Greek tyrant discussed previously did not begin oppressing the people once they had vanquished the nobles. Arguably, the likes of Agathocles, Nabis, Clearchus, and Cleomenes gave the people greater leverage against the tyrants themselves by invigorating and expanding their popular militaries. Indeed, in his discussion of Appius, Machiavelli explicitly invokes Nabis—here a "tyrant" rather than a civil prince (P 9)—whose "friendship" with the Spartan people enabled him to militarily hold off "the entirety of Greece and the Roman Republic" (D I.40). Whether or not Machiavelli's invocation of "all" tyrants is hyperbole, the passage above certainly raises the possibility that a new tyrant who has favored the people and eliminated the nobles might then successfully both oppress the people and maintain his rule.

Appius, of course, does exactly the opposite of what Machiavelli recommends in the civil principality chapter of *The Prince* when he switches sides from the people to the nobles: "by abandoning the people and favoring the nobles, Appius made a most obvious mistake" (D I.40). Recall that Appius oppressed the people as a senator, favored them on the path to becoming a tyrant, then egregiously oppressed them during his reign, with the aid of young nobles. What if Appius had successfully eliminated the nobles and *then* wished to commence oppressing the people? Machiavelli gives three options Appius might have taken, each of which entails enlisting a foreign or external source of power: hiring a personal bodyguard composed of foreigners (*satelliti forestieri*); arming peasants from the countryside (*contado*) to perform the tasks that generally the armed plebs of a city ought to do ("*faccia quello ufficio che arebbe a fare la plebe*");[10] or relying on a nearby foreign power to provide defense.

Machiavelli expresses ambivalence over the effectiveness of these modes, musing that one or another "might" secure a prince who confronts his own people as an enemy (D I.40). The first, of course, was more or less employed by both Appius and Walter: the former had a large number of lictors, and young nobles serve as his "satellites"; the latter had French soldiers and an armed contingent of plebs in his entourage. As I will discuss below, this is also the mode that Roman emperors, beginning with Augustus, would follow by maintaining the Praetorian Guard.

The second option, arming peasants to oppress the city, was relevant to Machiavelli's own experience: such recourse would have been available to Machiavelli's patron, Piero Soderini, had not the Florentine *ottimati* intervened to ensure that the gonfalonier would not personally command the militia that Machiavelli was recruiting from the Florentine *contado*. Florence's nobles, of course, had already ruled out using the city's plebs and guildsmen—which "ought" to be the case—as the basis for a militia. Indeed, Machiavelli seems to lament that in modern Italian cities, peasants and plebs are too segregated to serve together as a popular military resource. Reminding readers of a major source of the Roman Republic's military prowess, Machiavelli notes how in ancient times "the countryside and Rome were the same thing" (*sendo una medesima cosa il contado e Roma*) (D. I.40). Thus the option of arming the countryside against the city was unavailable to Appius, since Roman peasants were as much his enemies as were the Roman plebs. The third option, relying on support from another city, of course, raises the risk of foreign domination. Recall that Walter pursued a diplomatic pact of mutual defense with Florence's traditional rivals, Arezzo and Pisa, but this proved inconsequential to his efforts to maintain his tyranny.

In the next chapter of the *Discourses*, Machiavelli continues his ruminations over alternative courses of action that Appius might have pursued to preserve his tyranny (D I.41). Noting that Appius made multiple mistakes, Machiavelli singles out one as especially significant: the decemvir's rapid transition from treating the plebs with humility and kindness to treating them with pride and cruelty. If one wishes to transform oneself from appearing to be "a popular man" (*uomo popolare*) to one who actively oppresses the people, Machiavelli avers, one must do so "gradually and with credible pretense"; otherwise "everyone will recognize one's false spirit." Machiavelli further explains:

> If one has maintained an appearance of goodness for some time and then, for his own ends, desires to turn to wickedness, he should do so little by little, conducting himself as occasions permit. In this way, before one's alternative nature [*diversa natura*] deprives him of old favor, it provides him with so much new favor that one's authority does not decrease. Proceeding otherwise ensures ruin, as one is left friendless and unprotected. (D I.41)

The passage raises many more questions than it answers. What are the ends a tyrant might wish to pursue in undertaking such a transformation? Is oppressing the people an end in itself, or is it instrumental to some other desired or necessary end? What kind of micro-aggressions permit one to still, albeit temporarily, maintain the appearance of goodness? Additionally, what occasions justify resort to incrementally applied cruelty? Can one, for instance, resort to appropriation of property or molestation of women, even just slightly, in one's gradual turn toward oppressing the people? Can such wicked acts, which would, if performed at a stroke, certainly provoke hatred, be commenced without any detection if perpetrated bit by bit? In the absence of the capacity to make oneself physically invisible, exactly how would this be possible? Who are the new, powerful friends a prince might acquire that would permit him to maintain his authority? The three kinds of friends mentioned in the previous chapter—foreign bodyguards, armed peasants, and alien cities or princes—are no guarantees of success in the joint effort to oppress one's people and maintain one's state.

Machiavelli concludes that Appius ultimately failed because "he knew not how to do what he could have done" (D I.40). But exactly what that means is not entirely clear given the unsatisfactorily limited quality of the three options that Machiavelli hypothetically lays out for Appius in *discorso* 40, and the lack of specificity of the post facto advice he offers him in *discorso* 41. Readers are thus compelled to seek out other examples where Machiavelli discusses princes or tyrants who succeeded in maintaining their states despite not favoring their own people. The most prominent example, Septimius Severus, appears in Machiavelli's chapter in *The Prince* devoted to Roman emperors.

THE EMPEROR, THE PEOPLE, AND THE SOLDIERS

Chapter 19 of *The Prince* is the book's longest and, like the lengthiest chapter of the *Discourses* (D III.6), is largely devoted to conspiracies. The former chapter differs from the latter by more heavily emphasizing the need to avoid hatred, and by more extensively discussing the Roman emperors whose careers span the years AD 161-238. Machiavelli begins the chapter by reiterating his advice to civil princes-cum-tyrants provided throughout the rest of the book: maintain the favor of the common people by abstaining from molesting their women and appropriating their property, by checking the ambition of the nobles, and by keeping foreign enemies at bay (P 19). He invokes Nabis the Spartan yet again as the princely exemplar in these respects.

However, Machiavelli apparently departs from the world of "all cities," "all republics," and "all principalities," which, in his three major works, he declares to be invariably beset by conflicts between the two opposed humors of the *popolo* and the *grandi*. Chapter 19 introduces an alternative political universe, the world of the Roman emperors, in which a third humor emerges, a humor that entails a "third difficulty" princes must contend with: the "cruel and avaricious" humor of the soldiers, who exist completely apart from the people, and who exhibit a completely opposite motivation (P 19). In the Roman Republic, the Roman people (composed, as I noted above, of both peasants and plebs) were one with the Roman army, and therefore the people collectively confronted their humoral adversaries, the nobles, as citizen soldiers. Imperial Rome disjoined that popular civic-military entity such that domestic tumult was reconstituted in the form of an antagonism between the people, who seek security, and the soldiers, who seek plunder (plunder from the people as much as from foreign enemies). Thus, Machiavelli notes, the emperors struggled to contend with each humor in this new world-historical political configuration:

> While the people loved repose, and thus loved moderate princes, the soldiers loved princes of martial spirit—those who acted cruelly, insolently, and rapaciously toward the people so as to increase the wages of the cruel and avaricious soldiers. This situation ruined those emperors who either by nature or through skill could not earn a sufficiently great reputation to check both groups. (P 19)

Machiavelli reports that most emperors, especially "new men" without hereditary claims to the throne, adopted the "extraordinary" course of satisfying the soldiers' humor, "concerning themselves very little with harming the people" (P 19). It was necessary, they supposed, "to concentrate every effort on avoiding the hatred of the most powerful group," who at that time were the soldiers. As Machiavelli notes in the main chapter of the *Discourses* devoted to the Decemvirate, "in order to hold something with violence, he who does the forcing must exceed in power he who is forced" (D I.40). In chapter 9 of *The Prince*, Machiavelli advises civil princes to do what, apparently, Appius did not understand he should have done in the Roman Republic: princes should satisfy the humor of people, rather than that of the nobles, because the people are of greater number and hence of greater potential force—such a mode of proceeding entails the additional benefit of according with "decency" (*onestà*) (P 9). Now, in chapter 19, in the context of imperial Rome, Machiavelli declares that, even though the most powerful group, the soldiers, may be "corrupt," a prince must side with this most formidable actor, even if such an alliance "makes goodness your enemy" (P 19).

Still, Machiavelli points out, the strategy of permitting soldiers to abuse and despoil the people was successful only to the extent that a particular emperor managed "to maintain his reputation" with the soldiers (P 19). The prospects of success for a prince who inflicts "extraordinary" harms on the people, even when siding with a powerful army that is hostile to them, are limited. Of the cruel and rapacious emperors Machiavelli invokes—those who, "in satisfying the soldiers, were unsparing in the harms they visited upon the people"—three out of four "came to ruin." Commodus, Caracalla, and Maximinus suffered bad ends; only Septimius Severus prevailed.

Severus is the exception to the rule because, in Machiavelli's estimation, he possessed "such abundant virtue" that he maintained the friendship of the soldiers and, despite encumbering the people, "he always ruled felicitously because his virtues made both the soldiers and the people view him with great admiration" (P 19). Indeed, Machiavelli declares, under Severus "the people remained rather astounded and stupefied, while the soldiers remained reverent and satisfied." Apparently, in the context of a developing armed-subject population in the Romagna, Cesare Borgia could both "satisfy and stupefy" the people (P 7). But in the context of prevailing antagonism between the people and the military, only the army can be fully satisfied, and the best a prince can hope for is merely to amaze the people. Machiavelli deems Severus a universally feared and respected "new prince," one whose actions displayed the cunning of the fox and the ferocity of lion (cf. P 18): Severus's "very great reputation" kept the army from hating him, and it ensured that the people "never developed the hatred for him that his expropriations could have warranted" (P 19).

Machiavelli declares that "meticulous examination" of Severus's actions demonstrates how he satisfied the army and stupefied the people, avoiding the hatred of both (P 19). But the details that he provides concern only how Severus, on the one hand, manipulated and intimidated the Roman Senate and, on the other, deceived and eliminated rival claimants to the imperial throne. He provides none of the scrupulous attention to minute details of Severus's (or of the army's) interactions with the people of Rome that readers might hope for or expect. (Among the many historical figures that Machiavelli discusses in *The Prince*, Severus seems most like Nabis in this respect.) Certainly, Severus's ferociously intrepid military exploits would have impressed, indeed astounded, the Roman people: Machiavelli and his sources detail the intrigues and conquests that Severus, with breathtaking rapidity and reach, effected throughout eastern Europe, Italy, Syria, Byzantium, Parthia, and Britain. But Machiavelli leaves readers rather ill equipped to evaluate whether these military exploits are sufficiently astonishing to fully offset any hatred that Severus's domestic policies might otherwise have elicited from the Roman people.

If we consult Machiavelli's sources, Cassius Dio and Herodian,[11] for clarification, we find neither "extraordinary" nor wide-scale abuse perpetrated on the people by Severus, and relatively little by his Praetorian Guard. The historians recount avariciously motivated duplicity and violence that Severus directed against senators, wealthy citizens, and provincial nobles.[12] While both historians note that Severus greatly increased the numbers of soldiers in Rome,[13] they also emphasize that the emperor evenhandedly distributed vast, unprecedented sums of money both to the army and to the people.[14] Additionally, Severus maintained popular favor by holding elaborate public celebrations and exhibitions,[15] very much like the "*feste e spettacoli*" that Machiavelli declares a good prince should provide the people on appropriate occasions (P 21). Herodian even goes so far as to praise Severus's careful administration of laws and attention to civic governance whenever he was in the city.[16]

And therein may lie the rub. The Roman people were certainly happier and more secure while Severus remained in the city than when he traveled abroad on military campaigns—however much those exploits may have amazed them. In Severus's absence, either the emperor's praetorian prefect, Plautianus, or Severus's sons engaged in cruel and rapacious behavior—even if it is not clear how far throughout the city's population such abuse extended. Both Cassius Dio and Herodian report that Plautianus ruled violently and greedily while Severus was away; the former describes how he executed many prominent men, despoiled numerous citizens, and even castrated several nobles.[17] After Plautianus was executed for conspiring to depose Severus,[18] the emperor's sons, Antoninus and Geta, exploited the opportunity to engage in considerable rapacity: Cassius Dio reports that "they outraged women and abused boys, they embezzled money, and made gladiators and charioteers their boon companions."[19]

In sum, meticulous examination of Severus's career suggests that Machiavelli concludes the following about the man he considers Rome's most virtuous emperor: The people will not hate a prince who accumulates magnificent conquests abroad, so long as he also governs with generous provisions of bread and circuses, as well as judicious civil administration while at home—even if the prince's subordinates and relatives may mistreat them in his absence. Both Cassius Dio and Herodian chastise Severus for expropriating senators, rich citizens, and provincial nobles, as well as subject populations, to fund his impressive military adventures—but such plunder is no doubt what funds the ever increasing pay of his Praetorian Guard as well as the military feats, domestic spectacles, and public dispensations that astonish, and in some sense satisfy, his people.

In certain respects Severus stands not that far from Nabis, Machiavelli's consistent example for making and maintaining friendship with an armed people. Nabis used cruelty less well than Agathocles by failing to perform his executions/expropriations at a stroke to favor/support his subject soldiers. The same, it seems, applies to Severus, who resorts to intermittent, recurring expropriations of wealthy and prominent citizens to pay both his subjects *and* his soldiers. In short, it is more than slightly misleading of Machiavelli to place Severus among the emperors who were "unsparing in the harms they visited upon the people" (P 19).[20] Discrepancies between Machiavelli's account and his sources suggest that Severus relied less on popular maltreatment than Machiavelli implies. Indeed, one could plausibly conclude that Severus treats his people better than do any of the other emperors Machiavelli cites as favoring his soldiers.[21] For our purposes, he obviously treats the people better than did Appius, the decemvir, or Walter, the Duke of Athens.

CONCLUSION

A certain matter immediately becomes apparent when one consults Machiavelli's sources for his discussion of the Roman emperors in *The Prince*: the social bases of politics in imperial Italy already manifested the main deficiencies that Machiavelli attributed to modern Italy, deficiencies that his work often seems almost single-mindedly intended to redress. When describing Severus's entry into Italy to claim the imperial throne, Herodian observed the following:

> The invasion of so large an army terrified the Italian cities when they heard the news, since the inhabitants of Italy had long ago abandoned armed warfare in favor of the peaceful occupation of farming. During the days of the Republic when the senate appointed army commanders to their posts, all Italians used to bear arms and gained control of lands and seas in wars against Greeks and barbarians. . . . But when Augustus established his sole rule, he relieved Italians of their [military] duties, and stripped them of their arms; in their place he established a defensive system of camps for the empire, in which were stationed mercenary troops on fixed rates of pay to act as a barricade for the Roman empire.[22]

The separation of the people from the army inaugurated by Caesar Augustus was certainly not advantageous for the Italian people; nor, however, was it advantageous for Augustus's imperial successors, at least those Machiavelli names: of the ten emperors he invokes in chapter 19 of *The Prince*, eight came to ignominious ends, whether they favored the people or the army. Almost as if to erase this civically demilitarized history, which of course lived on in his own day, almost as if to purge its stench from his readers' nostrils, Machiavelli begins chapter 20 by fully rebuking the modes of Augustus that were maintained both by succeeding emperors and by the less than fully virtuous princes of modern Italy: "No new prince has ever disarmed but rather always armed his subjects. Once they are armed, after all, their arms become your arms. Distrusted subjects become faithful, faithful ones remain thus, and subjects become your partisans" (P 20).

Appius Claudius and Walter Brienne are new princes who are obviously deficient in the matter of armed subjects. Appius thought he could permit young nobles to abuse an armed populace who were necessary to defend his state; and then he missed the opportunity to at least impress, if not astonish, his citizen soldiers by leading them into battle when circumstances demanded it. Instead, he remained in the city, captivated by the illusion that nobles, old and young, whose manners Appius had corrupted and whose purses he had filled, would provide sufficient protection when he designed to civically debase and sexually defile the daughter of a soldier who was off defending his patria from the enemy—when in fact a more dangerous enemy to his tyranny—the people—resided at home.

Walter, rather than uniting the Florentines into a single civic-military base of power, prefers to keep the Florentine people divided between *plebe* and *popolani*, using the disenfranchised urban workers to terrorize the citizens enrolled in guilds. By adding foreign satellites to his domestic forces and enlisting enemy cities as diplomatic allies, Walter foolishly believed he could torture, despoil, and execute some citizens and corrupt others with uncivil feudal modes. But medieval Florence, while not a virtuous ancient republic, still possessed armed nobles and armed guildsmen with vast experience in fighting each other: former class adversaries who could at least temporarily unite to restore the name of liberty and to avenge the violence and dishonor with which the duke's Frenchmen had treated their women.

Machiavelli suggests that both Appius and Walter too quickly turned to cruelty once they abolished civic magistracies and established their tyrannies; but he also intimates that there are forms of cruelty too "extraordinary" to be perpetrated with impunity no matter how gradually a tyrant may proceed in committing them. Even if the decemvir and the duke had been prudent enough to follow the modes of Caesar Augustus in creating, or the modes of Septimius Severus in maintaining, the separation of popular and military humors under their tyrannies, Machiavelli suggests that they would nevertheless have needed to exhibit greater military *and* civil virtue to conclusively escape the hatred of their peoples and thereby avoid the loss of their states.

CONCLUSION

Since the sixteenth century, cynical assessments of Machiavelli's supposedly nefarious prescriptions for political leadership have been propagated by authors no less luminous than Gentillet, Marlowe, Shakespeare, Frederick the Great, and Diderot.[1] Such literary titans popularized the notion that Machiavelli instructed tyrants how—at any and all costs—to oppress and manipulate their subjects in the most unscrupulously self-aggrandizing fashion. In the late twentieth century, scholars associated with the Cambridge school of intellectual history, such as Quentin Skinner and John Pocock, admirably assailed this unqualified "tyrannical" interpretation of Machiavelli by emphasizing the place of liberty, the common good, and "republicanism" in his political thought.[2]

Unfortunately, Skinner and Pocock overcompensated in their efforts to morally rehabilitate Machiavelli from tyrannical stigma by overemphasizing citizen self-sacrifice and understating the crucial role played by entrepreneurial leaders in Machiavelli's political writings. A recent scholarly wave, which reads him as much more of a democrat than Skinner and Pocock do, has done little to fill the leadership lacuna in Machiavelli studies; moreover, it has offered few insights on the proper role of leadership in democratic politics.[3] In *The People's Princes*, I have attempted to contest and complement the tyrannical and the republican/democratic schools of interpretation. Machiavelli, I have argued, intended to educate *both* politically ambitious individuals and politically empowered citizenries on how to secure and enjoy the fruits of civic liberty; especially by collaboratively thwarting the oppressive agenda of oligarchic elites.

I have reconstructed Machiavelli's pedagogical method of "political exemplarity" by meticulously analyzing his case studies of leaders, both prudent and foolhardy, across history. Crucial for Machiavelli's mode of political exemplarity are not only the most illustrious leaders celebrated by historians (e.g., Moses, Romulus, Brutus, Camillus, Cesare Borgia, and Cosimo de' Medici), but also lesser-known figures who often prove much more consequential for his programmatic purposes (e.g., Agathocles, Nabis, Clearchus, Pacuvius, Giano della Bella, and Piero Soderini). Machiavelli's lessons for attaining political success and avoiding political ruin, I have argued, emerge from the explicit and implicit parallels and contrasts he sets out among his many ancient and modern examples of leadership; most important, his appraisals of how leaders negotiate the indignation of the common people, the insolence of domestic elites, and the imperial designs of foreign powers.

Machiavelli, I've shown, does not exalt but rather redefines, in a civic-serving fashion, traditional notions of "tyranny" in his assessments of virtuous princes. A Greek tyrant like Agathocles, Hiero, Nabis, Clearchus, or Cleomenes, who empowers his people both civically and militarily, is a tyrant in name only. He alleviates the oppression of his own people by domestic oligarchs, and he delays—and sometimes fully repels—domination of their polity by imperial aggressors such as other Greeks, the Carthaginians, and even the Romans. Machiavelli's ideal civil prince is prudent enough to abide by the modes of the so-called tyrant Agathocles, who effectively communicated to the Syracusans, "I require no bodyguards because the *people* are my bodyguards."[4] As we have seen, given the central lessons imparted by Machiavelli's infamous *piccolo libro*,[5] such a statement could have served as a fitting epigraph for the book known as *The Prince*.

I have defended Machiavelli's ultimate endorsement of Agathocles against both Cambridge school authors who denigrate the Sicilian as a usurper of a republic,[6] and democratically inclined interpreters who place the Syracusan's conduct beyond the boundaries of Machiavelli's moral horizon.[7] Since Machiavelli declares he is concerned first and foremost with "effectual truth" (P 15), I contend that every reader of *The Prince* must ultimately confront this incontrovertible fact: Agathocles is the only historical figure in the book who fulfills Machiavelli's fundamental requirements for political success (P 9, P 26). Agathocles frees his people from domestic oppression by Syracuse's oligarchs, and he delivers them from foreign domination by the Carthaginian Empire. Thus Machiavelli's initial qualified praise for Agathocles gives way to an "effectual," full-throated acclaim of the Syracusan over the course of the book—and indeed throughout his political writings. Whatever ethical niceties prevented previous writers from praising Agathocles (hesitations that Machiavelli initially parrots), the Syracusan's domestic and geopolitical success ultimately confirms Machiavelli's high estimation of his virtue and excellence.

To be sure, Machiavelli instructs us that salutary tyrants-cum-civil princes, like Agathocles and other Greek tyrants, cannot afford their subjects or citizens the sweetest fruits of a "free and civil way of life." There are limits to the civil benefits that, for example, a new prince like Cesare Borgia can grant his subjects in the Romagna. As we have seen, he cannot let the people themselves decide who, Borgia or Remirro, is responsible for, on the one hand, the "good government" they've received and, on the other, the disagreeable "rigors" they've endured to ultimately enjoy it. Borgia's princely leadership, I have intimated, shares certain characteristics with populism today. Contemporary populist leaders make decisions on behalf of the people; they consistently tell the people what they really want; and in doing so they effectively usurp the people's fully considered judgment.

The People's Princes explicates Machiavelli's notion that leaders must pursue immediate indispensability but eventually effect their own obsolescence. Machiavelli insists that they should make themselves indispensable to the common people in their rise to popular favor by securing tangible achievements that improve the people's well-being, thus enhancing their own present reputation. However, Machiavelli also insists that, to secure posthumous fame, leaders must make themselves obsolete so that the people are grateful to the leader, in retirement or posthumously, for helping to create the institutions that allow them to govern themselves—specifically, to govern themselves without relying exclusively on the political interventions of extraordinarily virtuous leaders.

Too often, "populist" as opposed to "democratic" leaders seek short-term political solutions that bolster their immediate popularity and support but then fail to initiate or endorse long-term solutions such as novel legislative, judicial, and electoral institutions that would allow the people to more directly rule themselves once the leader leaves office. Populist leaders, at best, tend to follow the examples of Giano della Bella, Michele di Lando, and Piero Soderini, who provide little more than stopgaps to the long-evolving process of oligarchic and plutocratic corruption in popular governments. Or at worst they act like ambitious populist leaders such as Corso Donati or Cosimo de' Medici, who attempt to steer democracy further out of the hands of the people for personal or partisan gain.

On the contrary, I have argued, genuinely democratic civic leaders ought to take their cues from Machiavelli's example of Furius Camillus or, especially, Pacuvius Calanus, who "opens the people's eyes," in the *Discourses*. Like the "prudent" Pacuvius, democratic leaders ought to locate institutional means for allowing common citizens to decide for themselves what they really want—for instance, wreaking vengeance on oppressive domestic elites or following optimal strategy against an impending foreign threat. The distinction between princely and civic leadership, best exemplified by my contrast between Machiavelli's Borgia and his Pacuvius, exposes the deficiency of the contemporary "populist" solution to the problem of popular judgment, which endeavors to partially close the people's eyes rather than fully open them.

Machiavelli illuminates the fine line between tyranny and statesmanship that an astute civic magistrate such as Pacuvius must walk when negotiating conflicts between elites and the people: such magistrates must not impulsively satisfy the raw, unrefined appetites of *either* the nobles or the people. Unlike tyrants such as Agathocles or Appius Claudius, who on their own initiative either liquidate or cosset politically obnoxious elites, Pacuvius instead enlists the assembled people themselves as ultimate judges in political trials of haughty elites, thereby simultaneously empowering common citizens and chastening oligarchic elites.

Ultimately, expressions of popular deference rather than pursuit of popular favor are most conducive both to princely success and to civic health in Machiavelli's model of leadership. As we have seen, Soderini attained the unceasing favor of the Florentine people, whereas Camillus was suspected by the Roman people of excessive ambition. But Camillus's voluntary exile and then frequent resignation of office secured for him both enduring fame and the civic enhancement of the Roman people. Soderini wished to hold Florence's highest office uninterrupted for the length of his life, and thus he sacrificed the existence of that office and of the republic he served. He feared that abdicating office temporarily—even if this would forestall a Spanish invasion of Florence and a Medici restoration in the city—might raise the intolerable risk that the people would never again place him in the supreme magistracy.

By deferring to the judgment of the people and bowing to the sovereignty of contingency through a well-timed return from exile and frequent abdications of dictatorial authority, Camillus wielded greater power than any individual could hope to attain in a civically virtuous republic—a form of power arguably superior to formal kingship. The Roman Republic and Furius Camillus, in Machiavelli's estimation, became history's most illustrious exemplars of civic liberty and civic leadership precisely because—not without risk of matters' turning out otherwise—citizens prudently learned to place "the full weight of the republic" on Camillus's shoulders, and he prudently learned to put his authority and reputation entirely "in the hands of the Roman people."

From Machiavelli's perspective, what scholars have recently called plutocratically generated "systemic corruption," or politically nefarious "oligarchic harm,"[8] is a constant, existential threat to any civic polity that has not already degenerated into a naked oligarchy. The only way to halt and roll back this corruption is for prudent leaders to mobilize the common people's "rage" over this situation in ways more effective than those attempted by the Gracchi or Michele di Lando. Civic leaders, Machiavelli insists, must enjoin citizens to use any leverage they possess—military service or labor power, for instance—to extract concessions from oppressive elites who would prefer to expand rather than diminish or relinquish their disproportionate economic power and political authority. Such concessions must include the establishment of institutions that, in Machiavelli's words, "halt the insolence of the few" and foster the judgment of the many, which is "rarely pernicious to liberty."

* * *

This book has drawn from Machiavelli an unapologetically partisan model of political leadership: Civic princes and common citizens must empower each other at the expense of rapaciously oppressive socioeconomic elites.[9] Let me conclude on a somewhat less partisan note by acknowledging that Machiavelli does not always evaluate leadership exclusively from the perspective of class politics. In the *Florentine Histories*, he expresses the conviction that leadership, indeed political engagement generally, whatever its ideological orientation, is inherently honorable and good. When assessing previous accounts of his city's history, Machiavelli reproves authors for being excessively circumspect about the past behavior of the forebears of Florence's still prominent families. Excessively worried about "besmirching the memories" of eminent Florentines, these historians, Machiavelli declares, "misunderstood that actions pertaining to governments and states bear greatness in themselves, and that however they are conducted or whatever their results, they always appear more honorable than blameworthy for those who perform them."[10]

Machiavelli here enjoins readers to recognize that involving oneself in politics, notwithstanding one's goals or modes of proceeding, is more praiseworthy than not involving oneself at all—whether out of indifference, fear of failure, or trepidation about making things worse. Getting one's hands dirty, in this conception of leadership, is more honorable than living content with anonymity or than endeavoring to retain one's moral purity through inactivity. Failure accompanied by great effort, even when animated by dubious motives, will win an individual greater acclaim than will inaction motivated by a pure heart. Hazarding risk in the political arena is itself worthwhile, perhaps even exhilarating, entirely apart from whether one achieves one's ultimately preferred political ends. The public and posterity will more often than not grant a politically adventurous individual the benefit of the doubt.

In this passage from the *Histories*, Machiavelli is surely addressing potential actors who have been rendered politically incapacitated under long-term and recently restored Medici rule in Florence. Many citizens who might otherwise step forward to participate in politics have no doubt been stultified by the suffocating hegemony of one family rule over what was once a rather vibrant modern republic. Machiavelli's injunction here is meant to arouse to action those individuals now inclined toward passivity, whatever their political proclivities. Any ambivalence over involvement in politics must be resolved on the side of action, Machiavelli insists—the esteem of the patria awaits you, whatever your ulterior motives or prospective effectiveness.

But this is not the lesson Machiavelli intends to impart to those more rare individuals who are naturally inclined to act consequentially in the political realm—those whose public spirit cannot be crushed by any regime, no matter how deeply entrenched or rampantly corrupt. An ideologically neutral view of leadership is *not* the message Machiavelli wishes to convey to individuals inwardly propelled to publicly exhibit their virtue. As I have made clear in the preceding pages, attentive readers of the *Histories*, as well as *The Prince* and the *Discourses*, will note that Machiavelli exhorts those with the temerity to enter politics to follow his model of popularly empowering and anti-oligarchic leadership.

In the *Histories*, Machiavelli may refrain from using "hateful words" to criticize Giano della Bella and Michele di Lando for failing to fully champion the people against oligarchic elites, but the implication is strong. There is no denying that, in *The Prince* and the *Discourses*, he spares Girolamo Savonarola and Piero Soderini not a single harsh word for that very failing. These examples, and the many others I have discussed, including far more prudent and severe ones like Lucius Brutus and Pacuvius Calanus, should illuminate Machiavelli's partisanly class-based view of political leadership.

ACKNOWLEDGMENTS

I owe a tremendous debt of gratitude to numerous people—colleagues, students, collaborators, friends, and family—who helped me conceive, develop, and complete this book.

Among the many generous scholars and friends in Europe who offered me hospitality and intellectual engagement, I thank Jérémie Barthas, Filippo Del Lucchese, Rainer Forst, Marco Geuna, Giovanni Giorgini, Dirk Jörke, Thomas Meyer, Francesca Russo, Camila Vergara, and most especially Gabriele Pedullà. I've attended various conferences over the past decade with the following accomplished North American Machiavelli scholars: Sean Erwin, Mark Jurdjevic, Daniel Kapust, Robyn Marasco, Alison McQueen, Katie Robiadek, and Yves Winter. Although a rather sober lot, I've managed to find modest amusement in their company. For decades now, a number of senior scholars have supported me in the development of what has (unintentionally) become a trilogy of Machiavelli books: Richard Bellamy, Bill Connell, Bill Hankins, Vicky Kahn, Harvey Mansfield, Carey Nederman, Philip Pettit, Ian Shapiro, Quentin Skinner, Steven Smith, Nadia Urbinati, and Martin van Gelderen.

My friends and colleagues in Hyde Park have been a constant source of inspiration and encouragement: Angus Brown, Chiara Cordelli, Adom Getachew, Daragh Grant, Will Howell, Joel Isaac, Deme Kasimis, Matt Landauer, Michèle Lowrie, Sankar Muthu, Robert Norton, Jennifer Pitts, Rocco Rubini, Emma Saunders-Hastings, Jim Sparrow, Sue Stokes, Nathan Tarcov, Lisa Wedeen, Jim Wilson, and Linda Zerilli. I am especially grateful to my Machiavelli students, from whom I've learned infinitely more than I could have ever taught them: Eero Arum, Andy Balbuena, Yuna Blajer, Agneska Bloch, Danielle Charette, Beatrice Fazio, Anthony Lanz, Will Levine, Amanda Maher, Sabrina Marasa, Luc Moulaison, Tejas Parasher, Marshall Pierce, Niklas

Plaetzer, Emily Salamanca, Max Benjamin Smith, and, especially, Gordon Arlen, Steven Klein, and Natasha Piano.

Portions of this book have been drawn from the following articles: "Subdue the Senate: Machiavelli's 'Way of Freedom' or Path to Tyranny?" *Political Theory* 40, 6 (December 2012): 717–38; "Faulty Foundings and Failed Reformers in Machiavelli's *Florentine Histories*," *American Political Science Review* 111, 1 (February 2017): 204–16; and "Machiavelli's Inglorious 'Tyrants': On Agathocles, Scipio, and Unmerited Glory," *History of Political Thought* 36, 1 (2015): 29–52. I thank SAGE Publications, Cambridge University Press, and Imprint Academic Publishers for permission to incorporate them here. Jacob Neplokh, Noelle Norona, J. W. Strasberg, and particularly Avery Broome provided invaluable research assistance as well as opportunities for the substantive exchange of ideas that significantly shaped the book. The efforts of my incomparable editor at the University of Chicago Press, Sara Doskow, her intrepid assistant, Rosemary Frehe, and production editor Caterina MacLean managed to improve the book's argument and put the manuscript into production in a remarkably short time. Theresa Wolner prepared an admirably detailed index. I also heartily thank Alice Bennett, whose extraordinary editing skills nearly made a great writer out of a merely good one.

My dearest friend, Bruce Western, although working in different precincts of the social sciences, has influenced this book in ways I hope he will readily and happily recognize. I lost my parents during the COVID-19 pandemic, but the support of my sister, Kara McCormick-Lyons, and her beautiful family helped me persevere in my work and in life more generally. My spouse, Alyssa Qualls, whose job is much more important than mine, made endless sacrifices to support the scholarship and teaching that means so much to me. My loving gratitude is commensurably infinite. Our eldest daughter, Annabelle, daily reminds me of the delicate joys to be found in unspoken bonds of devotion.

Finally, this book is dedicated to my youngest daughter, Susannah Francis McCormick, who brings happiness to our family and to anyone she meets, with ebullience, humor, mischief, and massive amounts of attitude.

NOTES

PREFACE

1. John P. McCormick, *Machiavellian Democracy* (Cambridge: Cambridge University Press, 2011); and John P. McCormick, *Reading Machiavelli: Scandalous Books, Suspect Engagements, and the Virtue of Populist Politics* (Princeton, NJ: Princeton University Press, 2018).

2. Contributions to the recent "democratic turn" in Machiavelli studies include Filippo Del Lucchese, *The Political Philosophy of Niccolò Machiavelli* (Edinburgh: Edinburgh University Press, 2015); Christopher Holman, *Machiavelli and the Politics of Democratic Innovation* (Toronto: University of Toronto Press, 2018); Ronald J. Schmidt, *Reading Politics with Machiavelli* (Oxford: Oxford University Press, 2018); Yves Winter, *Machiavelli and the Orders of Violence* (Cambridge: Cambridge University Press, 2018); Gabriele Pedullà, *Machiavelli in Tumult: The Discourses on Livy and the Origins of Political Conflictualism* (Cambridge: Cambridge University Press, 2018); and Camila Vergara, *Systemic Corruption: Constitutional Ideas for an Anti-oligarchic Republic* (Princeton, NJ: Princeton University Press, 2020). For critical evaluations of this scholarly literature, see Catherine H. Zuckert, "Machiavelli: Radical Democratic Political Theorist?," *Review of Politics* 81, no. 3 (Summer 2019): 499–510; Marc Stears, Jérémie Barthas, and Adam Woodhouse, "On Machiavelli as Plebeian Theorist," *Theoria* 66, no. 161 (December 2019): 108–16; and Katherine Robiadek, "For the People: Deepening the Democratic Turn in Machiavelli Studies," *Political Theory* 49, 4 (2021): 686–99.

3. Niccolò Machiavelli, *Il principe* (*De principatibus*), composed about 1513 and published in 1532, ed. G. Inglese (Turin: Einaudi, 1995), hereafter P; Machiavelli, *Discorsi*, composed about 1513–18 and published in 1531, ed. C. Vivanti (Turin: Einaudi-Gallimard, 1997), hereafter D; and Machiavelli, *Istorie Fiorentine*, composed about 1520–25 and published in 1532, ed. Franco Gaeta (Milan: Feltrinelli 1962), hereafter FH.

4. For recent engagements with Machiavelli's injunction that leaders "need to be needed" in order to secure their authority and maintain their rule, see Stephen Holmes, "Loyalty in Adversity," in *Machiavelli on Liberty and Conflict*, ed. David Johnston, Nadia Urbinati, and Camila Vergara (Chicago: University of Chicago Press, 2017), 186–206; and Gabriele Pedullà, *On Niccolò Machiavelli: The Bonds of Politics* (New York: Columbia University Press, 2023), 62–68.

5. See John P. McCormick, "Aristocratic *Insolenzia* and the Role of Senates in Machiavelli's Mixed Republic," *Review of Politics* 83, no. 4 (2021): 486–509.

6. I have reiterated arguments in favor of such institutions—class-specific magistracies and assemblies, citizen referenda, and, especially, popularly judged capital trials—in John P. McCormick, "The New Ochlophobia? Populism, Majority Rule and Prospects for Democratic Republicanism," in *Republicanism and the Future of Democracy*, ed. Yiftah Elazar and Geneviève Rousselière (Cambridge: Cambridge University Press, 2019), 122–42; John P. McCormick, "On Josiah Ober's Demopolis: Basic Democracy, Economic Inequality and Political Punishment," *Polis: The Journal for Ancient Greek and Roman Political Thought* 36 (2019): 535–42; and John P. McCormick, *Machiavelli und der populistische Schmerzensschrei: Aufsätze zur politischen Theorie*, trans. Mike Hiegeman (Frankfurt: Suhrkamp, 2023).

7. See *Plutarch's Lives, Volumes 1 and 2*, ed. Arthur Hugh Clough, trans. John Dryden (New York: Modern Library Classics, 2001). Erica Benner provides the most extensive analysis of Plutarch's influence on Machiavelli, but she draws primarily on Plutarch's *Moralia*: see Benner, *Machiavelli's Ethics* (Princeton, NJ: Princeton University Press, 2009), 8–10, 49–54, 63–90; and Plutarch, *Moralia*, trans. and ed. Frank Cole Babbitt et al. (Cambridge, MA: Harvard University Press [Loeb], 1927–2004), 16 vols. On the vast number of Plutarch's *Lives* available to Machiavelli in Latin and Italian translations, see Marianne Pade, *The Reception of Plutarch's Lives in Fifteenth-Century Italy* (Copenhagen: Museum Tusculanum Press, 2007), 89–178, 225–47, 259–342; Sophia Xenophontos and Katerina Oikonomopoulou, eds., *Brill's Companion to the Reception of Plutarch* (Leiden: Brill, 2019), 389–20; and Joanne Paul, "Machiavellian Counsel," in *Counsel and Command in Early Modern English Thought*, ed. Joanne Paul (Cambridge: Cambridge University Press, 2020), 71–96.

8. See Camila Vergara, "Corruption as Systemic Political Decay," *Philosophy and Social Criticism* 47, no. 3 (2021): 322–46.

CHAPTER 1

1. Niccolò Machiavelli, *Il principe* (*De principatibus*), composed about 1513 and published in 1532, ed. G. Inglese (Turin: Einaudi, 1995), hereafter P; Machiavelli, *Discorsi*, composed about 1513–18 and published in 1531, ed. C. Vivanti (Turin: Einaudi-Gallimard, 1997), hereafter D; and Machiavelli, *Istorie Fiorentine*, composed about 1520–25 and published in 1532, ed. Franco Gaeta (Milan: Feltrinelli, 1962), hereafter FH.

2. On Machiavelli's use of ancient sources generally, see Gennaro Sasso, *Machiavelli e gli antichi e altri saggi* (Milan: Ricciardi, 1987); on his departures from the writings of medieval and Renaissance Italian authors, see James Hankins, *Virtue Politics: Soulcraft and Statecraft in Renaissance Italy* (Cambridge, MA: Harvard University Press, 2019). For engagements with Hankins's account, see reviews by John P. McCormick, *Erudition and the Republic of Letters* 6 (2021): 299–329; Mark Jurdjevic, *Journal of Modern History* 93, no. 3 (September 2021): 668–70; Gabriele Pedullà, *Good Society* 31, nos. 1–2 (2022): 168–83; and Rocco Rubini, *European Legacy* 28, no. 1 (2023): 85–93.

3. For an overview of the ancient literature, see Christopher de Lisle, *Agathokles of Syracuse: Sicilian Tyrant and Hellenistic King* (Oxford: Oxford University Press, 2021).

4. Fine biographical accounts of Machiavelli include Roberto Ridolfi, *The Life of Niccolò Machiavelli*, trans. Cecil Grayson (Chicago: University of Chicago Press, 1963);

Sebastian de Grazia, *Machiavelli in Hell* (Princeton, NJ: Princeton University Press, 1990); Robert Black, *Machiavelli* (London: Routledge, 2013); Christopher S. Celenza, *Machiavelli: A Portrait* (Cambridge, MA: Harvard University Press, 2015); and Alexander Lee, *Machiavelli: His Life and Times* (Toronto: Picador, 2020). The best introductory study of Machiavelli's life and works is Gabriele Pedullà's *On Niccolò Machiavelli: The Bonds of Politics* (New York: Columbia University Press, 2023).

5. See John P. McCormick, "Machiavelli's Agathocles: From Criminal Example to Princely Exemplum," in *Between Exemplarity and Singularity: Literature, Philosophy, Law*, ed. Michèle Lowrie and Susanne Lüdemann (London: Routledge, 2015), 123-49.

6. On how Borgia fits into Machiavelli's narrative strands regarding religion, virtue, and popular perception see, respectively, John P. McCormick, "The Passion of Duke Valentino: Cesare Borgia, Biblical Allegory and *The Prince*," in McCormick, *Reading Machiavelli* (Princeton, NJ: Princeton University Press, 2018), 21-44; John P. McCormick, "The Enduring Ambiguity of Machiavellian Virtue: Crime, Cruelty and Christianity in *The Prince*," *Social Research* 81, no. 1 (Spring 2014): 133-64; and chapter 6 below.

7. Michèle Lowrie and Susanne Lüdemann, "Introduction," in Lowrie and Lüdemann, *Between Exemplarity and Singularity*, 1-15.

8. Rebecca Langlands emphasizes the situational quality of late republican/early imperial Roman engagements with exempla—specifically, the idea that circumstances largely dictate the appropriateness of actions performed by a political actor. See Langlands, "Roman *Exempla* and Situation Ethics: Valerius Maximus and Cicero *de Officiis*," *Journal of Roman Studies* 101 (November 2011): 100-122. In contrast, Machiavelli seems to endorse a narrower range of actions for individuals who confront circumstances that, in Machiavelli's rendering, are likewise more conceptually constrained. See also Matthew B. Roller, *Models from the Past in Roman Culture: A World of Exempla* (Cambridge: Cambridge University Press, 2019); and Rebecca Langlands, *Exemplary Ethics in Ancient Rome* (Cambridge: Cambridge University Press, 2020).

9. On Machiavelli's previously unappreciated reliance on Dionysius of Halicarnassus, see Gabriele Pedullà, *Machiavelli in Tumult: The Discourses on Livy and the Origins of Political Conflictualism* (Cambridge: Cambridge University Press, 2018).

10. See Livy I, Preface.

11. On Machiavelli's inversion of virtues and vices, see Eugene Garver, "After '*Virtù*': Rhetoric, Prudence and Moral Pluralism in Machiavelli," *History of Political Thought* 17, no. 2 (1996): 195-223; Cary J. Nederman, "Machiavelli and Moral Character: Principality, Republics and the Psychology of '*Virtù*,'" *History of Political Thought* 21, no. 3 (2000): 349-64; Mark Jurdjevic, "Virtue, Fortune, and Blame in Machiavelli's Life and *The Prince*," *Social Research* 81, no. 1 (Spring 2014): 1-30; and Quentin Skinner, "Machiavelli and the Misunderstanding of Princely *Virtù*," in *Machiavelli on Liberty and Conflict*, ed. David Johnston, Nadia Urbinati, and Camila Vergara (Chicago: University of Chicago Press, 2017), 139-63.

12. See Livy XXX.45.

13. Don Herzog surmises that Machiavelli's "mischievous presentation of Agathocles is just softening up the reader" for his subsequent endorsement of Hannibal's "inhuman cruelty" (P 17). See Donald J. Herzog, entry on Quentin Skinner, *The Foundations of Modern Political Thought*, in *The Oxford Handbook of Classics in Contemporary Political Theory*, ed. J. T. Levy (Oxford: Oxford University Press Online, 2017) (https://doi.org/10.1093/oxfordhb/9780198717133.013.19). In addition to cruelty, Agathocles

and Hannibal share the characteristic of far-flung military campaigns, two qualities that also conjure Machiavelli's figure of Septimius Severus (P 19), whom I discuss in chapter 8.

14. See D II.4, D 13, D 14, D 21, D 22.

15. Notable treatments of the Agathocles question include: Sydney Anglo, *Machiavelli—The First Century: Studies in Enthusiasm, Hostility, and Irrelevance* (Oxford: Oxford University Press, 2005), 51, 308, 627, 673; J. Patrick Coby, *Machiavelli's Romans: Liberty and Greatness in the Discourses on Livy* (Lanham, MD: Lexington Books, 1999), 233–36; Gabriele Pedullà, "Machiavelli's *Prince* and the Concept of Tyranny," in *Evil Lords: Theories and Representations of Tyranny from Antiquity to the Renaissance*, ed. Nikos Panou and Hester Schadee (Oxford: Oxford University Press, 2018), 191–210; Russell Price, "The Theme of *Gloria* in Machiavelli," *Renaissance Quarterly* 30 (1977): 588–631; Wayne A. Rebhorn, *Foxes and Lions: Machiavelli's Confidence Men* (Ithaca, NY: Cornell University Press, 1988), 17, 20; Gennaro Sasso, *Studi su Machiavelli* (Naples: Morano, 1967), 117–18; Sasso, *Niccolò Machiavelli, storia del suo pensiero politico* (Bologna: Mulino, 1980) 95, 347–49, 422–24; Jerrold E. Siegel, "*Virtù* in and since the Renaissance," in *The Dictionary of the History of Ideas*, ed. P. P. Weiner (New York: Scribner, 1974), 477–86; Quentin Skinner, *The Foundations of Modern Political Thought: Volume 1, The Renaissance* (Cambridge: Cambridge University Press, 1978) 119, 137–38; Quentin Skinner, *Machiavelli* (Oxford: Oxford University Press, 1981) 42; Quentin Skinner, *Machiavelli: A Very Short Introduction* (Oxford: Oxford University Press, 2000) 47; Peter Stacey, *Roman Monarchy and the Renaissance Prince* (Cambridge: Cambridge University Press, 2007) 135, 147, 296–97; Leo Strauss, *Thoughts on Machiavelli* (Glencoe, IL: Free Press, 1958) 47, 70, 243, 302n26, 310n530; Nathan Tarcov, "Quentin Skinner's Method and Machiavelli's *Prince*," *Ethics* 92, no. 4 (July 1982): 692–709; John Humphreys Whitfield, *Machiavelli* (Oxford: Blackwell, 1947) 80, 104; Miguel E. Vatter, *Between Form and Event: Machiavelli's Theory of Political Freedom* (Dordrecht: Kluwer, 2000), 16–17; and, especially, Victoria Kahn, "*Virtù* and the Example of Agathocles in Machiavelli's *Prince*," in *Machiavelli and the Discourse of Literature*, ed. A. R. Ascoli and V. Kahn (Ithaca, NY: Cornell University Press, 1993), 195–218.

16. See Hanna Fenichel Pitkin, *Fortune Is a Woman: Gender and Politics in the Thought of Niccolò Machiavelli* (Chicago: University of Chicago Press, 1984), 7–22.

17. Agathocles acquires mercenaries from Hamilcar to aid him in staging his coup; see D III.6, Justin XXII.4, and Diodorus XX.5. Throughout his career, Agathocles uses mercenaries in a way that ensures that, unlike in Machiavelli's modern Italy, the domestic authority controls the mercenaries rather than vice versa. See also De Lisle, *Agathokles of Syracuse*, 160–65.

18. Although Agathocles would often hold prominent citizens hostage while campaigning abroad. See also De Lisle, *Agathokles of Syracuse*, 32, 46, 157.

19. See Diodorus Siculus 19.9.6, 20.63.2–3. See also De Lisle, *Agathokles of Syracuse*, 61, 91.

20. For intriguing accounts of the many ways Machiavelli ignores, eschews, and flouts traditional notions of "tyranny," especially that of Bartolo da Sassoferrato, the one most relevant to the late medieval Italian context, see Jérémie Barthas, ed., *Della tirannia: Machiavelli con Bartolo* (Florence: Olschki, 2007), and Gabriele Pedullà, "Introduzione: L'arte fiorentina dei nodi," in *Il principe: Edizione del cinquecentennale con traduzione a fronte in italiano moderno di Carmine Donzelli*, ed. Gabriele Pedullà (Rome:

Donzelli, 2013), v–cxxi, esp. xl–xliv; and Hankins, *Virtue Politics*, 112–18, 484. See also Bartolus of Sassoferrato, "On Tyranny" (c. 1355), in *Florentine Political Writings from Petrarch to Machiavelli*, ed. M. Jurdjevic, N. Piano, and J. P. McCormick (Philadelphia: University of Pennsylvania Press, 2019), 85–104.

21. See Machiavelli on the French monarchy: P 19; D I.16, D I.58.

22. Recent accounts of Borgia's career include Marion Johnson, *The Borgias* (London: Macdonald, 2002), and Christopher Hibbert, *The Borgias and Their Enemies: 1431–1519* (Boston: Mariner Books, 2009). For a contemporary chronicle of the duke's exploits, see Francesco Guicciardini, *The History of Italy*, trans. S. Alexander (Princeton, NJ: Princeton University Press, 1984), 139–40, 150–57, 161–76, 182–89.

23. Again, consult, for instance, Guicciardini, *History of Italy*, 139–40, 150–57, 161–76, 182–89.

24. The most prominent negative accounts of Agathocles's career include Diodorus, *The Library of History: Diodorus of Sicily*, XIX–XX; and Polyaenus, *Stratagems of War*, 5.3, trans. R. Shepherd (Chicago: Ares, 1974), 194–95. More generous evaluations are offered by Justin, *Epitome of the Philippic History of Pompeius Trogus*, ed. R. Develin, trans. J. C. Yardley (Oxford: Oxford University Press, 1994), book XXII, and book XXIII, chaps. 1–2, 172–82; and by Polybius, who reproves the unavailable history of Timaeus for exaggerating Agathocles's faults. See Polybius, *Histories*, XII.15 (Oxford: Oxford University Press, 2010), 426.

25. It must be noted, of course, that Machiavelli does not necessarily equate success with either virtue or glory as such: Hannibal is an individual who, in Machiavelli's estimation, deservedly achieved both despite his ultimate military and political defeats (D III.10).

26. On Machiavelli's own attribution of theological qualities to Borgia's career, see John P. McCormick, "The Passion of Duke Valentino: Cesare Borgia, Biblical Allegory, and *The Prince*," in McCormick, *Reading Machiavelli* (Princeton, NJ: Princeton University Press, 2018), 21–44.

27. See Diodorus, *The Library of History*, 19.9.7, 20.101.2–3. See also De Lisle, *Agathokles of Syracuse*, 60.

28. Peter Stacey insists that Machiavelli fails to consider Agathocles, like Liverotto, fully virtuous because the Syracusan "rejects the republican ethic"; while Machiavelli may condone their respective behaviors in the sphere of princely politics, "a different form of reasoning applies to states called republics." See Peter Stacey, *Roman Monarchy and the Renaissance Prince* (Cambridge: Cambridge University Press, 2007), 297.

29. See John W. Oppel, "Peace vs. Liberty in the Quattrocento: Poggio, Guarino, and the Scipio-Caesar Controversy," *Journal of Medieval and Renaissance Studies* 4 (1974): 221–65; and Gabriele Pedullà, "Scipio vs. Caesar: The Poggio-Guarino Debate without Republicanism," in *Republicanism: A Theoretical and Historical Perspective*, ed. Marcello Fantoni and Fabrizio Ricciardelli (Rome: Viella, 2020), 275–305, at 281. See also Mark Jurdjevic, "Civic Humanism and the Rise of the Medici," *Renaissance Quarterly* 52, no. 4 (Winter 1999): 994–1020, at 1002–5.

30. If, for Machiavelli, there is ever such a thing as an inherently healthy republic: see D III.6.

31. Machiavelli notes how, in a manner quite unusual for the times, Valentino rapidly and extensively began arming his subjects. See Machiavelli, *Legazioni e commissarie*,

234 NOTES TO PAGES 18-20

3 vols., ed. S. Bertelli (Milan: Feltrinelli, 1964), 419, 455. See also Quentin Skinner, *Machiavelli: A Very Short Introduction* (Oxford: Oxford University Press, 2000), 20–21.

32. See Justin XXII.4, and Diodorus XX.4.8.

33. Perhaps most important, one characteristic in particular separates Agathocles from Borgia: Kahn successfully demonstrates that Machiavelli condemns the Syracusan far less substantially than interpreters conventionally suppose. Indeed, she understands Machiavelli to be more favorably disposed to Agathocles than to Borgia, suggesting that he presents the former as more popularly "representative," more robustly "proto-republican" than the duke, and indeed a better approximation of the civil prince, whom Machiavelli favorably describes in chapter 9. See Victoria Kahn, *Machiavellian Rhetoric: From the Counter-Reformation to Milton* (Princeton, NJ: Princeton University Press, 1994), 35–39. I am generally amenable to this position, as what follows makes clear; but several counterarguments are worth considering: Machiavelli explicitly identifies the people more closely with Borgia, via the title "Duke Valentino," than with any other figure in *The Prince*; Borgia betrays friends and allies after they have exhibited bad faith or caused him harm (cf., P 8), whereas Agathocles apparently does so without provocation; Borgia establishes civic institutions, whereas Agathocles, from a certain perspective, can be said to have undermined or destroyed them; and if Agathocles reigned longer than Borgia, it could be argued that this is due as much to the foundations provided by the respectively corrupt and thriving regimes that preceded their rule as to their own individual talents and efforts.

34. Machiavelli notes the checkered record of the Roman emperors who confronted circumstances where the soldiers were not identical to the people (as they had been in the republic): such emperors were forced to either indulge the soldiers' abuse of the people or protect the people from the soldiers; in either case, deposition or assassination was the usual outcome (P 19). See chapter 8 below.

35. Quentin Skinner is perhaps the most prominent scholar to insist that Machiavelli had little more than "contempt for Agathocles" and that he did not consider Agathocles virtuous. See Quentin Skinner, *The Foundations of Modern Political Thought*, vol. 1, *The Renaissance* (Cambridge: Cambridge University Press, 1978), 119, 137–38; Skinner, *Machiavelli* (Oxford: Oxford University Press, 1981), 42; Skinner, *Machiavelli: A Very Short Introduction* (Oxford: Oxford University Press, 2000), 47. This argument is elaborated by Peter Stacey, *Roman Monarchy and the Renaissance Prince* (Cambridge: Cambridge University Press, 2007), 135, 147, 296–97.

36. See John P. McCormick, *Machiavellian Democracy* (Cambridge: Cambridge University Press, 2011), 1–17, 21–35, 46–61.

37. See M. I. Finley, *Ancient Sicily*, 2nd ed. (London: Chatto and Windus, 1979), 101.

38. As both Victoria Kahn and Leo Strauss point out quite rightly. See Victoria Kahn, "*Virtù* and the Example of Agathocles in Machiavelli's *Prince*," in *Machiavelli and the Discourse of Literature*, ed. A. R. Ascoli and V. Kahn (Ithaca, NY: Cornell University Press, 1993), 195–218; and Leo Strauss, *Thoughts on Machiavelli* (Glencoe, IL: Free Press, 1958), 310n53.

39. See Victoria Kahn, "*Virtù* and the Example of Agathocles in Machiavelli's *Prince*," *Representations* 13 (Winter 1986): 63–83, as well as Kahn, *Machiavellian Rhetoric: From the Counter-Reformation to Milton* (Princeton, NJ: Princeton University Press, 1994), 26–39; and her reconsideration of Machiavelli's Agathocles in "Revisiting Agathocles," *Review of Politics* 75, no. 4 (Fall 2013): 557–72.

40. Kahn's interpretation casts serious doubt on, for instance, Pedullà's assertion that the Agathocles example is meant to demonstrate that "Machiavelli wants to make it clear that not all evil power can be justified in politics." See Pedullà, "Machiavelli's *Prince* and the Concept of Tyranny," 201.

41. Kahn, "*Virtù* and the Example of Agathocles," 71–74.

42. See D III.6, Justin XXII.4, and Diodorus XX.5.

43. Machiavelli's imagery here recalls an "upper room" that hosted a somewhat different last supper.

44. See Machiavelli, "A Description of the Method Used by Duke Valentino . . . ," in *Machiavelli: The Chief Works and Others*, ed. and trans. A. Gilbert (Durham, NC: Duke University Press, 1989), 1:163–70.

45. Diodorus (XXI.16) and Justin (23.2.3–13) disagree on whether Agathocles died a natural death or may have been poisoned. See de Lisle, *Agathokles of Syracuse*, 35–36.

46. See Alison Brown, *Medicean and Savonarolan Florence: The Interplay of Politics, Humanism, and Religion* (Turnhout: Brepols, 2011); Marcia Colish, "Republicanism, Religion and Machiavelli's Savonarolan Moment," *Journal of the History of Ideas* 60, no. 4 (1999): 597–616; Emanuele Cutinelli-Rèndina, *Chiesa e religione in Machiavelli* (Pisa: Istituti editoriali e poligrafici internazionali, 1998); Nathan Tarcov, "Machiavelli's Critique of Religion," *Social Research: An International Quarterly* 81, no. 1 (Spring 2014): 193–216; and Maurizio Viroli, *Machiavelli's God*, trans. A. Shugaar (Princeton, NJ: Princeton University Press, 2012).

47. This, of course, is one of the prevailing narratives of Machiavelli's *Istorie Fiorentine* (1525). See Christopher Lynch, "War and Foreign Affairs in Machiavelli's *Florentine Histories*," *Review of Politics* 74, no. 1 (December 2012): 1–26.

48. There is some tension on this point when Machiavelli discusses Agathocles in the *Discourses*: on the one hand, he cites the Sicilian as one who rose to power "from obscure or base fortune" more through fraud than through force (D II.13); on the other, he uses Agathocles as an example of a "prince of an army . . . who seized his patria at a stroke and through his forces" (D III.16). In the latter chapter, Machiavelli presents Agathocles as an individual who became prince more through force than "with deceit and art or with foreign forces."

49. Machiavelli notes that Valentino's "high intentions and spirit inclined him to do no other" than prove excessively deferential to the papacy (P 7). In this light, note how Machiavelli declares that subjects of ecclesiastical principalities "cannot think otherwise" than to continue living under religious rule (P 11).

50. This section is a condensed version of McCormick, "Subdue the Senate: Machiavelli's 'Way of Freedom' or Path to Tyranny?" *Political Theory* 40, 6 (December 2012): 717–38, and McCormick, "Machiavelli's Greek Tyrant as Republican Reformer," in *The Radical Machiavelli: Politics, Philosophy, and Language*, ed. F. Del Lucchese and V. Morfino (Leiden: Brill, 2015), 337–48.

51. See Polybius XIII.6–8, and Livy XXXII.19, XXXIII.44–45, XXXIV.22, 27.

52. According to Polybius, Hiero did not directly massacre these mercenary forces; he merely sent them to certain annihilation at the hands of enemy troops. See Polybius I.9.

53. Polybius I.8–16.

54. See Justin XXII.4 and Livy XXXIV.27.

55. On Hiero's and Nabis's foreign policies, see, respectively: Polybius I.8–16, Livy XXI.49–51, XXII.37, XXIII.21; and Livy XXIX.12, XXXV.25, XXXIV.31, XXXIV.41, XXXV.35.

56. The classic account of Machiavelli as a theoretician of the "economy of violence" remains Sheldon S. Wolin, "Machiavelli: Politics and the Economy of Violence," in Wolin, *Politics and Vision: Continuity and Innovation in Western Political Thought* (Boston: Little, Brown, 1960), 175–213.

57. See Polybius XIII.6–8.

58. See Strauss, *Thoughts on Machiavelli*, 310n53.

59. See Diodorus XXI.16.

60. Strauss suggests that Machiavelli deliberately fails to mention Agathocles's "pitiable end" and that Nabis "perished through a conspiracy." See Strauss, *Thoughts on Machiavelli*, 26. However, the classical sources conflict over the circumstances of Agathocles's death: Diodorus reports that he was poisoned; Justin claims he contracted a fatal disease. Even if the former is true, Agathocles's end is no more pitiable than that of, say, Moses or Romulus. Nabis did in fact succumb to an externally hatched conspiracy: former military allies assassinated him but failed to immediately install an alternative government in Sparta, owing to vigorous resistance from Nabis's subjects. In any case, Nabis was ambushed exactly where Machiavelli suggests a good prince always ought to be: exercising his troops (P 14).

CHAPTER 2

1. Niccolò Machiavelli, *Il principe* (*De principatibus*), composed about 1513 and published in 1532, ed. G. Inglese (Turin: Einaudi, 1995), hereafter P; Machiavelli, *Discorsi*, composed about 1513–18 and published in 1531, ed. C. Vivanti (Turin: Einaudi-Gallimard, 1997), hereafter D; and Machiavelli, *Istorie Fiorentine*, composed about 1520–25 and published in 1532, ed. Franco Gaeta (Milan: Feltrinelli, 1962), hereafter FH.

2. See, paradigmatically, Hans Baron, "Machiavelli: The Republican Citizen and the Author of 'The *Prince*,'" *English Historical Review* 76, no. 299 (April 1961): 217–53. For a comprehensive corrective to this view, see James Hankins, *Virtue Politics: Soulcraft and Statecraft in Renaissance Italy* (Cambridge, MA: Harvard University Press, 2019).

3. See, e.g., Quentin Skinner, "The Republican Ideal of Political Liberty," in *Machiavelli and Republicanism*, ed. Gisela Bock, Quentin Skinner, and Maurizio Viroli (Cambridge: Cambridge University Press, 1991), 293–309; Skinner, "The Rediscovery of Republican Values," in Skinner, *Visions of Politics*, vol. 2 (Cambridge: Cambridge University Press, 2002), 10–38. See also Peter Stacey, *Roman Monarchy and the Renaissance Prince* (Cambridge: Cambridge University Press, 2007) 314, and Stacey, "*Il Vivere Servo* in Machiavelli's Political Thought," paper presented at the conference "Machiavelli's *The Prince* at 500," EUI-Florence (May 29–31, 2013). For criticisms of this perspective, see Mark Jurdjevic, "The Guicciardinian Moment: The *Discorsi Palleschi*, Humanism, and Aristocratic Republicanism in Sixteenth Century Florence," in *Humanism and Creativity in the Renaissance: Essays in Honor of Ronald G. Witt*, ed. Christopher S. Celenza and Kenneth Gouwens (Leiden: Brill, 2006); and Gabriele Pedullà, "Humanist Republicanism: Towards a New Paradigm," *History of Political Thought* 41, no. 1 (2020): 43–95.

4. Regarding Machiavelli's political assault on traditional Florentine humanism, see James Hankins, *Virtue Politics* Mark Jurdjevic, "Machiavelli's Hybrid Republicanism," *English Historical Review* 122 (December 2007): 1228–57; and Danielle Charette, "Catilinarian Cadences in Machiavelli's *Florentine Histories*: Ciceronian Humanism,

Corrupting Consensus, and the Demise of Contentious Liberty," *History of Political Thought* 39, no. 3 (Autumn 2018): 439–64. On the political impact of civic humanism, see Mikael Hörnqvist, "The Two Myths of Civic Humanism," John Najemy, "Civic Humanism and Florentine Politics," and James Hankins, "Rhetoric, History, and Ideology: The Civic Panegyrics of Leonardo Bruni," all in *Renaissance Civic Humanism: Reappraisals and Reflections* (Cambridge: Cambridge University Press, 2000), 105–78; Mark Jurdjevic, "Civic Humanism and the Rise of the Medici," *Renaissance Quarterly* 52, no. 4 (1999): 994–1020; Anthony Grafton, "Humanism and Political Theory," and Nicolai Rubinstein, "Italian Political Thought, 1450–1530," both in *The Cambridge History of Political Thought, 1450–1700*, ed. J. H. Burns and Mark Goldie (Cambridge: Cambridge University Press, 1991), 9–29 and 30–65.

5. See Daniel J. Kapust, *Republicanism, Rhetoric, and Roman Political Thought: Sallust, Livy, and Tacitus* (Cambridge: Cambridge University Press, 2011), 101; Jonathan Zarecki, *Cicero's Ideal Statesman in Theory and Practice* (London: Bloomsbury, 2014), 5–11, 78–93; Gary A. Remer, *Ethics and the Orator: The Ciceronian Tradition of Political Morality* (Chicago: University of Chicago Press, 2017), 144, 236; Christopher Burden-Strevens, *Cassius Dio's Speeches and the Collapse of the Roman Republic* (Leiden: Brill, 2020), 281; and most extensively, Walter Nicgorski, *Cicero's Practical Philosophy* (South Bend, IN: University of Notre Dame Press, 2012).

6. See Leo Strauss, *Thoughts on Machiavelli* (Glencoe, IL: Free Press, 1958), e.g., 26, 28, 273. See also Giovanni Giorgini, *La città e il tiranno: Il concetto di tirannide nella Grecia del VII–IV secolo* (Milan: Giuffrè Editore, 1993), and especially Giorgini, "The Place of the Tyrant in Machiavelli's Political Thought and the Literary Genre of *The Prince*," *History of Political Thought* 29, no. 2 (2008): 230–56.

7. In contrast to Skinner, Eric Nelson and Jim Hankins have located the rise of "exclusivist republicanism" to eras much later than the Italian Renaissance. Nelson and Hankins have shown that there was greater fluidity than Skinner acknowledges between understandings of principalities and republics in virtually all traditional republican thinkers: for Nelson, it emerged in Dutch and English appropriations of Hebraic republicanism, and for Hankins it reached its apotheosis in the dogmatic antimonarchism of the French revolutionaries. See Eric Nelson, "'Talmudical Commonwealthsmen' and the Rise of Republican Exclusivism," *Historical Journal* 50, 4 (2007): 809–35; and James Hankins, "Exclusivist Republicanism and the Non-monarchical Republic," *Political Theory* 38, 4 (2010): 452–82.

8. Michèle Lowrie analyzes the role of repetition and reversibility in Roman discourses that posit the Gracchi, Marius, Caesar, and Cicero (among others) as exempla. See Michèle Lowrie, *Consequential Narratives: The Exemplum and State Violence from Cicero to Augustus* (forthcoming). See also F. Pina Polo, "The 'Tyranny' of the Gracchi and the Concordia of the Optimates: An Ideological Construct," in *Costruire La Memoria: Uso e abuso della storia fra tarda repubblica e primo principato*, ed. R. Cristofoli, A. Galimberti, and F. Rohr Vio (Rome: L'Erma di Bretscheider, 2017), 5–34.

9. On economic inequality as the primary source of political corruption in Machiavelli, see John P. McCormick, "'Keep the Public Rich and the Citizens Poor': Economic Inequality and Political Corruption in the *Discourses*," in McCormick, *Reading Machiavelli: Scandalous Books, Suspect Engagements, and the Virtue of Populist Politics* (Princeton, NJ: Princeton University Press, 2018), 45–68. See also Yves Winter, "Plebeian

238   NOTES TO PAGES 37-39

Politics: Machiavelli and the Ciompi Uprising," *Political Theory* 40, no. 6 (December 2012): 736–66; Julie L. Rose, "'Keep the Citizens Poor': Machiavelli's Prescription for Republican Poverty," *Political Studies* 64, no. 3 (2016), 734–47; Tejas Parasher, "Inequality and *Tumulti* in Machiavelli's Aristocratic Republics," *Polity* 49, no. 1 (January 2017): 42–68; Benedetto Fontana, "Machiavelli and the Gracchi: Republican Liberty and Class Conflict," in *Machiavelli on Liberty and Conflict*, ed. Camila Vergara, David Johnston, and Nadia Urbinati (Chicago: University of Chicago Press, 2017), 235–56; and Amanda Maher, "The Power of 'Wealth, Nobility and Men': Inequality and Corruption in Machiavelli's *Florentine Histories*," *European Journal of Political Theory* 19, no. 4 (2020): 512–31. On the relationship between economic inequality and oligarchic aggrandizement in Machiavelli, see Camila Vergara, *Systemic Corruption: Constitutional Ideas for an Anti-oligarchic Republic* (Princeton, NJ: Princeton University Press, 2020), 219 and 254.

10. See Plutarch, "Tiberius and Caius Gracchus."

11. Machiavelli notes elsewhere that the Gracchi's great uncle Tiberius Sempronius Gracchus once imposed the threat of capital punishment on any soldiers who ridiculed former slaves who had been enrolled in Roman legions (D II.26). Tiberius the nephew (whom Machiavelli does not expressly distinguish from his uncle, calling the latter simply "Tiberius Gracchus") apparently was unwilling to enlist similar severity against those, namely Roman senators, who would effectively make slaves out of their own citizen-soldiers.

12. Cleomenes, however, proves less adept than Agathocles or Nabis in pursuing redistribution at home *and* exerting military power abroad, as he was eventually overcome in the field by Macedonia. See Plutarch, "Agis and Cleomenes."

13. See Plutarch, "Agis and Cleomenes."

14. See Diodorus XIX.9 and Polybius XIII.6–8.

15. See Strauss, *Thoughts on Machiavelli*, 306n9.

16. See Mikael Hörnqvist, "*Perché non si usa allegare i Romani*: Machiavelli and the Florentine Militia of 1506," *Renaissance Quarterly* 55, no. 1 (2002): 148–91; John M. Najemy, "'Occupare la tirannide': Machiavelli, the Militia, and Guicciardini's Accusation of Tyranny," in *Della tirannia: Machiavelli con Bartolo*, ed. Jérémie Barthas, Quaderni di Rinascimento 42 (Florence: Olshki, 2007): 75–108; Jérémie Barthas, *L'argent n'est pas le nerf de la guerre: Essai sur une prétendue erreur de Machiavel* (Rome: École française de Rome, 2011); and Andreas Guidi, *Books, People, and Military Thought: Machiavelli's Art of War and the Fortune of the Militia in Sixteenth-Century Florence and Europe* (Leiden: Brill, 2020).

17. See Hörnqvist, "*Perché non si usa allegare i Romani*," 148, 156–81; and Barthas, *L'argent n'est pas le nerf de la guerre*, 329–98. Paul Rahe erroneously claims that Machiavelli neither desired nor intended to include citizens in his proposed militia project, but rather wished to exclusively arm peasants from the countryside. See Paul A. Rahe, "The Anatomy of an Error: Machiavelli's Supposed Commitment to a 'Citizen' Militia," in *Machiavelli Then and Now: History, Politics, Literature*, ed. Sukanta Chaudhuri and Prasanta Chakravarty (Cambridge: Cambridge University Press, 2022), 31–53. Hörnqvist and Barthas confirm that the latter policy was imposed on Machiavelli and Soderini by the Florentine nobles.

18. See Roberto Ridolfi, *The Life of Niccolò Machiavelli*, trans. Cecil Grayson (Chicago: University of Chicago Press, 1963), 80–88.

19. See Machiavelli, "Ai Palleschi" (1512), in *Opere I: I primi scritti politici*, ed. Corrado Vivanti (Turin, 1997), 87–89; and Machiavelli, "Memorandum to the Newly Restored Medici" (1512), in *Florentine Political Writings from Petrarch to Machiavelli*, ed. M. Jurdjevic, N. Piano, and J. P. McCormick (Philadelphia: University of Pennsylvania Press, 2019), 211–12.

20. We might wonder whether the metaphor of cutting the rich into pieces signifies not only the nobility's elimination but also the partitioning, parceling, and redistribution of their wealth to the people.

21. Clearchus, like Cleomenes, his fellow Greek tyrant in the *Discourses*, was less successful militarily than their counterparts, Hiero, Agathocles, and Nabis, in *The Prince*. This is not an unfamiliar pattern: Machiavelli emphasizes domestic issues in the former work and military ones in the latter—never one to the total exclusion of the other, of course. Compare, for instance, his criticisms of both Savonarola and Scipio on military grounds in *The Prince* (P 6, P 17) and on civic grounds in the *Discourses* (D I.45, D I.29).

22. Hankins finds Machiavelli's argument here quixotic. Hankins, *Virtue Politics*, 442. On Machiavelli's anticipation of his critique, see my review of Hankins in *Erudition and the Republic of Letters* 6 (2021): 299–329, at 313–14. I argue that Machiavelli's attention to Syracuse, Sparta, Heraclea, etc., attests to the fact that he believed, contrary to Hankins's assertion, that similar problems confronted both ancient and modern city-states. Both are beset by oligarchic corruption domestically and external threats from imperial hegemons. The difference that concerns Machiavelli is that ancient cities had armed populaces that could be mobilized to reduce oligarchic domination at home and withstand military threats from abroad. This is why Machiavelli advocates citizen militias in the Italian cities of his own day. In short, Machiavelli thought that apparently insurmountable contextual differences between ancient and modern cities could be fully reconciled by prudent civic-military reforms in the present.

23. Michèle Lowrie identifies the power to immortalize republican citizens as a form of revenge that emasculated citizens-cum-writers perpetuated on imperial elites in the Augustan period. See Michèle Lowrie, *Writing, Performance, and Authority in Augustan Rome* (Oxford: Oxford University Press, 2009), 183–84, 196–99.

24. I more intensively compare Machiavelli's accounts of Agathocles and Scipio in John P. McCormick, "Machiavelli's Inglorious Tyrants: On Agathocles, Scipio and Unmerited Glory," *History of Political Thought* 36, no. 1 (2015): 29–52.

25. Livy XXXVIII.52.

26. Polybius XII.15, quoting Timaeus.

27. P 8; see also Polybius XII.15.

28. Livy XXXVIII.24–25.

29. When his soldiers in Africa mutiny, Agathocles puts himself at their mercy, and they enthusiastically reaffirm his command. Thus he was both feared and loved. Diodorus 20.33–34.

30. Jane Chaplin argues that misreadings of exemplary figures and episodes are as central to the Roman tradition of exemplarity as are ostensibly "accurate" readings. See Jane D. Chaplin, *Livy's Exemplary History* (Oxford: Oxford University Press, 2001), 78, 82, 201.

31. Machiavelli's invocation of Fabius's criticisms of Scipio do not constitute an unqualified endorsement of Fabius's political prudence. In the *Discourses*, Machiavelli

attributes the glory Fabius gained as a military strategist to the fact that his natural inclinations conformed well to the times. There Fabius, like Scipio, is also revealed to be under the government of the Roman Senate—and also under the government of the people, who defied Fabius's insistence that Rome not invade Africa to defeat Carthage: "If Fabius had been king of Rome, he could easily have lost the war because he did not know how to vary his modes and customs according to varying times. But he was born in a republic comprised of diverse citizens and diverse humors" (D III.9).

32. Livy XXX.45; Petrarch, *Africa*, trans. T. G. Bergin and A. S. Wilson (New Haven, CT: Yale University Press, 1977), chap. 2, books 1, 2, 4. See also Petrarca, *De viris illustribus*, ed. C. Malta (Messina: Università degli studi di Messina, 2008), book 22.

33. Machiavelli's evaluation of Scipio vis-à-vis the example of Hannibal (especially in D III.21) enjoys a long history in scholarship on his political writings. See Robert Fredona, "Liberate diuturna cura Italiam: Hannibal in the Thought of Niccolò Machiavelli," in *Florence and Beyond: Culture, Society and Politics in Renaissance Italy*, ed. D. S. Peterson and D. E. Bornstein (Toronto: University of Toronto Press, 2018), 419–34.

34. See Marcia L. Colish, "Cicero's *De officiis* and Machiavelli's *Prince*," *Sixteenth Century Journal* 9 (1978): 81–93; Michelle Zerba, "The Frauds of Humanism: Cicero, Machiavelli, and the Rhetoric of Imposture," *Rhetorica* 22, no. 3 (2004): 215–40; Joy Connolly, *The State of Speech: Rhetoric and Political Thought in Ancient Rome* (Princeton, NJ: Princeton University Press, 2007); Daniel J. Kapust, *Republicanism, Rhetoric, and Roman Political Thought: Sallust, Livy, and Tacitus* (Cambridge: Cambridge University Press, 2014); and Gary A. Remer, *Ethics and the Orator: The Ciceronian Tradition of Political Morality* (Chicago: University of Chicago Press, 2017).

35. See John W. Oppel, "Peace vs. Liberty in the Quattrocento: Poggio, Guarino, and the Scipio-Caesar Controversy," *Journal of Medieval and Renaissance Studies* 4 (1974): 221–65; and Gabriele Pedullà, "Scipio vs. Caesar: The Poggio-Guarino Debate without Republicanism," in *Republicanism: A Theoretical and Historical Perspective*, ed. Marcello Fantoni and Fabrizio Ricciardelli (Rome: Viella, 2020), 275–305 at 281. See also Mark Jurdjevic, "Civic Humanism and the Rise of the Medici," *Renaissance Quarterly* 52, no. 4 (Winter 1999): 994–1020 at 1002–5.

36. According to Hankins, most humanists agreed that, among the greatest Roman commanders and citizens, Caesar was inferior in virtue to Scipio Africanus, even if they expressed moderate to high admiration for the dictator. Petrarch, for his part, equivocated on this question for much of his career before finally elevating Caesar over Scipio. Like Bartolus and many other humanists, Petrarch thought the wrong of Caesar's assassination far outweighed any offense the dictator himself committed. See Hankins, *Virtue Politics*, 125–27. Coluccio Salutati was Caesar's most vociferous defender, arguing that the dictator's just rule legitimated his unlawful usurpation of authority (*Virtue Politics*, 127–33). Perhaps the most fair-minded assessment of Caesar was written by Francesco Patrizi, who is unusual among the authors Hankins discusses for marking a distinction between the moral characters of Julius and Octavian Caesar. Unlike the inveterately cruel Augustus, Patrizi praises Caesar for his personal, military, and literary solicitude while not excusing his profligacy and ambition. See Hankins, *Virtue Politics*, 402–3. See also James Hankins, *Political Meritocracy in Renaissance Italy: The Virtuous Republic of Francesco Patrizi of Siena* (Cambridge, MA: Harvard University Press, 2023).

37. See Livy XXVIII.40–45.

38. See Machiavelli's other major discussion of Scipio Africanus, "Tercets on Ingratitude or Envy," in *Machiavelli: The Chief Works and Others,* ed. and trans. A. Gilbert
(Durham, NC: Duke University Press, 1989), 3:740–44.

39. See Livy XXVIII.51.

40. Livy XXVIII.52.

41. I will discuss Machiavelli's views on the appropriate moment when a civic magistrate should put himself, or his aristocratic adversaries, on trial in part 2 of this book,
where I examine the cases of Marcus Menenius and Piero Soderini.

42. Livy XXXI.4, XXXII.1.

43. See Strauss, *Thoughts on Machiavelli,* 245–46.

44. See Strauss, *Thoughts on Machiavelli,* 190.

45. Livy I.59–60, II.5.

46. Suetonius, *Lives of the Caesars,* 82.1–4.

47. Indeed, Machiavelli plainly states that the Roman Republic fell back into the
hands of "the party of the aristocrats" after Caesar's assassination (D I.52)—that is, until Cicero persuaded the Senate to lend Octavian Caesar excessive authority to move
against Mark Antony, leading to their own "destruction."

48. Suetonius 75.1–3.

49. See Chaplin on the role that misreadings and "accurate" readings of exemplary
figures play in the Roman tradition of exemplarity. Jane D. Chaplin, *Livy's Exemplary
History,* 78, 82, 201.

50. "E Cesare era uno di quelli che voleva pervenire al principato di Roma; ma,
se, poi che vi fu venuto, fussi sopravvissuto, e non si fussi temperato da quelle spese,
arebbe destrutto quello imperio."

51. Again, with the vociferous exception of Salutati: see Coluccio Salutati, "On the
Tyrant (1400)," in *Florentine Political Writings,* ed. M. Jurdjevic, N. Piano, and J. P. Mc-
Cormick, 56–84.

52. See, e.g., Sebastian de Grazia, *Machiavelli in Hell* (Princeton, NJ: Princeton University Press, 1989), 251. Some interpreters consider Agathocles's poor and abject origin to be the very reason he has not been more celebrated historically (e.g., P 14; D
I.10). Lefort and Coby suggest that Agathocles's low birth is what ultimately separates
him from figures who act in a similar manner and nevertheless attain glory, such as
Scipio, Moses, Romulus, and Borgia. See Claude Lefort, *Le travail de l'œuvre Machiavel*
(Paris: Gallimard, 1972) 380; and Patrick Coby, *Machiavelli's Romans: Liberty and Greatness in the Discourses on Livy* (Lanham, MD: Lexington Books, 1999), 234–35. But as I
have just explained, this is only part of the story.

53. See Fabio Raimondi, *L'ordinamento della libertà: Machiavelli e Firenze* (Verona:
Ombre Corte, 2013); Hörnqvist, *"Perché non si usa allegare i Romani,"* 148–91; and Najemy, *"'Occupare la tirannide': Machiavelli, the Militia, and Guicciardini's Accusation
of Tyranny,"* in *Della tirannia: Machiavelli con Bartolo,* ed. Jérémie Barthas, *Quaderni di
Rinascimento* 42 (Florence 2007): 75–108.

CHAPTER 3

1. Niccolò Machiavelli, *Discorsi,* composed about 1513–18 and published in 1531,
ed. C. Vivanti (Turin: Einaudi-Gallimard, 1997), hereafter D; as well as Machiavelli, *Il
principe (De principatibus),* composed about 1513 and published in 1532, ed. G. Inglese

242 NOTES TO PAGES 67–70

(Turin: Einaudi, 1995), hereafter P; and Machiavelli, *Istorie Fiorentine*, composed about 1520–25 and published in 1532, ed. Franco Gaeta (Milan: Feltrinelli, 1962), hereafter FH.

2. See John P. McCormick, *Machiavellian Democracy* (Cambridge: Cambridge University Press, 2011), and McCormick, *Reading Machiavelli: Scandalous Books, Suspect Engagements, and the Virtue of Populist Politics* (Princeton, NJ: Princeton University Press, 2018).

3. As Manlius Torquatus did (D II.16, D III.22), hence beneficially returning the republic to its "beginnings" (D III.1)—but as Cincinnatus, according to Livy, failed to do, using dictatorial authority to exonerate his son Caeso for oppressing the plebs. See Livy III.13–14.

4. See Machiavelli, *Decennali*, Epigram I, in *Machiavelli: The Chief Works and Others*, ed. and trans. A. Gilbert (Durham, NC: Duke University Press, 1989), 3:1463.

5. See Gabriele Pedullà, "Una 'tirannide elettiva'. Ovvero: Ciò che gli umanisti e Machiavelli hanno da insegnarci sulla dittatura e sullo 'stato di eccezione,'" in *Governo straordinario e stato di eccezione*, ed. Francesco Benigno and Luca Scuccimarra (Rome: Viella, 2007), 7-51; Marco Geuna, "Machiavelli and the Problem of Dictatorship," *Ratio Juris* 28, no. 2 (June 2015): 226–41; Marco Geuna, "Extraordinary Accidents in the Life of Republics: Machiavelli and Dictatorial Authority," in *Machiavelli on Liberty and Conflict*, ed. David Johnston, Nadia Urbinati, and Camila Vergara (Chicago: University of Chicago Press, 2017), 280–308; and Camila Vergara, "Crisis Government: The Populist as Plebeian Dictator," in *Mapping Populism: Approaches and Methods*, ed. Amit Ron and Majia Nadesan (London: Routledge, 2020), 210–20.

6. The issue of popular judgment speaks to Machiavelli's role in the historical development of the idea of "constituent power": that is, the power to refound and radically reform the basic structure of a polity, for instance by adding new offices to the constitution, by incorporating new groups into "the people," and by restructuring power arrangements among classes. See Filippo Del Lucchese, "Machiavelli and Constituent Power: The Revolutionary Foundation of Modern Political Thought," *European Journal of Political Theory* 16, no. 1 (2017): 3-23; Camila Vergara, "Populism: Plebeian Power against Oligarchy," in *Constituent Power: Law, Popular Rule, and Politics*, ed. Matilda Arvidsson, Leila Brännström, and Panu Minkkinen (Edinburgh: Edinburgh University Press, 2020), 183–98; and Camila Vergara, "Machiavelli's Republican Constituent Power," in *Machiavelli's Discourses on Livy: New Readings*, ed. D. P. Aurélio and A. S. Campos (Leiden: Brill, 2021), 143–61.

7. Consult Gilbert's research on the pro-oligarchic/antipopular republican preconceptions of the Florentine *ottimati* in this era, including members of the Rucellai and Buondelmonti families: Felix Gilbert, "Florentine Political Assumptions in the Period of Savonarola and Soderini," *Journal of the Warburg and Courtauld Institutes* 20 (1957): 187–214; Felix Gilbert, "The Venetian Constitution in Florentine Political Thought," in *Florentine Studies: Politics and Society in Renaissance Florence*, ed. Nicolai Rubinstein (Evanston, IL: Northwestern University Press, 1968), 442–62; and Felix Gilbert, "Bernardo Rucellai and the Orti Oricellari: A Study on the Origin of Modern Political Thought," in *History: Choice and Commitment*, ed. Felix Gilbert (Cambridge, MA: Harvard University Press, 2014), 215–46. For a roughly contemporary confirmation of these dispositions in Cosimo's and Zanobi's forebears, see Francesco Guicciardini, *The History of Florence* (c. 1508), trans. M. Domandi (New York: Harper, 1970), 144–45 and 299.

8. See Mark Jurdjevic, *Guardians of Republicanism: The Valori Family in the Florentine Renaissance* (Oxford: Oxford University Press, 2008), 1–45.

9. See Humfrey C. Butters, *Governors and Government in Early Sixteenth-Century Florence* (Oxford: Clarendon Press, 1985), 140–65; and John M. Najemy, *A History of Florence: 1200–1575* (Oxford: Blackwell, 2006), 414–41.

10. See Mikael Hörnqvist, *"Perché non si usa allegare i Romani*: Machiavelli and the Florentine Militia of 1506," *Renaissance Quarterly* 55, no. 1 (2002): 148–91; John Najemy, "'Occupare la tirannide': Machiavelli, the Militia, and Guicciardini's Accusation of Tyranny," in *Della tirannia: Machiavelli con Bartolo, Quaderni di Rinascimento* 42 (Florence: Leo S. Olschki, 2007), 75–110; and Jérémie Barthas, *L'argent n'est pas le nerf de la guerre: Essai sur une prétendue erreur de Machiavel* (Rome: École française de Rome, 2011), 329–98. More recently, see Andrea Guidi, *Books, People, and Military Thought: Machiavelli's Art of War and the Fortune of the Militia in Sixteenth-Century Florence and Europe* (Leiden: Brill, 2020); and Sean Erwin, *Machiavelli and the Problems of Military Force: A War of One's Own* (London: Bloomsbury Academic, 2022).

11. Other erstwhile popular champions, according to Machiavelli, did in fact lose such a reputation with the people: most notably, Giorgio Scali (P 9), Savonarola (P 6, D I.45), and Virginius (D I.45).

12. See Eero Arum, "Machiavelli's *Principio*: Political Renewal and Innovation in the *Discourses on Livy*," *Review of Politics* 82, no. 4 (2020): 525–47.

13. Livy XXXVIII.52.

14. An act not unlike the one that began Christianity—presumably one of the few "good things" in that sect's "beginnings" that, in Machiavelli's estimation, contributed to its longevity.

15. Plutarch, *Life of Brutus*, par. 5.2.

16. Especially members of the Strozzi family: see Melissa Meriam Bullard, "Marriage Intrigues," in *Filippo Strozzi and the Medici: Favor and Finance in Sixteenth-Century Florence and Rome* (Cambridge: Cambridge University Press, 1980), 45–60; Butters, *Governors and Government in Early Sixteenth-Century Florence*, 65; and Najemy, *History of Florence*, 414–18.

17. The *compagnacci*, younger members of the anti-Savonarolan *arrabiati*, were originally armed political partisans of Lorenzo de' Medici. See W. R. Lloyd, "Savonarola: His Friends and Enemies," in *The Flower of Christian Chivalry* (London: Strahan, 1871), 59–122; Pasquale Villari, *Life and Times of Girolamo Savonarola*, trans. Linda Villari (London: T. Fisher Unwin, 1897), 325–34; and Najemy, *History of Florence*, 397.

18. As Robert Black observes, "Piero Soderini had gained support to become life-termed gonfalonier precisely because he had no children and could not therefore establish a dynasty." See Black, "Review: Machiavelli, Some Recent Biographies and Studies," *English Historical Review* 127, no. 524 (February 2012): 114.

19. In the midst of the republic's final crisis, on August 27, 1512, the gonfalonier did win a vote of confidence in the Great Council; the people resoundingly supported Soderini's continuation in office. See Najemy, *History of Florence*, 421.

20. If such proud, prominent, privileged, and powerful individuals do ever die it is usually through extraordinary means employed outside the law: through assassinations or their foiling, or through summary execution (see D I.7 and D III.6).

21. See Machiavelli, *Second Decennale*, 1463.

22. See Gilbert, "Venetian Constitution in Florentine Political Thought," 484.

244 NOTES TO PAGES 89–101

23. The office of lifetime gonfalonier was initially proposed by the quasi-senatorial Council of the Eighty. See Najemy, *History of Florence*, 387, 405, and 421.

24. Livy I.35.

25. See Gilbert, "Bernardo Rucellai and the *Orti Oricellari*," 101–31.

26. Livy, I.40–41.

27. See Butters, *Governors and Government in Early Sixteenth-Century Florence*, 51–52; and Najemy, *History of Florence*, 407–12.

28. Machiavelli gestures in some but not all of these directions in his memoranda to the Medici: see Machiavelli, "*Ai Palleschi*" (1512), in *Opere I: I Primi Scritti Politici*, ed. Corrado Vivanti (Turin 1997), 87–89; and Machiavelli, "Memorandum to the Newly Restored Medici" (1512), in *Florentine Political Writings from Petrarch to Machiavelli*, ed. M. Jurdjevic, N. Piano, and J. P. McCormick (Philadelphia: University of Pennsylvania Press, 2019), 211–12.

29. See Stephen D. Bowd, "The Strategy of Terror," in *Renaissance Mass Murder: Civilians and Soldiers during the Italian Wars* (Oxford: Oxford University Press, 2018), 54–62.

30. Livy, XXX.30–31.

31. Although many members of the Great Council had extensive business interests in France. See Butters, *Governors and Government in Early Sixteenth-Century Florence*, 268–71.

32. Bullard, *Filippo Strozzi and the Medici*, 64.

33. On the vote of confidence for Soderini in the Great Council and the Eighty in August of 1512, see Najemy, *History of Florence*, 421.

CHAPTER 4

1. Niccolò Machiavelli, *Il principe* (*De principatibus*), composed about 1513 and published in 1532, ed. G. Inglese (Turin: Einaudi, 1995), hereafter P; Machiavelli, *Discorsi*, composed about 1513–18 and published in 1531, ed. C. Vivanti (Turin: Einaudi-Gallimard, 1997), hereafter D; and Machiavelli, *Istorie Fiorentine*, composed about 1520–25 and published in 1532, ed. Franco Gaeta (Milan: Feltrinelli, 1962), hereafter FH.

2. Camillus's example contrasts with that of, again, Cincinnatus, who used his dictatorial authority to excuse his son, Caeso, from punishment for oppressing the plebs. See Livy III.14.

3. Livy V.49; Plutarch, *Life of Camillus*, I.1.

4. According to Plutarch, Camillus suggests changing the venue of Manlius's trial so that the plebeians could not see the Capitol that Manlius had saved and hence would more readily condemn him to death. Plutarch, *Life of Camillus*, 36.5.

5. Exodus 32:26–28.

6. Strauss misunderstands the relation of Savonarola's invectives to Valori's fall from power. See Leo Strauss, *Thoughts on Machiavelli* (Glencoe, IL: Free Press, 1958), 18–19.

7. Popular favor ultimately did Soderini no good: on August 27, 1512, the gonfalonier won a resounding vote of confidence in the Great Council; the people enthusiastically supported his continuation in office. Less than a week later four sons of Brutus, whom he should have tried for treason, stormed the palace, threatened to assault him, and compelled his resignation and exile. See Najemy, *History of Florence*, 421.

8. In D III.23, Machiavelli declares that Camillus failed to avoid "the shoal" of unnecessarily offending the people; here in D III.30 he writes that Camillus successfully steered away from "the shoal" of ordering the people in a militarily disorganized fashion.

9. See Christopher Lynch, "Machiavelli on Reading the Bible Judiciously," *Hebraic Political Studies* 1, no. 2 (2006): 162–85.

10. See Mikael Hörnqvist, "*Perché non si usa allegare i Romani*: Machiavelli and the Florentine Militia of 1506," *Renaissance Quarterly* 55, no. 1 (2002): 148–91; John M. Najemy, "'Occupare la Tirannide': Machiavelli, the Militia, and Guicciardini's Accusation of Tyranny," in *Della tirannia: Machiavelli con Bartolo*, ed. Jérémie Barthas, *Quaderni di Rinascimento* 42 (Florence: Olshki, 2007): 75–108; and Jérémie Barthas, *L'argent n'est pas le nerf de la guerre: Essai sur une prétendue erreur de Machiavel* (Rome: École française de Rome, 2011), 329–98.

11. Livy VI.7.

12. Both Livy and Plutarch insist that Camillus was equating himself with Jupiter. See Livy V.23 and Plutarch, *Life of Camillus*, V.6. But the plebs, stinging from being expected to repay the dictator's debt to Apollo, may have readily thought that he was invoking the grandeur of that deity.

13. D III.24; Livy, V.32.

14. Livy V.48–49.

15. Livy V.49; Plutarch, *Life of Camillus*, I.1.

16. Machiavelli, *Art of War*, book I. Indeed, Machiavelli underscores that, for any city to be "ordered well," its citizens must not be "compelled to fight unwillingly"—that is, to take up soldiering as a profession rather than as a civic duty. See Yves Winter, "The Prince and His Art of War: Machiavelli's Military Populism," *Social Research* 81, no. 1 (2014): 165–91; and Winter, *Machiavelli and the Orders of Violence* (Cambridge: Cambridge University Press, 2018), 66–88.

17. See Barthas, *Argent n'est pas le nerf de la guerre*.

18. As in the notable contrasting examples of Pisa and Prato (D I.38). In the *Florentine Histories*, Machiavelli tersely recounts: "Death was always a truer friend to the Florentines than any other, and likewise a more powerful benefactor than their own virtue" (FH III.29).

19. Matthew 18:20.

20. See William Parsons, *Machiavelli's Gospel: The Critique of Christianity in "The Prince"* (Rochester, NY: University of Rochester Press, 2016), 286.

21. See Christopher Hibbert, *The Borgias and Their Enemies: 1431–1519* (New York: Houghton Mifflin Harcourt, 2008), 30.

22. See John P. McCormick, *Reading Machiavelli: Scandalous Books, Suspect Engagements, and the Virtue of Populist Politics* (Princeton, NJ: Princeton University Press, 2018), 54–57.

23. Livy VI.5.

24. Livy VI.14.

25. Livy V.9, V.26.

26. Plutarch, *Life of Camillus*, 10.5–11.1.

27. Plutarch, *Life of Camillus*, 7.1–7.5; see Livy V.20.

28. Plutarch, *Life of Camillus*, 2.1–2.6; Livy V.26–27.

29. Plutarch, *Life of Camillus*, 2.1–2.6.

30. Livy V.29.

31. Livy VI.42; Plutarch, *Life of Camillus*, 42.1–5.

32. Plutarch insists on this as fact: *Life of Camillus*, 24.1–3. Livy hopes it was so: Livy V.46. See also Livy V.51 for Camillus's proclaimed dedication to Rome's patria and religion.

CHAPTER 5

1. Niccolò Machiavelli, *Il principe* (*De principatibus*), composed about 1513 and published in 1532, ed. G. Inglese (Turin: Einaudi, 1995), hereafter P; Machiavelli, *Discorsi*, composed about 1513-18 and published in 1531, ed. C. Vivanti (Turin: Einaudi-Gallimard, 1997), hereafter D; and Machiavelli, *Istorie Fiorentine*, composed about 1520-25 and published in 1532, ed. Franco Gaeta (Milan: Feltrinelli, 1962), hereafter FH.

2. See Amanda Maher, "What Skinner Misses about Machiavelli's Freedom: Inequality, Corruption, and the Institutional Origins of Civic Virtue," *Journal of Politics* 78, no. 4 (2016): 1003–15; John P. McCormick, "'Keep the Public Rich and the Citizens Poor': Economic Inequality and Political Corruption in the *Discourses*," in McCormick, *Reading Machiavelli: Scandalous Books, Suspect Engagements, and the Virtue of Populist Politics* (Princeton, NJ: Princeton University Press, 2018), 45–68; Yves Winter, *Machiavelli and the Orders of Violence* (Cambridge: Cambridge University Press, 2018), 148–52; Gabriel Pedullà, *Machiavelli in Tumult: The Discourses on Livy and the Origins of Political Conflictualism* (Cambridge: Cambridge University Press, 2018), 42–54, 73–83; and Camila Vergara, *Systemic Corruption: Constitutional Ideas for an Anti-oligarchic Republic* (Princeton, NJ: Princeton University Press, 2020).

3. See Pedullà, *Machiavelli in Tumult*, 10–27.

4. On the substance of this debate in D I.5, see John P. McCormick, *Machiavellian Democracy* (Cambridge: Cambridge University Press, 2011), 46–53.

5. See McCormick, *Machiavellian Democracy*, 51–52.

6. For my differences with Gabriele Pedullà on whether Machiavelli believes the people can behave as oppressively as the nobles, see our contributions to "The Political Logic of Conflict: A Debate on *Machiavelli in Tumult* by Gabriele Pedullà," *Storica* 27, no. 81 (2021): 109–75 at 139–45 and 167–69. See also John P. McCormick, "Aristocratic *Insolenzia* and the Role of Senates in Machiavelli's Mixed Republic," *Review of Politics* 83, no. 4 (2021): 486–509.

7. See D II.9–10, D II.19–21, D II.24, and D II.32.

8. Mansfield readily accepts the nobles' response that the people and the dictator were in fact acting "extraordinarily," but it is not clear on what grounds. See Harvey C. Mansfield, *Machiavelli's New Modes and Orders: A Study of the Discourses on Livy* (Chicago: University of Chicago Press, 2001), 48. If he means the use of the dictatorship itself, Machiavelli later identifies the office as an *ordinary* institution that addresses *extraordinary* circumstances (D I.34). If he means that the people had no legal authority to change the focus of Menenius's investigation, this is technically true, but "the people" in the sense of the *populus Romanus* theoretically have the authority to do whatever they want. Moreover, Mansfield speculates that the plebeian dictator is seeking the consulship for himself, but Machiavelli's readers would likely know that dictators almost always previously served as consuls. See Arthur Kaplan, *Dictatorships and "Ultimate" Decrees in the Early Roman Republic, 501-202 B.C.* (New York: Revisionist Press,

1977), 2; and Richard E. Mitchell, *Patricians and Plebeians: The Origin of the Roman State* (Ithaca, NY: Cornell University Press, 1990), 137.

9. Machiavelli demonstrates that, rather than make any concession on their appetite to oppress, the nobles dissemble, deflect, and feign vulnerability, declaring that "the restless spirit of the plebs" is the most dangerous threat to republics and that the people's propensity to raise up champions "whom they use as sticks to beat down the nobility" is the greatest injustice posed by class conflict (D I.5).

10. See Gabriele Pedullà, "Una 'tirannide elettiva'. Ovvero: Ciò che gli umanisti e Machiavelli hanno da insegnarci sulla dittatura e sullo 'stato di eccezione,'" in *Governo straordinario e stato di eccezione*, ed. Francesco Benigno and Luca Scuccimarra (Rome: Viella, 2007), 7-51; and Marco Geuna, "Machiavelli and the Problem of Dictatorship," *Ratio Juris* 28, no. 2 (June 2015): 226-41.

11. John M. Najemy, "Society, Class, and State in Machiavelli's *Discourses on Livy*," in *The Cambridge Companion to Machiavelli*, ed. John M. Najemy (Cambridge: Cambridge University Press, 2010), 96-111 at 103.

12. Livy IX.6.

13. Or perhaps Machiavelli does not care at all whether their verdict is partisan. In the world there is none but the vulgar (P 15). Appearances and results are all that matter. As Machiavelli attests in his letters, he views things from the standpoint of the people, a view that is in crucial moments correct. See Niccolò Machiavelli, "Caprices for Soderino" (September 1506), in *Machiavelli's "The Prince,"* trans. William J. Connell (New York: Bedford/St. Martin's, 2005), 121-24; and Niccolò Machiavelli to Francesco Guicciardini (15 March 1526), in Machiavelli, *Lettere*, ed. Franco Gaeta (Milan: Feltrinelli, 1961), 407-8.

14. Gabriele Pedullà does not go as far as Dionysius of Halicarnassus in exaggerating the extent to which the dictatorship did or should serve as a tool of the Roman nobility against the plebeians. See Pedullà, *Machiavelli in Tumult*, 102, 146, and Pedullà, "Reply," in "The Political Logic of Conflict: A Debate on *Machiavelli in Tumult* by Gabriele Pedullà," *Storica* 27, no. 81 (2021): 167-69. But he largely neglects the ways Machiavelli presents the dictatorship as an instrument of the people against the nobles. See McCormick, contribution to "The Political Logic of Conflict," 139-41.

15. Furthermore, the episodes examined in this chapter might also prompt Pedullà (among others) to reconsider his depiction of Machiavelli as an entirely uncritical, unqualified advocate of imperial republics. See *Machiavelli in Tumult*, 6, 173-74. See also William J. Connell, "Machiavelli and Growth as an End in Itself (Telos) for the State," *Revista de Estudios Politicos* 167 (January 2015): 13-32. Machiavelli's position on empire might be much more complicated: Pedullà and Connell fail to fully address two related issues that are also very salient in the *Discourses*: (1) that it is possible for republics to expand too much, and (2) that territorial expansion eventually causes the corruption and fall of the Roman republic. See McCormick, "Political Logic of Conflict," 141-45.

16. For guidance in consulting editions of Livy most likely to have been available to Machiavelli, I rely on Ronald T. Ridley, "Machiavelli's Edition of Livy," *Rinascimento* 27 (1987): 327-39. In Livy's original Latin, the dictator and master of horse are named Caius Maenius and Marcus Folius, while, in the editions Machiavelli likely consulted, their names are Caius Menenius and Marcus Follium. Machiavelli either mistakenly or deliberately changes Caius to Marcus in the *Discourses*.

17. Livy IX.6.

18. Another interesting aspect of Livy's account: when accusing the people of pursuing, through purportedly corrupt means, offices they supposedly do not deserve, the nobles invoke the term "new men," which had class-political resonance in both ancient Roman and modern Florentine contexts. The appellation applies to individuals who were the first in their families to attain high office in Rome, such as Marius and Cicero, and political influence in Florence, such as, say, Bernardo del Nero and Machiavelli himself. See John M. Najemy, *A History of Florence, 1200–1575* (Oxford: Wiley/Blackwell, 2006), 365.

19. Livy IX.6.

20. Livy IX.26.

21. Livy II.32.

22. It is worth noting that Machiavelli, in advocating for a Florentine militia in 1498, tacitly subverts the moral of the parable: in the militia statute he drafted, Machiavelli asserts that the Monte, the republic's central financial institution, was the city's "heart," and that no particular members should disproportionately benefit from it. This is an implicit criticism of the Florentine *ottimati*, who, in being granted exorbitantly favorable loans to fund mercenaries, were themselves the vaguely parasitic limbs "of this body we call the city." See Jérémie Barthas, *L'argent n'est pas le nerf de la guerre: Essai sur une prétendue erreur de Machiavel* (Rome: École française de Rome, 2011), 291–308, especially 295. Although he does not recognize the connection with Livy's Menenius Agrippa and the parable of the body, Barthas convincingly demonstrates the connection with Machiavelli's reflections on money and militias in the *Discourses* (D II.10 and D II.30).

23. Livy II.32.

24. Livy II.33.

25. Livy II.52.

26. Livy IV.53.

27. Sallust, *Jugurtha* 27.1–5.

28. Sallust, *Jugurtha* 30.1–3.

29. See Patricia J. Osmond, "Sallust and Machiavelli: From Civic Humanism to Prudence," *Journal of Medieval and Renaissance Studies* 23, no. 3 (1993): 407–38; and Benedetto Fontana, "Sallust and the Politics of Machiavelli," *History of Political Thought* 24, no. 1 (Spring 2003): 86–108. See also Daniel Kapust, "Cato's Virtues and *The Prince*: Reading Sallust's 'War with Catiline' with Machiavelli's *The Prince*," *History of Political Thought* 28, no. 3 (Autumn 2007): 433–48.

30. Sallust, *Jugurtha*, 30.3.

31. Sallust, *Jugurtha*, 31.2.

32. Sallust, *Jugurtha*, 31.2, 7.

33. Sallust, *Jugurtha*, 31.2, 7.

34. Sallust, *Jugurtha*, 31.9–12, 25.

35. See McCormick, *Reading Machiavelli*, chap. 3, n. 5.

36. Sallust, *Jugurtha*, 31.15–16.

37. Sallust, *Jugurtha*, 31.21–23. On Machiavelli's understanding of aristocratic insolence, see John P. McCormick, "Aristocratic *Insolenzia* and the Role of Senates in Machiavelli's Mixed Republic," *Review of Politics* 83, no. 4 (2021): 486–509.

38. Sallust, *Jugurtha* 31.17.

39. Sallust, *Jugurtha* 31.18–20.

40. Sallust, *Jugurtha* 32.1.

41. Sallust, *Jugurtha* 34.1.

42. Appian, *The Civil Wars*, trans. J. Carter (London: Penguin, 1996), 32.1.

43. See Livy, "Periochae to Book 60" (www.livius.org/li-ln/livy/periochae/periochae00.html); Appian, *Civil Wars*, 1.18; *The Oxford Classical Dictionary*, ed. S. Hornblower and A. Spawforth (Oxford, 2003), 614; Plutarch, "Gaius Gracchus," in *Makers of Rome*, trans. I. Scott-Kilvert (London: Penguin, 1965), 184–92. On the possibility that Machiavelli surreptitiously supports antipatrician agrarian reforms in Rome, despite apparent statements to the contrary, see Eric Nelson, *The Greek Tradition in Republican Thought* (Cambridge: Cambridge University Press, 2004), 75–86.

44. See Jeffrey A. Winters, *Oligarchy* (Cambridge: Cambridge University Press, 2011), 21.

45. According to Livy, Cincinnatus used his dictatorial authority to oversee a trial that exonerated his son, Caeso, for abusing plebeians, resulting in the banishment of the individual who purportedly gave false testimony against him. See Livy III.29. Menenius likewise might have used the dictatorship to settle a personal score emerging from class conflict.

46. See Najemy, *History of Florence*, 421.

47. See Barthas, *L'argent n'est pas le nerf de la guerre*, 295.

48. See James B. Atkinson, "Niccolò Machiavelli: A Portrait," in *Cambridge Companion to Machiavelli*, 14–31, at 18–21.

49. See Mikael Hörnqvist, *"Perché non si usa allegare i Romani*: Machiavelli and the Florentine Militia of 1506," *Renaissance Quarterly* 55, no. 1 (2002): 148–91. James Hankins confirms that Machiavelli's endorsement of popular militias was singularly uncompromising in his political context. The few other Italian advocates of popular militias, like Matteo Palmieri and Francesco Patrizi, for instance, were much more amenable to continued reliance on mercenary arms than was Machiavelli. See Hankins, *Virtue Politics: Soulcraft and Statecraft in Renaissance Italy* (Cambridge, MA: Harvard University Press, 2019), 259–63. Moreover, Hankins demonstrates that most mainstream advocates of civic-military reforms like Leonardo Bruni were focused on elite rather than popular civic-military initiatives: Hankins shows that Bruni's *De militia* (c. 1420) was not, as often understood, intended to revitalize Florence's popular neighborhood and guild militias, but rather to encourage the rearming of individual nobles within the city's Guelf party. See Hankins, *Virtue Politics*, 241.

CHAPTER 6

1. Niccolò Machiavelli, *Il principe* (*De principatibus*), composed about 1513 and published in 1532, ed. G. Inglese (Turin: Einaudi, 1995), hereafter P; Machiavelli, *Discorsi*, composed about 1513–18 and published in 1531, ed. C. Vivanti (Turin: Einaudi-Gallimard, 1997), hereafter D; and Machiavelli, *Istorie Fiorentine*, composed about 1520–25 and published in 1532, ed. Franco Gaeta (Milan: Feltrinelli, 1962), hereafter FH.

2. Hans Baron, "Machiavelli: The Republican Citizen and the Author of 'The Prince,'" *English Historical Review* 76, no. 299 (April 1961): 217–53. For a recent invaluable essay on the dating of *The Prince*'s composition, see Jérémie Barthas, "Machiavelli e la restaurazione dei Medici a Firenze. Per un nuovo paradigma interpretativo," *Rivista storica italiana* 131 (2019): 761–811.

3. Quentin Skinner, *Foundations of Modern Political Thought*, vol. 1, *The Renaissance* (Cambridge: Cambridge University Press, 1978), 183.

4. See Livy XXIII.2–4. Among other difference between their accounts, Livy presents Pacuvius as having a more dubious civic-moral character than does Machiavelli.

5. For a formidable rebuttal of this perspective, see Quentin Skinner, *Machiavelli* (Oxford: Oxford University Press, 1981); and, more recently, Skinner, "Machiavelli and the Misunderstanding of Princely *Virtù*," in *Machiavelli on Liberty and Conflict*, ed. D. Johnston, N. Urbinati, and C. Vergara (Chicago: University of Chicago Press, 2017), 139–63.

6. On Machiavelli's assertion about the necessity of popularly judged, capital trials for civic liberty, see John P. McCormick, "Machiavelli's Political Trials and the 'Free Way of Life,'" *Political Theory* 35, 4 (August 2007): 385–411; and McCormick, "Of Tribunes and Tyrants: Machiavelli's Legal and Extra-legal Modes for Controlling Elites," *Ratio Juris* 28, 2 (June 2015): 252–66.

7. See Harvey C. Mansfield, *Machiavelli's New Modes and Orders: A Study of the Discourses on Livy* (Chicago: University of Chicago Press, 2001), 145. See also Mansfield, *Machiavelli's Virtue* (Chicago: University of Chicago Press, 1996), 251. Similarly, Vickie Sullivan imputes to Machiavelli a "devilish delight" in exposing and ridiculing the people's supposed credulity in circumstances where elites apparently manipulate them. See Vickie B. Sullivan, *Machiavelli, Hobbes, and the Formation of a Liberal Republicanism in England* (Cambridge: Cambridge University Press, 2004), 53. For the master's own suggestion that Machiavelli does not, appearances to the contrary, elevate the people's judgment over that of the nobles, see Leo Strauss, *Thoughts on Machiavelli* (Glencoe, IL: Free Press, 1958), 137, an argument I challenge in chapter 5 of McCormick, *Reading Machiavelli: Scandalous Books, Suspect Engagements, and the Virtue of Populist Politics* (Princeton, NJ: Princeton University Press, 2018), 144–75.

8. Proponents of this view include Miguel E. Vatter, *Between Form and Event: Machiavelli's Theory of Political Freedom* (New York: Fordham University Press, 2014), and Miguel Abensour, *Democracy against the State: Marx and the Machiavellian Movement* (Cambridge: Polity, 2011).

9. Arendt's idiosyncratic translation of the ancient Greek term *isonomia*, or "legal equality," as "no-rule" is the intellectual genesis of contemporary "radical" democratic theory in its recent agonistic, post-Marxist, postmodern, or poststructuralist forms. See Arendt, *On Revolution* (London: Penguin, 1965), 30–31. Wolin conceives of "democracy" as an existential moment rather than a political regime; and Rancière insists that democracy cannot be realized in any institutional form but rather manifests itself most robustly in the people's fervent, intransigent opposition to the state. See Sheldon S. Wolin, "Norm and Form: The Constitutionalizing of Democracy," in *Athenian Political Thought and the Reconstruction of American Democracy*, ed. J. Peter Euben, John Wallach, and Josiah Ober (Ithaca, NY: Cornell University Press, 1994), 29–58; Sheldon S. Wolin, "Fugitive Democracy," in *Democracy and Difference: Contesting Boundaries of the Political*, ed. Seyla Benhabib (Princeton, NJ: Princeton University Press, 1996), 31–45; and Jacques Rancière, *Hatred of Democracy*, trans. Steve Corcoran (London: Verso, 2007). For a critique of this approach to democratic theory as it concerns Machiavelli, see John P. McCormick, "Teorie anti-istituzionali di democrazia 'radicale': I post-marxisti europei," in *Democrazia machiavelliana:*

Machiavelli, il potere del popolo e il controllo delle élites, ed. John P. McCormick (Rome: Viella, 2020), 20–29.

10. Among the unfortunate results of the "radical" appropriation of Arendt's reading of democratic Athens is, for instance, Wolin's and Rancière's insistence that apportionment of public offices through lottery was the realization of "no-rule" rather than an attempt by the Athenian demos to distribute "rule" much more widely than nondemocracies do; that is, rather than serving as a "noninstitution" that defies the principle of "rule" as such, distributing magistracies through lottery actually institutionalized the democratic principle "to rule and be ruled in turn." See Wolin, "Norm and Form," 43; and Rancière, *Hatred of Democracy*, 41, 54. See Ella Myers, "Presupposing Equality: The Trouble with Rancière's Axiomatic Approach," *Philosophy and Social Criticism* 42, no. 1 (January 2016): 45–69.

11. See McCormick, *Machiavellian Democracy*, chaps. 3–5; and McCormick, "Teorie anti-istituzionali di democrazia 'radicale': i post-marxisti europei."

12. Perhaps the simplest refutation of the attempt by Vatter, Abensour, and others to sharply separate popular contestation of authority from concrete popular rule is Machiavelli's own insistence that "all the *laws* made in favor of freedom arise from the disunion between the *popolo* and the *grandi*" (D I.4; emphasis added). Throughout the *Discourses*, Machiavelli describes "laws" as concrete instantiations of hard-won democratic gains—always necessary for liberty's attainment but by no means permanently sufficient for its preservation. Such gains are secured and expanded by further popular contestation, by greater apportionment of formal governing power to the people, and by additional legal enactments conducive to liberty in the future. Put simply, Machiavelli did not, as the "radical" democratic literature too often does, confuse popular government with anarchy.

13. See John P. McCormick, "Machiavelli, Popular Resistance and the Curious Case of the *Ciompi* Revolt," in *Penser et agir à la Renaissance*, ed. V. Ferrer and P. Desan (Geneva: Librairie Droz, 2020), 369–90; and McCormick, "Review of Yves Winter, *Machiavelli and the Orders of Violence*," *Constellations* 27, no. 2 (June 2020): 313–16.

14. See McCormick, *Machiavellian Democracy*, chap. 3, "The Benefits and Limits of Popular Participation and Judgment," 65–90.

15. Machiavelli has a penchant for inviting readers to evaluate the episodes he recounts largely, or even entirely, in light of the initial setting he provides for such episodes. Compare, for instance, the way he introduces the Pacuvius/Capua episode here (D I.47) with the way he introduces the Liverotto/Fermo episode in *The Prince* (P 8). In the former, he writes, "one may invoke [a] noteworthy example that occurred in Capua after Hannibal defeated the Romans at Cannae . . ."; in the latter he introduces Liverotto's usurpation of Fermo's republic with the words, "In our time, during Alexander VI's reign. . . ." I suggest that Hannibal hovers over the entire Capua episode in the same manner that Alexander, or rather the papacy, hovers over the entire Fermo episode. See John P. McCormick, "The Enduring Ambiguity of Machiavellian Virtue: Cruelty, Crime, and Christianity in *The Prince*," *Social Research* 81, no. 1 (2014): 133–64.

16. In the wake of 2016's Brexit referendum in Britain, scholars have emphasized the importance of forcing a positive choice between specific options rather than merely asking for an affirmation or rejection of the status quo. Many suggest that the Brexit referendum yielded a flawed, irresponsible outcome because it entailed a simple "yes/no" choice, without requiring an alternative, substitute "yes" choice in the event of

an initial "no" vote. See Simon Kaye's blog post, "Deal > Remain > No-deal > Deal: Brexit and the Condorcet Paradox" (https://blogs.lse.ac.uk/politicsandpolicy/brexit -condorcet/), as well as several essays contained in Francis Cheneval and Alice el-Wakil, eds., "The Institutional Design of Referendums: Bottom-Up and Binding," special issue of the *Swiss Political Science Review* 24, no. 3 (September 2018): 215–369.

17. The presence of an external enemy apparently induces the Capuan people to accept the idea that civic unity affords them a better chance of not being oppressed by outsiders. On the salutary civic effects of external enemies, see Ioannis D. Evrigenis, *Fear of Enemies and Collective Action* (Cambridge: Cambridge University Press, 2007).

18. In language that any contemporary reader would have recognized as evoking Florence's traditional electoral "bagging" procedures, Machiavelli's Pacuvius has the names of all the senators placed "in a bag" (*borsa*) rather than, according to Livy, "in an urn" (*in urnam*) (Livy XXIII.2). However, while Florentine committees of scrutinizers, or *accoppiatori*, would traditionally judge the suitability of the candidates whose names were drawn from the bags, Machiavelli here has the assembled people serve as *accoppiatori*—deciding not simply whether the candidate was worthy of office but whether he was worthy of execution (D I.47). On Florentine electoral procedures, see John M. Najemy, *Corporatism and Consensus in Florentine Electoral Politics, 1280–1400* (Chapel Hill: University of North Carolina Press, 1982); and Nicolai Rubinstein, *The Government of Florence under the Medici, 1434 to 1494* (Oxford: Clarendon, 1998).

19. For invaluable insights into the Machiavelli-Borgia relationship, see Skinner, *Machiavelli*, 9–19, 26, 37, 45–47, 50. Peter Breiner provides a helpful literature review on Borgia as Machiavelli's *nuovo principe* in "Machiavelli's 'New Prince' and the Primordial Moment of Acquisition," *Political Theory* 36, no. 1 (February 2008): 66–92.

20. Recent interpreters who view Machiavelli's depiction of Borgia as mostly satiric or ironic include John M. Najemy, "Machiavelli and Cesare Borgia: A Reconsideration of Chapter 7 of *The Prince*," *Review of Politics* 75, no. 4 (Fall 2013): 539–56; and Erica Benner, *Machiavelli's Prince: A New Reading* (Oxford: Oxford University Press, 2014), 94–111. For a vigorous refutation, see Mark Jurdjevic, "Machiavelli and Guicciardini on Cesare Borgia's 'Good Government': Chapter 7 of *The Prince* Revisited," *Machiavelliana* 2 (2023): 79–108.

21. See Richard Bellamy, "Dirty Hands and Clean Gloves: Liberal Ideals and Real Politics," *European Journal of Political Theory* 9, no. 4 (2010): 412–30; and Bellamy, "The Paradox of the Democratic Prince: Machiavelli and the Neo-Machiavellians on Ideal Theory, Realism, and Democratic Leadership," in *Politics Recovered: Realist Thought in Theory and Practice*, ed. Matt Sleat (New York: Columbia University Press, 2018), 166–93.

22. On the historical and conceptual evolution of the definitions of "demagogue" and "statesman," see Melissa Lane, "The Origins of the Statesman-Demagogue Distinction in and after Ancient Athens," *Journal of the History of Ideas* 73, no. 2 (2012): 179–200.

23. See FH III. Livy's Pacuvius Calavius says as much himself: "You may now impose justice on this despicable and disreputable senate . . . without risking your lives in vain attempts to storm the houses of individual senators, fiercely guarded by their clients and slaves. Punish them such as they are here and now: unarmed, unaided, and confined in the Senate chamber." Livy XXIII.2.

CHAPTER 7

1. Niccolò Machiavelli, *Istorie Fiorentine*, composed about 1520–25 and published in 1532, ed. Franco Gaeta (Milan: Feltrinelli, 1962), hereafter FH; Machiavelli, *Il principe* (*De principatibus*), composed about 1513 and published in 1532, ed. G. Inglese (Turin: Einaudi, 1995), hereafter P; Machiavelli, *Discorsi*, composed about 1513–18 and published in 1531, ed. C. Vivanti (Turin: Einaudi-Gallimard, 1997), hereafter D.

2. See, paradigmatically, Victoria Kahn, "*Virtù* and the Example of Agathocles in Machiavelli's *Prince*," *Representations* 13 (Winter 1986): 63–83. See also, more recently, Harvey C. Mansfield, *Machiavelli's Effectual Truth* (Cambridge: Cambridge University Press, 2023).

3. See, in this spirit, Marta Celati, "Imitation and Allusion in Machiavelli's *Istorie fiorentine*: Between Contemporary Sources and Classical Models," in *Imitative Series and Clusters from Classical to Early Modern Literature*, ed. Colin Burrow, Stephen J. Harrison, Martin McLaughlin, and Elisabetta Tarantino (Berlin: De Gruyter, 2020), 205–22.

4. Not to mention Hiero, Agathocles, Nabis, and Cleomenes, discussed in chapters 1 and 2.

5. Although they differ to varying degrees on how dramatically they believe Machiavelli changed his political orientation, the following writers all agree that his views did in fact fundamentally transform in a more "pessimistic" or "conservative" direction: Francesco Bausi, *Machiavelli* (Rome: Salerno, 2005); Robert Black, *Machiavelli* (London: Routledge, 2013); Mario Martelli, "Machiavelli e Firenze dalla repubblica al principate," in *Niccolò Machiavelli: Politico storico letterato*, ed. J.-J. Marchand (Rome: Salerno, 1996), 15–31; Giovanni Silvano, "Florentine Republicanism in the Sixteenth Century," in *Machiavelli and Republicanism*, ed. G. Bock, Q. Skinner, and M. Viroli (Cambridge: Cambridge University Press, 1990), 41–70. I engage this interpretive wave in "On the Myth of the Conservative Turn in Machiavelli's *Florentine Histories*," in John P. McCormick, *Reading Machiavelli* (Princeton, NJ: Princeton University Press, 2018), 69–108.

6. See John M. Najemy, "Machiavelli and the Medici: The Lessons of Florentine History," *Renaissance Quarterly* 35, no. 4 (1982): 551–76. See also Najemy, *Machiavelli's Broken World* (Oxford: Oxford University Press, 2022), 274–381.

7. As Mark Jurdjevic puts it in a formidable extension of Najemy's thesis, "nothing in Machiavelli's treatment" of individual actors in the *Histories* "suggests that he had even the dimmest hopes that they might do otherwise" than they actually did in the circumstances he describes. See Mark Jurdjevic, *A Great and Wretched City: Promise and Failure in Machiavelli's Florentine Political Thought* (Cambridge, MA: Harvard University Press, 2014), 33. Jurdjevic seriously qualifies his agreement with Najemy in Jurdjevic, *Regimes of the Many and the Few in the Political Thought of Machiavelli and Guicciardini* (Toronto: University of Toronto Press, forthcoming).

8. Najemy's and Jurdjevic's argument concerning Machiavelli's supposedly changed views on political leadership constitutes part of the broader scholarly trend, mentioned above, whose participants assert that the *Histories* constitutes a dramatic shift in Machiavelli's political writings. For instance, Bausi, Martelli, Silvano, and, most forcefully, Black suggest that because Machiavelli had joined the Florentine political establishment in the 1520s, having been more or less co-opted by the city's elite, his writings changed to accommodate its more princely or more patrician political preferences. Consequently, on this view, works like the *Histories* purportedly reflect these

changes in Machiavelli's political orientation: he became more critical of the people rather than the nobles of republics, and he became more pessimistic concerning the Roman republican model, generally, than he was in earlier works.

9. Leo Strauss and Gennaro Sasso make impressive cases for the conceptual unity of Machiavelli's thought: see Leo Strauss, *Thoughts on Machiavelli* (Glencoe, IL: Free Press, 1958); Strauss, "Niccolò Machiavelli," in *The History of Political Philosophy*, ed. Leo Strauss and Joseph Cropsey (Chicago: University of Chicago Press, 1987), 296–317; and Gennaro Sasso, *Niccolò Machiavelli*, vol. 2, *La storiografia* (Bologna: Il Mulino, 1993).

10. This infamous statement by Machiavelli concerning the composition of the *Histories* is relevant here, even if it somewhat belies what I take to be the largely systematic quality of his rhetoric of praise and blame in the book: "For a long time I have not said what I believed nor do I ever believe what I say, and if indeed sometimes I do happen to tell the truth, I hide it among so many lies that it is hard to find." Machiavelli to Francesco Guicciardini, May 17, 1521, in *Machiavelli: The Chief Works and Others*, ed. Allan Gilbert (Durham, NC: Duke University Press, 1989), 3:971.

11. See Christopher Lynch, "Machiavelli on Reading the Bible Judiciously," *Hebraic Political Studies* 1, no. 2 (2006): 162–85.

12. Strauss persuasively argues that Machiavelli occludes the distinction between founders and reformers—specifically, the distinction between seemingly extraordinary "new princes" or "heroic founders" and apparently more ordinary "continuous founders" or "founder-captains." See Strauss, *Thoughts on Machiavelli*, 44–45, 70, 104–15, 130, 133, 165–66, 203, 250. In some sense Brutus and Camillus (D III.12) are every bit as much founders of Rome (like Romulus) as they are mere reformers. Likewise, the Spartan reformer Cleomenes, Machiavelli intimates, stands in a similar relation to the Spartan founder Lycurgus (D I.2, I.10).

13. See Giovanni Giorgini, "Machiavellian Variations, or When Moral Convictions and Political Duties Collide," *Journal of Ethics* 27 (2023): 461–75.

14. See Sverre Bagge, "Actors and Structure in Machiavelli's *Istorie Fiorentine*," *Quaderni d'Italianistica* 28, no. 2 (2007): 45–87; Ana Maria Cabrini, "La storia da non imitare: Il versante negativo dell'esemplarità nelle *Istorie Fiorentine*," in *Cultura e scrittura di Machiavelli* (Roma: Salerno, 1997), 197–220; Salvatore di Maria, "Machiavelli's Ironic View of History: The *Istorie Fiorentine*," *Renaissance Quarterly* 45, no. 2 (Summer 1992): 248–70; Felix Gilbert, "Machiavelli's *Istorie Fiorentine*: An Essay in Interpretation," in Gilbert, *History: Choice and Commitment* (Cambridge, MA: Harvard University Press, 1977), 135–53; Martine Leibovici, "From Fight to Debate: Machiavelli and the Revolt of the Ciompi," *Philosophy and Social Criticism* 28, no. 6 (November 2002): 647–60; Timothy Lukes, "Descending to Particulars: The Palazzo, the Piazza and Machiavelli's Republican New Modes and Orders," *Journal of Politics* 71, no. 2 (April 2000): 520–32; Marina Marietti, "Une Figure Emblématique: Michele di Lando vu par Maquiavel," *Chroniques* 69/70 (2002): 129–38; Mark Phillips, "Barefoot Boy Makes Good: A Study of Machiavelli's Historiography," *Speculum* 59, no. 3 (July 1984): 585–605; Yves Winter, "Plebeian Politics: Machiavelli and the Ciompi Uprising," *Political Theory* 40 no. 6 (December 2012): 736–66; and Winter, *Machiavelli and the Orders of Violence* (Cambridge: Cambridge University Press, 2018), 167–91.

15. To be sure, Machiavelli does not insist that a founder/reformer must kill *all* of the nobility to be successful. But he certainly implies that killing more than one is

necessary to instill the fear required to induce temporary good behavior among aristocratic survivors, who may consequently be mollified by honors and rewards. The conspirators Brutus executed did not constitute all of Rome's nobility, and eliminating the lords of the Romagna did not preclude Cesare Borgia's efforts to buy off the nobility of papal Rome (P 7). Indeed, throughout *The Prince* Machiavelli elaborates on the appropriate meting out of favors to elites necessary to maintain a prince's security (e.g., P 9, P 20). The point is that Michele's acquiescence to Ser Nuto's death was not enough to secure the plebs' continued loyalty; and the elaborate favors he bestows on the popular nobles, without executing any of them, seem to embolden them in ways that, as we will shortly observe, prove disadvantageous for both Michele and the plebs.

16. Michele likely intends to use a Ghibelline city like Empoli as a power resource against Florence's Guelf Party, whose agents in the Eight of War he had recently dismissed from government. Nevertheless, there are ways Michele might have made this clear to the plebs, especially by treating the popular nobles, allied both with and against the party, more severely than he did.

17. See the role played by the provosts (*proposti*) in Machiavelli, "Discursus on Florentine Matters After the Death of Lorenzo de' Medici the Younger" (1520), in *Florentine Political Writings from Petrarch to Machiavelli*, ed. M. Jurdjevic, N. Piano, and J. P. McCormick (Philadelphia: University of Pennsylvania Press, 2019), 211–12.

18. See, e.g., Leonardo Bruni, *History of the Florentine People*, vol. 3, ed. and trans. James Hankins (Cambridge, MA: Harvard University Press, 2007), 6–15.

19. See Niccolò Rodolico, *La democrazia fiorentina nel suo tramonto (1378–1382)* (Florence: Zanichelli, 1905), 199–206; and Rodolico, "The Struggle for the Right of Association in Fourteenth-Century Florence," *History* 7 (1922): 178–90. On this and other differences between Machiavelli's account of Michele's career and those of other historians, see Mark Phillips, "Barefoot Boy Makes Good: A Study of Machiavelli's Historiography," *Speculum* 59, no. 3 (1984): 585–605.

20. See Christopher Lynch, "War and Foreign Affairs in Machiavelli's *Florentine Histories*," *Review of Politics* 74, no. 1 (Winter 2012): 1–26. See, more generally, Christopher Lynch, *Machiavelli on War* (Ithaca, NY: Cornell University Press, 2023).

21. The most extensive analysis of Machiavelli's use of allegory in *The Prince* (and to some extent the *Discourses*) to demonstrate the force of Christianity and to argue for the necessity of overcoming it is William B. Parsons, *Machiavelli's Gospel: The Critique of Christianity in "The Prince"* (Rochester, NY: University of Rochester Press, 2016). On Machiavelli's critique of Christianity in the *Histories*, see Harvey C. Mansfield, "Party and Sect in Machiavelli's *Florentine Histories*," in *Machiavelli's Virtue* (Chicago: University of Chicago Press, 1996), 137–75.

22. Machiavelli's famous remarks on the wanton behavior of the princes of the church in D III.1 could be seen, in this respect, as applying to more conventional princes as well—at the very least, Machiavelli asserts that Christian morality inhibits modern peoples from effectively deterring modern princes, clerical and secular, from engaging in egregiously oppressive behavior. See Emanuele Cutinelli-Rendina, *Introduzione a Machiavelli* (Rome: Laterza, 1999).

23. See the dedicatory letter to the *Florentine Histories* and Machiavelli's "Discursus on Florentine Matters," composed at approximately the same time.

CHAPTER 8

1. Niccolò Machiavelli, *Istorie Fiorentine*, composed about 1520–25 and published in 1532, ed. Franco Gaeta (Milan: Feltrinelli, 1962), hereafter FH; Machiavelli, *Il principe* (*De principatibus*), composed about 1513 and published in 1532, ed. G. Inglese (Turin: Einaudi, 1995), hereafter P; Machiavelli, *Discorsi*, composed about 1513–18 and published in 1531, ed. C. Vivanti (Turin: Einaudi-Gallimard, 1997), hereafter D.

2. I argued in part 1 that Machiavelli countenanced a very specific kind of tyranny. Especially illuminating on this point is Giovanni Giorgini, "The Place of the Tyrant in Machiavelli's Political Thought and the Literary Genre of *The Prince*," *History of Political Thought* 29, no. 2 (2008): 230–56.

3. On the Roman tradition of exemplarity with and against which Machiavelli works, see Jane D. Chaplin, *Livy's Exemplary History* (Oxford: Oxford University Press, 2001), especially 78, 82, 201; Rebecca Langlands, "Roman *Exempla* and Situation Ethics: Valerius Maximus and Cicero's *De officiis*," *Journal of Roman Studies* 101 (November 2011): 100–122; and Michèle Lowrie and Susanne Lüdemann, "Introduction," in *Between Exemplarity and Singularity: Literature, Philosophy, Law*, ed. Lowrie and Lüdemann (London: Routledge, 2015), 1–15.

4. See John M. Najemy, "Machiavelli between East and West," in *From Florence to the Mediterranean and Beyond: Essays in Honour of Anthony Molho*, ed. D. R. Curto, E. R. Dursteler, J. Kirshner, and F. Trivellato (Florence: L. S. Olschki, 2009), 127–45; and Lucio Biasiori and Giuseppe Marcocci, eds., *Machiavelli, Islam and the East: Reorienting the Foundations of Modern Political Thought* (New York: Palgrave Macmillan, 2018). Although see also Isaac Gabriel Salgado, "Mind the Gap: A Machiavellian Lesson in Anti-racism," *Polity* 55, no. 3 (2023): 544–67.

5. See John P. McCormick, *Reading Machiavelli: Scandalous Books, Suspect Engagements, and the Virtue of Populist Politics* (Princeton, NJ: Princeton University Press, 2018), 73–78.

6. James Hankins declares that Machiavelli "directly blames" the entire Florentine people, without qualification, "for consenting via acclamation to Walter's tyranny, thus granting it at least a veneer of legitimacy." Hankins, *Virtue Politics: Soulcraft and Statecraft in Renaissance Italy* (Cambridge, MA: Harvard University Press, 2019), 484. Yet Machiavelli more than slightly intimates that the episode in question was a charade: he describes how Walter had prearranged for armed guards to permit him, but not the sitting priors, to enter the Palazzo; it is therefore very likely that the unidentified individual who nominated the duke for lifetime lordship, and many members of the crowd who acclaimed him, were in fact Walter's creatures (FH II.35).

7. Rinuccini and Savonarola catalog Lorenzo's courtly excesses in great detail—without ever mentioning his name. See Alamanno Rinuccini, "Liberty" (1479), and Girolamo Savonarola, "Treatise on the Constitution and Government of the City of Florence" (1498), in *Florentine Political Writings from Petrarch to Machiavelli*, ed. M. Jurdjevic, N. Piano, and J. P. McCormick (Philadelphia: University of Pennsylvania Press, 2019), 156–78 and 179–204. On the myriad types of sotto voce critiques of Lorenzo's rule prevalent during and after his reign, see James O. Ward, *Hidden in Plain Sight: Covert Criticism of the Medici in Renaissance Florence* (New York: Peter Lang, 2019).

8. On the role gender plays in Machiavelli's political thought and "republicanism" generally, see Hanna Fenichel Pitkin, *Fortune Is a Woman: Gender and Politics in the*

Thought of Niccolò Machiavelli (Chicago: University of Chicago Press, 1999); Maria J. Falco, ed., *Feminist Interpretations of Niccolò Machiavelli* (University Park, PA: Penn State Press, 2004); and Melissa Matthes, *The Rape of Lucretia and the Founding of Republics: Readings in Livy, Machiavelli, and Rousseau* (University Park: Penn State Press, 2007).

9. See McCormick, *Reading Machiavelli*, 73–78.

10. Machiavelli's declaration that plebeians "ought" to be recruited for military service refutes Paul Rahe's claim that Machiavelli was not devoted to popular militias. See Paul A. Rahe, "The Anatomy of an Error: Machiavelli's Supposed Commitment to a 'Citizen' Militia," in *Machiavelli Then and Now: History, Politics, Literature*, ed. Sukanta Chaudhuri and Prasanta Chakravarty (Cambridge: Cambridge University Press, 2022), 31–53. Aristocratic apprehensions over Machiavelli's Florentine militia project compelled him and Soderini to assiduously avoid any references to the ancient Roman citizen army, even if Machiavelli harbored hopes of imitating the Romans in practice, should the militia eventually be extended to the city: see Mikael Hörnqvist, "*Perché non si usa allegare i Romani*: Machiavelli and the Florentine Militia of 1506," *Renaissance Quarterly* 55, no. 1 (2002): 148–91, at 185–86.

11. Cassius Dio, *Roman History*, vol. 9, books 71–80, trans. Earnest Cary (Cambridge, MA: Harvard University Press [Loeb], 1927); and Herodian, *History of the Empire*, vol. 1, books 1–4, trans. C. R. Whittaker (Cambridge, MA: Harvard University Press [Loeb], 1969). Exactly how much of Cassius Dio was translated into Latin in the fifteenth century is unknown. See Hankins, *Virtue Politics*, 364. Angelo Poliziano's Latin translation of Herodian's entire history circulated widely in the 1490s. See Edward C. Echols, *Herodian of Antioch's History of the Roman Empire* (Berkeley: University of California Press, 1961), 8.

12. Cassius Dio, Epitome of Book LXXV.2.1–2; Epitome of Book LXXV.8.4; Herodian, III.5.5–6; III.8.7.

13. Cassius Dio, Epitome of Book LXXV.2.1–2; Epitome of Book LXXV.2.4–5 (where the historian emphasizes Severus's employment of non-European soldiers in his bodyguard); Herodian, III.13.4.

14. Cassius Dio, Epitome of Book LXXVII.1.1 (remarking that, "in fact, no emperor had ever before given so much to the whole population at once"); Herodian, II.14.4–5; III.8.4; III.8.9–10; III.10.2.

15. Cassius Dio, Epitome of Book LXXVII.1.3; Epitome of Book LXXVII.1.5; Herodian, III.8.9–10; III.10.2 (emphasizing elaborate featuring of gladiators and exotic animals).

16. Herodian, III.10, line 2.

17. Cassius Dio, Epitome of Book LXXVI.14.1–4.

18. Severus was not, after all, the supremely astute fox that Machiavelli presents him to be; he thwarts Plautianus's conspiracy only by accident. This is much like Machiavelli's presentation of Nabis, when he fails to mention that the Spartan tyrant was killed in a conspiracy launched by erstwhile foreign allies.

19. Cassius Dio, Epitome of Book LXXVII.7.1. See Herodian, III.13, line 6.

20. Leo Strauss typically exaggerates when he describes Machiavelli's Severus as the best example of "an able Roman emperor who had the support of the soldiers" and who, furthermore, "was *under no compulsion to consider the people at all*." See Strauss, *Thoughts on Machiavelli* (Glencoe, IL: Free Press, 1958), 46; emphasis added. The figure of Severus functions as something of a talisman in the literature inspired by Strauss's

interpretation of Machiavelli, for it purportedly confirms that Machiavelli was not in reality the popular partisan he otherwise seems to be. See, for example, Harvey C. Mansfield, *Machiavelli's Virtue* (Chicago: University of Chicago Press, 1998), 187.

21. See the near civil war described by Herodian that previous emperors permitted to ensue between the people and the soldiers: Herodian, I.12.5–12; II.2.4–5; and II.6.1–5. And then there is the unprecedented massacre of the Roman people perpetrated by the Praetorian Guard at Caracalla's command: Herodian, IV.6.4–5. Contemporary scholars estimate the number of civilians murdered at 20,000. See Eric R. Varner, *Mutilation and Transformation: Damnatio Memoriae and Roman Imperial Portraiture* (London: Brill, 2004), 168.

22. Herodian, II.11.3–5, pp. 215–16.

CONCLUSION

1. See Victoria Kahn, *Machiavellian Rhetoric: From the Counter-Reformation to Milton* (Princeton, NJ: Princeton University Press, 1994); and Kahn, "Machiavelli's Afterlife and Reputation in the Eighteenth Century," in *The Cambridge Companion to Machiavelli*, ed. John M. Najemy (Cambridge: Cambridge University Press, 2010), 239–55.

2. See J. G. A., Pocock, *The Machiavellian Moment: Florentine Political Thought and the Atlantic Republican Tradition* (Baltimore: Johns Hopkins University Press, 1975); Quentin Skinner, *Past Masters: Machiavelli* (New York: Hill and Wang, 1981); and *Machiavelli and Republicanism*, ed. G. Bock, M. Viroli, and Q. Skinner (Cambridge: Cambridge University Press, 1990).

3. For a criticism of the recent "democratic turn" in Machiavelli studies along these lines, see Catherine H. Zuckert, "Machiavelli: Radical Democratic Political Theorist?" *Review of Politics* 81, no. 3 (Summer 2019): 499–510. More sympathetic assessments are offered by Marc Stears, Jérémie Barthas, and Adam Woodhouse, "On Machiavelli as Plebeian Theorist," *Theoria* 66, no. 161 (December 2019): 108–16; and Katherine Robiadek, "For the People: Deepening the Democratic Turn in Machiavelli Studies," *Political Theory* 49, 4 (2021): 686–99.

4. See Diodorus XIX.9.7, XX.63.3.

5. Niccolò Machiavelli, Letter to Francesco Vettori, December 10, 1513.

6. See Quentin Skinner, *The Foundations of Modern Political Thought*, vol. 1, *The Renaissance* (Cambridge: Cambridge University Press, 1978), 119, 137–38; Skinner, *Machiavelli* (Oxford: Oxford University Press, 1981), 42; Skinner, *Machiavelli: A Very Short Introduction* (Oxford: Oxford University Press, 2000), 47; and Peter Stacey, *Roman Monarchy and the Renaissance Prince* (Cambridge: Cambridge University Press, 2007), 135, 147, 296–97.

7. See Gabriele Pedullà, "Introduzione: L'arte fiorentina dei nodi," in *Il Principe: Edizione del cinquecentennale con traduzione a fronte in italiano moderno di Carmine Donzelli*, ed. Gabriele Pedullà (Rome: Donzelli, 2013), v–cxxi, especially xl–xliv; and Pedullà, "Machiavelli's *Prince* and the Concept of Tyranny," in *Evil Lords: Theories and Representations of Tyranny from Antiquity to the Renaissance*, ed. Nikos Panou and Hester Schadee (Oxford: Oxford University Press, 2018), 191–210 at 201.

8. See Gordon Arlen, "Aristotle and the Problem of Oligarchic Harm: Insights for Democracy," *European Journal of Political Theory* 18, no. 3 (2019): 393–414; and Camila

Vergara, "Corruption as Systemic Political Decay," *Philosophy and Social Criticism* 47, no. 3 (2021): 322–46.

9. Straussian scholars have maintained, and no doubt will continue to insist, that Machiavelli was, in significant ways, actually a champion of the nobles against the people: see Daniel N. Levy, *Wily Elites and Spirited Peoples in Machiavelli's Republicanism* (Lanham, MD: Lexington Books, 2014); Zuckert, "Machiavelli: Radical Democratic Political Theorist?"; and Max J. E. Morris, "The Wisdom of the People and the Elite: John McCormick and Leo Strauss on Machiavelli," *Theoria: A Journal of Social and Political Theory* 70 (2023): 33–52.

10. Niccolò Machiavelli, *Istorie Fiorentine* [1523], ed. Franco Gaeta (Milan: Feltrinelli 1962), Proemio.

INDEX

abdication, 53, 67-69, 92, 96-103, 119, 123-24, 126, 134-36, 173, 223, 244n7. *See also* exile

Achaean League, xv, 43

Agathocles the Sicilian: and Borgia, 3-5, 9, 13-18, 21-22, 25-27, 29, 231n6, 233n22, 234n33; and citizens/people, 62, 221, 232n18; as civil prince, successful, 195; and civil principalities, 19, 29-33, 61, 98; and Clearchus, xvi, 4, 40-41, 151, 155-57; condemned, 4-6; condoned and endorsed, 6; as consul, 5; contempt for, 234n35; as controversial figure, 3; and corruption, 36-37, 51; as criminal petty tyrant, 10, 44; criminality of, 4-5, 8-18, 20-21, 29, 31-32, 41, 44, 47; criticisms of, xvi, 19-20; cruelty of, xvi, 4, 6, 9-18, 31-32, 46-47, 231-32n13; death of, 32, 235n45, 236n60; denunciation of, 20-21; endorsement of, 221; as exemplum, 3-33, 35-36, 62, 230-36nn; and exploitation of high office, 40; far-flung military campaigns of, 231-32n13; faults of, 233n24; and force, 235n48; and glory, 4, 10-11, 44-48, 241n52; and good government, 15, 63; and government of senate, 48-53; as Greek tyrant, xv-xvi, 4, 6, 9-10, 35-38, 44, 55, 140, 151, 155-56, 195, 197, 221-22, 223, 239n21; and Hannibal, 231-32n13; hardships and dangers endured by, 5, 59-61; and Hiero, 3, 9, 30-37, 43-44; humble origins and low birth of, 30, 47, 241n52; impressive long-term success of, 9; independence of, 59; interregnums of, 33; and Julius Caesar, xvi, 4, 18, 37; and killing/murders, 17-18, 21, 23, 29; and Liverotto, 3-5, 9, 14, 22-29, 31, 41; as magistrate, 3, 6; and mercenaries, 232n17; and Michele, 184-85; and military, 12, 15, 18, 22, 30-32, 62-63, 197, 211, 231-32n13, 239n21, 239n29; mischievous presentation of, 231n13; and Nabis, 3-5, 9, 29-33, 35-38, 41-44, 51, 57-59, 62, 98, 197, 238n12; negative accounts of career, 233n24; as new prince, 184; and nobility, 26-27; and papal parricide, 22-29; and patria, 32; pitiable end, 236n60; policies of, praised, 43; and political exemplarity, xiii; political success of, 4, 29-33, 221; as praetor, 10-11, 47, 184-85; praise for, 6, 21-22, 221; as prince, 3-4, 6, 13; as princely exemplum, xv, 3-33, 230-36nn; princely interregnums of, 33; and prominent citizens held hostage, 232n18; and Scipio, 4-5, 7, 44-53, 239n24; self-affiliation with, xix, 5, 59-61; and Senate, 111; supreme command and senate, 40; and Syracusan